W9-DCM-950

**Research Methods
in the Social and Behavioral Sciences**

Research Methods
in the Social
and Behavioral Sciences

Russell A. Jones
University of Kentucky

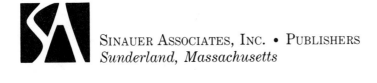
SINAUER ASSOCIATES, INC. • PUBLISHERS
Sunderland, Massachusetts

RESEARCH METHODS IN THE SOCIAL AND BEHAVIORAL SCIENCES

Copyright © 1985 by Sinauer Associates Inc.

This book may not be reproduced in whole or
in part by any means without permission from
the publisher. For information address
SINAUER ASSOCIATES INC.
Sunderland, MA 01375

Library of Congress Cataloging in Publication

Jones, Russell A.
    Research methods in the social and behavioral
sciences.

    Bibliography: p. 381
    Includes index.
    1. Social sciences – Research – Methodology.   2. Social
psychology – Research – Methodology.   I. Title.
H62.J62   1985   300´.72   85-14247
ISBN 0-87893-370-0 (pbk.)

Printed in U.S.A.

5 4 3 2

For three generations of friends . . .

Karen,
F.M.,
Wanda,
Doris, &
Helen

Contents

Preface

A physician who knew how to use only one diagnostic instrument would never be licensed to practice medicine. There are a few problems such a physician might identify, but the vast majority of physical and mental disorders would escape notice. Similarly, anyone interested in investigating behavior must master more than one methodology. Otherwise, they are going to miss an awful lot. Behavior is complex and multidetermined, and no one methodological approach is, by itself, adequate. Experiments, interviews, and participant observation, for example, complement each other; and each, when used appropriately, can help in attempts to understand and explain social behavior. The major purpose of the discussion that follows is to make clear the variety of methods available to anyone interested in research on social and behavioral processes. But, methods are not to be used randomly; one must also develop an appreciation for the sorts of hypotheses and questions that can be most profitably investigated with each.

Chapter One begins with a general discussion of the personal and situational determinants of behavior, a discussion that underlines its complex nature. That very complexity can be a fertile source of hypotheses, however; and hypothesis generation is one of the most exciting parts of research. It is not necessary to be a genius to come up with interesting ideas for investigation. One of the major goals of the first chapter, in fact, is to demystify the whole research process. Research methods are simply procedures and techniques that will help in obtaining evidence, in as unbiased a manner as possible, on the questions of interest. The general research strategy described in Chapter One (and recommended wholeheartedly) is this: When some phenomenon occurs that needs explaining, think up as many plausible explanations as possible to account for it and devise the necessary methods for gathering evidence on the validity of those explanations. The ideal to be pursued is triangulation of measurement—to obtain evidence for the hypothesis or explanation using several different methods. Chapter One will try to make clear why that procedure is good.

Following the introductory chapter, the body of the book consists of a series of chapters, each devoted to a particular research method. The basic format of these chapters is the same. The method is defined and then illustrated with a detailed description of a research application. In each case, examples were selected that not only would illustrate the important methodological points but also would be of interest from a substantive point of view. (There is some fascinating research being carried out on social and behavioral processes.) Along with the illustrative research in each chapter, the advantages and disadvantages of each method are discussed. Thorough familiarity with the good and the bad aspects of each method is essential for it will enable the investigator to make intelligent choices among available methods for specific research purposes.

Individual chapters are devoted to the following methods: (1) participant observation, (2) nonparticipant observation, (3) content analysis and archival research, (4) survey research, (5) quasi-experiments and field experiments, (6) evaluation research, (7) laboratory experiments, and (8) simulation. The selection of this ordering of the methods was intentional. The progression is from the simple to the more complex methods.

Interspersed in the above sequence is a general methodological chapter on the interview. This chapter follows the chapter on archival research and content analysis because the interview is a basic tool of nearly all the methods discussed subsequently, including survey research, evaluation research, and experimentation. How questions are worded, the manner of the interviewer, the setting, the respondent's motivation, and a host of other factors can affect the validity of the information obtained in any interview. Both art and science are involved; and with a little effort, both components can be mastered.

The chapter arrangement should also make clear how each method controls for some of the sources of bias that were uncontrolled in those preceding it. Unfortunately, there is no perfect method, none that is completely free of bias. That, of course, is one of the main reasons for having a variety of methods—but more about that later.

Acknowledgments

A number of people have been instrumental in the process of completing this book. I would like to thank them all, beginning with John Amacker and Clyde Hendrick for their initial prompting and encouragement. Robert Helmreich, Alice Eagly, and Julia G. Hall provided additional encouragement in the form of favorable comments on the prospectus for the book. Sylvia Wrobel, whom I tried to entice to be a coauthor, wrote a first draft of what has become Chapter Five before joining the move to the Sunbelt. John V. Haley wrote a computer program that generated the table of random numbers found in the Appendix. Joanne Ries and Beverly Morris helped track down obscure references and made innumerable trips to the local interlibrary loan office. David Kravitz, Mark Peyrot, Susan Nakayama, Glen Rogers, and Marianne Miller all read and commented on various chapters. Steve Penrod, Phil Tetlock, and Julia Hall provided detailed critiques of the entire first draft. Jodi Simpson's editing helped smooth out some of my more awkward constructions. Ann Scott, Saundra Jones, and Irma Fox cheerfully made the transition from Selectric to word processor while continuing to transform almost illegible handwriting into first-rate copy. Carlton Brose of Sinauer Associates has been helpful in too many ways to name. And my wife, Karen, has put up with it all. Thanks.

RUSSELL A. JONES

**Research Methods
in the Social and Behavioral Sciences**

1

Investigating Social Behavior

The Nature of Research

The Complex Nature of Behavior

Thinking about the Causes of Behavior

Research Strategy

The Ethics of Research

Summary

Recommended Readings

Several years ago, a panel of distinguished social and behavioral scientists convened in Estes Park, Colorado to ponder the problem of how to improve the education of those who were interested in research on human behavior. What skills should such people master? To what bodies of literature should they be exposed? How much math is necessary? How much needs to be known about experimental design and statistics? Who is capable of doing good research on human behavior? Need only geniuses apply?

The timing of this conference is of interest because it gives some hints as to the types of answers they might have been expected to give to the above questions. The Korean War had been over for only five years, and *brainwashing* was a household word. The North Koreans and Chinese were believed to have developed powerful techniques for manipulating and controlling human behavior and thought processes. They seemed to know more about the physiology of the brain and how it influenced behavior than we did. Less than a year prior to the conference, the Russians had launched the first Sputnik; and there was a national outcry that the United States was losing the race into space because we were not teaching our high school students enough mathematics and physics. Given this atmosphere, you might try to guess what the panel had to say about what they believed to be absolutely essential in teaching people how to do good research on social and behavioral processes.

Were you to guess that they recommended a return to basics, a renewed emphasis on the philosophy of science and logic, a firm grounding in precise quantitative techniques for assessing behavior, and a solid background in physics, biology, and mathematics (with, perhaps, a couple of short courses in how to hold a clipboard, look serious, and keep one's lab coat clean), you would be wrong.

The first thing the panel did was analyze the process of how good research is carried out; and they concluded that the process is distinctly different from the stereotype of what research appears to be. You are probably well aware of the stereotype. It is perpetuated by numerous television series and old movies in which bright, attractive, but unusually intense men and women are to be seen carrying out crucial experiments, carefully scrutinizing the results, discussing the implications of their findings in hushed tones before revealing the new discovery to a thankful world, and, finally, retreating back into the lab to continue their quest for truth. There are several interesting components to this TV version of science. There is usually the implication that elaborate equipment is an essential— banks of flashing lights, electronic paraphernalia, and, at least, a computer terminal if not an actual computer. Further, the whole process is depicted as being quite formal, rather cut-and-dried. You stick the data into the magnificent machine, which analyzes and interprets them, and the truth is revealed unto you in the form of a printout or (more dramatically) an electronic display.

The Nature of Research

In fact, nothing could be further from the truth. Research is simply not like that. It is an informal, messy-looking process. It is so different from the stereotype that it has even been suggested – somewhat facetiously – that the history of science be rated X (Brush, 1974) and kept from impressionable young students because it does such violence to the image of scientists as careful weighers of evidence pro and con, concerned only with being objective. The most important parts of research are, in fact, subjective and have little to do with elaborate quantitative analyses or expensive laboratory equipment. The essential components of research – where it begins and where it leads – have to do with observations of phenomena and the development of hunches, ideas, and questions about the hows and whys of things. Why do females generally excel in verbal skills and males in mathematics? Is it all a function of social learning? Is there a genetic component? Why did SAT scores decline in the 1970s? [Wharton (1977) has noted that at least 79 different explanations have been offered in response to this last question.]

Once an idea or a potential explanation is developed for some phenomenon, you usually want to try it out, to see whether or not it works. Research methods are the tools for doing that. They are simply techniques and skills that help you find answers to your questions, that help you check on your hypotheses. Thus, there is nothing mysterious about scientific research, it is simply a broad term that refers to any of a number of ways of taking a systematic approach to finding out about things. The crucial part is the question itself. All of the research methods, all of the fancy equipment are simply aids for testing out answers to questions. As Pirsig (1974) put it, a mechanic who blows the horn to check on the battery is informally conducting true research. He assumes that if the battery is okay, the horn will blow. He is testing a hypothesis by putting the question to nature: Does the horn blow? The danger is that you may conclude more from your findings than is warranted. If, for example, the horn fails to blow and the mechanic were to conclude that a new battery is needed, then there is the very real possibility of money being wasted. There may simply be a loose connection between the battery and the horn. As you shall see, the major value of research methods is that they help you clarify the conditions under which you seek answers to your questions. Thus, they help you avoid concluding more than is justified from the answers you receive. For a well-known example of political foot-in-mouth disease, caused by inferring more than one should from some research, see page 5.

Research on human behavior is important because it helps us understand ourselves and others. Not only is it obviously important, it can also be fun, and anybody who is interested can do it. You do not have to be a genius. In fact, that panel of distinguished researchers mentioned earlier suggested that above a certain optimum level—such as that of the average college student—intelligence may be less important in conducting good research than curiosity, nonconformity, and a tendency to question authority. Further, when dealing with research on human behavior and social processes, there is no clear dividing line that marks it off from the sort of informal research that you have all been doing all your life. From observing and reading to asking your friends and conducting informal experiments, you have learned a great deal about human behavior, and in the process you have learned a great deal about how to learn about human behavior. If you had not, you probably would not have been able to function well enough to get out of the first grade, much less into college. Thus, rather than an introduction to research methods in the social and behavioral sciences, you might want to think of this text as a guide to continuing education, or even advanced study.

The Complex Nature of Behavior

The study of human behavior and social processes is quite different from, say, the study of physics. Physics is often considered to be the epitome of what a science should be like. For years it was held up as the model for the social and life sciences to imitate. But, physics deals with inanimate matter, not people. People are all too animate. They have plans, purposes, and goals. They interpret and give meanings to aspects of their worlds. They are not like blocks of wood to be slid down inclined planes so that friction can be assessed. (Friction might, however, be created should some naive investigator try asking people to do that.)

For an example of this basic difference, consider almost any social exchange between two people, for example, a smile or a pat on the back. What is really important is the interpretation of the act—what it is taken to mean—and that cannot be determined by the physical characteristics of the act alone. Whether a smile is taken as an expression of friendliness, of condescension, or of evil intent is partly a function of what Gergen (1980) referred to as the RETROSPECTIVE CONTEXT, that is, those events believed to have led up to a smile. But, the meaning attached to a smile is also subject to infinite revision; and those revisions are a function of the EMERGENT

SPEED KILLS–OR IS IT WET HIGHWAYS?

In 1956 the State of Connecticut instituted a severe crackdown on speeders to see if more rigorous enforcement of speed laws would decrease the number of traffic-related deaths. At the end of the year, 40 fewer lives had been lost on the highways in Connecticut than in 1955 and the Governor, Abraham Ribicoff, issued the following statement: "With the saving of 40 lives in 1956, a reduction of 12.3 percent from the 1955 motor vehicle death toll, we can say that the program is definitely worthwhile" (Campbell, 1969b).

Thus, cracking down on speeders was followed by a clear decrease in traffic death tolls. But was Ribicoff's statement justified? He clearly implied that cracking down on speeders caused the decrease in traffic deaths. What are some other possibilities? Campbell (1969b) described several:

1. In 1956, there may have been less rain and snow, with resulting clearer and dryer roads than in 1955. One possible consequence would be fewer accidents in 1956.
2. In addition to cracking down on speeders, Connecticut may have instituted a fasten-your-seat-belt campaign so that fewer fatal injuries occurred, but not necessarily fewer accidents.
3. Death rates may have been steadily declining from year to year even prior to the crackdown.

There are other possibilities, but the point here is simply that Ribicoff's implication that the crackdown caused the reduction in deaths cannot be justified by the simple fact that the reduction followed the crackdown.

CONTEXT, that is, events that follow a smile. What was taken for friendliness may later be seen as having been an expression of condescension.

Thus, the problem of meaning, or interpretation, makes the study of human behavior both more complex and more interesting than the study of inanimate matter. As McKearney (1977, 1978) pointed out, however, behavior becomes meaningful only when you learn something about its functional significance, what it is intended to accomplish.

People and Situations

If you could ignore what people are trying to accomplish by behaving in particular ways, that is, if you could ignore their purposes, their plans, their motives, then research on human behavior might be quite simple. But as any good detective will tell you, motives cannot be ignored. Quite the contrary, discovering a motive is often the key to solving a case. Sherlock Holmes once was puzzled by a man chasing around London trying to find a particular Christmas goose – not just any goose, but one particular goose. Inquiry revealed that (1) the man worked in a hotel in which a large diamond had recently been stolen from a guest, (2) the man's sister ran a small goose farm not far from the hotel, and (3) several days after the theft the man's sister had sold all her geese. Holmes began to suspect that the man was a thief who had chosen an unusual hiding place for his booty. By attributing a motive to the man, his behavior was made meaningful; and, needless to say, Holmes was correct.

People are rational beings, and you need to keep that in mind. They are not simply automata who respond to situations. Quite often behavior that appears unusual has a reasonable explanation, and the task of research is to ferret out the data that will help bring those explanations to light, data that will help make the seemingly bizarre understandable. It is not always easy, but you must begin with the assumption that it can be done.

Take an example. To an outsider, the Hindu refusal to eat beef seems very odd. How can it be that those millions of cows wander around the countryside in India and that, at the same time, famine is endemic there? Why don't the people just eat some of those cows? It comes as something of a surprise that those sacred cows have to be kept alive, at all costs, or India's rather shaky economy would collapse. According to Harris (1974), India has 60 million farms. Each needs at least one pair of oxen or water buffalo for traction animals. There are only 80 million traction animals available, however – a shortage of 40 million. This shortage of draft animals is a serious threat to the Indian peasant farmer because, should he lose an ox, he would be unable to plow and would lose his farm. Oxen, of course, come from those sacred zebu cows, and even a skinny old cow can breed. Further, Harris points out that India's cattle produce 700 million tons of recoverable manure, about half of which is used for fertilizer and the rest as fuel for cooking. The annual thermal equivalent of the cow dung being used for cooking would be 27 million tons of kerosene, 35 million tons of coal, or 68 million tons of wood – resources that India simply does not have. Also, the cows are effective scavengers, and what they eat is usually not fit for human consumption. There is more to the story, but the point is simply that even apparently nonfunctional aspects of human behavior often have reasonable explanations.

On a general level, it seems to be the case that most explanations of human behavior have at least two components. Behavior is seen as being a function of both the person and the situation in which the person is immersed (Cronbach, 1957; Bowers, 1973). It is a truism that very few situations influence everybody in the same way. Consider a restaurant or a movie. Ask 10 people what they think of a particular restaurant and you will get 10 different opinions – often with little overlap. Some people will base their evaluation on the prices, some on the quality of the food, some on the service, some on the range of selections, some on the atmosphere, some on the noise level. People react to situations differently, of course, because of who and what they are, because of what they bring to the situation in terms of past experiences, genetic endowment, expectations, preferences, and even such fleeting phenomena as whether they are having a good day or a bad day.

What this means for research is that when trying to understand why a person behaved in a particular way in a particular situation you need to examine more than just the characteristics of the person and the characteristics of the situation. You need to pay particular attention to the fit between the two. As an illustration, consider the relationship between a group leader's personal style (i.e., managing and controlling versus relaxed and permissive) and the group's performance. Fiedler (1955, 1973) found that the nature of this relationship depends on whether the group situation is favorable or unfavorable to the leader. For Fiedler, GROUP SITUATION refers to three variables: (1) whether the leader has good or poor interpersonal relations with key group members, (2) whether the task confronting the group is highly structured or not, and (3) whether the leader has much or little power and authority over the group members. His reasoning was that in situations where all of these variables are favorable (a structured and clear task, good interpersonal relations with important group members, and a powerful leader), the group will be ready to get on with the task and a straightforward and directive leader is likely to be more effective. When the conditions are very poor for the leader, a directive, controlling leader will also be most effective because someone with the strength to step in and get the group organized and underway is needed. On the other hand, when conditions are only moderately favorable (or moderately unfavorable), a permissive, considerate leader might be most effective. Here the task is ambiguous or relations with group members are uneasy. The situation calls for someone who can coordinate conflicting views and smooth ruffled feathers. Thus, a person who is an effective leader in one situation might be the worst possible leader in another situation.

What, then, is the goal of research in the social and behavioral sciences? Stated very broadly, it is the development of explanatory concepts that help you understand individual behavior and social processes, concepts that help make life intelligible (Cronbach, 1975; Gergen, 1978). Fiedler's explanation of the relationship between a leader's style, the group situation, and group effectiveness has made the results from a number of studies understandable. His explanation has helped behavioral scientists interpret and make sense of an important set of person–situation interactions. It is important to note, however, that somebody may come along tomorrow with a better explanation than Fiedler's. That would be genuine scientific progress. For an example, see the Discussion on page 9.

Multidisciplinary Reality

Science is a creative enterprise in which progress often consists, as in the Discussion, of looking at some old data in a new way. It sounds simple, and it can be. However, discerning relationships among apparently diverse phenomena can be inhibited by a number of things, both psychological (Adams, 1980) and institutional (Straus, 1973). The common core of these blocks to creative thinking seems to be a tendency to oversimplify the multidimensional and multidisciplinary nature of reality. Do not misunderstand. Simplification is important, even essential, for day-to-day existence. We simply do not have the time or energy to react to every person or object in all their glorious uniqueness. If we did take the time, we might never get past breakfast each morning—inspecting and tasting each cornflake, evaluating each for crispness, flavor, similarity to other cornflakes, dissimilarity to Cheerios, to oatmeal, to Rice Krispies. We would go crazy. A cornflake is a cornflake, and we have better ways to spend our time. But, psychological and institutional practices that may be generally beneficial can still inhibit creativity.

Consider the way in which STEREOTYPING can keep you from seeing a person or a thing in more than one way. Once you have categorized an object as a *chair*, say, it is hard to think of any use for it other than to sit on—or, possibly, to stand on to reach something on a shelf. With people, labels are even worse because they often become self-fulfilling prophecies (Jones, 1977). The way in which you categorize someone influences your behavior toward them which, in turn, influences their behavior—often in such a way as to validate the label that started the whole vicious circle. Eisenberg (1972) gave an excellent example of this process:

> So long as the "nature" of insanity was thought to be violent, and so long as the insane were chained, beaten, and locked in cells, madmen raged and fumed. With the introduction of the "moral treatment" of the insane at the beginning of the 19th century, violence in mental asylums markedly abated. A century later, the "nature" of insanity was perceived as social incompetence; the sick were "protected" from stress, and the institution assumed responsibility for all decision-making. Misguided benevolence stripped the patient of adult status and generated automaton-like compliance; the result was the chronicity of the back wards of our state hospitals. A generation ago, the concept of the therapeutic environment, with its rediscovery of self-government and personal responsibility as the bases for attaining competence, began to reverse the cycle of self-perpetuating hospitalization.

FACTS ARE NOT ENOUGH

Good science – whether it is social, physical, or biological – is more than just piling up documented instances of empirical relationships. The census bureau does that and does it quite well. They can tell you how many people in the United States under the age of 16 live in homes with only one parent present. How many people over 65 live alone. How many households with eight people have only one bathroom. And so on, ad infinitum. It is important information and it can indeed be useful to some social scientists, but it is not science.

The thing that distinguishes science from the mere collection of facts is the search for explanations of those facts, the search for understanding. It is important to note that the terms *explanation, understanding,* and *theory* imply more than prediction. People could predict that the sun would rise in the east long before they understood why. The development of theoretical explanations that can integrate and make intelligible large bodies of isolated facts is the major way in which science advances.

Consider this example. For most of the twentieth century, one of the problems that has interested a number of social scientists is the effect of the presence of others on an individual's performance. The data were very unclear. Sometimes the presence of others appeared to facilitate one's performance and sometimes it appeared to inhibit. For many years the only generalization one could draw was that the presence of others had an effect, even when no competition was involved. Often it was found that even within the same setting, the presence of others facilitated performance on some tasks and inhibited performance on others.

In reviewing the pertinent research, Zajonc (1965) discovered a single thread of consistency in the results. The learning of new responses always seemed to be inhibited by the presence of others, whereas the performance of familiar responses seemed to be facilitated by the presence of others. Zajonc argued that there is a general class of psychological processes known to increase the likelihood of occurrence of dominant (or, well-learned) responses. This class consists of drive, arousal, and related processes. If it could be shown that the presence of others is physiologically arousing (and it could), this would account for the findings on social facilitation because arousal is known to facilitate dominant responses. But what about social inhibition? Zajonc reasoned that in ambiguous situations, or learning situations in which the individual has not yet mastered the task, the dominant responses are usually incorrect. If performance accuracy is used as the criterion, the presence of others will inhibit correct responding because their presence facilitates dominant responses.

Zajonc's (1965) formulation has been extended and refined by Cottrell (1968), Cohen and Davis (1973), and others, but it remains an excellent example of how an insightful theoretical development can bring order to apparent chaos.

Thus, you need to be doubly watchful about the biasing effects of stereotypes on your thinking. They may partially induce the very reality you think you perceive.

There are a number of other perceptual blocks that can inhibit creativity. Adams (1980) identified three that are particularly troublesome: (1) delimiting a problem area too closely, (2) failure to see a problem from various viewpoints, and (3) not utilizing all sensory inputs. These are quite closely related. All involve the unwitting acceptance of unnecessary constraints on your approach to a problem. As an illustration, Adams used this puzzle: Without lifting your pencil from the paper and using no more than four straight lines, connect the nine dots shown below.

When most people see this problem for the first time, they assume that you are not to go outside the boundary set by the dots themselves—even though that is neither stated nor implied in the puzzle. Once you overcome that self-imposed constraint, there are a number of possible solutions, two of which are given below.

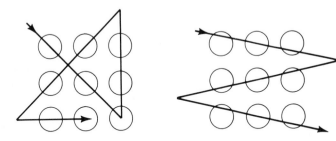

In the second solution, an additional assumed constraint has been broken. The puzzle only said connect the dots, but most people assume that means the lines must go through the center of each dot.

If you impose unnecessary restrictions on yourself when dealing with such simple puzzles, it should come as no surprise that you have great difficulties breaking out of conventional ways of looking at behavior and social processes, especially those that you are personally familiar with and involved in. Watzlawick, Beavin, and Jackson (1967) pointed out that a key ingredient of therapy with distressed married couples is often nothing more exotic than getting the partners to see how the other person views the situation. The wife who nags *because* her husband is so withdrawn usually behaves differently when she realizes that from her husband's point of view withdrawal is a *response* to her nagging, not its cause. Seeing the relationship from the other person's perspective can help clarify the dynamics involved. People usually behave, however, as if their own perspective on an issue were the only one possible, and that may blind them to some exciting, creative possibilities.

Koestler (1976) noted that the sudden switch of perspectives that is the source of much creative thinking is also the source of most humor. What usually happens in a joke is that the punch line puts a new meaning to something that has preceded it:

> San Francisco Car Salesman: With this car you could be in L.A. in 4 hours!
> Customer: But why would I want to go to L.A.?

The salesman, of course, was making a point about the car's speed. The customer's response was on another dimension, stemming from the reference to Los Angeles. According to Koestler, this is a typical pattern in jokes. One is set up by focusing attention and expectations in one direction, then brought up short by an ending that switches the focus. Koestler's point is that humor and creativity are very closely related and the key to both is the ability to break with conventional expectations and see something from a different perspective.

Unfortunately, there are not just individual perceptual blocks to this, but institutional ones as well. Consider the typical university or college. There are departments of psychology, sociology, anthropology, education, communication, political science, philosophy, history, and physiology, each focusing on some aspect of human behavior, each with a separate body of knowledge, each with a different tradition of research and theory, and each rarely looking at what the others are doing. It is absolutely absurd.

The reasons for this state of affairs are not hard to find. As Straus (1973) has pointed out, the departments in universities have become entrenched as administrative units, which means they control the budgets and such not-so-subtle powers as the hiring and firing of faculty. Further, because the university department is typically identified with a specific discipline, the administrative functions of a department function to preserve what may be outdated disciplinary identities and inappropriately compartmentalized teaching. For example, basic research methods courses could just as well be taught in a psychology department, a sociology department, an education department, a political science department, and a variety of others.

It is important to remember, then, that the disciplines most departments represent are arbitrary subdivisions of knowledge. Pick a topic you find interesting (sex roles, memory, group interaction). Each of these topics has been the subject of research by psychologists, anthropologists, historians, educators, physiologists, and philosophers. To assume that any one of these disciplines has a better, or more valid, perspective on any of these topics is simply unjustified. Imagine the potential for fresh new approaches if you were to cultivate the habit of looking at any topic from a variety of perspectives!

Thinking about the Causes of Behavior

That panel of experts mentioned earlier did note that in learning how to do research it is important for you to develop competence in designing, executing, and interpreting a variety of different types of research. This book should help. But, they also noted that much more important than any of this is the development of CREATIVITY: the ability to look for and see new relations, to reformulate or synthesize facts already known, to develop new perspectives on old problems. Although it is true that few of us are in the same league with Leonardo da Vinci, it is also true that creative thinking can be practiced and improved. As Adams (1980) noted, the way to improve one's skill at anything is to be continually conscious of one's performance and keep trying to do better. How can you do that?

Observation

The first step in creative thinking about the hows and whys of behavior is simply to *pay attention*. The necessity for careful observation can hardly be overemphasized. Particularly when dealing with human behavior, we are likely to get caught in the trap of thinking we know more than we really do because much that goes on around us is really unnecessary for us to attend to in terms of our usual day-to-day routines. We learn to ignore whole chunks of behavior of those around us. That is typically a useful habit, but it is one you need to be able to suspend at will so that you can attend to the details of behavior when you need to. Beveridge (1957) even went so far as to say that well-developed habits of observation are more important in research than is a great store of academic knowledge.

One might argue that all research methods are simply ways for helping you increase the precision of your observations. Sloppy habits of observation are not only unscientific, they can lead to embarrassing consequences, as illustrated in the following anecdote (Beveridge, 1957).

A Manchester physician, while teaching a ward class of students took a sample of diabetic urine and dipped a finger in it to taste it. He then asked all the students to repeat his action. This they reluctantly did, making grimaces, but agreeing that it tasted sweet. "I did this," said this physician, . . . "to teach you the importance of observing detail. If you had watched me carefully you would have noticed that I put my first finger in the urine but I licked my second finger."

A serious obstacle to accurate observation is the influence of preexisting beliefs, such as the stereotypes discussed earlier. There is a good deal of evidence that people often see and remember only what they expect to see. For example, Cohen (1977) asked students to rate each of a number of behaviors in terms of whether a *waitress* or a *librarian* would be more likely to exhibit it. A number of the behaviors clearly differentiated the two. A waitress was seen as being very likely to wear a uniform, not to wear glasses, to eat hamburger, and not to eat roast beef. Librarians, on the other hand, were seen as likely to wear glasses and eat roast beef but not to wear a uniform or eat hamburger. Based on these and similar items, Cohen constructed a script for a 20-minute videotape of a woman and her husband eating dinner and talking. The tape was produced so that it contained a number of behaviors that had previously been rated as being typical of a waitress and a number of behaviors typical of librarians. Some new subjects were then recruited and asked to look at the tape and answer a few questions about it. However, prior to seeing the tape, half of the subjects were told that the woman they would be viewing on the tape was a waitress and half were told that the woman they would be viewing was a librarian. As you may have guessed, those who thought they were watching a waitress were later more accurate in remembering stereotypical waitress behaviors from the tape than they were in remembering stereotypical librarian behaviors. A parallel effect occurred for those who thought they were watching a librarian.

As you shall see in Chapter 9, the influence of EXPECTATIONS on what you think you see is not confined to naive subjects in a laboratory experiment. There is a mass of evidence that experimenters may see only what they expect to if they are not careful (Rosenthal, 1976). Fortunately, there are techniques available that help prevent that, and they will be explored in some detail later.

The line between errors of observation and errors of inference is a very unclear one—it is often difficult to tell where observation ends and inference begins. Seeing what we expect to see, for example, might just as well be termed an error of inference as of observation, that is, we infer that what we expected to see was really there. Whichever way you classify it, there is a very real tendency to fill in gaps in your observations based on how things normally occur or how they have occurred in your past experience. The danger, of course, is that things may change. They do not always continue on their normal course, and your past experience with the thing you are observing may not be typical.

In addition, your desires may interfere with accurate observation and inference. Consider the task of judging the logical validity of a syllogism such as this:

> Republicans are successful inflation fighters.
> Reagan is a Republican.
> Reagan will be successful in curbing inflation.

It has been found that people who agree with the conclusions of such syllogisms are more likely to accept invalid arguments as logical. On the other hand, people who disagree with the conclusions are more likely to err by rejecting valid arguments. A syllogism, of course, may be perfectly logical, even if you disagree with its conclusion (Janis & Frick, 1943). It will probably come as no surprise to you that the desires, emotions, and ambitions of people engaged in research can cloud their vision and bias their interpretations. One of the things that separates good researchers from bad ones, however, is that the good ones devise ways of checking themselves. Darwin, for example, would make a special note when he came across data unfavorable to his ideas. He knew he was more likely to conveniently forget such facts (Beveridge, 1957).

There are many other kinds of observation errors. You may, for example, simply miss some detail because it blends so well with its surroundings, that is, it does not stand out sufficiently to be noticed. Trying to find a penny that has been dropped in dirt the same color as the penny is an example. This observational bugaboo is termed the inability to distinguish figure from ground, a name that comes from the fact that objects of perception are always seen against a contrasting background. Optical illusions, such as those illustrated in Figure 1, are another source of inaccurate observations. In the figure, do the inside horizontal lines in A appear curved? Do those in B appear equal? Which line is longer in C, the vertical or horizontal? Which diagonal is longer in D? If you have never seen these illusions before, you might want to check your answers with a ruler.

Observation and inference are the bases for a pair of important concepts having to do with the development and testing of ideas, induction and deduction. INDUCTION involves going from the specific to the general. For example, you might notice that most of your friends have tastes very similar to your own, that most of your father's friends appear to be about the same age, and that most college professors seem to hang around with other college professors. From these isolated observations you might formulate a general proposition something like "people seem to be attracted to similar others." You would have exemplified the process of induction. DEDUCTION, on the other hand, involves applying a general principle to a specific instance. If you have already developed the principle that similarity leads to attraction, you might predict that travel groups composed of alumni

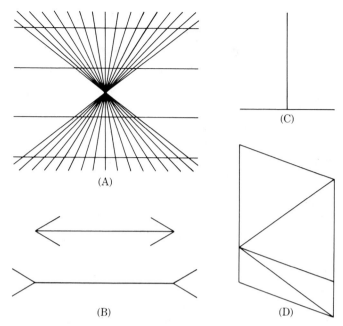

Figure 1 OPTICAL ILLUSIONS reinforce the point that we may be mistaken about what we think we see, even when the evidence is right in front of us.

from a single university will like each other better – and, hence, have a better time on their trip – than will randomly composed groups. Induction and deduction are intricately woven into everyday life, and you use them all the time. Horse race fans who do not know much about horses typically use an inductive approach when placing their bets. They may, for example, look at how many races a horse has already won – "he's won five races so he'll win this one." Bettors who know more about horses (or like to think they do) will usually use a deductive approach. They want to know about things like the horse's bloodlines. How fast was the sire when he was racing?

Neither induction nor deduction is infallible, of course, a fact that racetrack owners will gleefully confirm. With induction you may find that the specific instances you have examined are a peculiar, unrepresentative sample of those you could have examined. Thus, the general principle you have induced from them may not be very general after all. This difficulty will be examined in more detail in Chapter Six. With deduction, on the other hand, the general principle (fast horses sire fast horses) that you attempt to apply to a particular situation may be wrong. Even such a master of deduction as Sherlock Holmes sometimes operated with false premises.

He once deduced that a man he was looking for was a man of exceptional intelligence. The basis for this deduction was his belief that a large head was a sure sign of high intelligence and he had the man's hat, which was enormous. It is now known, of course, that head size and intelligence are not necessarily related.

Precise observation is important, then, but it is not enough. There needs to be some organization to your observations. Random collections of facts are almost totally useless—unless you want to be a contestant on a quiz show. Understanding seems to be advanced primarily by purposeful observation, by curiosity about answers to specific questions.

Curiosity and Sources of Ideas

To say that understanding is advanced primarily by purposeful observation does not mean that chance is unimportant in research. As Cronbach (1975) has pointed out, you need to cultivate an "open-eyed, open-minded appreciation of the surprises that nature deposits in the investigative net." There have been many examples of research workers making observations that could have had genuinely important consequences had they become curious about the meaning of what they were seeing. If they had only stopped for a moment and asked themselves, "What does that mean? Why did that happen?" Beveridge (1957) has noted that prior to Sir Alexander Fleming's discovery of penicillin, the first of the modern miracle drugs, many people had noticed the little green mold that sometimes formed on bacterial colonies in laboratory petri dishes and that seemed to kill the bacteria. Fleming's predecessors treated it as a nuisance, whereas Fleming became curious about it—especially about the fact that it seemed to inhibit the growth of bacteria.

Even when you are unable to immediately follow up observations of interest, you need to store them in question form so that later observations can be screened for their pertinence to the question. Some people make it a point to jot down things that pique their interest; they keep a notebook of things they are curious about. Darwin, of course, was a master of this. While he was sailing toward South America on H.M.S. *Beagle*, he noticed a large number of spiders in the rigging of the ship one day and was curious about how they could have gotten so far from land. Some weeks later at St. Fe, he was watching a spider on top of a post when it suddenly sent out a number of threads from its spinners. These diverged upward from the spider's body like ribbons blown by the wind. When the spider released its grip on the post it sailed away, borne by the wind. Darwin was not idly watching a spider on a post. He had been curious about how spiders could arrive on board the *Beagle* when it was in midocean. He was seeking an answer to a specific question.

Curiosity about things is the source of all research. Darwin himself was often exasperated by people who did not share his enormous curiosity. He could not understand why many people never seemed to wonder about why some springs were hot and others were cold, why there were earthquakes and volcanoes, why mountains existed in one area but not in others.

Curiosity alone may be too diffuse to be of much use; it needs to be given focus and direction. One of the best ways to do that is to make a list of possible explanations for the thing you are curious about and look for evidence on the validity of your explanations. This will be discussed more fully in the following section, but first a word about generating potential explanations. That is a very important part of the process because the potential explanations you begin with will determine what sort of evidence you seek, which, in turn, will very likely determine what you find. Also, as McGuire (1973) has noted, it is hardly worth developing a great methodological arsenal if the explanations you want to examine are trivial. What is not worth doing is not worth doing well.

In the following pages the terms *explanation* and *hypothesis* will be used interchangeably; and, again, be sure to note that a simple prediction is neither. You may be able to predict many things that you do not understand. Many people find their curiosity engaged by just such phenomena, and the creative process begins when they start trying to explain them. Often curiosity is piqued, given focus, and articulated into hypotheses only as a result of confrontations with data of various sorts. Concreteness and familiarity with the thing to be explained are essential. It is very difficult to come up with good hypotheses about drug addiction if you know nothing about the life situations and styles of drug addicts, if you know nothing about the functions that drugs can serve for people, or if you know nothing of the physiological effects of drugs.

Suppose you were to find yourself in a situation in which something unusual occurs, something you do not understand. A careful analysis of the elements of the situation may be a fruitful source of hypotheses about the event. Such an analysis, of course, is a way of becoming intimate with the problem, a way of forcing yourself to be very precise and concrete about what actually happened. Consider this example. While eating dinner at a large New York restaurant, one of Freud's colleagues, A. A. Brill, developed the hypothesis that what appears to be telepathic communication between two people in the same setting may be explained by their simultaneously seeing something in the situation which *independently* triggers the same thought in each (Freud, 1938). It happened like this. As he and his wife were eating, Brill casually remarked that he wondered how a friend of theirs was liking Pittsburgh. His wife was quite surprised and claimed that she had just been thinking the same thing. For a while Brill was mystified, but careful inspection of the setting revealed a man, seated toward the rear of the restaurant, who bore a remarkable resemblance to their friend in Pittsburgh. Apparently, busy with eating and talking, Brill and his wife had not noticed the man consciously, but his visual image had triggered the same association for both of them.

Careful analysis of the components of a specific situation is conceptually very similar to the sort of intensive case study carried out by many psychiatrists and clinical psychologists during the course of psychotherapy with an individual patient. Such long-term, in-depth studies of individual lives can be fertile sources of hypotheses about the forces that shape behavior.

Another important source of hypothesis formation is the use of *analogy*, borrowing some principle from one area of knowledge and seeing if it can be applied in another. One of the best examples of this is McGuire's (1964) work on inducing resistance to persuasion. McGuire noted that for many diseases people are immunized by actually having a very weak case of the disease – the principle of vaccination. Vaccination works by stimulating the body's defense against the particular disease so that if the individual is later exposed to the disease, the defenses will be better able to combat infection. It occurred to McGuire that, by analogy, a similar principle might operate in the area of persuasion and attitude change. That is, one might use the vaccination analogy to derive hypotheses about producing resistance to persuasion. To adhere to the analogy, however, it was necessary to use beliefs that subjects had seldom, if ever, heard being attacked because vaccination is for diseases to which the person has not previously been exposed. McGuire found an appropriate category of beliefs to fit the analogy, that is, cultural truisms. Without going into all the details of McGuire's research, it should be noted that the analogy proved quite useful. One finding, for example, was that people were more resistant to changing their beliefs following a mild attack on those beliefs (vaccination) than they were following receipt of a message supporting their beliefs. The mild attack seemed to stimulate their defense of the belief. Analogies can be an excellent source of hypotheses. Original, creative research often begins with the perception of an analogy between two things previously thought to be unrelated.

A particularly intriguing source of hypotheses about human behavior is the careful dissection of some bit of folk wisdom or *rule of thumb*. This is a somewhat ticklish area for many social scientists. They, apparently, do not want to be contaminated by dealing with what everybody already knows. If they do deal with such things, it may be only to dredge up examples of instances in which common sense is mistaken (e.g., Jones & Gerard, 1967). The motivation seems to be nothing more than a need to prove that social science is really scientific. It all seems a little silly, however, because in the study of human behavior and interpersonal relationships, the greatest body of knowledge available is contained in the day-to-day experience of people. Hence, rules of thumb and folk wisdom are not only important, they are crucial sources of hypotheses. You need to make such folk wisdom more precise, to try to understand its limits, to dissect it, to analyze it. There is little to be gained by merely scoffing at it.

One of the forms in which folk wisdom comes down to us is the APHORISM, a pithy saying that is assumed to express an important truth or principle. It is often the case that an interesting hypothesis about behavior can be extracted from such sayings. What, for example, is the hypothesis contained in this quotation from John Stuart Mill? "One can, to an almost laughable degree, infer what a man's wife is like from his opinions about women in general." Stated formally, the implicit hypothesis has nothing to do with husbands and wives or even with males and females. It has to do with one's perspective and might be phrased, "Everyone assumes that their experience is typical" – an idea that has some interesting implications (Page 20). As an exercise, see if you can formulate the general hypotheses contained in the aphorisms listed below, all of which come from a selection by Auden and Kronenberger (1966).

A beautiful woman should break her mirror early. (Gracian)

Tell me to what you pay attention and I will tell you who you are. (Ortega y Gasset)

The "silly" question is the first intimation of some totally new development. (Whitehead)

Truths turn into dogmas the moment they are disputed. (Chesterton)

The hypotheses implicit in these aphorisms have led to some exciting research on labeling and the consequences of stereotyping (Snyder & Swann, 1978), the influence of personality on perception (Bruner, 1951), scientific revolutions (Kuhn, 1970), and the polarization of attitudes (Myers & Bishop, 1970). The point here, however, is that folk wisdom remains a vast, and largely untapped, reservoir of hypotheses for those curious about human behavior.

There are many other sources of hypotheses. Conflicting and apparently contradictory research results are another. When one investigator finds that TV violence does not instigate or legitimize aggression among viewers and another investigator finds that it does, a genuine intellectual puzzle is posed. What accounts for the discrepancy? Perhaps the levels of violence differed in the studies. Maybe there were differences between the viewers questioned in the two studies. Maybe . . . and so it goes. Many of the possible explanations may be testable; strategies may be devised for obtaining evidence on their plausibility.

THE "SOMEONE WHO" ARGUMENT

According to Nisbett and Ross (1980), in our attempts to understand the world around us we are often overly influenced by concrete, sensory data. We fail to recognize that the data we are exposed to, the things we see with our own eyes or hear with our own ears, may be unusual, biased, or even unique. Consider this scenario from Nisbett, Borgida, Crandall, and Reed (1976).

> Suppose you wish to buy a new car and have decided that on grounds of economy and longevity you want to purchase one of those solid, stalwart, middle-class Swedish cars – either a Volvo or a Saab. As a prudent and sensible buyer, you go to *Consumer Reports*, which informs you that the consensus of their experts is that the Volvo is mechanically superior, and the consensus of the readership is that the Volvo has the better repair record. Armed with this information, you decide to go and strike a bargain with the Volvo dealer before the week is out. In the interim, however, you go to a cocktail party where you announce this intention to an acquaintance. He reacts with disbelief and alarm: "A Volvo! You've got to be kidding. My brother-in-law had a Volvo. First, that fancy fuel injection computer thing went out. 250 bucks. Next he started having trouble with the rear end. Had to replace it. Then the transmission and the clutch. Finally, sold it in three years for junk."

What would your reaction be in this situation? Chances are you might have some serious second thoughts about buying a Volvo. Logically, however, you should not be bothered very much. Presumably the frequency of repair records in *Consumer Reports* were based on a large number of cars. Finding out that your friend's brother-in-law got a lemon would not change Volvo's overall record very much. Yet, people apparently give such vivid, concrete information as the friend's report more weight than it deserves. When confronted with summary statistics such as those found in *Consumer Reports* or the *Surgeon General's Report on Smoking*, people often respond with

> Yes, but I know *someone who* smokes a pack a day and is seventy-four years old.
> Yes, but I know *someone who* dropped out of school in the ninth grade and is now making $100,000 a year.
> Yes, but I know *someone who* ...

When someone tries to convince you with such arguments, you should ask yourself how representative their example is. Do *most people* who drop out of school in the ninth grade end up making so much money?

Research Strategy

When you become curious about some aspect of human behavior, how do you proceed? There is a great deal of information about behavior and social processes already available, of course, so there are many things that you might be able to just go look up in some reference book. Suppose, for example, you were interested in the frequency of abortions. Are abortions rare occurrences or not? How does the number of abortions compare to the number of live births in various parts of the country? Answers to questions like this are easily available. The Center for Disease Control, a branch of the U.S. Public Health Service, publishes an annual summary of morbidity and mortality statistics for the U.S. In 1977, there were 325 reported legal abortions for every 1000 live births in the country, but there was tremendous variation in this ratio from state to state—from 54 to over 1000 abortions for every 1000 live births (Center for Disease Control, 1978).

The answers to most questions about behavior, however, are not quite so easily found. Usually what you want to know is a little more involved than a simple rate of occurrence, although that can be quite important to know. If you are like most of us, chances are you are more interested in the hows and whys of behavior. Why do some women and not others get abortions? Why was Carter defeated in his bid for a second term? How can I improve my study skills? How does racial prejudice originate and how is it maintained? To answer questions like these you may have to do some original research. The answers to these questions are likely to be quite complex, and even though some things are already known about each of them, much remains to be learned. But, where do you begin?

Multiple Hypotheses

When you are curious about some aspect of behavior, whether it is your own behavior or that of someone else, one of the best ways to begin your effort to understand it is simply to sit down and write out as many plausible explanations for the behavior as you can. Make a list. It is worth forcing yourself to spend some time on this because many people have a tendency to take the first reasonably coherent explanation that comes to mind and run with it, that is, they assume that it must be *the* explanation. This technique of listing possible explanations is not new. Almost 100 years ago, Chamberlin (1890) christened it the METHOD OF MULTIPLE WORKING HYPOTHESES and strongly advocated the self-conscious development of every rational explanation of the phenomenon of interest.

In addition to keeping you from jumping too quickly into some ill-advised data-chasing expedition (the scientific equivalent of the wild goose chase), taking the time to list all the plausible explanations you can think of for some behavior has other advantages. Perhaps most important is that it is likely to make clear to you that the behavior or social process in question does not have a single, simple cause. Adequate explanations of behavior usually involve several factors, and the relative contributions of these causal factors may vary, depending on the circumstances. The explanation for behavior, in short, is likely to be complex (Figure 2). Such a concern for the multiple causes of behavior make research both more interesting and more difficult. You will find that you become less concerned with isolating *the* cause of the behavior in question and more interested in understanding the conditions under which one cause predominates and how those conditions differ from the ones under which a second cause predominates. As McKearney (1977, 1978) pointed out, EQUIFINALITY is an important characteristic of behavior. That is, the same behavior may be produced by a number of different means. For example, Byrne (1971) has shown that several different kinds of similarity – in attitudes, in values, in economic status – may lead to attraction between people. However, interpersonal attraction may also be produced by things other than similarity. In fact, certain kinds of dissimilarity may lead to attraction.

Before you go any farther, try it. Suppose that last October, the police department in your town began a home-cruiser program. Off-duty police officers were allowed to drive their patrol cars home and, as long as they paid for the gas used, could use the cars as they would their own – to go shopping, to the movies, to buy groceries, and so on. The idea was that this would make the police much more visible, with cruisers parked in residential areas and at shopping centers and, generally, on the streets. The hoped-for consequence of this increase in visibility, of course, was a decrease in crime. In January, after a three-month evaluation of the program, the mayor called a press conference at which it was announced that the program was a smashing success. Between October and January there had been a sizable decrease in burglaries, car thefts, muggings, and vandalism throughout the city. You read this in the paper the next day and it arouses your interest. Was the home-cruiser program a success? How many explanations can you think of that might account for the decrease in crime referred to by the mayor? (See Figure 2 in Chapter 4.)

There are some obvious possibilities. One is that crime generally decreases in cold weather, especially outdoor crime like car thefts, muggings, and vandalism. Thus, the late fall and winter weather between October and January may deserve the credit. You also should not rule out the possibility that the mayor was right, that the ubiquitous police cars made some would-be criminals think twice about the wages of sin and forego the crime they had contemplated. Another potential explanation is that crime had been steadily decreasing in the city, even prior to October,

"I think you should be more explicit here in step two."

Figure 2 EXPLAINING THE RELATIONSHIP BETWEEN EVENTS is essential to the advancement of understanding. (Cartoon © Sidney Harris.)

because of stepped-up patrols by on-duty policemen. Perhaps several new industries had opened up, providing jobs for the unemployed.

Whether you are interested in the evaluation of the home-cruiser program or the question of why you do not seem to have many friends, once you have generated a number of possible explanations, the next step is the same. You use all the ingenuity you can muster to devise methods for gathering evidence on the validity of your various hypotheses—*one, all, some,* or *none* of which may turn out to be adequate. The task of the chapters that follow is to acquaint you with the variety of methods that are available. As you shall see, each method has certain advantages and certain disadvantages. The purpose in acquainting you with this wealth of ways for answering questions about behavior is to help you make intelligent choices about which method or methods would be appropriate for answering a given question.

First, however, a few words about CRITICISM are in order. When you are trying to develop explanations, being too critical of your ideas may hinder progress. If you stifle an idea just because it appears to be a little far-out, you may be ensuring that you will not come up with any new perspectives on the question of interest. At the stage of hypothesis generation or theoretical analysis, then, you need to encourage the free-flow of ideas. A little bone-cracking, audacious thought is needed, and Gergen (1980) has suggested several strategies that might help improve the quality of your hypotheses. Consciously try looking at the question from several points of view; consider the assumptions behind the question and extend them to the borders of absurdity; try fitting the question into some new analogies. Save your critical powers until later, because you will need them.

Specifically, you will need them when you are selecting or constructing a method to evaluate your explanations. That is the time to be critical, to look for loopholes, to play the skeptic–not to play, to *be* the skeptic. Will the method you select really provide an answer to your question or will it simply help you amass ambiguous information? Samelson (1980) has argued that at this point most people engaged in research on human behavior are *not sufficiently critical*. They are often too ready to accept the evidence in favor of a particular explanation if they find it congenial. That, of course, is one of the main reasons for entertaining several explanations simultaneously. It helps avoid the trap of becoming unduly attached to any one.

As you can probably guess, it is a difficult balance to maintain: nurturing and encouraging ideas, hypotheses, theories, but demanding rigor and precision in their evaluation. But the real purpose of all the research methods to be discussed, all the fancy equipment and paraphernalia of logic and design and sampling and measurement, is simply "to make sure Nature hasn't misled you into thinking you know something you don't actually know" (Pirsig, 1974). The following chapters will help you hone your critical skills with respect to particular methods and help you learn what questions you should ask in trying to design a technique for evaluating your ideas. There are, however, a couple of general research strategies that need to be introduced before looking at specific methods, strategies that will help you ensure that you are not misled into thinking you know something that you do not.

Triangulation and Replication

Suppose you have come up with a hypothesis that you would like to check out, one that you would like to gather some evidence on to see whether it is accurate. For example, you might be curious about the relationship between intelligence and creativity (mentioned at the beginning of this chapter). Specifically, you might question the implications of some of the comments and hypothesize that the highly intelligent are generally more observant, less constrained by social norms, more inclined to question authority, and, thus, more creative. The problem you would immediately have to face is referred to as OPERATIONALIZATION. That is, when you want to measure concepts such as *high intelligence* or *inclined to question authority* or *creativity*, you must be able to point to something and say, "I am willing to take this as an example of the concept." To operationalize a concept, then, is to specify instances of that concept in the world around you.

There are three things to note about this definition. First, it is imperative that you be as clear and as precise as possible about how a particular concept is being operationalized. To say that *high intelligence* is indicated by someone doing well on an IQ test would not be acceptable. What does *doing well* mean, and which test are you talking about? Second, people may argue with you about the particular index you have chosen as your operationalization of a concept. The evidence may indicate that what you have chosen as an index of the concept is flawed in some way. If you were to choose grade point average (GPA) as an index of intelligence, you would probably catch a lot of flak about GPA being more a function of motivation than intelligence. Third, it should be noted, if it is not already clear, that it is possible to operationalize a concept in more than one way. How many different behaviors can you think of, for example, that might be taken as indications of a *disposition to question authority*?

Fortunately, the fact that such concepts can usually be operationalized in several different ways has led to a general research strategy for checking on our observations and holding our biases at least partly in check. The strategy is called TRIANGULATION OF MEASUREMENT or MULTIPLE OPERATIONISM (Webb, Campbell, Schwartz, & Sechrest, 1966). Although the names are forbiddingly polysyllabic, the technique is really quite simple. Operationalize your concepts in several different ways and seek evidence on your hypothesis with several different methods. That is all that is involved. This is an important strategy because there is no research method without bias—as you will see in the chapters that follow—and different methods have different biases. Thus, when you can obtain evidence for your hypothesis using two or more different methods, you can rightfully have more confidence in its accuracy than when only one method is employed.

Another way of saying this is to pose it as a problem of replication. Suppose you were to observe some phenomenon—say, that friends tend to be similar to each other. If, the following day, you were to observe the same people in the same situation and conclude that friends tend to be similar to each other, you would be conducting an EXACT REPLICATION of your observations. Exact replications are not very informative. If your observation of the relationship between similarity and friendly behavior was due to some peculiarity of the situation, then observing the same situation again will not eliminate the peculiarity. Perhaps the people you saw were rehearsing their parts in a play. If you can observe a relationship between similarity and friendship in several different situations, among several different kinds of people, at several different times of the year, you can be more positive that the relationship really exists. It is rather unlikely that all those people were rehearsing for that same play. Looking for the relationship in different situations, with different subjects, under different circumstances, and using different techniques of measurement is what is meant by triangulation of measurement or CONCEPTUAL, as opposed to exact, REPLICATION (Jones, 1966).

For example, suppose you had developed the idea that in forming an impression of another person we often pay too much attention to their overt behavior and not enough attention to how that behavior has been forced by the situation, by the role that the person has been put in. The issue of interest, then, might be phrased as the extent to which the social roles we play in our day-to-day existence make us appear to have qualities and characteristics that we do not really possess. What are some of the ways in which you might investigate this?

You might select participant observation (a method to be discussed in the following chapter), as Goffman (1961) did when he became assistant athletic director of a large mental hospital in Washington, D.C. For the year that he spent there, observing and taking notes on all facets of the role of mental patients, Goffman focused most of his attention on the manner in which both the institution and the staff stripped away all supports that could have enabled patients to maintain or regain a normal self-concept. He found that mental hospitals disrupt nearly all the activities that allow people to think of themselves as normal, responsible adults with some degree of self-determination and freedom of action. Further, this disruption begins even before the patients are fully admitted. The admission process is often what Goffman refers to as a BETRAYAL FUNNEL, in which the soon-to-be patients find themselves odd person out in a triad consisting of a psychiatrist, the patient's next of kin, and the patient. The next of kin, who may have suggested hospitalization, is not likely to be able to provide a realistic picture of what life in the hospital will be like and the extent to which the patient's personal freedom will be curtailed. Hence, one side effect of the admissions process is that the patients are likely to become embittered about and distrustful of this person.

At each stage of the admissions process, there is a further loss of adult status: personal possessions are taken away, institutional clothes are issued, and often the patients must even request permission to go to the bathroom. Patients soon learn that they must defer to all staff members and nearly all aspects of life on the wards are regimented and done in the company of others. Thus, the patients are denied control over their own time and energy. Those who had been work-oriented on the outside become demoralized because there is nothing to do but sit around or engage in petty activities, such as playing cards or watching TV, and these only at specified times.

To an observer, it appears that these people belong just where they are. Judging only from their behavior, they appear irresponsible and childlike. They have to be told what to do, they never take the initiative, and most of their activities are trivial ways of wasting time. Goffman's major point, of course, is that the patients he observed were, in effect, made to behave as they did by the nature of the institution in which they found themselves.

There are ways other than participant observation, however, to investigate this question of whether you really fail to consider the impact of the situation in which you observe another's behavior. For example, Ross, Amabile, and Steinmetz (1977) designed a laboratory experiment that is conceptually very closely related to Goffman's study at St. Elizabeth's Hospital. Ross and co-workers recruited Stanford University undergraduates to participate in a quiz game; one member of each pair was assigned the role of contestant and one the role of questioner. The questioners were instructed to compose a set of difficult, but potentially answerable, questions on any topic they desired. Thus, they were free to select questions on isolated, esoteric bits of trivia that they happened to know ("What's the name of the post at the end of a banister?" "Which former presidents of the United States died on the same day?"). The contestants were to try to answer such questions. During the actual quiz, the questioners gave the contestants 30 seconds to answer, then indicated whether the answer given was correct, and supplied the correct answer when it was not. Immediately following the quiz, the subjects rated themselves and their partners on their level of general knowledge. As may be seen in Figure 3, the results indicated that contestants rated themselves as significantly less knowledgeable than their partners. This occurred in spite of the fact that the contestants knew the questioners had been given the task of selecting questions about isolated bits of knowledge that they happened to possess. Had the roles of questioner and contestant been reversed, the new questioners could easily have dreamed up questions that they could answer but that their partners could not. As it was, the contestants failed to consider the self-presentational advantage enjoyed by their questioners. In a subsequent experiment, Ross and co-workers were able to demonstrate that observers who watched the quiz game and who heard the instructions given the questioners also estimated that the questioners were significantly more knowledgeable than the contestants.

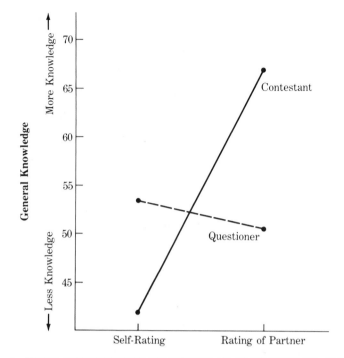

Figure 3 SELF-ASSESSMENT OF GENERAL KNOWLEDGE. Following a quiz in which the questioners made up the questions, both questioners and contestants rated themselves and their partners on how much knowledge they believed they and their partner possessed. (From Ross, Amabile, & Steinmetz, 1977.)

This is not to imply that triangulation of measurement necessarily involves the use of two research methods as different as the approaches of Goffman and Ross et al. That would be ideal because the greater the difference in the methods, the less the chance that they share the same biases. It is much more common, however, for an investigator to employ variations on a single methodological theme in the attempt to operationalize a concept in different ways. For example, Langer (1975) was interested in what is referred to as the ILLUSION OF CONTROL. Her idea was that people often confuse situations in which the outcomes are determined by sheer chance with those in which they can exert some control over the outcome. As a result, they often behave in chance situations as if skills and other such performance-relevant phenomena make a difference. They do not, of course. In a series of experiments, Langer operationalized this idea in several different ways. Consider two examples: In one experiment subjects drew for high card (a chance-determined event) against an opponent who was either neatly attired and apparently competent or sloppily dressed, awkward and apparently incompetent. With a chance event, the apparent competence of one's opponent should make no difference, but it did. Subjects were unwilling to bet as much on the draw when facing a competent opponent as they bet when facing an incompetent opponent. In a second experiment Langer found that subjects allowed to select their own ticket from a box of lottery tickets were significantly more reluctant to part with the chosen ticket than those who had simply been handed a ticket from the box. All tickets had precisely the same chance of winning, but apparently the act of selecting the ticket gave subjects a feeling of greater control over the outcome—just as having an incompetent opponent did.

Thus, concepts may be operationalized in different ways, and it is good research strategy to do so. Whether you are interested in similarity of friends or situations that appear to coerce certain behaviors or confusions of skill-determined and chance-determined outcomes, if you can think of a couple of ways in which the concept would manifest itself, your research will be on a firmer foundation than if you operationalize the concept in only one way.

Building and Testing Theories

The purpose of research in the social and behavioral sciences is essentially the same as the purpose of the research on your own and others' behavior that you have been doing most of your life. Both are concerned primarily with the development of concepts, explanations, hypotheses, and theories that will help make life intelligible, that will help us to understand behavior. You know what a concept is, and in this book the terms *explanation* and *hypothesis* are used interchangeably. That leaves theories. One of the things that scares people off when someone starts discussing theory is that they envision an elaborate, hard-to-understand superstructure made up of varying amounts of hot air and gas, which—perhaps because of such a composition—rarely touches ground. Such a preconception is unfortunate and, usually, just plain wrong. A THEORY is nothing more than a possible explanation for some phenomena. Theories can vary enormously in scope, that is, in the range of facts they seek to explain; but at bottom a theory is purely and simply a proposed explanation. A detective who is investigating a murder and suggests that it was committed in the course of a robbery is putting forward a theory that may or may not be accurate; but it is a theory nonetheless. Such a theory usually directs the search for evidence. If the murder was committed by a robber, it was *probably* not premeditated and *probably* not committed by the victim's spouse.

Within the broad purpose of theory development, however, there are several different aspects of the research process that will engage your attention and effort to varying degrees in various stages of research. Be forewarned that separation of these three aspects is to some extent artificial; they usually fade into each other almost imperceptibly. But, definitions are in order. For convenience these different emphases of the research process are referred to as description, theoretical elaboration, and verification. DESCRIPTION is often thought of as being the first stage of research: a careful chronicle of some situation or event, with meticulous attention to detail. In anthropology, for example, a researcher might go to live in a different culture, such as that of Haiti, and write a detailed, descriptive account—termed an ETHNOGRAPHY—of what life is like there. Ethnographies and other descriptive data, anecdotes, observations, personal experiences, readings, and any other kinds of information you may have— including the results of previous research of your own—are used to begin the process of THEORETICAL ELABORATION, which is the generation of proposed explanations to account for what has been observed (or read about, or heard). Finally, VERIFICATION is simply the process of seeking evidence that indicates that your hunch or guess or proposed explanation was indeed correct. Perhaps a few examples will enhance these definitions.

Some of the best examples of description are to be found in the writings of reporters and journalists such as Tom Wolfe (1976) and Lillian Ross (1969) and in biographies and autobiographies of both the famous and the infamous. A good description is very concrete and, if successful, makes the reader feel that he or she can almost see the scene being described. Consider how much you learn in Ross's (1981) brief description of a group of Indiana teenagers arriving in New York City.

> A few Sundays ago, in the late still afternoon, a bright yellow school bus, bearing the white-on-blue license plate of the State of Indiana and with the words "BEAN BLOSSOM TWP MONROE COUNTY" painted in black letters under the windows on each side, emerged into New York City from the Holland Tunnel. Inside the bus were eighteen members of the senior class of the Bean Blossom Township High School, who were coming to the city for their first visit. The windows of the bus, as it rolled into Canal Street, were open, and a few of the passengers leaned out, deadpan and silent, for a look at Manhattan. The rest sat, deadpan and silent, looking at each other. In all, there were twenty-two people in the bus; eleven girls and seven boys of the senior class; their English teacher and her husband; and the driver (one of the regular bus drivers employed by the township for the school) and his wife.

The key to good description, then, is precise and accurate detail. Careful observation of numbers, names, expressions, colors, positions, sounds, and—most difficult of all—the absence of each of these is the stuff from which descriptions are made.

Quite often the description of some social phenomenon will raise a question in your mind; and when that happens, the process of theory building is likely to begin. All you have to do is speculate a little about the answer to your question and you are on your way. For example, during a 1971 lecture tour of Italy, Tom Wolfe (1976) noted that the Italian students he talked with seemed to be absolutely amazed that in America hippies actually left home and lived communally according to their own rules. Wolfe was struck by the fact that in Italy many students seemed to live radical, even wild, lives during daylight hours, but . . .

> They were in radical organizations and had fought pitched battles with the police, *on the barricades*, as it were. But by 8:30 p.m. they were back home, obediently washing their hands before dinner with Mom and Dad and Buddy and Sis and the Maiden Aunt. When they left home for good, it was likely to be via the only admissible ticket: marriage. Unmarried sons of thirty-eight and thirty-nine would still be sitting around the same old table.

Someone reading such a passage is bound to wonder about why the rebelliousness of youth does not extend to breaking with the family in Italy as it often does in the United States. Are there differences in social or religious structures that might account for the difference? Maybe in Italy everyone, including parents, sees the government as the enemy. Hence, rebellion might be rewarded and condoned by families more so than it is here. That is sheer speculation, of course, but it is a potential explanation for Wolfe's observation, and, most important, you could test it.

Note that if Wolfe's description is biased in some way, you might build an elaborate set of hypotheses to explain something that did not even exist. That is why accurate description and observation are so crucial in research. Theory, as Glaser and Straus (1967) pointed out, must be firmly grounded in the data of the real world. If the description that piques your curiosity and gets you started spinning out possible explanations is itself a misrepresentation of reality, chances are your explanations will be totally worthless. No one needs an explanation of why males live longer than females, because females live longer than males.

When building your theories, it is good to remember that explanations have several qualities, some of which are unnecessary, but nice, and others of which are both nice and necessary. Simplicity is one of the former and testability one of the latter. Simpler explanations are always preferable to complex ones, provided they can account for the data equally well. The simpler the explanation, the easier it is to understand and test. To test a complex, many-faceted explanation one would have to obtain evidence on all of its components, and that, by definition, would be more difficult than gathering evidence on only one. In the early part of this century, a cartoonist named Rube Goldberg became famous for designing elaborate, intricate devices that were intended to achieve relatively simple results.

His name, in fact, became a pejorative term for unnecessarily complex explanations and apparatus. For an example of one of Goldberg's inventions, see Figure 4. "Less is best," then, as far as hypotheses go. It should be kept in mind, however, that human behavior is itself complex, so you should not shy away from complex explanations when they appear warranted.

In contrast to simplicity, testability is not an option. It is a must. Hypotheses must be testable, and that is where the third aspect of the research process comes in: VERIFICATION. The goal of research is to in-

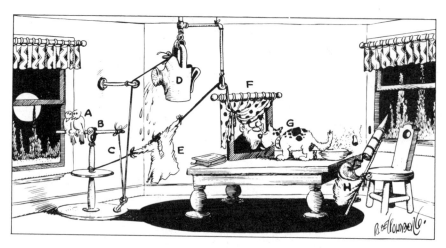

Self-Emptying Ashtray of the Future

Bright romantic moon brings love birds (A) together on perch (B), causing string (C) to upset sprinkling can (D) and wet shirt (E). Shirt shrinks, unveiling portrait (F). Dog (G), seeing portrait of his master, wags tail, brushing ashes from tray into asbestos bag (H). Smoldering butts ignite rocket (I) which carries bag of ashes out the window into the far reaches of the sky.

This should encourage young couples to start families, because the children can wear the shrunken shirts.

Figure 4 A RUBE GOLDBERG INVENTION. As with many overly elaborate explanations, such inventions work (if at all) only under a very precise set of circumstances. This ash tray would not work, for example, if there were no love birds in the area; if the shirt were Sanforized; if the dog did not like his master; or if the butts in the ash tray had already gone out. Similarly, overly complex explanations often do not generalize well to situations different from those that suggested them. (Cartoon by Rube Goldberg © King Features Syndicate, Inc.)

crease our understanding of behavior and social processes, and until proposed explanations are tested, they remain mere possibilities. Until they are verified, we have no way of knowing whether they add to our understanding or detract from it. The latter is, unfortunately, a real danger. Untested explanations, especially plausible ones, may actively detract from our understanding by inducing us to believe we know more than we really do and lulling us into complacency. After all, if we know why something occurs, it is a waste of time, energy, and money to try to demonstrate what we already know. Plausible, untested explanations about behavior do more than dampen our motivation for research, however. They may induce us to behave in ways that distort social situations and change them from what they would have been had we bothered to try to check our beliefs. Liebow (1967) gives an illustration of how this can work:

> Owners of small retail establishments and other employers frequently anticipate employee stealing and adjust the wage rate accordingly. Tonk's employer explained why he was paying Tonk $35 for a 55–60 hour workweek. These men will all steal, he said. Although he keeps close watch on Tonk, he estimates that Tonk steals $35–40 a week. What he steals, when added to his regular earnings, brings his take home pay to $70 or $75 per week. The employer said that he did not mind this because Tonk is worth that much to the business. But if he were to pay Tonk outright the full value of his labor, Tonk would still be stealing $35–40 per week and this, he said, the business simply would not support.

By expecting Tonk to steal, his employer defined the employment situation in such a way—paying a substandard wage—that Tonk had to steal to support himself. The employer's assumption that Tonk would steal regardless of what he was paid remained untested. It could have been true or false.

Untested assumptions and explanations for behavior, then, may so distort reality that they appear to be correct even when they are not. The research methods described in the chapters that follow will provide you with a useful bag of tools to test your hypotheses, verify your impressions, check on your hunches, and be very precise about separating what you know from what you do not. As you will see, the best method depends on many things—including the circumstances, what you are interested in, and how much time and energy you are willing to invest. One of the characteristics that distinguishes a good researcher from a poor one is the ability to select, or, more often, *design* a method appropriate to the question or hypothesis of interest. This book will help you learn how to do that. Before proceeding, however, you should be alerted to a topic of considerable importance in the conduct of research. It is a topic that will be returned to again and again in the context of each of the methods.

The Ethics of Research

The need for knowledge about human behavior and social processes can hardly be overestimated. Pick up any newspaper and the acuteness of that need is likely to overwhelm you: Reports of violence, drug addiction, discrimination, poverty, international conflict, and the consequences of poor decision-making and individual psychopathology fill the pages. Even the classified ads bear testimony to the climbing divorce rate, social disorganization, and endemic loneliness. Further, many of the major health problems of today are caused by factors that are, or could be, under the control of individuals. Sexton (1979), for example, points out that for nine of the ten[1] leading causes of death in the United States there is reason to believe that specific *behavioral* factors contribute to the magnitude of the death rate.

Would you argue with the statement that you need to understand much more than you do about behavior? Research on decision-making that identifies the type of errors you are likely to make may help improve the quality of the decisions you make tomorrow. Research on drug addiction that identifies the functions addiction serves and how it occurs may help prevent it or, at least, help others understand the phenomenon and react more appropriately. The problem is that although you may agree that knowledge and understanding are ideals worthy of pursuit, there are other ideals that you may, at times, value even more highly. When such a conflict of ideals occurs, the issue of whether or not one should conduct the research in question may be said to pose an ethical dilemma. Quite literally, you have to ask yourself, "Can the research be ethically justified?" As Diener and Crandall (1978) have pointed out, the field of ETHICS is simply the study of our values and how they can best be realized.

On a general level, two values most likely to conflict with the value we place on increasing our knowledge and understanding of behavior are the following: (1) you should never harm another person, and (2) each individual has a right to privacy. As examples of research that highlight these conflicts, consider the two following synopses.

1. In the late 1950s and early 1960s, Berkun, Bialek, Kern, and Yagi (1962) conducted some research on psychological stress among new Army recruits at a large, undeveloped, mountainous military reservation in California. Within days after reporting for duty and prior to any training whatsoever, the men were loaded onto buses and taken to the isolated reservation. They were told merely that they were to be used to test some new "concepts of atomic-age warfare and that they would be called upon

---

[1]The exception is "diseases of early infancy," but even here there is reason to believe that the mother's behavior—alcohol abuse during pregnancy—is a factor.

to perform individually rather than as units." In one situation, the men were taken individually to a lonely outpost and told their job was to spot passing aircraft, identify them with the aid of a booklet provided, and relay the information via radio to the Command Post. While a subject was in this position he *inadvertently* became the target of artillery fire. The subject was led to believe that transmissions from his radio were not being heard, but he could hear frantic conversations between the Command Post and others about the idiots in artillery, conversations reinforced by a series of increasingly close dynamite explosions (incoming artillery) that went off near the subject's outpost.

2. In a book called *Tearoom Trade: Impersonal Sex in Public Places*, Humphrey (1970) reported on his observation of homosexual activity in public restrooms. For a period of some months he became a *watchqueen*, one who stands near the doors and/or windows and warns the participants when a stranger approaches. Watchqueens are generally voyeurs, people who obtain sexual gratification by observing the sexual organs or actions of others, so Humphrey was able to witness hundreds of acts of fellatio without being expected to participate. His major interest, however, was in identifying the social characteristics of the people who did take part in such activities. Consequently, he made notes of license numbers and other identifying characteristics and traced these men so that he could find out where they lived. Later he disguised himself, and under the ruse of conducting an innocuous door-to-door survey, he interviewed the men.

When they were published, both of the above studies aroused a great deal of critical comment. Subjects in the Berkun et al. (1962) research had been alarmed, even terrified by what they thought was happening to them. Did the researchers have the right to do that? Was the knowledge gained about the effects of acute psychological stress on cognitive and physiological functioning—numerous measures were taken as soon as the "shelling" stopped—sufficiently important to justify the overpowering fear experienced by the subjects? In the study by Humphrey (1970), subjects did not, in fact, experience any harm as a result of the research—although the potential for harm in the form of blackmail and its consequences was quite real had Humphrey misplaced his notes. The issue that critics have raised with respect to Humphrey's research is invasion of privacy (von Hoffman, 1970). Was the knowledge gained about the otherwise normal, law-abiding lifestyles of many of the participants in the tearoom trade sufficiently important to justify the manner in which it was obtained?

The dilemmas posed by the studies of Berkun et al. (1962) and Humphrey (1970) can in many instances be avoided by the use of informed consent. INFORMED CONSENT is a procedure in which people are given an explicit choice about whether or not they would like to participate in the research *prior* to participation but *after* they have been fully informed of any potential harmful effects of the research and made aware that they are completely free to withdraw from the research at any time. For a great deal of research on behavior and social process, informed consent is ideal because it enlists the cooperation of participants while at the same time alleviating any anxieties about what they are letting themselves in for. If you are interested in short-term memory, for example, and want to find out whether caffeine has any effect on the ability to recall numbers, you can tell potential participants that the research would require that they drink a cup of coffee, wait 15 minutes (for it to take effect), then try to repeat backward some groups of numbers that you will read to them. If they do not like coffee (or you), have not got an hour to spare, or cannot stand numbers games, they can say, "No thanks."

On the other hand, there are instances in which informed consent may be impossible, undesirable, or unnecessary. Informed consent may be impossible because the researcher does not know all the potential harmful effects or because the participants are incapable of understanding what is involved or because the atmosphere in which the research takes place is not really conducive to a free choice to participate or not. If you contemplate doing research in which any of these three things are true, you should ponder whether or not the research can be ethically justified. Informed consent may be undesirable in certain contexts because it would change the behavior of interest. Knowing that you are interested in how aging affects memory may cause many older people to become apprehensive and not do as well as they could on memory-related tasks. It is this category of research — research in which distortions may be introduced into the results by knowledge of what the researcher is interested in — that causes the most difficulty. We shall return to it repeatedly in the chapters that follow as we examine the *ethical* and *methodological* complications that it introduces into the various ways of doing research.

Finally, informed consent may simply be unnecessary for research that investigates public behavior, involves no harm or inconvenience to subjects, and in which all subjects remain anonymous. No one would object, for example, if you wanted to look at the effects of cable TV on reading habits by examining book sales and library withdrawals before and after the introduction of cable TV into your town.

Summary

There is a discrepancy between the stereotype and the reality of research; and there is no clear dividing line between scientific research on human behavior and the sort of informal research you have been doing all your life. Research begins with questions, curiosity about the hows and whys of behavior, and proposed explanations. The value of the research methods to be discussed in the following chapters is that they help you be very precise about the conditions under which you have found answers to your questions. Thus, they help you avoid concluding more than is justified.

It is necessary to be precise about the conditions surrounding behavior because it is the functional significance, or meaning, of behavior that is important. The reasons why something was done, the motives behind the action, are crucial; and that makes research on human behavior both more difficult and more exciting. On the general level, behavior is usually seen as being a function of both the person and the situation in which the person is immersed. The goal of research in the social and behavioral sciences is the development of explanatory concepts that will help you understand the complex interrelationships of individuals influencing and being influenced by a constant stream of social situations. Testable explanations are the goal.

Developing explanations for behavior is a creative process, and your own creativity can be improved by overcoming a few common blocks. The first step is to realize that reality is multidisciplinary. Nobody has a monopoly on the best way to explain behavior. The second step in nurturing your creativity is to learn how to observe closely and well. Pay attention to what is going on around you. Your expectations about what is going to occur will often prevent you from seeing what does occur. It is a habit you have to kick. Close observation of a number of isolated instances of behavior and the formulation of an underlying general principle that is inherent in them all is referred to as induction. Deduction is the opposite— applying a general principle to a specific instance. Neither is infallible, but careful observation and accurate inference are important to both.

Observation and accurate description of behavior are important, and they are usually the first step in research; but they are definitely not enough. Understanding seems to be advanced primarily by purposeful observation, by curiosity about answers to specific questions. Thus, the general research strategy that I have advocated involves two additional steps: (1) When you are curious about some aspect of behavior, make a list of as many plausible explanations for it as you can. (2) When you begin gathering evidence on a proposed explanation, operationalize you concepts in more than one way. The research process, then, involves three phases: description or observation, theory building, and verification.

A great deal remains to be learned about human behavior, but the value you place on knowledge may conflict with other ideals. Such conflicts are the sources of ethical dilemmas. Informed consent can resolve many, but not all, of these dilemmas, and in the chapters that follow I shall pay particular attention to those situations in which informed consent is impossible or undesirable.

Recommended Reading

Several books discuss topics we have mentioned in this chapter. With the exception of the book by Nisbett and Ross, the following books are available in paperback. With the exception of the book by Kuhn, they all contain extensive bibliographies that you can use as a guide to the topics you find interesting. With no exceptions, they all are worth looking into.

Adams, J. L. *Conceptual blockbusting: A guide to better ideas* (2nd ed.). New York: Norton, 1980.

James Adams is a Professor of Engineering at Stanford and teaches courses in design. His book is a delightful, profusely illustrated guide to the intellectual, cultural, emotional, and environmental blocks to creative thinking. In his own words the aim of the book is "to let you learn something about how your own mind works in a conceptual situation and to give you some hints on how to make it work better." Woven into his discussions of blocks to creativity are numerous exercises, games, and examples that not only help to clarify the issues but are just plain fun to try. Do you want to invent some gadget that will make you a million dollars, but do not know what the world needs? Try making a *bug list*, all the things you can think of that really bug you–chairs that will not slide on the floor, dirty aquarium sides, broken shoelaces, soppy soap dishes. It may help you think of some things to invent. Got a problem you cannot solve? Try switching your problem-solving language from verbal to mathematical or from mathematical to visual.

Diener, E., & Crandall, R. *Ethics in social and behavioral research*. Chicago: University of Chicago Press, 1978.

This book is an outstanding introduction to the range of ethical issues encountered by those who do research in the social and behavioral sciences. The topics discussed include such central concerns as the need for informed consent, how research may conflict with the right to privacy, the use of deception, and the social responsibilities of scientists. With each of these, and with the other issues discussed, the authors present a balanced view, enumerating the pros and cons in a careful, scholarly manner, but always making clear the course of action that they believe to be most appropriate. Numerous illustrations of questionable ethical practices are provided so that the discussions are made concrete and vivid for the reader. The examples used are drawn from a variety of disciplines, including anthropology, education, psychology, and sociology.

Harris, M. *Cows, pigs, wars, and witches: The riddles of culture*. New York: Vintage, 1975.

Harris presents an informative and entertaining analysis of the ways in which the parts of a culture, including apparently bizarre behaviors, mesh into a coherent, intelligible whole. The core of the book consists of 11 chapters, in each of which the origins and functions of some unusual feature of behavior are carefully dissected. The message in each case is that when viewed in the cultural context these behaviors are not in the least bizarre. Rather, they are eminently rational and contribute to the group's survival. Harris' writing style makes the book read more like a collection of fascinating short detective stories than a series of anthropological essays.

Nisbett, R., & Ross, L. *Human inference: Strategies and shortcomings of social judgment.* Englewood Cliffs, NJ: Prentice-Hall, 1980.

It has been argued in Chapter One that research in the social and behavioral sciences is quite similar to normal, everyday processes involved in trying to understand the world around you. Nisbett and Ross document a number of psychological processes that can interfere with both. There is evidence, for example, that you may be overly influenced by the vividness of information in trying to make a decision. Similarly, there are predictable systematic distortions in memory, distortions that can get you into trouble when you have to recall information learned earlier in order to make a judgment. You may attend to different things when observing someone else behave than you do when it is your own behavior that is of interest. What you have attended to, of course, will influence your beliefs about how and why the behavior was performed. These are just a sample of the errors discussed, errors that you need to be aware of in order to combat their influence. We shall discuss several topics from their book in the chapters that follow.

Kuhn, T. S. *The structure of scientific revolutions* (2nd ed.) Chicago: University of Chicago Press, 1970.

When the first edition of Kuhn's book was published in 1962, it became a classic almost overnight. Now you can hardly find a discussion of the nature of research and scientific progress that does not mention Kuhn's views. His major point is that the important advances in science have always involved what he refers to as *paradigm-shifts*, the imposition of a totally new *conceptual* framework on findings and data that had become increasingly difficult to understand within the old framework. A familiar example is the shift that occurred several hundred years ago away from the view that the earth was the center of the solar system. The *theory* put forth by Nicolaus Copernicus, that the earth and the other planets revolved around the sun, could account for the data available at the time in a simpler, more elegant manner. What Copernicus suggested, of course, was looking at what was already known from a dramatically different perspective. Kuhn's book is important, and if you really get interested in research, it is well worth reading.

2

Observing Social Behavior

Historically, participant observation was associated primarily with anthropology. The name is still used interchangeably with FIELDWORK and FIELD RESEARCH, as in "going out into the field," that is, away from civilization. It was, at first, a rather natural extension of the work of explorers, missionaries, sailors – anyone who had been to some exotic, faraway place. In the 1800s, for example, the published journals of missionaries who had spent time in Africa, of sailors who had been around Cape Horn, and of explorers who had steamed up the Amazon were among the most popular books in both England and America. Everyone wanted to know what those places were like. How did people live there? What did they do? Thus, as we gradually found out about the existence of other peoples and places and ways of life around the world, we simultaneously realized that we knew nothing about them. As Lofland (1971) points out, to know about is not really to know. But, several generations of anthropologists have been valiantly trying to fill the knowledge gap by going out to live in some of those exotic places, seeing what life there was like, and coming back to describe it and explain it and contrast it with our own peculiar ways. The realization that there were whole areas of our own society about which very little was known and within which fieldwork might be useful developed somewhat later.

But, think about it for a moment. Suppose you wanted to know what life was like for hospitalized mental patients – how they are treated, how they spend their time. How would you find out? Statistically speaking, chances are pretty good that you have one or more ex-mental patients among your acquaintances. So, you could just ask them. You could also read autobiographical accounts by ex-patients, such as Beers's *A Mind That Found Itself.* In addition, you might arrange a tour of the facilities at the nearest psychiatric hospital. But even if you did all of these things, you would not have a very good picture of what life on a psychiatric ward was really like.

Participant Observation

There is a better way, and in the early 1970s it was tried by a psychologist at Stanford University and seven of his friends and co-workers: They had themselves admitted to the psychiatric wards of a number of different hospitals. Each gained entry, as an apparent patient in need of treatment, by claiming to hear voices saying such things as "empty" or "hollow." Once on the wards, however, all eight pseudopatients stopped simulating any symptoms. They behaved as normally as possible. During the course of their stays, which averaged 19 days, the pseudopatients took notes and systematically recorded what went on around them. They wrote down the number and types of drugs given, how much time the staff spent on the ward, how their fellow patients behaved. One of the things that became clear from the notes is that once a person has been labeled schizophrenic, as most of the pseudopatients had on entry, interpretation of that person's subsequent behavior is strongly colored by the label. For example, Rosenhan (1973) noted that patients would often congregate outside the cafeteria entrance half an hour or so before mealtime. There is nothing mysterious about that. Life on the wards was so dull that meals were one of the few things that could be anticipated with pleasure. But on observing their behavior, one of the ward psychiatrists commented that it was typical of the oral-acquisitive nature of the schizophrenic syndrome.

Take another example. Suppose you were interested in doomsday cults. Specifically, suppose you were curious about what happens when the predicted disaster—usually the end of the world—does not occur on schedule. Again, you could do some reading. Or, you might try to find people who once belonged to a cult and interview them. But again it would be better to join such a group and see for yourself. One October, a number of years ago, a team of social scientists did just that (Festinger, Riecken, & Schachter, 1956). They became participant observers in a group predicting that a cataclysmic flood would occur on December 21st of that year, a flood that would inundate most of the western part of the United States. This prophecy had been revealed to the group's leader, Mrs. Marian Keech, through automatic writing. Festinger and his colleagues were interested in what would happen when Mrs. Keech's prediction proved false, and to find out they joined the group. They were there, observing and sneaking out to the back porch to make notes, when the night of December 21 came and went with everybody dry as a bone.

"Aha!" you say. So, this participant observation is sort of like being a reporter. You hang around where something interesting is happening, ask questions, make a few notes, and then write up what went on. Well—yes and no.

There is more involved, but there are definite parallels (see the Discussion on page 44). Participant observation does require that you enter into the routine of the people or situation under study, usually for a rather extended period of time. The point is to develop INTIMATE FAMILIARITY (Lofland, 1971) with their world—how they see things, what is important to them, how they spend their time. Observing and systematically recording things that happen, informally or formally interviewing all those who might have information pertinent to the events under study, and gathering relevant auxiliary information are all parts of what is involved. Note that the emphasis is on discovery, on finding out what life is like for people in the setting of interest, on learning, *not* on testing preconceived ideas. Those things are also a part of the way good reporters operate. Similarly,

━━━━━━━━

INVESTIGATIVE REPORTING AS A RESEARCH METHOD

One of the best-selling books of the 1970s was *All the President's Men* by Carl Bernstein and Bob Woodward, two *Washington Post* reporters who described their investigation of the Watergate burglary and cover-up. Using that book as a vehicle, Levine (1980) has recently pointed out a number of parallels between the tactics employed in such reporting and those required in qualitative scientific research, such as participant observation.

Investigative reporting is, quite simply, a search for evidence that will justify the publication of a news story. Thus, like the participant observer, one of the first problems faced by the reporter is a problem of ACCESS – how to get to the information needed, how to find the people who might know what you need to know. Bernstein and Woodward were quite inventive in this area. For example, they talked to desk clerks, bellmen, maids, and waiters at the Watergate complex; they checked out a group of people who had served in the Army with one of the burglars; they checked every name and telephone number found in the burglars' address books. In other words, they made use of INFORMANTS (people who might be able to tell them something about the events of interest), and they tracked down potential informants by systematically piecing together information about the social networks of the burglars.

Bernstein and Woodward were also quite conscious of the necessity to vary their interview style depending on whom they were talking with and about what. They were not at all hesitant, for example, to confront reluctant interviewees with adverse information that required comment. The responses to this confrontational style of interviewing were often quite informative. In that connection, the reporters became acutely aware that nonverbal communication was almost as crucial as verbal. The perceived emotional state of an informant provides critical information.

The problem for both the investigative reporter and the participant observer is that information obtained via informants or hunches derived from an interviewee's demeanor must be assessed for accuracy. Informants can lie, as some did to Bernstein and Woodward. Hunches may be incorrect. For the reporters the major check on the quality of the evidence they obtained was the editorial review process. Editors at the *Post* cross-examined them on the details of each story before allowing publication, a process that Levine claims is analogous to the editorial review that occurs when a scientific article is submitted to a journal. In the long run, publication itself is a check for accuracy because other reporters working on the story for other papers will confirm or refute what is claimed. As Levine (1980) put it, "In investigative reporting, as in science, the more powerful control is not the research design but the social control inherent in independent review, criticism, and attempts at replication of the reported observations."

both participant observers and reporters can choose from a variety of roles, that is, the modus operandi can range from complete openness about who they are and why they are there to complete secrecy and, perhaps, the assumption of a disguise.

What separates participant observation as a research method from reporting is that a reporter's work is usually complete when a story or narrative of events has been constructed. The participant observer's work is only about half done at that point. The participant observer uses that narrative and the raw materials on which it is based to develop what Lofland (1976) referred to as DISCIPLINED ABSTRACTIONS, which are analytic concepts derived from the firsthand observation of specific episodes and events. They are disciplined in that they must be tied to, or grounded in, specific observations. You must be able to point to something that occurred, something that is recorded in the narrative, and say, "Here, this is an example of what I'm talking about." The scientific goal, then, is to use what you have seen and heard and experienced to generate explicit and articulate abstractions. Perhaps an example will help make this clear.

Responses to Token Women

A TOKEN, when the term is applied to a person, usually refers to someone who is identified by ascribed characteristics, such as race or sex, and who is a member of a group in which all the other members differ from the token on one such ascribed characteristic. Thus, a black faculty member in an otherwise all-white academic department would be a token, as would a female baseball player on an otherwise all-male team.

But, how does the presence of a token influence what goes on in the group? Does it make any difference that one of the group members is obviously different from the rest? And what about the token's feelings? As part of a large study of a major company, which she refers to as Industrial Supply Corporation (INDSCO), Kanter (1977a, 1977b) had an opportunity to collect some data bearing on these questions. She gained access to the sales division of INDSCO, a division consisting of over 300 men and only 20 women. Because the sales division was geographically decentralized into a number of field offices, the skewed ratio of men to women in the sales force meant that each field office had only one female, or at most two, on the sales staff.

Kanter's involvement with INDSCO stretched over a five-year period. She began as an ouside research consultant, hired by the company for specific ad hoc purposes. As she became more acquainted with the experiences of INDSCO's men and women, her agenda broadened to trying to understand the complex social reality represented by the corporation and its impact on the people who experienced it. Toward that end, she spent hundreds of hours observing the interactions of male and female members of the sales division, participating in training groups with them, sitting in on sales meetings, and taking part in informal social gatherings. She also collected a variety of auxiliary information about the company and the employees' perceptions of it and of each other. She designed a mail survey, one that took over two hours to complete, and sent it to 205 of the sales workers and managers. She personally interviewed the first 20 women to enter the sales force. She was given access to the results of an earlier survey of employees' attitudes, to recordings of group discussions, to performance appraisals, to a variety of public documents about the company. She also just hung around the company whenever she had the chance and talked to people. She recorded everything possible that occurred in her presence, as she puts it, "almost automatically . . . because, as all good consultants know, it is wise to keep complete notes and collect as much system information as possible in order to be maximally helpful to clients."

As Kanter's familiarity with the sales division grew, she began to see that being the only woman in a setting in which one's peers, superiors, and customers were all male had certain consequences. First, the proportional rarity of the token women made them stand out, they were simply more *visible* than a typical male member of the sales force. As one of the saleswomen put it:

> I've been at sales meetings where all the trainees were going up to the managers—"Hi, Mr. So-and-So"—trying to make that impression, wearing a strawberry tie, whatever, something that they could be remembered by. Whereas there were three of us [women] in a group of fifty, and all we had to do was walk in and everyone recognized us.

The major result of their greater visibility was that they were under considerably greater pressure to perform. Their every move was noticed, they could not just fade into the shadows occasionally, as their male colleagues could. There was also a symbolic component to the extra pressure because they were seen as representatives of a category, saleswomen. When they made a mistake, or lost an account, or did not seem sufficiently motivated, their behavior was taken as "typical" of their category [women]. That did not happen for the men, of course, because there were always other examples of their category around who had not made a mistake or who had not lost an account recently or who were sufficiently motivated.

Second, the presence of a lone woman in a sales office seemed to lead to polarization. The men in the office seemed to become more aware of their similarities to each other and their differentness from the token woman. The result was that merely being male seemed to be on their minds more than it would have otherwise; hence, maleness and masculinity were exaggerated around the office, and the woman was further isolated. As Kanter (1977a) put it, "Ironically, tokens, unlike people of their type represented in greater proportion, are thus instruments for under*lining* rather than under*mining* majority culture." One of the ways in which this manifested itself was in meetings, when one of the males was about to tell another off-color joke or swear or ask if everybody wanted to go have a drink. They would stop, look at the woman, and ask, "Is it okay to swear?" or "Do you mind if I tell a little joke?" or "You're not one of those women's libbers, are you?" Thus, the women were constantly reminded that they were different, that this was really a man's world they were in.

Third, it seemed to Kanter that the characteristics of individual women were often distorted to fit preexisting stereotypes about women as a group, a process referred to as ASSIMILATION. The result was that each woman tended to be pushed into one of a relatively limited number of roles within her group: mother, seductress, pet, iron maiden. This role encapsulation limited their freedom of expression and the ways in which they could demonstrate competence. When your colleagues seek you out only to tell you their problems, for example, they will never find out how much you know about the business. Another way in which the tendency to typecast the female tokens manifested itself was for the woman to be given respon- sibilities for areas that were stereotypically female concerns. In one of the most blatant examples of this, a group of four sales trainees (three males, one female) were to be assigned as summer replacements. The men were assigned to replace salesmen, the woman was asked to fill in for a secretary. Temporarily, you understand. Only after "long and heated discussion" was the sales manager made to see the error of his ways.

Kanter's research resulted in more than a history of INDSCO or a reporting of what was said and done in a variety of specific instances, although both of those things were included. In addition, Kanter used her intimate knowledge of the sales division, its personnel, and their interrela- tions to develop a series of concepts that would give meaning to what she had seen and heard. The concepts serve to place her research within a more general framework. The visibility of the token women led to unusual per- formance pressures; the presence of a lone woman in a group of male col- leagues polarized the group and led to an exaggeration of the dominant culture, maleness in this case, within the group; the characteristics of in- dividual women were assimilated to preexisting stereotypes, a process resulting in role encapsulation and consequent limitations on their freedom. Thus, Kanter's research resulted in a set of DISCIPLINED ABSTRACTIONS, con- cepts closely tied to her observations, but serving to place those observa- tions within a broader theoretical context. The development of such disciplined abstractions is the scientific goal of the whole operation. It is what takes participant observation beyond reporting. The hope, of course, is that those higher level concepts (visibility, role encapsulation) may help investigators understand what goes on in other situations that have a similar structure. As a case in point, there is reason to believe that the high levels of stress experienced by black executives, who constitute only 4 percent of the nation's managers, stem in part from processes similar to those identified by Kanter (Campbell, 1982).

With the why clearly in mind, then, let us take a look at the how of participant observation. What is involved in getting it done?

Where the Action Is

Several years ago, George C. Scott (1980) said that fame had deprived him of what he considered to be one of the most important tools of actors. Having become so well-known that he is recognized almost everywhere he goes, he can no longer develop his feeling for how a scene should be played, for example, by unobtrusively observing similar real-life scenes. He can no longer tune his ear for dialogue by sitting in a bar and listening to strangers talk. The point, of course, is that when you want to learn how people behave at bar mitzvahs or Quaker weddings or New Year's Eve parties, you have to go to a few. When you want to discover what life is like on the graveyard shift, you have to be there from midnight to 8 a.m. (and one night is not enough). The first rule of participant observation, then, is that you have to go where the action is in order to learn about it. It is not going to come to you.

Sounds obvious. But you would be surprised at how many experts on criminology have never talked with a real criminal (Polsky, 1969) or how many economic analysts appear to believe that an armchair and a little deductive logic are acceptable substitutes for business and banking experience (Bergmann, 1982). Having been married for almost 30 years, I am amazed by the existence of marriage counselors who have never been married (or who have never lived with someone for an extended period of time). But whatever your interest, once you have made the decision to seek out the action, the first order of business is developing what Lofland (1971, 1976) referred to as INTIMATE FAMILIARITY.

Developing Intimate Familiarity

There are three phases involved in developing intimate familiarity: doing your homework, gaining entry, and immersion in the setting.

In some respects, doing you homework is like planning a vacation. Once you have decided that you would like to spend a couple of weeks in England, say, it would probably be a good idea to buy one of Fodor's famous travel guides and do a little reading: sights to see, places to stay, prices, how to get around. It would be a mistake to wait until you stepped off the plane at Heathrow or Gatwick to decide whether you are going to spend the first night in London or Dover. The importance of those kinds of practical decisions should not be underestimated. A little bit of planning, such as sketching out a rough itinerary, can make the difference between a pleasant vacation and a real hassle. But if you really want to get something out of your vacation, then a more thorough preparation is called for. A good book or two on English history would help. If you are an architecture buff, you might read up on Sir Christopher Wren and then plan your itinerary to see a few of his buildings. If you are a literature fan, you might reread some Shakespeare and plan to spend a day or two in Stratford. The point, of course, is that such preparation will help you appreciate more fully the things you see and do. You will have some pegs to hang impressions on. You will know what to look for.

With participant observation, the danger in doing too much homework ahead of time is hinted at in that last sentence: you will know what to look for. If you are looking for something specific within the ambiguities of human interaction, chances are you will find it. You probably will not even have to look very hard. Chances are also pretty good that you will miss a lot of more interesting and important things. For that reason, many fieldworkers are somewhat apprehensive about the biases introduced by carrying too many preconceptions into the field with you. Whyte (1951), for example, said a fieldworker needs only a minimum of theoretical orientation before beginning to observe. As he put it, theory should emerge from the observations themselves. But the theory that you hope will emerge from participant observation will generally have to do with the how of social behavior. How does a teacher control a classroom? How do people end conversations? How do mental patients get around institutional rules? So, it is okay to learn as much as you can about the context and history of the setting you are going to observe ahead of time. But try to make no assumptions about what will actually be going on within the setting. That is what you are there to find out. Think about it this way. If possible, learn about the what and why ahead of time. Then use participant observation to learn how—how whatever it is that is supposed to get done really gets done.

Having done your homework, the next step is gaining entry to the setting you want to observe. It can be a tricky business, and nearly all veteran fieldworkers have horror stories about mistakes made in the process. Wax (1971), for example, accepted the hospitality of an Indian family, the Goodhorses, during the initial stages of her stay on the Thrashing Buffalo Reservation. Things began to go wrong almost immediately. The community seemed to turn a cold shoulder to her inquiries and no progress was made for weeks on end. Eventually, Wax discovered that the good Goodhorses "were notorious not only for cheating and defrauding white people but for cheating and defrauding the more unfortunate and helpless of their fellow Indians." Moving off the Goodhorse land and into an abandoned schoolhouse brought a dramatic change in the community's attitude toward Wax and her research. The point, of course, is that there are internal conflicts in many settings and it is a mistake to align yourself with either side when you want to study the community or setting as a whole. Of course, when you are only interested in observing one side, say the Democratic campaign machine, that is a different story.

The major problem of gaining entry is what Whyte (1951) called personal acceptance. Whyte noted that at one point during the fieldwork that resulted in *Street Corner Society* it became known that he was writing a book about the community. Whether or not that was perceived to be a good thing by any particular member of the community seemed to depend entirely on whether or not that person liked Whyte himself. Whyte's major tactic for gaining acceptance was to obtain the backing of KEY PEOPLE, relatively high status members of the community who vouched for him and whose support conveyed to others that it was okay to talk to him. A related tactic for gaining acceptance is to use what Lofland (1971) referred to as "preexisting relations of trust" as a route into the setting. For example, in the illustration cited earlier, the relationships Kanter established as a research consultant for INDSCO were instrumental in her gaining access to the sales division.

Of course, acceptance by members of a setting who know you are doing research is quite different from the situation in which you choose to conceal your purpose, as Rosenhan and his colleagues did in their study of psychiatric wards. That is when participant observation becomes morally hazardous. As long as people know you are doing research, they will not necessarily expect you to do everything they do, although they will – and have a right to – expect you to accept them on their own terms. However, if you have chosen to conceal your identity, things can get pretty sticky. If the group or any of its members engage in any illegal or immoral activities, you may be expected to do so as well or, at least, not to tell. If they find out at some later point in time that you were not really one of them after all, they are likely to feel betrayed – even if you never violated their trust and they never did anything wrong.

My advice? Avoid concealing your identity. Let people know who you are and why you are there. It will forestall all sorts of problems. It will also give you greater freedom to move around, ask questions, and be pleasantly, naively, nosy. You will still have to demonstrate to people that you can be trusted to be discreet and that you are sincerely interested in them and their activities. That should be easy, however, because if you are not sincerely interested in them, you should not be there. And remember, your task is to observe and to learn, not to pass judgment.

When the setting is at all unusual, or different from settings in which you have some experience, it is going to be difficult at first. It will be something like listening to someone speak a language you do not understand. In that case, it is hard to tell where one word (or sentence) ends and another begins, let alone follow the topic being discussed. With participant observation, the connections among the intersecting streams of behavior that you observe are not likely to be immediately apparent. They will emerge only as you become thoroughly familiar with the setting and the people in it. The challenge, from your point of view as an observer, is to recognize the patterns of behavior in what you are seeing and hearing. And, note well, you must assume that there is an underlying order, even though at first it all appears to be utter chaos. The more closely you look, the more patterns you are likely to see (see page 52).

To help identify the patterns, Lofland (1971, 1976) has suggested that it may help to self-consciously attend to the following six types of things:

1. Acts: relatively brief actions that take place, such as typing a letter or making a sandwich.
2. Activities: actions of major duration, lasting days or even months, such as taking a course or building a patio.
3. Meanings: what the participants say they are doing, such as trying to get through school; or keeping the wolf from the door.
4. Participation: each person's holistic involvement in the setting. The dean of a college, for example, is likely to be more fully involved in a range of activities within the college than is a typical faculty member.
5. Relationships: who spends time with whom, what kinds of interrelations exist among the several people in the setting.
6. Settings: you also need to ask yourself about the setting as a whole, what is it an example of?

Most of these will become obvious, of course, as you spend time in the setting, talk to people, and ask questions. But remember, these are just the elements, the building materials from which you must construct those disciplined abstractions mentioned earlier. Two things are involved in converting these raw materials into something useful: taking field notes and developing an analytic filing system.

Field Notes and Filing

Quick now. What did you have for lunch the first Tuesday of last month? What did you do that afternoon? What programs did you look at on TV

Issues and Discussions ━━━━━━━━━━━━━━━━━━━━━━━━━━━━

SEGMENTING THE STREAM OF BEHAVIOR

Darren Newtson (1973, 1976) and his colleagues (Newtson, Engquist, & Bois, 1977) have focused attention on the perceptual processes involved when we try to make sense of what another person is doing. The basic assumption behind Newtson's research is that we do not passively take in information about the behavior we are observing. Rather, we actively participate in the perceptual process by organizing the ongoing observed behavior into meaningful segments or actions. Thus, to a large extent we control the amount and kind of information obtained when observing another's behavior and may literally generate more or less information from a given behavioral sequence, depending on such things as our expectations and attentiveness.

In some of his research, Newtson has asked people to watch videotapes of others performing simple behaviors, such as sitting at a desk writing or crossing a room and closing a door. Using a mechanical device synchronized with the videotapes, some observers were asked to segment the observed behaviors into the smallest units they found natural and meaningful. Others were asked to mark off the largest units they found natural and meaningful. The two groups of observers ended up with quite different impressions of the person on the videotape. The small unit observers were much more confident of their impressions and had clearer, better differentiated impressions of the person observed. So, pay close attention to the behavior you are observing.

The purpose in observing behavior, of course, is to gain enough information from what we are watching to understand what the observed person is doing. As a sequence of behavior becomes predictable, Newtson has found that observers gradually begin to segment the behavior into larger and larger units. It is as if they feel they do not have to pay so much attention, because now they know what is going on. But, beware! If you fall into that habit, you may give your first impressions—when you are paying rapt attention—too much weight.

that night? If you are like most of us, chances are you cannot answer any of those questions. You might be able to if you are a creature of habit: you never eat lunch, you have a class every Tuesday from one to three, and you always look at the CBS News on Tuesday night. But even if those things are true for you, you probably would not be able to recall what was on the news that day. However, the odds are a little better that you might indeed be able to reconstruct what was said in class that afternoon. That is assuming that you are a good student and took notes. It is amazing what a few good notes can do for your memory.

In fact, it is precisely because memory is so fallible that note-taking is a crucial skill for participant observers. According to Lofland (1971),

"Aside from getting along in the setting, *the fundamental concrete task* of the observer is the taking of field notes" (emphasis added). Field notes involve a little more than the sorts of notes you are probably used to taking in class. For example, your class notes for that Tuesday last month probably contain no information on what you were wearing, what the instructor was wearing, who sat next to whom, which students asked questions, which students were late, whether or not anyone laughed at the instructor's jokes, what color the walls of the room were, and whether the room was dirty or clean. The field notes of a participant observer who sat in on that same class would contain *all* that information *and more.* Field notes are running descriptions of events, people, things seen and heard and felt and tasted and smelled. Put simply, they should be concrete, exhaustive descriptions. Everything has to go in, whether or not you think any particular item is important.

That is a tall order, and the taking of good field notes is indeed a demanding task. How are you to do it? If you are busy writing away in your notebook, you are going to miss a great deal of what you should be observing. Note-taking can also be disruptive in many situations. Imagine the consequences of whipping out your pad and pencil just as someone is starting to sound off about what a creep the boss is. Thus, most experienced fieldworkers recommend that during the course of a day, say, when you are observing, you only jot down occasional notes, phrases, key words. But, pay careful attention. Observe closely. Ask questions when you need to. Then, at the end of the day—and certainly no later than the following morning—find a private place, get out your pen, your notebook, your jottings, and let it flow. That is when you write it all down, in exquisite, descriptive detail from beginning to end. Obviously, the ratio of field notes to hours of observation will vary, depending on what you are observing, how many people there are, and how much action is taking place. But, just to give you a rough guideline, Lofland (1971) said that at a minimum you should have two single-spaced typewritten pages for every hour of observation.

Fieldworkers differ among themselves on whether it is better to type, dictate, or write out the notes in longhand. Whyte (1951), for example, recommended dictation, whereas Lofland (1971, 1976) claimed that typing is the only way. However, if you are fortunate enough to have access to a computer with a word processing program, that will be hard to beat. The advantages of the computer stem from the ease of revision and the ability to move blocks of text from place to place in your notes without retyping. But, whichever technique you choose, you will find that both as you are observing and as you are working on the field notes, ideas will occur about processes, questions will come up that you may not be able to answer at the time, hypotheses and hunches will be suggested. Put them all in your notes, but separate them by brackets from the descriptive material or put them neatly in the margins at appropriate places. These ideas, questions, and hunches will form the basis from which you will construct your analytic files.

To keep this from getting too abstract, let me illustrate some of what is involved with the help of Figure 1. First, look at panel A. You will see that you are going to need multiple copies of each day's notes. That should not be too difficult to arrange, given the recent proliferation of copying machines. And, of course, keeping your notes in a computer file will enable you to print out multiple copies quite easily. One copy of the notes must be kept intact, in chronological order. That means you need to be sure to put the date and approximate times of your observation on each day's notes. We shall get to what you do with the other copies in a moment. First, read through the brief excerpt of notes depicted in Figure 1A. You will notice typographical errors, ungrammatical expressions, and, yes, even incomplete sentences. That does *not* mean you need to develop that style. The point is that field notes are for your eyes only. You do not need to waste time going back and correcting typographical errors or searching for the most felicitous way of expressing yourself. Nobody is ever going to see the field notes but you, so just get the facts down. You will also note that there is a rather tedious quality to the notes. That is perfectly all right. Much of everyday life has a tedious quality to it, and the purpose of field notes is to help you capture what life is really like in the setting you are observing.

Now, look at Figure 1B. There you see two general categories of files: mundane files and analytic files. MUNDANE FILES are geared to the specifics of what you are observing: people, settings, organizations. They help you keep track of all the information you have about certain key features and people. Of course, if there were a large number of people in the setting, you probably would not have a file on each one, only the more important, central characters. The others you might lump into categories–*Clowns, Complainers, Idealists*–and keep a file on each category. ANALYTIC FILES are those in which you keep track of instances from your notes that docu-

Figure 1 FIELD NOTES AND FILE ORGANIZATION. In the example, multiple copies of each day's field notes (A) are needed so that a copy can be filed under each relevant category (B). One copy must be added to the ongoing complete set of field notes, which are crucial for establishing context. The mundane files are valuable for keeping observations on specific people (Dora, Ralph, John), places, and organizations (planning committee). Copies must also be placed in the analytic files, which are based on your own emerging ideas about important processes, strategies, and concepts (commitment, milking the system) that occur within the setting. The set of analytic files is likely to expand as new ideas and concepts emerge.

Multiple Copies of Notes   (A)

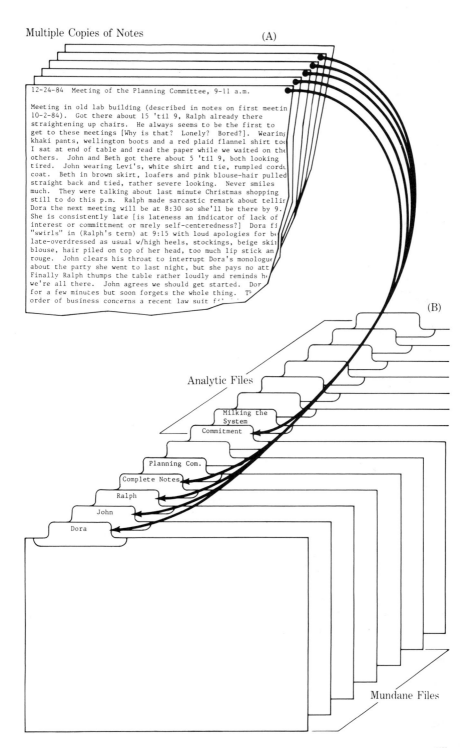

12-24-84 Meeting of the Planning Committee, 9-11 a.m.

Meeting in old lab building (described in notes on first meetin
10-2-84). Got there about 15 'til 9, Ralph already there
straightening up chairs. He always seems to be the first to
get to these meetings [Why is that? Lonely? Bored?]. Wearing
khaki pants, wellington boots and a red plaid flannel shirt too
I sat at end of table and read the paper while we waited on the
others. John and Beth got there about 5 'til 9, both looking
tired. John wearing Levi's, white shirt and tie, rumpled cordu
coat. Beth in brown skirt, loafers and pink blouse-hair pulled
straight back and tied, rather severe looking. Never smiles
much. They were talking about last minute Christmas shopping
still to do this p.m. Ralph made sarcastic remark about tellir
Dora the next meeting will be at 8:30 so she'll be there by 9.
She is consistently late [is lateness an indicator of lack of
interest or committment or mrely self-centeredness?] Dora fi
"swirls" in (Ralph's term) at 9:15 with loud apologies for be
late-overdressed as usual w/high heels, stockings, beige skir
blouse, hair piled on top of her head, too much lip stick an
rouge. John clears his throat to interrupt Dora's monologue
about the party she went to last night, but she pays no att
Finally Ralph thumps the table rather loudly and reminds he
we're all there. John agrees we should get started. Dor
for a few minutes but soon forgets the whole thing. Th
order of business concerns a recent law suit f

                                                                (B)

Analytic Files

        Milking the
         System
      Commitment

   Planning Com.

 Complete Notes

    Ralph

   John

  Dora

                                            Mundane Files

ment and support your developing ideas about the interpersonal processes, tactics, and strategies that operate within the setting and make it work (or keep it from working). The set of analytic files will gradually expand as you become familiar with the setting and ideas occur to you about what is going on. You must keep asking yourself for explanations of what you see happening. In the example discussed earlier, Kanter was able to make sense of her observations with three primary analytic concepts: visibility, polarization, and assimilation. A great deal of what happened to the token women in the INDSCO sales force could be accounted for quite well with these three abstract notions: (1) visibility led to increased performance pressure, (2) polarization led to exaggeration of the dominant (male) culture, and (3) assimilation led to role encapsulation.

There are no guarantees, however. After immersing yourself in the setting, observing carefully, asking appropriate questions, and learning to take good field notes, you may still draw a blank. You may end up without the foggiest notion of how to explain what is going on. That is not very likely, but it is possible. Just remember, do not take anything for granted. Do not be afraid to ask yourself, and others, naive questions. You are there to learn. There are, of course, some things that we know will interfere with your learning. Anticipation of them may help prevent ending your observation empty-handed (or, empty-headed).

Pitfalls for the Unwary

Francis Bacon once said that it is easier to evolve truth from error than from confusion. Keep that in mind. It may provide some consolation in your first efforts at fieldwork because, as you will see, there are ample opportunities for error. For convenience, I have grouped the more serious ones into two broad categories: the psychological and the interpersonal, with ethical problems being a special case of the latter.

Psychological Pitfalls

The taking-in of information by observation is usually referred to as PERCEPTION and, as Erdelyi (1974) pointed out, there are actually a number of different processes involved: attention, encoding or interpretation, short-term memory, and rehearsal of what has been stored in short-term memory. Unfortunately, each of these processes is subject to bias.

Take ATTENTION, the process of concentrating on some aspect of your surroundings. In most situations there is simply more information available than we can handle. We are overwhelmed with sights, sounds, and smells and have to select small portions of what is available to attend to and encode. The aspects of a situation we choose to attend to are a function of many things, such as our interests and our experience. There is some evidence, however, that in many situations we do not choose at all. Sometimes it seems as if situations choose for us by drawing our attention to certain of their features. Taylor and Fiske (1975, 1978) noted that, all too often, we unthinkingly devote the lion's share of our attention to whatever or whomever happens to be the most salient stimulus in our environment, to whatever or whomever is easiest to attend to.

As a demonstration of this phenomenon, Taylor and Fiske asked students to watch some simple interactions, such as a conversation between two people. They manipulated the salience of the people conversing by varying the seating positions of the observers. Thus, some observers were seated so that they were looking directly at one of the two participants but could only see the back and side of the second participant. Other observers were seated so that they were looking directly at the second participant but could only see the back and side of the first. Still other observers were seated so that they could see both participants equally well. This arrangement is diagrammed in Figure 2. Following the conversation, observers were asked a number of questions about what they had heard and were asked to rate the participants on a number of scales. The major result was that Observers 1 and 2 (who were facing Participant A) rated A as having been more responsible for the nature and direction of the conversation, whereas Observers 5 and 6 (who were facing Participant B) rated B as having been more responsible. Observers 3 and 4, who could see both participants equally well rated them as having been about equally responsible for the tone and topics of conversation. As Taylor and Fiske (1975)

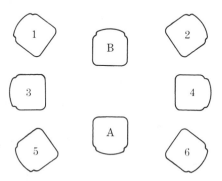

Figure 2 SEATING ARRANGEMENT OF OBSERVERS (1-6) around conversing participants (A, B). The observers' interpretations of who had the most influence in the conversation were strongly affected by their vantage points. (From Taylor & Fiske, 1975.)

noted, "Where one's attention is directed in one's environment influences what information is perceptually salient. Perceptually salient information is subsequently overrepresented when one imputes social or causal meaning to one's perceptual experience." Thus, you must be very careful not to fall into the trap of paying too much attention to the salient features of the setting. Make a conscious effort to distribute your attention to all aspects of the situation.

The second component of the perceptual process, the encoding or interpretation of what you observe, is also subject to distortion. It is impossible to go into any situation with your mind a complete blank. Even if you know nothing more than the name of the setting in which you are going to be observing, you are likely to have some definite expectations about what you will find there. Those expectations, in turn, are likely to color your interpretations. It is a difficult bias to overcome, because we quite often make inferences based on expectations so quickly, so unconsciously, that we confuse them with observations. We really see what we expect to see. Consider this example. Rubin, Provenzano, and Luria (1974) asked the parents of newly born infants (less than a day old) to rate their young sons and daughters. Objective comparisons established that the male and female infants did not differ in weight, length, color, reflex irritability, or heart and respiratory rates. Even so, the parents, especially the fathers, rated their sons as firmer, larger-featured, better coordinated, more alert, and hardier. The daughters were perceived to be softer, finer featured, more awkward, more inattentive, weaker, and more delicate. They, indeed, saw in their newly born just what they expected. (For another example of reading in, see page 59.)

There is a related way in which expectations may blind us to what is really out there to be observed. On the basis of one or two items of information about a person, we may categorize them as being a certain type. We then expect them to behave in congruent ways, and those expectations may interfere with our ability to see and utilize new information about the person, especially information that would contradict the initial categorization. For example, Dailey (1952) asked subjects to read autobiographical sketches written by stimulus persons and to predict how the stimulus persons would respond to specific items on a personality inventory. The criterion in each case was how the stimulus person had actually responded. Some subjects made predictions after reading half of the autobiography and again after reading all of it. Others made predictions only after reading all the information. The latter group did significantly better. Thus, premature conclusions based on a small amount of information may prevent you from learning as much as you should from additional data. The moral, of course, is try to keep an open mind as long as possible when observing. Do not fall victim to the PRIMACY EFFECT, that is, do not

GEORGE IN THE AFTERNOON

Several years ago, the actor George Segal agreed to be interviewed by the 26 students enrolled in a nonfiction writing class at the University of California at Santa Barbara. He answered their questions for an hour and twenty minutes and, the following week, each student was required to turn in a 1000-word report on what had been said, done, and seen during the session. The class instructor, Barry Farrell (1975), was so struck by the diversity of their impressions of what Segal had looked like and said that he took a sentence or two from each report and strung them all together. The result was a telling illustration of the extent to which apparently objective reports of an event are influenced by the style, focus of attention, and intepretations of the reporter. Consider the following:

> I was struck by his candid but pleasant arrogance. He had no false pretenses or pompous mannerisms. The blond-haired actor was reverberating with the taut worry of a struck tuning fork. Could this calm, composed man be the same George Segal who pulled down his pants on the Black Bird set? Segal wasn't always this suave.

> Segal rested languidly on a desk top. He perched atop a desk. He assumed a commanding place on top of a table in front of the class. He clung to the table, knuckles curled tightly around its edges. His hands were resting motionless in his lap, but he seemed to be knitting all the flying, scattered vibrations into a low-keyed OM.

> Always in complete control. Segal fielded ridiculous questions with professional ease. He stooped to answer familiar questions. Serious questions that touched on conflicts were treated as jokes or ignored. . . . I was rankled by the interview. It was stilted and tight. His observations were colorful and lucid. Statements of double meaning were in abundance. The bass note was sincerity and cool. It was clear that he had learned the necessity of humility along the way. Who had more right to snobbism, sophistication, and conceit?

It is hard to believe they all saw and participated in the same interview. That, of course, is the point. Physically, they did, but, psychologically, they did not. Each brought different experiences, tastes, prejudices, preferences, expectations, and desires to the situation. More than beauty is in the eye of the beholder.

let the first things you learn about a setting or the people in it have undue influence on your impressions. First impressions may be seriously distorted.

Reconstructing a day's events from a few jotted notes taken at odd moments during the day can also be a hazardous enterprise as far as accuracy is concerned. Shweder (1975) provided some important evidence on this point, using data originally collected by Newcomb (1929) in a summer camp for boys. The camp lasted for about three and one-half weeks and, during that time, the day-to-day behaviors of each camper were recorded by six observers. The observers noted every occurrence of each of 26 separate behaviors exhibited by the boys. Some examples of the behaviors recorded are the following:

Speaks with confidence of his own abilities

Spends more than an hour of the day alone

Painstaking in making up his bed

Talks more than his share of the time

Gets into scraps with other boys

These observations, noted as soon as possible after they occurred, constitute the actual behavior of the boys. In addition, at the end of the entire camp session, each of the six observers was asked to give an overall rating to each boy on each of the 26 behaviors. The latter ratings constitute what Shweder termed the rated behavior of the boys, and these ratings were made purely on the basis of memory, that is, without looking at the earlier recordings of actual behavior. Finally, Shweder asked some graduate students to look at the 26 behaviors and, for each possible pair of those behaviors, to rate the conceptual similarity of the behaviors themselves. These ratings constitute what Shweder referred to as the PREEXISTING CONCEPTUAL SCHEME, that is, the expectations about which behaviors are similar or related or likely to be exhibited by the same person. The major results of interest are the following. First, the actual behavior of the boys did not correspond very closely to what the observers remembered three weeks later. Memory is unreliable. Second, the preexisting conceptual scheme did correspond very closely to the rated behavior. Not only is memory unreliable, there is a systematic, predictable distortion in memory in the direction of our expectations about what-is-likely-to-be-related-to-what. So, you must devise ways of checking on yourself. Writing up field notes promptly, as soon after observation as possible, will help. It will not completely solve the problem.

The potential observer biases we have been discussing are internal ones. They all stem from normal psychological processes, imperfections in the ways we take in, manipulate, and try to make sense of the information available to us. The other major category of potential observer biases is more external in nature. The problems here stem from the nature of the observer's relations with other people in the setting being observed.

Interpersonal and Ethical Pitfalls

Moving into a strange setting and trying to learn its nuances and subtleties can be a frightening experience. The more different the setting is from what you are used to, the more frightening it is likely to be. Nothing can be taken for granted. Everything has to be learned from scratch. In fact, it is not at all unusual for beginning field workers to feel overwhelmed by the task. Commenting on her own first experience in the field, Margaret Mead (1949) once said:

> For my first two months in Samoa, as I learned to speak the language, eat the food, and interpret the postures and the gestures of the people, I found myself often saying under my breath, "I can't do it. I can't do it."

Similarly, Wax (1971) noted that for the first six weeks in the field she felt as if she were losing her mind. Carpenter (1965) said he felt like a mental defective during his first months among the Eskimos.

Such feelings seem to be the rule, although there are, as always, exceptions. The culprit seems to be a complete lack of any meaningful social relationships during the initial stages of research. Even when people have agreed to allow you to be present, you are initially only *in*, but not *of* the setting. According to Wax (1971) it is only with the establishment of a few genuine personal relationships that those feelings of incompetence and lack of progress are likely to pass. That makes sense, of course, because what you are there to learn are the nuances and subtleties of social life–which means you must participate in and observe that life up close. If the others in the setting merely tolerate your presence at public events and are polite to you, you will not learn what you need to know. You must win the confidence and friendship of at least a few people in the setting so that they will explain things to you, share confidences, help you meet others who can assist you, and tell you when you blunder.

There is a potential problem, however, that you need to be aware of. Given your marginal, *in* but not *of*, status in the setting, you may attract some of the more peripheral characters. That is, there is a real danger that the people most likely to gravitate toward you will be those who are themselves marginal for one reason or another. You would not want to disregard what these people have to say, of course, but you would need to keep it in perspective. You would need to take into account, for example, their status, or lack of status, in the setting. You would also not want to be perceived as attending only to those who are malcontent. People might begin to question your motives for being there.

But, even in building relationships with the more central, well integrated members of the setting, there is the potential for bias. There is ample evidence (e.g., Byrne, 1971) that we are most attracted to those who are similar to us in any of a variety of ways. Thus, it is quite likely that there will be some people in the setting with whom you more easily and naturally establish a good rapport. There will be others whom you find it somewhat more difficult to talk to. The danger, of course, is that you will rely too heavily on what the former have to say and not give equal time – or credibility – to the latter.

As you become known and accepted within the setting, a new problem arises. Ideally, the setting and the interactions within it should be unaffected by your presence. That may be an impossible ideal. People who treat you in a relatively normal manner will expect you to reciprocate. Having helped you by telling you about the setting, showing you around, answering your questions, and introducing you to others, they have a right to expect that you will help them, should the occasion arise. Lofland (1971) said there is probably no way to avoid performing some service for others within the setting, assuming you want to maintain your acceptability. Look at it as an opportunity to learn more about what is going on. Wax (1971), for example, let Indian children wait in her house for the school bus on cold winter mornings. She took the opportunity to talk to them about school and a variety of other topics. Whyte (1951) was elected secretary of a club he was observing. He was reluctant to accept, but did so because it gave him an excuse for openly taking copious notes while meetings were in progress.

You could argue, of course, that the mere presence of an observer influences the setting. People behave differently around strangers, particularly strangers doing research. They do indeed. That is one reason why you should not expect to go into a setting and learn all about it in a week or two. It will take time and after a few months, you will no longer be a stranger. Of course, in some situations, there is the possibility of concealing the fact that you are doing research. There is ample precedent for that (see Figure 3). It would hasten your acceptance into the setting. The ethical and interpersonal problems created by such undercover research seem to outweigh the advantages, however. Unless you are really an odd bird, for example, you are bound to make a few friends while doing your observing. Those people are likely to feel used or betrayed when they find out you were just doing research, and they probably would find out when you leave. Also, suppose they reveal something to you that is immoral or criminal? How would you handle that?

Having it known that you are an observer keeps everything above board. You will no doubt still make friends, but there will be no sense of being duplicitous on your part or, later, no sense of having been used on theirs. It will also make it easier for everyone when you choose to draw the line and say thanks just the same but you would just as soon not par-

Policeman attempts to arrest policewoman

Associated Press

LOS ANGELES — A policewoman and a male officer, each unaware of the other's identity, tried to arrest each other while working undercover in a vice crackdown, police said.

The two officers were working in the Hollywood area on Sunday as part of a crackdown on prostitution when the male officer approached the policewoman in the belief she was a prostitute, said Lt. Dan Cooke.

The man allegedly asked the woman if she would perform a sex act for a specific sum and she agreed, then both identified themselves as police officers, Cooke said Tuesday.

"I guess they both tried to place each other under arrest," said Cooke, who explained that the officers did not recognize each other because they work at different stations.

No arrests were made, he added.

Figure 3 USE OF UNDERCOVER AGENTS to obtain evidence of criminal activity is a form of participant observation. As noted in the text, however, concealment of your reason for being in a setting is not recommended. (From *The Lexington Leader*, June 16, 1982 © The Associated Press)

ticipate in that particular activity. Asking dumb questions, taking notes, and, generally, being nosy are also more acceptable behaviors if everybody knows what you are doing.

When Observation Is Appropriate

The major attraction of participant observation for many people is that it gives you a meaningful, coherent picture of a setting. You get to see the whole, in all its complex dynamic reality and not just bits and pieces. Becker and Geer (1970) even went so far as to state that participant observation is the yardstick by which the completeness of data gathered in other ways should be measured. That is a slight overstatement, as Trow (1970) pointed out. Becker and Geer seemed to assume that all events could be studied by participant observation, which, of course, is not so. Suppose you were interested in suicide rates in different groups? Or, the relationship between economic cycles and mob violence? Suppose you wanted to learn how Democrats feel about birth control? Participant observation is simply not an appropriate technique for finding answers to such questions.

Perhaps one way to define when it is appropriate, then, is to be clear about when it is inappropriate. According to Pearsall (1970), it is inappropriate with large populations, events of long duration, very infrequent events, and activities that are simply inaccessible to observers. So, with groups that are small enough so that you could really get to know the people involved in a reasonable period of time and who are willing to put up with your presence, participant observation may be feasible. Some examples? Well, Margaret Mead's fieldwork in Samoa took nine months and her detailed observations were confined to a group of girls living in three contiguous villages. Coombs and Goldman's (1973) study was of one 12-bed intensive care unit and was carried out over a single summer. The doomsday cult mentioned earlier (Festinger et al., 1956) was observed over a two-month period from October to December, and most of the observations were done in the prophet's household. Clearly the groups observed tended to be fairly small and the time periods fairly limited. There is sometimes the possibility of part-time observation carried out over more extended time periods. Polsky (1969), for example, carried out his observations of poolrooms and hustlers over a number of years, while working as an editor and book publishing executive. You do not necessarily have to change your entire life, then, to do participant observation. It depends on what you are interested in.

There is another consideration in deciding whether participant observation is an appropriate procedure in a particular situation. That is: Do you have an axe to grind? Do you want to prove something about the situation? If you do, participant observation is definitely not for you! Because of the multiple opportunities for bias in participant observation, it should be used only when you genuinely want to learn what is going on in a setting, only when you can approach the setting with an open mind. Given the tremendous amounts of information available in dynamic social settings, the ambiguities inherent in most interactions, and the limited perspective and biases of a single observer, you could find evidence to fit almost any preconception if you looked hard enough. For an example, see page 65. Thus, if you already know what is going on and you just want to gather a little information to prove it, do not bother. You will waste your time, and everybody else's as well.

On the other hand, if you are really curious, if you really would like to know what is going on in the particular setting and how it gets done, then participant observation may be just the thing. Try it.

Summary

Participant observation emerged as an extension of the descriptive narratives brought back by explorers of faraway places. There are a number of parallels between participant observation and reporting. Both involve the development of intimate familiarity with a setting, the systematic recording of observations, and the gathering of auxiliary information. What

THAT OLDER FELLOW IN THE
SECOND ROW SURE LOOKS FAMILIAR!

Until his retirement in 1974, Ludwig Eichna served as chairman of the Department of Medicine at the State University of New York Downstate Medical Center. The following year he reentered that very same medical school with the first-year class and, until May, 1979, when they graduated, he did everything they did (academic things, at least). He attended all lectures, conferences, seminars, reports, and labs. He was present for patient workups and presentations. He did duty in operating and delivery rooms. He was on call nights and weekends. He even took all examinations, oral and written, that the students did. He also did something that the students did not do—he kept an extensive log of his (and their) activities for the four-year period. Having himself been to medical school some decades earlier, Dr. Eichna's purpose was to assess changes in, and the current state of, medical education. Four years of participant observation was his method of choice and, no doubt, it was an arduous four years, given the tightly packed schedule of a typical medical student.

Unfortunately, the value of Eichna's (1980) conclusions about his experiences are somewhat ambiguous. There are several reasons for this. First, he notes that prior to his retirement as Chairman of the Department of Medicine he had been "increasingly dissatisfied with the course and results of medical school education." Such an attitude is hardly conducive to an open, unbiased assessment of current practices. One wonders whether Eichna embarked on the research not to learn, but to prove. Second, one might question the wisdom of the decision to become a participant observer at the same school where he had been a powerful member of the administration. Imagine the effect on junior faculty of his presence in their classroom. There they are, day after day, lecturing their former chairman on the fine points of medicine. Chances are that Eichna heard more than his share of excruciatingly correct, but nervously delivered lectures. The point, of course, is that what he saw and heard may not have been typical, it may have been biased because of his presence (given who he was). Third, Eichna presents his findings in the form of eight Principles, with commentary on each. That's fine. A participant observer is indeed supposed to go beyond simple reporting. Observations are to be used as the basis for analysis, for extracting themes, for abstracting principles. But the principles must be tied to specific observations of specific situations, and the reader needs to be given the particulars. Eichna never does that. For example, he repeatedly states that "clinical subjects increasingly intrude into biological science time," but he never gives a specific example of a course in which this occurred or an instructor who gave up class time to a clinical colleague or the date and text of a decision by the curriculum committee to take time away from a biological science course.

distinguishes the two is the scientific goal of the participant observer, that is, the development of disciplined abstractions.

Kanter's fieldwork in the sales force at INDSCO is an example of the development of disciplined abstractions. The INDSCO sales force was made up of approximately 300 men and only 20 women. The situation of, and reactions to, the token women seemed to reflect the operation of three basic processes: (1) visibility, which led to increased performance pressures, (2) polarization, which led to an exaggeration of the dominant (male) culture, and (3) assimilation, which led to role encapsulation for the females.

The key to participant observation is developing intimate familiarity with some specific social setting. Three things are involved: doing your homework, gaining entry, and immersion in the setting. The point is to learn how–how whatever it is that is supposed to get done in the setting really gets done. To do that you have to be personally accepted, not just administratively accepted. So that you do not forget what you are learning, your second most important task (gaining acceptance is, of course, number one) is the systematic taking of field notes–every day, without fail. Multiple copies of the field notes are necessary for sorting and cross classifying into your mundane and analytic files. The mundane files are used to deposit information on specific aspects of the people and setting. The analytic files are the basis for development of disciplined abstractions. As ideas begin to occur about processes operating within the setting, you create files in which to deposit copies of notes pertinent to each idea.

There are two general classes of pitfalls that can create problems for the unwary participant observer: (1) those stemming from imperfections in the way you take in and process information and (2) those stemming from relations, or lack of relations, with other people in the setting. The first class of pitfalls includes the dangers of devoting too much attention to the most salient aspects of a setting, of letting your expectations bias what you think you see, and of trusting your memory. The interpersonal difficulties include the initial marginal status of the observer and the lack of social relations, both of which can seriously impede progress. You also need to recognize varying perspectives within a setting but you should not give undue weight to the view of those with whom you most quickly and/or most easily establish rapport.

Finally, participant observation is not appropriate for use with large populations, events of great duration, infrequent events, and activities inaccessible to observers. It is also not appropriate when you have something to prove.

Recommended Readings

Two of these books were written by sociologists and two by anthropologists. The fifth was written by a journalist. Both Thompson and Goffman are prolific writers, and if you cannot find the two books that are listed here, any of their other books would be worthy substitutes.

Goffman, E. *Asylums: Essays on the social situation of mental patients and other inmates.* Garden City, NY: Doubleday-Anchor, 1961.

In the mid-1950s, Erving Goffman spent a year observing the day-to-day activities of inmates and staff at St. Elizabeth's Hospital in Washington, D.C. St. Elizabeth's is roughly the equivalent of a large state mental hospital, except that it is supported by the Federal Government and the District of Columbia is not a state. In any event, Goffman chose to participate in the life of the hospital as a member of the staff—he started out as assistant athletic director—rather than as an inmate, so that he might have more freedom of movement and greater access to all levels of hospital life. One of the things to note about this book, is how Goffman intersperses data from his own observations with anecdotes and excerpts from literature, biographies, and a variety of other sources. It not only makes for very interesting reading, it has the effect of tying his observations and analyses into a larger body of knowledge, thereby increasing the relevance and generality of his data. Note also the difference between this book and the one below by Hunter Thompson. Thompson stays almost entirely at the level of pure description. Goffman uses his observations for purposes of analysis, to develop concepts and ideas that will help in understanding life in other institutions and that will help in understanding how institutions do what they do to people.

Polsky, N. *Hustlers, beats, and others.* Garden City, NY: Doubleday, 1969.

If you could read only one chapter about fieldwork before setting out to do your thing, the third chapter of Polsky's book is the one I would recommend. It is both an impassioned defense of the need for the type of data obtained only via participant observation and some practical suggestions about the best ways to proceed. Although he focuses primarily on research within deviant subcultures, his recommendations can be applied more generally. Sample advice: "Most important when hanging around criminals—what I regard as the absolute 'first rule' of field research on them—is this: Initially, keep your eyes and ears open *but keep your mouth shut.* At first try to ask no questions whatsoever. Before you can ask questions, or even speak much at all other than when spoken to, you should get the 'feel' of their world by extensive and attentive listening . . . (even then) if the researcher is a compulsive talker or otherwise longwinded, if he can't shut up for considerable periods, he will be seriously handicapped." Another nice feature of the book is that in writing about his own research on poolroom hustlers, Polsky provides a model of how participant observation can be done part-time, over a period of years, while one is also engaged in other more mundane pursuits, such as holding down a job and keeping food on the table.

Scheper-Hughes, N. *Saints, scholars, and schizophrenics: Mental illness in rural Ireland.* Berkeley, CA: University of California Press, 1979.

According to the World Health Organization, the rate of psychiatric hospitalization in Ireland is the highest of any country in the world. When I first read that, it seemed very odd to me. Why Ireland? Taken in isolation, any single fact about a culture may seem extremely puzzling. One of the strong points of participant observation is that it helps you understand the context, the setting within which isolated aspects of a culture are cast. It often happens that once that full context is understood, the part that previously seemed so peculiar makes perfect sense. In an effort to understand more about that high rate of psychiatric hospitalization, Nancy Scheper-Hughes—together with her husband and three small children—spent a year in the small village of *Ballybran* on Ireland's rugged west coast. The year was spent in intimate contact with villagers and village life, coupled with intensive interviewing of several groups, and extensive reading of Irish history and folklore. The pattern that emerged, and which is movingly described in this book, is a melancholy one, but it is one within which that high incidence of psychiatric problems makes sense. The book is an excellent example of the use of participant observation.

Thompson, H. *Hell's Angels: A strange and terrible saga.* New York: Ballantine Books, 1967.

If you have never read any of Hunter Thompson's books, you should try this one at least. It is not only fun to read, it is informative about a style of life you will probably never have the opportunity to experience. Thompson is a journalist, and for the better part of 1965 he hung out with a group of Hell's Angels in San Francisco, getting material for this book. He rode with them, drank with them, and—well—did other things with them. The story of that year is a fascinating example of what is variously referred to as *pop sociology* and *gonzo journalism*. My major reason for recommending the book, however, has to do with writing style. One of the most difficult tasks for the novice participant observer is learning how to capture observed situations on paper, that is, in field notes and in later reports of the research. Thompson is a master of description. The scenes he depicts are so vivid you sometimes think you can smell the motorcycle grease and hear the roar of an unmuffled engine whipping through traffic at 90 miles an hour. But do not get too caught up in reading the story. Pay attention to how the vividness is conveyed. One key is the use of detail. Another is the use of direct quotations; he lets people speak for themselves. Thompson is also not afraid to use a little nonstandard English if it will communicate his meaning and that, after all, is the point.

Wax, R. H. *Doing fieldwork: Warnings and advice.* Chicago: University of Chicago Press, 1971.

Forewarned is forearmed. Thus, one of the things that veteran fieldworkers recommend is that you read some personal accounts of field research before you embark on your own. If you take that advice, you may decide that Murphy[1] was a fieldworker. As Rosalie Wax put it, "It might be wise for beginning fieldworkers and their employers and supervisors to assume that a fieldworker is likely to encounter a great deal of difficulty getting his work underway." She backs up that statement by relating her own experiences in research, experiences that stretch over a quarter of a century. The problems often stem from the fact that there are so many things in a field setting that the researcher is (1) unable to control and (2) does not know about. It takes time to find out enough about a community, say, to know who would be the best people to talk to, who should be avoided, who is currently not speaking to whom. It also helps to know that good fieldwork still gets done – eventually – and that other people have had the same problems.

[1]Murphy's First Law: If anything can go wrong, it will.

3

Using Observation
to Test Ideas

People interested in the behavior of animals have long been aware that a great deal can be learned by a little careful, unobtrusive observation. For example, in a study that began in the early 1960s, Jane Van Lawick-Goodall (1971) and her associates spent years observing the behavior of chimpanzees under completely natural conditions. Their tireless tramping through jungle grass, peering through telescopes, climbing trees, taking pictures, and perching on mountaintops were rewarded with a number of significant findings. It was discovered that chimpanzees eat meat, whereas previously they had been thought to dine exclusively on fruits and nuts. They were seen using tools and even – surprise – making tools. Note that the researchers were not participants in chimpanzee society. They observed from a distance and, generally, they tried to keep their presence on the periphery from influencing what was going on.

Van Lawick-Goodall's chimpanzee watching is an example of the type of research used in ETHOLOGY, an old but recently revitalized field of study concerned with the behavior of animals in their natural settings. As Miller (1977) has noted, ethology can contribute greatly to our knowledge of the diets, activities, sleep cycles, temperature preferences, and habitats of a variety of animal species. For many animals, such data are incredibly difficult to obtain and, as a consequence, very little is known about them. Think about it for a moment. How would you find out how much time blue whales spend sleeping or how long a typical antelope lives? Our knowledge of the habits of blue whales, antelopes, and hundreds of other animals is so limited that any new tidbit of information is valuable.

The reason for mentioning ethology is that it forms a bridge between participant observation (Chapter Two) and our current concern with the use of observation to test specific ideas. In ethology, the observer is usually no longer a participant, but the goal is still the global one of trying to understand how the animal lives in its natural habitat. Similarly, participant observation with humans is most useful in settings that are unfamiliar to the observer. The approach of both the ethologist and the participant observer, then, is empirical. They are there to learn all there is to learn, to take in all available information about the setting.

In contrast, there are vast areas of everyday life about which we already appear to have more information than we can handle. What is needed is some way of sorting things out, of separating fact from fancy. The approach needed here is called a RATIONAL APPROACH. It involves formulating a specific question and deciding which behaviors you need to observe in order to answer the question. Thus, the continued discussion of observation in research needs a couple of changes in emphasis. The focus shall be on situations in which the observer (1) is not, or is only minimally, a participant and (2) has narrowed his or her interest down to a specific question for which an answer is sought via watching (systematically, of course) what people do. It is important to note that the kind of observation being discussed here is nothing very esoteric. As Heyns and Lippitt (1954) said, it is simply the scientific use of a skill that you already have. The *scientific* qualifier does imply that you are going to have to be a little more rigorous, a little more demanding of yourself (and others) in using it. But, there is no new or occult skill to be developed.

People Watching

The source of the specific question of interest can vary. What piques your curiosity may leave someone else bored, and vice versa. What strikes you as peculiar and in need of explanation, others may take completely for granted. But, generally speaking, there are two starting points for research, that is, two major categories of questions.

The first category consists of those questions or hypotheses that are raised by or derived from a theory. The goal of your observation in this case will be to clarify or test the theory. For example, Wicklund and Gollwitzer (1982) have proposed a theory about how people behave when they become aware of a sense of incompleteness in their image of themselves, a discrepancy between the way they are and the way they would like to be. What is likely to happen, according to the theory, is that they will engage in what are referred to as SELF-SYMBOLIZING BEHAVIORS, behaviors designed to convey to themselves and others that they really are a jogger or an intellectual or an anthropologist or whatever it is they wish they were. You can probably think of several situations in which observations bearing on this theory could be made. One possible prediction is that new medical doctors, those right out of school, are more likely to dress and act like "real" doctors than people who have had their degree for several years. The neophytes, for example, might never be seen without their white coats, stethoscopes, name tags, and beepers. Their senior colleagues might be a little more relaxed about dress. Note that if your prediction does come from a theory, as does this example about self-symbolizing among new doctors, and your intent is to test or clarify the theory, you will be engaged in what is referred to as BASIC RESEARCH.

The second starting point for research, the second category of questions about how and why people do the things they do, consists of those questions arising from the need to make an intelligent decision in a specific situation. For example, if you were thinking about opening a filling station and had a choice of three or four locations, you might want to spend some time observing traffic patterns at each of the potential sites. Are some of the sites more accessible to motorists than others? Are there differences in total traffic flow past the various sites? In gathering that information you would be conducting APPLIED RESEARCH, research intended to help you make the best decision possible about what to do in that particular situation.

Note that it is the source of your question, not the methodology employed to answer it, that determines whether you are doing basic or applied research. Unfortunately, there has been a great deal of silliness propagated about basic versus applied research – with the pure basic people tending to look down their noses at those mucking about with applied problems. Ideally, of course, there should be a continuous interplay between the two: findings from applied research being used to generate theoretical ideas, which are tested and clarified in basic research, then extended to practical settings to help understand processes there and suggest directions for further applied research. As Lewin (1951) once put it, such cooperation is possible only "if the theorist does not look toward applied problems with highbrow aversion or with a fear of social problems, and if the applied [researcher] realizes that there is nothing so practical as a good theory."

Regardless of whether the question that has captured your attention is a basic, theoretical one or a practical, applied one, there is always a common goal. That goal is valid information with which to answer the question and, as McGuire (1969) pointed out, considerable creative ingenuity may be required to obtain it. It may stimulate your creativity to consider the different types of behavior that can, in fact, be observed and used to answer your questions.

Varieties of Behavior for Observation

According to Weick (1968), those doing observational research have been unnecessarily narrow in their choices about which behaviors to record. They have relied too much on language, on what people say. That is certainly an understandable bias, since language is what makes us human. Verbal behavior is, indeed, the single most important category of behavior to observe and we shall discuss it in detail in the section Observational Systems, that is, the entire second half of this chapter. People do talk, but they also express themselves in a variety of other ways. Each of these alternative modes of expression can serve as the basis for observational measures, depending, of course, on what it is you are interested in. The three categories of behavior that we shall consider here, behaviors that can be systematically observed in testing your ideas, are (1) nonverbal, (2) extralinguistic, and (3) spatial.

Consider NONVERBAL BEHAVIOR first. It is an area of research in which there has been a growing interest in the past few years. Many people appear to be rediscovering the importance of all the little gestures and cues described by Freud, years ago, in *The Psychopathology of Everyday Life*. He described (1938) a category of behavior that most people seem to think of as chance occurrences (leaving a button unbuttoned, tics of various sorts, fingering one's beard – things done absent-mindedly, with no conscious intention or purpose). Freud, however, believed that such behaviors were not chance at all, but symptomatic. He believed they give "expression to something which the actor does not suspect in them, and which, as a rule, he has no intention of imparting to others, but aims to keep to himself." Similarly, Goffman (1959) distinguished between an impression that you give (your conscious attempts to communicate particular information about yourself) and an impression that you give off (the not-so-conscious nuances that may undercut the definition of the situation you wish to maintain).

The variety of nonverbal behaviors that can be observed and, possibly, used as indicators of social and psychological processes is almost infinite: facial expressions, eye contact, aspects of dress, grooming, types of gait, body positions. But, some caution is required. As Friedman (1982) noted, there is often room for disagreement about what particular nonverbal behaviors really mean. Take body position, for example. What does it mean if someone leans forward rather than backward when interacting with others? It could mean that they like the person they are interacting with, but it could also mean about 50 other things: They are nervous; they have a sore back; the chair is uncomfortable; they cannot hear well. You see the problem. Unfortunately, many people using nonverbal behaviors in observational research act as if they did not see the problem. They offer seemingly plausible analyses of what a specific nonverbal behavior means and let it go at that. But, that will not do. Even though it seems reasonable that leaning toward rather than away from someone indicates liking, you must establish that as a fact if you want to use leaning forward as your index of liking. One way to do that would be to observe interactions between people known to like each other and people known to dislike each other. If more leaning forward occurred among the former, you would have some evidence to support your use of leaning forward as a measure of liking. The point really applies to all behaviors you plan to observe – nonverbal, verbal, overt bodily movement, extralinguistic. You must document that the behavior is a valid indicator of whatever it is you are taking it to indicate.

EXTRALINGUISTIC BEHAVIORS, the noncontent aspects of speech, constitute a special class of nonverbal behaviors. As you are probably well aware, it is not just what you say, but how you say it that conveys information to a listener. Tone of voice, loudness, rate of speaking, dialect, tendencies to interrupt, pronunciation, and a variety of other such markers are included here and are available for use as observational measures. For example, consider the letters *th* as they appear in words such as *thing*, *three,* and *third.* Labov (1970) pointed out that there are at least three systematic variations in the pronunciation of this combination: (1) the fricative, in which the breath is quickly forced through a narrow opening between the teeth and lips, (2) the affricative, in which the breath is more slowly released, and (3) the stop, in which the outgoing breath is completely stopped. The fricative is usually considered correct, or at least the most prestigious. Labov recorded speech samples in four different situations from lower class, working class, lower middle class, and upper middle class respondents in New York City and scored the samples on the pronunciation of *th.* A score of 0 was given for each fricative, a 1 for each affricative, and a 2 for each stop. Thus, the higher the score, the "poorer" the pronunciation. The results appear in Figure 1. As the figure shows, there are both social class and situational variations in pronunciation. The pronunciation of upper middle class subjects was relatively consistent and correct, regardless of whether they were engaging in casual conversation, reading, or pronouncing words from a list. In contrast, the casual conversation of

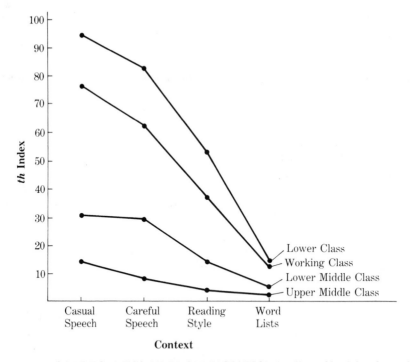

Figure 1 CORRECTNESS OF PRONUNCIATION is affected both by the social class of the speaker and by the situation in which the speech is given. The *th* index is a measure of the correctness of pronunciation: the higher the index, the poorer the pronunciation. (From Labov, 1970.)

lower class subjects was very poor on this index. When asked to pronounce words from a list, however, these subjects pronounced the words very much like the upper middle class subjects.

There are a couple of reasons for selecting Labov's study to illustrate an extralinguistic behavior that could be observed and recorded. The first is to make the point that accurate observation of such behaviors often requires the observer to make fine discriminations, such as between the fricative *th* and the affricative. Needless to say, the finer the discriminations required, the greater the likelihood of errors. This may partially explain why people have been hesitant to use nonverbal and/or extralinguistic behaviors in observational research. That is, such behaviors are generally more subtle than, say, verbal behaviors, such as asking a question, giving an opinion, or gross bodily movements. The second reason for mentioning Labov's study is that it illustrates one solution to the problem of observing such subtle behaviors. Labov *recorded* the subjects reading and speaking. Thus, he could replay the recordings as often as necessary for him to score a particular *th* – or to have others check all of his scoring. Videotapes, audio recordings, and photographs can be quite helpful in research. We shall mention them again in connection with observer training, assessment of reliability (below), and content analysis (in the next chapter).

Usually somewhat more easily observable than nonverbal or extralinguistic behavior is the third category of behavior mentioned earlier, SPATIAL BEHAVIOR. People structure their use of space with surprising regularity. It is surprising because, like many other nonverbal behaviors, it is usually done without conscious awareness. For example, individuals appear to maintain varying distances from others, depending on the nature of their relationship with the others. The study of interaction distance and the variables that affect it is termed PROXEMICS, a word coined several years ago by Edward Hall (1966). According to Hall, there are four different spatial zones surrounding people, and only certain types of interactions occur within each of these zones: intimate (less than 18 inches from the other person), personal (18 inches to 4 feet), social (4 to 12 feet), and public (12 to 25 feet). It is highly unlikely, for example, that you would carry on an intimate conversation with someone who was 20 feet away. There are several thriving areas of research related to spatial behavior: research on crowding (Burger et al., 1983), on reactions to invasions of one's personal space (Sommer, 1969), and on territoriality (Altman, 1975). The point here, however, is simply to alert you to the possibility of using such behaviors as indications of social and psychological processes.

There are, of course, literally thousands of behaviors that could be made the focus of your observations. Again, the ones you choose to observe will be a function of the question of interest. But, there are some additional considerations, and we have already introduced you to a couple. You have to establish that the behavior you wish to observe is a valid indicator of whatever it is you are taking it to indicate. The behavior also should be easy to observe, if possible, and clearly discriminable from other behaviors. As Cone and Foster (1982) put it, the behaviors of interest should be accessible to the observer. (For some devices that may help make behaviors accessible, see page 79). These are rather obvious, but important, points. There is another issue, however, that is sometimes not so obvious. It has to do with the influence of the observer on the behavior being observed, that is, the issue of the reactivity of observation.

Avoiding Reactivity

One of the major concerns about the use of direct, first-hand observation in research is that, in most settings, the presence of an observer is OBTRUSIVE. The word itself means "tending to push self assertively forward; brash; intrusive; undesirably noticeable." And, as Kazdin (1982) has noted, the fear is that awareness of being observed will create changes in the behavior of those observed. If it does, then any conclusions based on those observations will, at best, be suspect. Obtrusive assessment or observation, then, may create a reaction in those observed.

Such reactive effects show up in a variety of places, even in those supposedly unconscious nonverbal gestures and nuances discussed earlier. The problem is that most people are aware that others read significance into such behaviors (Schlenker, 1980). Hence, they may attempt to control those nonverbal aspects of their behavior in order to project a certain image. If they are successful, any observational measure based on recording the occurrence of those gestures and expressions would be of questionable validity. Thus, whatever behaviors you plan to focus on in an observational study, you need to worry a little about whether those behaviors are likely to be a part of an act put on for your, or other's, benefit. In particular, you cannot assume that because many nonverbal behaviors are performed unconsciously that they all are.

As Kazdin (1982) noted, however, reactive effects are not well understood. Although it is plausible that the presence of an observer and the awareness of being observed are likely to alter the behavior of those observed, such alterations do not always occur. Thus, the issues really are (1) what kinds of behaviors are most likely to be affected by observation, (2) how can reactive effects be detected when they are present, and (3) how can they be prevented? Let us consider them one at a time.

One of the major reasons reactive effects occur is because people generally are concerned about the impressions they make on others. They are concerned about how others will judge them. In Rosenberg's (1965)

REMOTE OBSERVATION VIA RADIO TELEMETRY

Radio telemetry refers to the conveying of information from one place to another via radio transmitters and receivers (Miklich, 1975). Your first associations to that definition may be things like Dick Tracy comics, James Bond movies, and CB-equipped 18-wheelers. But, in the past few years, radio telemetry has proved quite useful in research requiring the observation or monitoring of individuals as they go about their normal activities. Miklich, Chai, Purcell, Weiss, and Brady (1974), for example, reported a study in which boys at a rehabilitation center for asthmatic children were asked to wear radio transmitters for several days. The idea was to see if various emotional and/or interpersonal situations were likely to trigger asthma attacks. It turned out that anger and excessive excitement did occasionally precipitate such attacks, but not all the time and not for everyone.

There are problems in using such devices, however. One has to do with the awareness of being monitored by those asked to wear the radio transmitters. It is quite possible that that awareness may change their behavior: They may become self-conscious and inhibited – not doing or saying certain things that they would normally do or say. However, Purcell and Brady (1966) claimed that people adapted to the miniature transmitters very quickly and after a day or two seem to forget that they were wearing the radios and that someone was eavesdropping. Whether or not you could count on such adaptation occurring would depend on who you were monitoring and what normal activity is for them.

There are some intriguing possibilities for such equipment. The Associated Press (1983) reports that a judge in Albuquerque, New Mexico has begun using an electronic handcuff to monitor the whereabouts of convicted drunk drivers who have been placed on probation and told to stay home, that is, out of the bars and off the streets, when not at work. Each handcuff emits a signal that is picked up by a receiver attached to the probationer's home telephone. If the wearer goes more than 1000 feet from the telephone, a signal is transmitted to a central computer via the phone lines and the next day the probation officer gets a report on the midnight wanderings. Even though you may not be too excited about electronic handcuffs, the story illustrates another problem with radio telemetry for remote observation. That is, the units are generally very low power and, in order to be used over any distance, they need to be coupled with a telephone. In the study by Purcell and Brady, mentioned earlier, the subject wore radio transmitters that broadcast their conversations to a nearby receiver. The receiver, in turn, relayed the conversations via telephone lines to a remotely located tape recorder.

phrase, they suffer from EVALUATION APPREHENSION. It follows that the presence of an observer is likely to increase the occurrence of socially desirable behaviors and decrease the occurrence of socially undesirable behaviors. SOCIALLY DESIRABLE BEHAVIORS are just what the name implies–those behaviors that are socially sanctioned and approved: coming to a full stop at stop signs, being polite, dressing appropriately. Most state police appear well aware of the evaluation apprehension–social desirability link. Parking a patrol car beside the highway is usually sufficient to slow traffic down to 55 mph for a mile or two in both directions. Similarly, diet centers and weight reduction spas apparently owe part of their success to the clients' knowledge that each week they are going to have to weigh in in front of other people. The threatened embarrassment of having put on a few pounds instead of taking them off helps motivate adherence to the weight reduction plan.

That last example suggests another possible mechanism underlying reactive effects, an attention–feedback–regulation mechanism. Conceptually, at least, this is independent of evaluation apprehension although the two would often lead to the same prediction if the behaviors being observed were socially desirable or undesirable. The ATTENTION-FEEDBACK-REGULA-TION idea is simply that the presence of an observer calls attention to certain behaviors, that is, those being observed. The person being observed begins to notice (self-feedback) what he or she is doing and, as a result, changes (self-regulation) how it is done or even what is done. Another possible explanation for the reactive effects of observation involves a phenomenon described briefly on page 9. That is, work by Zajonc (1965), Cottrell (1968), and others has suggested that the presence of an observer may be arousing. Unfortunately, that alone can be sufficient to produce changes in the observed behavior. Physiological arousal is known to facilitate the performance of dominant, well-learned responses and to inhibit efforts to learn new tasks or perform less well-mastered tasks.

Whatever the explanation for reactivity in a particular situation, it is your responsibility as a researcher to demonstrate that your observations are not contaminated by its subversive influence. The easiest way to detect the presence of reactivity effects involves a little deception. That is, you put observers into the setting for a while and then withdraw them, but you continue to observe surreptitiously the behavior of interest. For example, suppose you were interested in the effects of a drug such as Ritalin on the classroom behavior of hyperactive children (Collins, Whalen, & Henker, 1980), but you were worried that such children might be particularly sensitive to the presence of a stranger in the classroom. To check on that you might arrange to be present in the back of the class observing on alternate days. Then, on the other days, you might observe from a remote location via a TV camera mounted unobtrusively in the classroom.

If the behavior of the hyperactive kids was essentially the same on the days you were present and on the days you were not, you could feel confident that your presence was not affecting their behavior. Of course, to avoid reactive effects being produced by the TV camera, it would be best for it to be a permanent fixture in the classroom and for no one to know (except you) when it would be turned on. In a study patterned along these lines, Roberts and Renzaglia (1965) tape-recorded counseling sessions under several different conditions. In one, both client and counselor knew that the recording was being made. But, in another, neither client nor counselor was aware that the session was being recorded. The nature of the interaction did vary in several respects when the results from these conditions were compared, a finding indicating that knowledge of being recorded did indeed produce reactive effects.

A number of people have suggested ways to avoid or, at least, minimize reactive effects. Purcell and Brady (1966), for example, suggested that allowing time for participants in the setting to get used to being observed helps. They asked young boys to wear radio transmitters for an hour each day and found that, after the first two or three days, the boys paid little attention to the transmitters. Kazdin (1982) claimed that reducing the degree of obtrusiveness will also help control reactivity. In a classroom setting, for example, observing from the rear is preferable to observing from the front. It may also help to pick behaviors for observation that are not intrinsically socially desirable or undesirable. And then, of course, there is the possibility of concealment, of simply not letting people know that what they are doing is being observed. Henle and Hubble (1938), for example, eavesdropped on students in college dormitories by hiding observers under the beds. Dykman and Reis (1979) simply noted the seats chosen in a classroom by students on whom they had some previously collected personality data. The students with the most positive self-concepts tended to pick seats near the front of the room, but the point here is simply that the students did not know anyone was paying attention to where they sat.

The idea of surreptitious observation is distasteful to many people. But, before you reject that option, let us examine it a little more closely. There are also a couple of other ethical issues that arise in connection with observation and that need to be discussed.

Some Ethical Considerations

Remember, the topic of this chapter is observation of naturally occurring behavior, behavior *in situ*. What that means is that you, as the observer, do not influence the situation in any way. You introduce no new or foreign elements. You ask no questions. You tell no lies. The major ethical problem, then, is whether your observations will constitute an invasion of privacy for the people in the situation.

One solution, of course, is to let them decide. Ask them if they mind being observed doing whatever it is you want to watch them do. If you take this approach, there are a couple of pitfalls. One we have just discussed, that is, the potential reactive effects produced by their knowledge of being observed. If you can demonstrate that such effects are minimal or nonexistent, then getting the INFORMED CONSENT of the people you want to observe may indeed be the way to go. As noted in Chapter One, obtaining informed consent simply means giving people an explicit choice, prior to participation, of whether or not they would like to participate in the research. You also need to tell them of any potential harmful effects and let them know they are free to withdraw from the research at any time. If you decide to try that, however, you need to be especially sensitive to another ethical consideration. That is, do the people of whom you are making this request really have the freedom to say no? If they do not, then do not ask.

People should not be coerced, even subtly, into participating in research. Noncoercion is an important principle and it is one that has been much abused. Prisoners being asked by prison administration officials to take part in research, military personnel volunteering for research projects, and, yes, even students fulfilling course requirements by taking part in research are all questionable practices. In each of these, and similar, situations, the request cannot really be turned down. After collecting information on a number of incidents in which people had been coerced into research participation, the Committee on Ethical Practices in Research of the American Psychological Association (APA, 1973) formulated the following principle:

> Ethical research practice requires the investigator to respect the individual's freedom to decline to participate in research or to discontinue participation at any time. The obligation to protect this freedom requires special vigilance when the investigator is in a position of power over the participant. The decision to limit this freedom increases the investigator's responsibility to protect the participant's dignity and welfare.

Note that this and the other principles formulated by the committee were all hotly debated. They are not cast in stone but are the result of compromises between conflicting values: need for knowledge, freedom of inquiry, self-determination, right to privacy. In that spirit of debate, some believe the last sentence of the principle should have been left off. That is, some believe you should never make "the decision to limit this freedom."

But, sometimes informed consent does seem unnecessary. Surely there are behaviors you can observe without obtaining informed consent. You do it every day. Obviously there are limits, both ethical and legal. Wiretapping, for example, is clearly out of bounds. It is legally beyond the pale.[1] But where is that ethical/legal boundary?

For most people, the location of that boundary has to do with the notion of privacy, which is defined as the individual's ability to selectively control access to information about his or her beliefs, attitudes, and behavior (Altman, 1975; Reubhausen & Brim, 1965). If you were to stand up in class and start reading from your diary, people might be embarrassed or they might think you were behaving inappropriately, but they would not think your privacy had been invaded. On the other hand, if your roommate were to stand up in class and start reading from your diary (without your permission), your privacy would indeed have been invaded. The key to privacy, then, is that individuals must be able to choose how much or how little to reveal about themselves. As Kelman (1977) put it, the individual should not be deprived of control over his or her self-presentation, and the information obtained about the individual should have no damaging consequences for them.

What that means for research is that public behaviors are usually considered to be fair game for observation (McCarthy, 1981). But be careful. The right to privacy is not completely relinquished in public. The behavior of coming out of a hotel arm-in-arm with a member of the opposite sex may be public, but to record that behavior with a camera, say, so that the individuals could later be identified could conceivably have damaging consequences for them. So, it should not be done. In general, research in which specific individuals are identified as having been at a certain place at a certain time or in the company of certain others is considered to be an invasion of privacy. Kelman (1977) noted that there are also social norms that operate in public to secure areas of privacy and that these norms should not be disregarded in observational research. For example, if you were in a restaurant and the people at the next table were talking loudly enough for you to hear, it would be perfectly acceptable to make notes on such overheard conversations. But, to use covertly a listening device to enhance the audio level of conversations lost in the din of plates and silver would not be acceptable. By talking at a level so that their conversation is indeed lost in the surrounding din, people invoke a measure of privacy for themselves—even though they are in a public place (see page 84).

Thus, even if you are observing naturally occurring public behavior, questions may still arise as to whether or not your observations constitute an invasion of privacy. If there is any doubt about the research you are planning, one thing you should not do is trust your own judgment. You

---

[1]It is interesting to note that some legal limits, such as the prohibition against recording jury deliberations, were in fact enacted in reaction to specific social science research projects (Strodtbeck, James, & Hawkins, 1957; Burchard, 1958).

PHOTOGRAPHIC ETHICS AND SAMPLE BIAS

In the past few years there has been an increasing use of photography and videotaping in research in anthropology, sociology, and psychology. One of the characteristics of a photograph, of course, is that any individuals depicted can usually be easily identified – even when masked by one of those little black rectangles across the eyes. This can present a problem because many of the photographs that are likely to be useful in research are ones that are taken covertly, that is, without the knowledge of the people being photographed.

One possible solution of the ethical problem posed by covertly taken photos and tapes is to go ahead and make them and then ask the people pictured for their permission to use them. According to Webb, Campbell, Schwartz, Sechrest, and Grove (1981), this was the procedure used by Alan Funt to secure materials for his television program "Candid Camera." People would be covertly videotaped responding to contrived situations in which they were often made to appear ludicrous – such as having an arm reach out of a mailbox and take a letter they were about to deposit. For many people, having others see how they responded to such situations could have been acutely embarrassing and would have constituted an invasion of their privacy. Hence, it was imperative to obtain their permission before showing the taped segments on TV.

But if someone refused permission, there was no problem. Funt's crew simply kept filming until they found someone who was willing. That solution is not possible in research, however. As Webb et al. (1981) noted, if any sizable number of people refuse to grant permission, a bias is introduced. The people who refuse may differ in some systematic way from those who agree. Thus, any conclusions based only on photos, tapes, or other observations of the latter group would be highly suspect because they would be unrepresentative.

are likely to pay too much attention to the possible usefulness, either practical or theoretical, of the research. Others, such as potential research participants, may focus more clearly on the possible ethical risks involved. Thus, one of the suggestions of that committee on ethical practices in research that was mentioned earlier was this: Always obtain the advice of other people who are concerned about the potential risks to participants (APA, 1973). But, do not forget, even if those others see no problem and say go ahead, you will be the responsible party if problems do arise. So be careful; that is, always respect the privacy of those whose behavior you do observe.

One of the things that may help you respect the privacy of those observed is to remember that any particular behavior is usually related to a variety of other behaviors, attitudes, beliefs, and values. Thus, whether or not the behavior you are focusing on seems to be revealing something that the person would like kept secret may not be immediately obvious to you, but it might be to the person being observed. That is one of the reasons why it is a good idea to discuss what you plan with others before beginning your research. They may help you see the implications of what you have in mind.

The idea that there are systematic relationships among behaviors is an important point. So far, the examples mentioned in this chapter have dealt with single aspects of behavior. The research has taken one aspect of behavior, such as the way *th* is pronounced, and related it to some other information, such as the social class of the speaker (Labov, 1970). Dykman and Reis (1979) noted where students sat in a classroom and related that to scores on a measure of self-concept that they had previously obtained. The attention to individual aspects of behavior was intentional. It was supposed to get you thinking analytically about the varieties of behaviors that could be observed. It was also intended to introduce you to a couple of general bugaboos that plague all observational research, the problems of reactivity and protection of privacy. But, it is clear that individual aspects of behavior do not occur in isolation. In fact, most observational systems focus on several different behaviors simultaneously. That vastly increases their power, of course, but it also multiplies the problems.

Observational Systems

The central component of all observational systems is what Hawkins (1982) called a BEHAVIOR CODE. It is a detailed description of the behaviors and events to be observed and recorded and includes a precisely specified set of rules about how those observations are to be made. The purpose in developing a behavior code is to enable observations to be made that are not so dependent on the particular characteristics and interests of the observer. That is, with a good behavior code, two or more people watching the same set of events unfold should end up having seen and recorded the same things. The code tells them what to look for and it does so in language that is as unambiguous as possible. The price you pay for using a behavior code, then, is tunnel vision. You focus on only a few specific behaviors that are of interest. In the process, of course, you miss a great deal of what occurs. But the benefit is that you, and others, can really have faith in what you say about those specific behaviors–provided you follow a few simple rules in developing and using the behavior code. Before describing those rules, let us look at an example.

An Illustration: Making the Elderly Dependent

That title may strike you as odd, because surely no one would try to make the elderly dependent. It is generally believed that the longer we can maintain some degree of independence the better off we are. The better off those around us are, also. In fact, there is evidence that nursing home residents who assume more responsibility for their own care are both happier and healthier than their more passive, dependent peers. Rodin and Langer (1977), for example, found that simply encouraging residents to carry out such simple tasks as caring for plants in their rooms had long-term beneficial effects on mood, activity levels, and health. It may be, however, that well-meaning people who believe their job is to care for the elderly inadvertently encourage dependence and passivity.

That could happen very easily. One of the well-established facts about behavior in both animals and humans is that what follows a given behavior makes a difference. Behavior followed by rewarding consequences is likely to occur again; behavior followed by punishing consequences is less likely to occur again. Technically, this set of relations between behaviors and consequences is referred to as the OPERANT PARADIGM, so named by B. F. Skinner years ago (1938) to reflect the idea that some behaviors operate on the environment to produce certain effects. You do not need to remember the jargon as long as the idea is clear. Some behaviors are learned and maintained because performing them is followed by rewarding events (REINFORCEMENT). Other behaviors are never learned, or if already known, are lost (EXTINCTION), because performing them is never followed by reward, that is, is never reinforced.

To determine whether those ideas might help explain the development of dependence among nursing home residents, Barton, Baltes, and Orzech (1980) set up an observational study to examine naturally occurring interactions between residents and staff in a home for the elderly. The study focused on two categories of resident behavior in relation to personal maintenance: independent behavior and dependent behavior. Similarly, two categories of staff behavior were to be noted: independence-supportive behavior and dependence-supportive behavior. There was a fifth category, other, for all other staff and resident behaviors. Barton et al. (1980) defined these categories as follows:

Independent behavior refers to a resident's self- or other-initiated execution of bathing, dressing, eating, grooming, toileting tasks or components thereof without assistance.

Dependent behavior refers to a resident's request for or acceptance of assistance in bathing, dressing, eating, grooming, or toileting.

Independence-supportive behavior refers to staff verbal encouragement of or praise for a resident's execution of personal maintenance tasks without help. It also refers to staff discouragement of or scolding for a resident's request for assistance or nonattempts of execution of self-maintenance tasks.

Dependence-supportive behavior refers to staff assistance in a resident's personal maintenance, praise for a resident's acceptance of assistance, or discouragement of a resident's attempts to execute personal maintenance tasks without help.

Other behavior is used to code staff or resident behavior that is not related to personal maintenance tasks.

Thus, there were four basic types of behavior of interest and a fifth, catch-all category for everything else.

The observation was done in a nursing home in rural Pennsylvania. Thirty-six residents with an average age of 70 were observed interacting with 17 nursing staff members. With only four observers, Barton et al. were unable to observe what went on in the home around the clock. So they decided to observe the interactions between residents and staff for 1.5 hours each morning and did so for 23 days. On any given day, two of the four observers were each assigned to a randomly selected staff member. The observer followed the staff member from room to room and categorized the behaviors taking place in the first two minutes of each encounter with residents into the five categories above. At the end of each daily session, the two observers watched and coded the same staff–resident interaction in order to check the reliability of their coding,[2] that is, the extent to which they agreed on how the behaviors observed should be categorized.

While watching resident–staff interactions, the actual categorization of behaviors was done by pressing keys on a small, hand-held electronic device. For example, if a resident was observed performing independent behavior, key 1 would be pressed. If a staff member was seen performing independence-supportive behavior, key 2 would be pressed. Each category, of course, was assigned a different key. The recording device had a memory, like many small calculators, so it kept a running tab of how many times each key had been pressed. Another useful feature of this particular gadget was that it also recorded the sequence in which the keys were pressed. As you will see, this allowed Barton et al. to look at sequences of behavior. That is, if a resident behaves independently, does the staff member then perform an independence-supportive behavior?

The major results of this study are depicted in Figure 2. As you can see, for residents the most likely behaviors are those categorized as independent. In contrast, the most frequent behaviors for the staff are those supportive of dependence. Further, because the recording devices used kept track of the sequence of behaviors categorized, it was possible to look at relationships between staff and resident behaviors. That is, what was a staff member likely to do immediately after a resident performed a de-

[2]Reliability here was calculated separately for each behavior category. Agreements on occurrence and nonoccurrence of the category were divided by agreement plus disagreement. For coding of residents' behavior the mean reliability over all sessions was .78; for coding of staff behavior the mean reliability was .81.

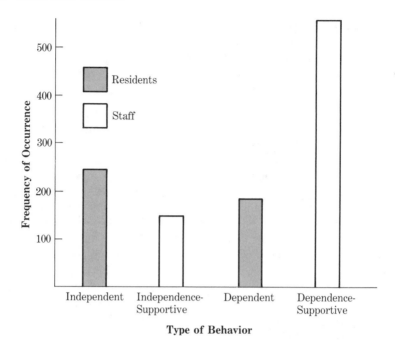

Figure 2 FREQUENCY OF BEHAVIORS by residents and staff of a nursing home. Residents more frequently displayed independent behavior, whereas the staff displayed dependence-supportive behavior most often. (From Barton, Baltes, & Orzech, 1980.)

pendent behavior? As you might guess from the figure, when a resident behaved in a dependent manner, staff members were most likely to behave in a dependence-supportive manner. Unfortunately, even when a resident behaved in an independent manner, staff members were also most likely to follow that with dependence-supportive behavior. As Barton et al. (1980) noted, it appears that attempts at independence among the residents are not supported by nursing staff behavior. While such staff behavior may appear kind and helpful in the short run, it may have the long-term consequences of increasing dependence among the residents.

As mentioned earlier, the heart of any observational system is the set of categories into which your observations are coded. Barton et al. used four content categories. Note that if they had observed precisely the same set of interactions between residents and staff with a different set of categories, they would have had an entirely different study – and an entirely different set of conclusions. For example, they might have been interested in the relationships between health and spontaneous expressions of statisfaction and dissatisfaction among the residents. If so, the observers would have coded the resident–staff conversations into a set of positive and negative categories having to do with, say, food or facilities or presidential politics or last night's TV programs. The point, again, is simply that the categories into which your observations are to be coded are the keys to the whole enterprise. Hence, they need to be constructed and used with care.

Category Construction and Observation Training

The construction and use of a set of categories to record observation of behavior is very similar to a method of research called content analysis. The major difference, as you will see in the following chapter, is that content analysis is employed on printed text. It is also sometimes used on videotapes or films, but usually not on live, ongoing behavior. Conceptually, however, content analysis and the use of a category system for coding observed behavior are so much alike that about halfway through Chapter Four you may start wondering why the two have been separated here.

They have been separated because there is an important difference in the nature of the categories that can be employed. With printed material, you can read it several times, examine your categories repeatedly, think about the big picture, and even ponder the meaning of life before coding any particular phrase or sentence into a category. Not so with live behavior, especially if you are observing the interactions of a group of four or five people. There is no time for contemplation. If you do not pigeonhole a particular behavior into one of your categories immediately, it is lost forever. Thus, the set of categories, the behavior code in Hawkins's (1982) phrase, usually must consist of relatively simple, clearly observable behaviors when you are observing the action live. The four categories employed by Barton et al. (1980) that we cited earlier illustrate this simplicity quite well. The behavior of the residents was simply categorized as independent, dependent, or other. If they themselves executed the tasks of bathing, dressing, and so forth, it was independent. If they asked for or accepted aid in doing these things, it was dependent. In contrast to such relatively simple judgments, the categories employed in content analysis can require the coder to make much more complex discriminations. For example, in a content analysis of presidential speeches, which we shall describe in more detail later, Tetlock (1981) employed a set of categories designed to assess complexity of thought. Coders were required to read excerpts of speeches and decide whether they exhibited DIFFERENTIATION (the ability to see different aspects of a problem) and/or INTEGRATION (the perception of links or connections among those differentiated aspects). In addition, the coders had to decide whether there was a little or a lot of each of these two qualities present in the speeches. Unless you are blessed with an unusually good memory, those would be difficult judgments to make on the spur of the moment while continuing to listen to the rest of the speech and making the same judgments about each part of the remainder.

So, the first rule of constructing your category set is *keep it simple.* Do not ask more of yourself – or others who may be observing for you – than is humanly possible. As Reid (1982) put it, you should begin with the simplest set of categories conceivable, that is, the simplest set that will enable you to answer the question of interest.

One thing you should look into in this connection is the possibility that someone else has already developed a set of categories that you could use. That would save you some time and effort. For example, suppose your casual observations had suggested that females tend to behave differently depending on whether they are in all-female groups or in both-sexes (mixed) groups. Specifically, your impression might be that they tend to make fewer suggestions, to be more generally positive, and to be less openly critical when interacting with males. To see whether this impression was indeed accurate, you would need to do some systematic observation and recording of both mixed and all-female groups. And, lucky you, it just so happens that there is a well-known coding scheme (referred to as Interaction Process Analysis) that would be ideally suited to your purpose. That scheme was developed by Robert Bales (1950, 1970) and his associates at Harvard and is depicted in Figure 3. As you can see in the figure, the set includes both verbal and nonverbal aspects of behavior. In using Bales's system, observers classify each intelligible unit of behavior in a group into one of the 12 categories. In addition, they record who initiated each unit of behavior and to whom it was directed.

If your interest is such that an existing category system can be used, there is another advantage. That is, in addition to saving you the time and effort that would have gone into making your own, by using an existing system your research is more likely to fit into a coherent body of literature. If, for example, you were able to use Bales's categories, you would find that there is a stream of relevant research reports extending back over four decades. Many of those would be very helpful because they give information on how to train observers to use the categories and the reliability that can be achieved in coding interaction into the categories. That information, of course, would benefit you personally. In a similar vein, there is a benefit to others if you use an existing system. Your results will then be more easily comparable to other results in the literature because they will have been obtained using the same basic procedures.

But suppose you have examined the literature carefully, and there is nothing that seems to fit exactly what you had in mind. How do you begin to develop you own? The first step is to be very explicit about the behaviors you want to observe. Each category must be labeled and defined in great

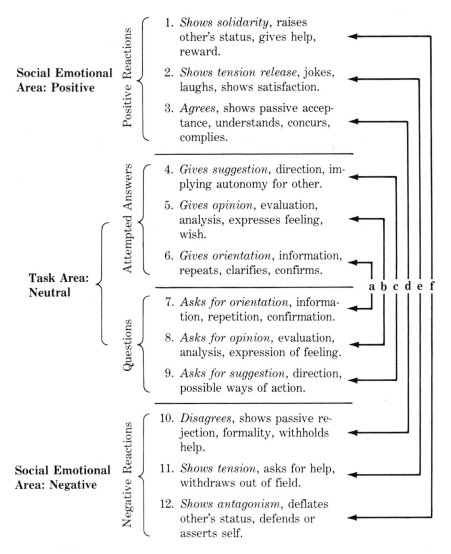

Key

a Problems of Orientation
b Problems of Evaluation
c Problems of Control

d Problems of Decision
e Problems of Tension Reduction
f Problems of Reintegration

Figure 3 CATEGORIES FOR OBSERVING AND CODING GROUP IN-
TERACTIONS. The categories define relatively molar, meaningful units, even
though quite different behaviors might be included in the same category. For example, a nod of the head and the statement "I agree" would both be placed in
Category 3. (From Bales, 1950.)

detail. Dictionary-like definitions are necessary but definitely not sufficient. As Hawkins (1982) has pointed out, you are going to have to elaborate on those definitions, to point out how the behaviors that fit into each category differ from the behaviors that fit into other categories. Also, you will need to give some examples of behaviors in each category. The point, of course, is to remove as much ambiguity as possible and thereby increase the likelihood that different observers using the system will all categorize any given behavior in the same way. As an example, consider Bales's (1970)

Issues and Discussions ———————————————————————

HOW TO SCORE INTERACTION CATEGORY 10

Disagreement is an act with negative implications. But not all acts with negative implications are classed as disagreement in Category 10. Disagreement is defined more specifically in terms of where it comes in interaction sequences. Disagreement is the *initial* act of conveying the information to the other that the content of his proposition (his statement of information, opinion, or suggestion) is not acceptable, at least not immediately; for example, "No." "I don't think so." "I disagree." "I don't agree." "I can't accept that." "Well, . . ." "But. . . ." Sometimes the information is repeated by a combination of two or three of these kinds of reactions. In this case a separate score is given for each act. Disagreement is a *reaction* to the other's action. The negative feeling conveyed is attached to the content of what the other has said, not to him as a person. And the negative feeling must not be so very strong, or the act will seem unfriendly.

Mild degrees of disagreement are included, such as showing surprise, temporary disbelief, astonishment, amazement, or incredulity; for example, "What!" "You don't say!" "That can't be!" "Would you believe it!" One may also disagree by omission, failing to pay attention when the other is speaking, failing to give a requested repetition, or the like. Either verbal or nonverbal indications that the member is skeptical, dubious, cautious about accepting the proposal, hesitant, or critical, may be included as disagreement, provided the implications of ascendance or of hostility are absent. When these indications are present, the act should be scored as seeming unfriendly.

Unless there is repetition of disagreement as described above, only the *initial* act after the other speaks is marked as disagrees. The propositions that follow in making the argument, in the form of information about the situation, analysis of the facts, opinions, alternative suggestions, and the like, are scored in their regular category, *unless* the tone of voice, the facial expression or bodily attitude conveys negative feeling. Whenever the observer sees or hears any actual signs of negative feeling or emotion directed at the other person, the act should be scored as seeming unfriendly.

But the simple fact that an argument stands in logical opposition to the discussion (below) about how to score Category 10 in Figure 3. These are thorough instructions, but not excessively so. They give examples of things that would fit into the category, examples that would not, and even specify the context to be taken into account, that is, only the immediately preceding statement. The point, of course, is to try to anticipate all of the questions an observer might have about when, precisely, to code an act or behavior into that category. Such detailed definitional-instructions must be developed for every category you plan to use. Often these instructions

---

content of the other's argument does not require that the argument be scored as Disagrees. For example, suppose that one person gives some information to another. Then the other reacts by saying, "I don't think so. It seems to me that there were more than that. In fact, I remember seeing at least five." The first reaction would be scored as disagrees, assuming there were no signs of negative feeling toward the other as a person. The second act would *not* be scored as disagrees, but as giving opinion, since it is neutral, and a conjecture. The third act would be scored as giving information, on the assumption that it is also neutral because it reports a concrete observation. The thing to note is that *after the initial act of disagreement, the scoring reverts to the neutral categories based upon the interaction form of the acts.* After an initial act of disagreement, "the slate is wiped clean," so far as relations of logical contradiction are concerned. If the slate were not wiped clean, one would have to continue to follow logical contradictions in an argument indefinitely. Finally, it might happen that everything said would be in logical contradiction to something said earlier. The category Disagrees would have become a "sink" into which all interaction would be drawn.

The frame of reference within which disagreement is judged is thus short in time, consisting of one or more acts during which a logical position is taken, and the initial act only of the rejoinder. The frame of reference for judging agreement is similar. If the reaction is an agreement, after the initial act of agreement, the scoring reverts to the neutral categories based upon the interaction form of the acts. Unless, that is, there is an emotional tone of seeming friendly.

Assume that another person's act of giving information is followed by these three acts: "I don't think so. It seems to me we should be more careful! You have no right to go around saying things like that!" The first act might be scored as disagrees, although in the context that follows one might also have felt some negative feeling in the phrase "I don't think so," in which case it might be scored as seeming unfriendly. The next two remarks, in any case, seem clearly to imply some negative feeling toward the other and so should be scored as seeming unfriendly. (From Bales, 1970.)

are bound together in what is referred to as an observer's manual, which brings us to the issue of observer training.

In training observers–yourself included–to use a category system, the first step is to have them memorize the manual–word for word! There are several reasons for this. The first is simply so observers will be completely familiar with the definitions of each category. The second is that it is important for observers to understand that the definition of any particular category is partially determined by its place in the system as a whole. Independance-supportive behavior, in the set of categories used by Barton et al., is defined with respect to what is categorized as independent behavior. "Disagrees" in the Bales system (Figure 3) depends in part on what is taken as "Gives Opinion." As Heyns and Lippitt (1954) put it, "it is as important for the observer to understand and remember the total system and the theoretical relationships among the categories as it is . . . to retain in detail the specific definitions for each one." There is more to be said about the relationships among categories in the following chapter on content analysis. For now, just remember that what has been said about individual category construction here will be just as relevant there and what will be said about the system as a whole there is relevant here.

Once observers are thoroughly familiar with the category definitions, the next order of business is practice using the system. Practice, and lots of it. It is one thing to know the definitions and quite another to use them in categorizing the characteristics of live action. There is the pressure of time. Observers have to learn to use the system quickly and efficiently, to categorize an item of behavior and move on to the next. Observers also need to learn to stay calm, to not get upset when they realize they have missed something. They have to let it go and pay attention to what is happening at the moment. But practice alone is not enough, in spite of the old adage that practice makes perfect. Practice only makes you tired. Practice with corrective feedback makes perfect. Reid (1982) proposed that the preparation of videotapes or films depicting the kinds and range of behavior to be observed with the system is quite useful in training observers. They can watch and code the action on the tape and their coding can then be compared–behavior by behavior–to what is known to be on the tape. Misclassifications, omissions, and other errors can be discussed and then they can try it again. And again. And again, until they get it right.

In sum, you need simple categories, clear definitions, thorough familiarity with the system, and practice using it. The point of these requirements is to give you faith that different observers using the system to observe the same behavioral sequences all see and record identical things as having occurred. Another way of saying this is that the goal of developing such a system is to make observations independent of the particular observer (see page 95). As Hawkins (1982) put it, a well-developed and

SEARCHING FOR GOOD OBSERVERS

Sensitive, precise observation is an asset that would obviously be valuable in many different kinds of research. It should come as no surprise, then, that for many years psychologists have been interested in the possibility of identifying good observers. The early efforts in that direction usually consisted of generating lists of traits that were thought to characterize good observers. Allport (1937), for example, believed that such people were generally intelligent, detached, insightful, and mature – among other things. Although plausible, such lists are not particularly helpful in selecting observers or in training someone to become better at observation. How, for example, would you teach someone to be insightful?

As Boice (1983) noted, few of these early lists were based on actual research. More often they were based on impressions and distilled clinical wisdom. Those are valuable sources of hypotheses, of course, but they are not substitutes for data. What is needed, first of all, are some techniques for reliably identifying successful observers. One effort in this direction is the work of Rosenthal, Hall, DiMatteo, Rogers, and Archer (1979), who have developed a test of accuracy in perceiving nonverbal messages. Called the PONS, for Profile of Nonverbal Sensitivity, it consists of 220 brief film segments of a young woman displaying various nonverbal behaviors. A person taking the PONS test tries to identify what the woman is doing in each segment by selecting one of two choices such as (1) nagging a child or (2) expressing jealous anger. It has been found that subjects scoring higher on the PONS are, among other things, less dogmatic, more extraverted, more interpersonally democratic and encouraging, and more interpersonally sensitive as judged by friends and relatives.

But, being able to identify successful observers is only the first step. What is needed next is an assessment of what it is that makes them successful, that is, what do good observers do that makes them good? What observational skills do they employ? It is all well and good to say that good observers have insight, but the important question is what produces that insight? For example, are good observers better at remembering details, details that may later be combined to form a coherent impression and produce that "Aha!" flash of insight? Or, to take another possibility, do good observers simply spend more time looking at and listening to the person or persons they are observing? As Boice (1983) put it, it is surprising how little is known about the skills that make an observer good.

correctly used category system should take you beyond the impressionistic stage of observation. With such a set of categories, observation becomes systematic and replicable, that is, reliable. Let us look at this notion of reliability, and some of the problems in establishing it, a little more closely.

Varieties of Reliability

RELIABILITY concerns the extent to which observations and other forms of measurement are repeatable. As Hartman (1982) has noted, it would be nice if we could forget about the notion of reliability and just discuss observer accuracy. But we cannot, because usually there is no criterion against which to assess true accuracy. If you have films or videotapes of the events you are observing and recording using a system of categories, then you could assess accuracy. Without them, you must fall back on trying to assess observer reliability instead.

According to Weick (1968), an ideal observational study would require four different kinds of reliability assessments. The first is to check on the extent to which different observers watching and coding the same events agree in what they record. This is usually referred to as interobserver agreement, and, of the four, it is clearly the most important. Because, as Weick noted, if you cannot achieve interobserver agreement, something is clearly amiss. Without it, there is no guarantee that anything real is being recorded. The second type of reliability that is nice to document involves comparing the data produced by the same observer(s) watching similar events at two different times. If the events are really similar, these data will tell you whether or not the observers are being consistent over time. Be sure to note the *if* in that sentence because if the events are not similar, the observers will appear inconsistent when, in fact, they are not. The third type of reliability assessment mentioned by Weick is a comparison of the codings produced by different observers watching similar events at different times. This seems to be rarely done and, if you think about it for a moment, you can probably guess why. The potential ambiguities are just too numerous: different observers, different events, different times. If the observers turned out to have quite different codings, it would be impossible to tell why. The fourth type of reliability check is an examination of the data from individual observers watching single events unfold. This is an internal check on the consistency of each observer. For example, the observer's task may be to watch and code teacher-pupil interactions for an hour each morning. It would be nice to know that they are applying the category system in the same manner during the last 15 minutes as they applied it during the first 15 minutes. Note, again, that this assumes that in the last 15 minutes of the hour the behaviors of the teachers and pupils are similar to their behaviors in the first 15 minutes. If they are, reliable observers would produce similar codings for the two periods.

Interobserver agreement is not only the most important of the varieties of reliability; it is by far the most commonly reported. There is a problem you should be aware of, however—a phenomenon called OBSERVER DRIFT.

If observers are able to see each other coding, or if they discuss the various behaviors being coded too much, they may well come to agree with each other in what and how they code, but drift away from what the manual says they should be doing. Thus, they would have high reliability–they agree with each other–but they would not be coding behaviors correctly. So, you should not place too much faith in interobserver agreement. If at all possible, obtain some measure for accuracy of coding. For example, it would have been nice if Barton et al. had filmed or videotaped a few of the staff–resident interactions in their nursing home study. Then they could have coded the filmed interactions–very carefully–and used those codes as criteria of accuracy. Observer codings of those same live interactions could then be compared to the codings of the filmed versions.

If you do not have the fancy equipment or if it is simply impossible to develop criteria against which coding can be compared, there are still several things you can do to prevent observer drift. Reid (1982) suggested that you not allow observers to watch each other as they code or to discuss disagreements about coding unless someone thoroughly familiar with the coding system is present. He also said that frequent review sessions and quizzes on the category definitions are a good idea–just to keep everyone on their toes.

There is an interesting irony involved in establishing and checking on the reliability of observers. As was pointed out earlier, one of the major problems with direct observation is the possibility that it will produce reactive effects. However, to check that the observers are doing their task properly, you must observe them. Hence, there is the possibility that your observations may change the behavior of the observers. When they know they are being checked, they will cut out the horseplay, pay more attention to the task, and do a bang-up job of observing and coding. When they know they are not being checked, they may relax and take the whole thing a little less seriously.

Some evidence on this comes from a study by Serbin, Citron, and Connor (1978) in which 17 undergraduate observers observed three teachers and 14 children in each of four classes. Each met for two or three half-day sessions each week. During each class, four or five observers coded teacher–child interactions, the observations being made from behind a one-way mirror. The teachers each wore microphones that transmitted on different FM frequencies. When assigned to observe a particular teacher, an observer simply plugged into an FM receiver in the observation room and tuned to that teacher's frequency. For the first two weeks of the study, pairs of observers were assigned to observe the same teachers at the same time. This was thus an overt assessment period, because each observer knew that his or her observations were being checked against the other's observations. Beginning with Week 3, however, observers did not know when their observations were being checked. A checker simply tuned into the same teacher at various times and coded her interactions—the same interactions that the assigned observer was coding simultaneously. The results of these reliability checks are depicted in Figure 4, where you can see that there was a significant drop in reliability when the covert assessments began. In addition, immediately after each session (during both the overt and covert periods), observers were given feedback about how their codings compared with the other observer or the checker. As the figure shows, with this continued feedback their reliability gradually improved during the covert assessment period.

In addition to regular feedback and letting observers know that they will be checked periodically, there are several steps that can be taken during the development of an observational system that will ensure that it can be used reliably. As Heyns and Lippitt (1954) noted, the less inference required of an observer, the higher the interobserver agreement. They also note that the less an observer has to do, the higher the reliability of coding. Both of these are versions of a piece of advice given earlier, that is, keep the category system as simple as possible. The fewer the categories and the more easily observable the behaviors to be coded, the better.

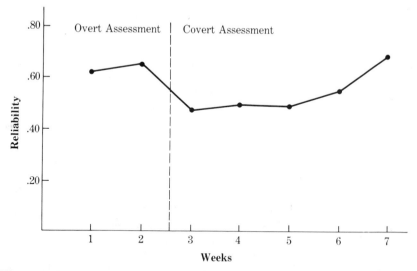

Figure 4 RELIABILITY OF OBSERVER CODING depends on whether the observers know their coding is being checked. Despite a drop in reliability from the overt to the covert assessment periods, the reinstitution of feedback (weeks 3–7) improves reliability. (From Serbin, Citron, & Connor, 1978.)

Summary

Ethology, the study of the behavior of animals in their natural settings forms a link between participant observation and the focus of this chapter, that is, the use of observation by nonparticipants to test specific ideas. The approach advocated here is the rational approach, which involves formulation of a specific question and decisions on which behaviors to observe in order to answer the question. The source of your question, not the methodology chosen to answer it, determines whether you will be doing basic or applied research. Basic research stems from questions intended to test or clarify theory. Applied research stems from questions arising from the need to make an intelligent decision in a specific situation.

Although most observational research has focused on verbal behavior, there are a variety of other kinds of behavior that can be reliably observed. These include nonverbal, extralinguistic, and spatial behaviors. The only reason, apparently, that verbal behavior has been so overutilized is that it is, generally, the easiest to observe. Whatever behavior you do choose to observe, it is absolutely crucial to document that the behavior is a valid indicator of whatever it is you are taking it to indicate.

One of the major problems with the use of direct, first-hand observation in research is that, in most settings, the presence of an observer is obtrusive. That may create changes in the behavior of those observed and, thus, bias the conclusions based on the observations. Such reactive effects may be due to evaluation apprehension, an attention-feedback-regulation cycle, or social facilitation. Whatever the explanation, it is your responsibility as an observer to demonstrate that your observations are not contaminated by reactivity. There are several ways of avoiding or minimizing reactive effects, including unobtrusive observation and concealment.

The ethical concern most often discussed in connection with observation is invasion of privacy. One way to avoid the possibility that you will be invading someone's privacy is to secure their permission, via informed consent, for observing. If you choose that route, you need to be sure that there is no hint of coercion involved. For observation of public behaviors, informed consent is not necessary as long as specific individuals are not identified. Just to be safe, however, you should discuss your research with others before you begin. Specifically, you should seek the advice of other people who are concerned about the potential risks to participants.

Individual aspects of behavior rarely occur in isolation. Consequently, most observational systems focus on several different behaviors simultaneously. A study by Barton et al. of the interactions between nursing home residents and staff illustrates such an observational system. In this study it was found that staff members were quite supportive of dependent behaviors among residents but failed to encourage independent behavior. The central component of the Barton et al. study was a set of four categories for coding staff–resident interactions. Such behavior codes, or category systems, must include detailed descriptions of the behaviors to be observed and recorded as well as a set of rules about how the observations are to be made.

If you cannot find a ready-made behavior code that suits your purposes, there are several things to remember about constructing and using such sets of categories. The first is to keep it as simple as possible. You cannot expect observers to make complex, subtle discriminations while observing and recording live behavior. You also need to define each category thoroughly (i.e., elaborately, with lots of examples) and have the observers memorize those definitions. You need to give the observers lots of practice using the system. You also have to identify the observers' mistakes, provide corrective feedback, and have them try coding again – and again.

There are several kinds of reliability. In the absence of any technique for assessing accuracy of observation, interobserver agreement is the most important and most common substitute. In establishing a respectable level of interobserver agreement, one of the things to watch for is observer drift: observers agreeing with each other, but drifting away from using the categories as they were intended to be used. There must be continuous monitoring of observers, with continuous feedback. Both monitoring and feedback improve their performance.

Recommended Reading

These books are available in paperback. Each elaborates on topics that we have only touched upon in this chapter and each is well worth reading. The first, by Brinberg and Kidder, is part of a monograph series that you might want to look into. The series is published by Jossey Bass, and each issue (four a year) is organized around a single methodological topic. Titles from the last few years include *Generalizing from laboratory to life, Ethics of human research, Problems with language imprecision,* and *Unobtrusive measurement today.* As with most edited efforts, the individual contributions vary wildly in quality, but you can usually find two or three chapters in each issue that are worth reading.

Brinberg, D., & Kidder, L. (Eds.) *New directions for methodology of social and behavioral science: Forms of validity in research* (No. 12). San Francisco: Jossey Bass, 1982.

If I were forced to pick out the two most important concepts in research, I would choose observation and validity. We have spent a considerable amount of time on observation in the preceding chapters. In contrast, the notion of validity has just barely been introduced. We shall return to it repeatedly, however, in the chapters that follow and shall elaborate on its multiple forms. The volume by Brinberg and Kidder is a good introduction to those multiple forms of validity. It will help you sort out the many names – internal validity, construct validity, external validity, concurrent validity, predictive validity, face validity, ecological validity, and more – and see how they are related. McGrath and Brinberg, for example, argued that there are really just three basic issues involved: correspondence, robustness, and value. The question of correspondence is that of fit between things, say, between your ideas and the ways you choose to investigate them. The question of robustness is that of generalization. Can you extrapolate your findings, say, to other groups of people or to related domains of inquiry? The question of value is one often raised by Senator Proximire, that is, are the events and phenomena that are the subject of research both real, or true, and important? If you do not make it through the entire volume, at least read the chapter by Kidder. It is an interesting discussion of the many faces of face validity.

Hall, E. T. *Beyond culture.* Garden City, NY: Doubleday, 1977.

As we have seen, the conditions under which your observations are made should be spelled out as precisely as possible. The reason, of course, is that such explicitness makes it easier for others to duplicate the circumstances and, hopefully, the results of your research. From a methodological point of view, the value of Hall's book is that it discusses many of the facets of culture that we find it difficult to be explicit about. Much of our daily existence is so taken-for-granted that it has simply slipped out of awareness. As Hall puts it, his focus is on the "nonverbal, unstated realm of culture," and in this book he ranges over a variety of topics: how we structure time, how we use space, how we move, the extent to which we do or do not rely on imagery in our thinking, how we violate our biological inheritance, and how difficult it is to communicate with someone who does things differently from the way we do. It is all fascinating. But, the thing to pay particular attention to is the powerful influence of our implicit assumptions about the nature of the world on what we see and how we interpret what we see.

Lorenz, K. *King Solomon's ring.* New York: New American Library, 1972 [Originally published, 1952].

Many of the early studies of animal behavior were severely criticized because they were carried out in what, for the animals, were peculiar, unnatural environments. The observations of chickens, for example, that led to the concept of a PECKING ORDER were carried out in barnyards. There nearly all of the inhabitants are female, they are often cooped up in a relatively small, fenced enclosure, and they are fed at predetermined times. Under more natural conditions, they would spend their days roaming freely over a wide area in search of food, and their behavior might or might not be similar to that seen in a chicken coop. Konrad Lorenz is an Austrian ethologist who has spent much of his life observing animal behavior under conditions more natural than chicken coops. For example, to study the social behavior of jackdaws, Lorenz built an aviary in the roof of his house, an aviary equipped with a trap door for access to the outside so that the birds could come and go as they pleased. His observations confirmed the existence of a dominance hierarchy among these free-flying jackdaws. Thus, the existence of a pecking order among birds does not appear to be an aberration brought on by domestication and confinement. The book ranges far beyond the social behavior of jackdaws, however, and makes delightful reading: If you would like to learn a little more about the naturalistic observation of animal behavior, this is a good place to start.

McCain, G., & Segal, E. M. *The game of science* (3rd ed.). Monterey, CA: Brooks/Cole, 1977.

As you are no doubt aware by now, my major concern is with the techniques of science, the nitty-gritty of research and how it actually gets done. The book by McCain and Segal offers an enjoyable, and quite personal, introduction to the larger picture, to science as a social institution. They include a variety of topics, including a number of brief historical sketches, the relationship between science and technology, and an interesting typology of scientists themselves. According to McCain and Segal, there are PLAYERS, OPERATORS, COACHES, and BYSTANDERS. The Players are the good guys, the ones pursuing research because of its sheer fascination. They are the ones who are really into it. The Operators, as you can guess from the somewhat pejorative label, are a slightly disreputable bunch. They are after nothing but recognition, and the authors take a dim view of their intellectual abilities and contributions. The Coaches are those who seem to prefer to disseminate scientific knowledge to others. They include teachers and textbook writers – a vastly underrated group. The Bystanders are the most puzzling, however. They are the ones who spend years getting the necessary training, but then never use it. They leave the field. They go into business, take up farming, or just drop out. McCain and Segal also discuss the distinction between basic and applied research, a distinction that may not be quite as clear as they suggest. But, it might. Read the book and see what you think.

Radner, B., & Radner, M. *Science and unreason.* Belmont, CA: Wadsworth, 1982.

What do the studies of biorhythms and creationism have in common? According to this book, both are examples of pseudoscience. Their claims are founded in evidence that will simply not stand close inspection. You are no doubt aware of a number of other pseudoscientific beliefs. There is the mysterious Bermuda Triangle, for example, into which planes and ships are supposed to vanish at an alarmingly high rate. There is the view that the gods mentioned in various ancient myths were actually astronauts, visitors from other planets. There is even a group of people, members of the International Flat Earth Research Society, who – to this day – are promoting the view that the earth is flat. Ridiculous! Of course it is, but where do you draw the line? Some of the claims of modern science are themselves rather bizarre. So how is one to judge what is a genuine, though odd, scientific theory and what is pseudoscience? The Radners offer a number of guidelines, markers that will help you draw that line. Practitioners of pseudoscience, for example, seem to have a penchant for irrefutable hypotheses, ideas that can never be put to the test and demonstrated to be incorrect. How could you ever prove that the earth was not visited by extraterrestrial beings 3000 years ago? There are other clues to what is pseudo – and what is real – science. But, read the book. You will learn something about the fringe. All things are not possible.

4

Archival Research and Content Analysis

Learning from the Past

Content Analysis

Summary

Recommended Readings

The word *research* comes from an old French word, *recerchier*, which meant to seek out or to search again. Archival research and content analysis, the methods to be discussed in this chapter, stem rather directly from this original meaning. Both usually involve the reexamination of existing materials. ARCHIVAL RESEARCH utilizes the vast store of records generated in any literate society – crime statistics, health statistics, marriage applications, unemployment data, production data – to examine systematically questions and hypotheses of current interest. Similarly, CONTENT ANALYSIS utilizes texts of all sorts – books, diaries, speeches, newspapers and magazine articles – for the same purpose. As you shall see, neither archival research nor content analysis is limited exclusively to preexisting materials. Investigators can and do ask people to generate materials, to write out self-descriptions or to keep diaries, for example, which are then subjected to content analysis. For the most part, however, content analysis and archival research still deal primarily with preexisting records and texts.

Working with such sources of data has a distinct advantage. If the data were collected for a purpose other than what you have in mind and if they have already been collected and filed away, then it is impossible for you to bias the data collection process. In that sense, the use of preexisting records and texts is relatively nonreactive or unobtrusive. Research or measurement is said to be reactive when the research produces a change in the process or object of interest that would not have occurred otherwise (Sechrest & Phillips, 1979). For example, suppose you were interested in voter apathy and decided to interview a number of people on election eve about their voting intentions. Chances are that the questions on your interview schedule would remind some people who had forgotten that the election was tomorrow. Your research on voter apathy would, thus, be reactive. It would have produced an effect on the voter turnout the following day. On the other hand, examining court records to see if juries composed of experienced jurors are more likely to convict defendants than juries composed of inexperienced jurors (Dillehay & Nietzel, 1982), would be completely nonreactive. There is no way that the examination of records months or years after a trial can influence the outcome of the trial.

Archival research and content analysis are generally less reactive than other research methods. They usually make use of data generated as a by-product of other endeavors and/or data collected for other purposes, but that can have its problems. If the data were collected or produced for some other purpose, chances are they will not be ideal for the purpose you have in mind. You have to be a little creative in making them speak to the question of interest to you – but we are getting ahead of ourselves. Let us take archival research and content analysis separately, although, as you will see, they have a great deal in common.

Learning from the Past

Between Pennsylvania and Constitution Avenues in Washington, D.C., just a couple of blocks from the Capitol, is a building that houses the National Archives. In the main exhibition hall, a steady stream of tourists – cameras at the ready – peer through tinted glass at three of the most famous documents in American history: the Declaration of Independence, the Constitution, and the Bill of Rights. Although the display does attract many tourists, the purpose of the National Archives is actually to preserve and make available for research the permanently valuable records of the United States Government. In fact, the National Archives and Records Service has over a dozen records centers and operates six presidential libraries, such as the Lyndon B. Johnson Library on the campus of the University of Texas at Austin. The sum is an incredible storehouse of information about all aspects of the nation's past – government, laws, people, wars, economics – information available to anyone with a serious research purpose.

Most dictionaries define the term ARCHIVES, in fact, as public records and documents. I would define it a little more broadly than that to include public and private records of any sort. But even if you stick with public records only, it is hard to conceive of the sheer mass of information that is out there. In addition to those maintained by the National Archives and Records Services, there are literally hundreds of thousands of archives scattered across the country: city, county, and state governments, universities, businesses, churches, synagogues, social clubs, and professional societies all maintain records that could be helpful in attemps to understand a little more about people.

Employing that information intelligently, however, can be a tricky business. The problem, the source of the difficulty in using archival data, is that the most interesting questions about human behavior can rarely be answered with a simple descriptive statistic, although such bare data about people and their peculiarities can have a fascination all their own (see page 106). If all you want to know is something on the order of whether large or small cities have higher crime rates, however, you probably do not need a course in research methods to find out. Consult the FBI's *Uniform Crime Reports*, which are published annually, and you will find that not only do small cities have lower crime rates than do large cities, they even have lower crime rates than do suburban and rural areas (Archer, Gartner, Akert, & Lockwood, 1978).

But, as mentioned in Chapter One, the world wants explanations. Why do smaller cities have lower crime rates? Why do suicide rates peak in the springtime? They do and have done so for at least 100 years (Schachter, Redington, Grunberg, Apple, & Schindler, 1980). On such questions, it is

Issues and Discussions ────────────────────────────────

THE LURE OF LISTS

Want to know the top 10 air aces of World War I? Twelve Nazi war criminals who are still at large? The 11 hottest cities in the world? General Custer's ranking in his graduating class at West Point?

You will find these and a wealth of other such tidbits of information in *The Book(s) of Lists* (Nos. 1, 2, and 3) by the Wallace family, one of the most entertaining uses of archival material to appear in recent years. The books are just what their titles claim to be – *lists:* 13 famous people who never graduated from grade school; the 12 all-time best-selling books; Arnold Palmer's favorite golf holes; the 10 actors and actresses most often nominated for an academy award; Margaret Mead's favorite anthropology books. There is a fascination about reading these compilations that is hard to explain – but fascinating they are. They quickly became best sellers. The irony in that is that so many people still seem to think of archives as dusty bins filled with reams of boring materials. It is amazing what a little selection and organization can do. The lists challenge and interest by inviting comparison with your own knowledge and opinions. You no doubt know that water boils at 212° Fahrenheit, but did you know that the temperature of the Red Sea is 95° Fahrenheit, a temperature maintained by hot water seepages around its floor. Custer, by the way, was at the bottom of his graduating class – dead last, you might say.

rare that archival records speak for themselves. As Fischhoff (1980) has noted, records have to be delicately coaxed to shed any light on such issues. As for suicides and springtime, you might suggest that the April 15th deadline for paying taxes is a possible explanation. That possibility can be ruled out, however, because suicides peaked in the springtime even before there was an income tax (Schachter et al., 1980).

Do not misunderstand. You need descriptive information about the past to help you understand a variety of phenomena, and your major sources of such information, of course, are the multitudinous archives referred to earlier. But you should not assume that archives are useful only for such descriptive purposes. With a little ingenuity and a little careful thought about what data are there, archives can also help you tremendously in the search for the explanations of behavior, for understanding why people do the things they do. Consider the following example.

An Illustration: Threat and Authoritarianism

Following World War II, when the extent of the Nazi atrocities against the Jews became known, a number of personality and social psychologists began trying to understand how it could have happened. Was it a quirk of the German character? Are there specific conditions under which humans become so inhumane? Utilizing questionnaire data and intensive clinical interviews, the investigators pieced together a picture of what has come to be known as the authoritarian personality, a picture characterized by a bizarre pattern of ideas and beliefs. The authoritarian seemed at once to admire science and rationality and yet was filled with irrational and unscientific beliefs. Such people seemed to be both enlightened and superstitious. Further, they appeared fiercely individualistic and yet abjectly afraid of being different; strongly independent, but inclined to bow to authority. The authoritarian syndrome, as sketched by Adorno, Frenkel-Brunswik, Levinson, and Sanford (1950), was, thus, a complex web of contradictory impulses.

Adorno and his colleagues went on to identify a number of specific markers of authoritarianism. In contrast to others, authoritarians seemed (1) to greatly admire power and strength, (2) to have a cynical contempt for humankind, (3) to believe in mystical determinations of one's fate, (4) to maintain submissive attitudes toward anyone in power, (5) to reject those who violate in-group values, (6) to oppose efforts to examine the subjective and interpersonal aspects of experience, and (7) to be especially harsh toward those who violate sexual norms. Of particular interest, however, was the suggestion by Adorno et al. that environmental threats – such as an economic depression, a war, a natural catastrophe – would bring about increases in authoritarianism. Someone who seemed relatively normal during good times might become rigidly authoritarian and punitive when the chips were down.

An interesting idea, but can it be tested? You could bring people into a lab setting, have them anticipate receiving electric shock (a threat), and ask them to make judgments about various out-group members. You could then compare those judgments to similar judgments made by people not anticipating shock. That, in fact, has been done, but it seems rather anemic in comparison to the horrors that prompted the initial research on the authoritarian personality. There are ethical constraints on such laboratory research, constraints that would keep you from really threatening subjects to see what their reactions might be. Some sort of pervasive threat with serious potential consequences for the individual would be needed to give the hypothesis that threat leads to increased authoritarianism a real test.

It occurred to Sales (1973) that the economic disaster of the 1930s might have been just such a threat. The 1920s had been a time of unparalleled prosperity for the United States, but in the 1930s, the bottom fell out. Unemployment more than tripled from the 1920s to the 1930s and the per capita income slid downward. Bread lines and soup kitchens were common during the 1930s and the prospect of a global war was becoming increasingly real with Hitler's rise to power and his subsequent territorial claims for Germany. Thus, Sales chose a number of indices or markers that seemed to correspond to aspects of the authoritarian syndrome described above and compared the values of these indices for the 1920s and the 1930s.

For example, if authoritarians tend to demand submission to in-group values, then it should follow from the hypothesis that a time of increased threat (the 1930s) should lead to greater demands for toeing the party line than a time of low threat (the 1920s). Sales found that only eight states passed statutes requiring loyalty oaths from school teachers in the 1920s. During the 1930s, however, 17 states passed such laws. This occurred in spite of the fact that at the beginning of the 1930s there was a smaller remaining pool of states without such laws than at the beginning of the 1920s. Thus, it appears that, as expected, increased demands for submission to in-group norms occurred during the 1930s.

A second index Sales chose was the amount of support for police forces during the 1920s and 1930s. If authoritarians condemn those who violate in-group values, it should follow that they will support forces in society charged with apprehending and punishing the violators. During the times of increased threat, authoritarian tendencies should increase, which implies that support for such forces should increase. Looking at the proportion of the New York City and Pittsburgh budgets devoted to police, Sales found that during the 1920s police were allocated a significantly smaller percentage of the budget in these cities than during 1930s. Although this fits with the hypothesis, it is ambiguous until some additional information is brought to bear. First, was crime on the increase? Consulting the *Uniform Crime Reports for the United States*, Sales found that, in fact, there was actually a decline in crime between the 1920s and 1930s. The second type of data needed is information on other aspects of the budgets. Maybe Pittsburgh and New York were generally increasing expenditures for services—police, garbage collection, fire departments—and cutting back in other areas. Selecting the fire department allotment for comparison, Sales found the fire departments' shares of the budgets actually declined from the 1920s to 1930s. Thus, it appears that, relative to other city services and in the face of a decline in crime (but in line with the hypothesis), in the 1930s New York City and Pittsburgh increased their support for police to a level higher than that given in the 1920s.

Another index that Sales selected was designed to see whether there was an increase in the harshness with which sexual offenders were treated during the period of increased threat (the 1930s). Going through the court records of Allegheny County, Pennsylvania, he found that during the 1920s, rapists received sentences averaging 3.41 years in prison. During the 1930s, the average sentence for rape was 4.65 years. For a major nonsexual crime selected for comparison purposes, no such increase in sentence length occurred between the 1920s and 1930s. Again the result is in line with the hypothesis.

Sales employed a series of additional indices taken from archival sources to test the hypothesis about the relationship between environmental threat and authoritarianism. Figure 1 depicts the results for two of the additional measures. Each of the indices used has limitations, of course; none of them is an infallible indicator. The result with each, however was generally in line with the hypothesis. In threatening times, authoritarianism seems to increase. Sales's use of multiple indicators, each of which has its own unique problems and sources of error, increases our confidence that the relationship between threat and authoritarianism is real.

There is more to Sales's research. He did a similar analysis comparing the years 1959–1964, a period of low threat in the United States, with the years 1967–1970, a period of high threat. Again the results derived from the analysis of a variety of indicators of authoritarianism (numbers of books on astrology, circulation of conservative periodicals, length of sentences for rape) were generally supportive of the hypothesis that authoritarianism increases during periods of high threat. Again confidence in the reality of the relationship between threat and authoritarianism is incremented a little by the comparison of these two additional time periods. If the relationship had held only for the 1920s to 1930s comparison, you might have

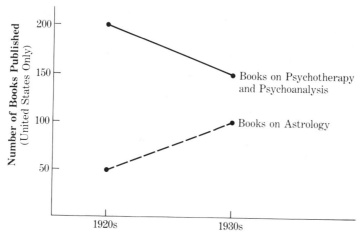

Figure 1 THE NUMBER OF BOOKS PUBLISHED ON ASTROLOGY increased during bad times while the number of books published on psychotherapy and psychoanalysis decreased. These data are consistent with the authoritarian syndrome discussed in the text. The hypothesis predicted that if threatening times (the 1930s Depression) increase authoritarianism, interest in astrology should increase and interest in psychotherapy should decrease. (From Sales, 1973.)

suspected that it was spurious. You might have believed that there was something peculiar about the 1920s or 1930s that made it appear that authoritarianism and threat were related, when, in fact, they were not. The additional data from the 1960s help establish the generality of the hypothesis.

Some additional confirmation comes from Padgett's and Jorgenson's (1982) analysis of the number of articles on astrology and mysticism appearing in the popular press in Germany between World War I and World War II, that is, between 1918 and 1940. As markers of economic threat, they chose percentage of unemployed trade union members, real wages of miners, and industrial production. The number of articles on astrology and mysticism increased as unemployment increased and as wages and production fell. Of course, it is possible that as more and more people were laid off the demand for magazines and newspapers of all types increased. People who are out of work do have more time on their hands, and they might spend it reading. To rule out this possibility, Padgett and Jorgenson also tabulated, from the German equivalent of the *Reader's Guide to Periodical Literature*, the number of articles on cooking and the number of articles on gardening appearing during the same time period. Neither of these increased with economic threat. In fact, the articles on cooking decreased with economic threat; more articles on cooking appear during times of prosperity.

As noted in Chapter One, when the same result is obtained using several different measuring instruments, several different research methods, or several different indices of some hypothetical phenomenon, the likelihood that the result is erroneous, artifactual, or unrepresentative of the real state of affairs is greatly diminished. The variety of indicators used by Sales and by Padgett and Jorgenson to look at the consequences of perceived threat is an excellent example of what has been advocated here all along, TRIANGULATION OF MEASUREMENT. Operationalize your concepts in several different ways and seek evidence on your hypotheses with several different methods. With archival research OPERATIONALIZATION translates into deciding on exactly what information you are going to extract from the records, what index or marker you are going to use.

Deciding on an Index

The indices in archival research are, in several respects, analogous to what geologists refer to as outcroppings. An outcropping is a projection of bedrock or some other stratum of stone through the soil. It is like the tip of an iceberg—it is not of great interest for itself, but for what it signifies. A small outcropping of coal, for example, may mean that miles of rich veins of ore lie hidden just beneath the surface. A geologist who recommended setting up an expensive mining operation on the basis of citing one small outcropping, however, would probably not be taken too seriously. Other evidence in support of the inference that those veins were really there would have to be found before such a massive expense could be justified– other outcroppings, borings that yielded coal, soundings, information on other coal found in the vicinity.

Similarly, the indices used in archival research are seldom of intrinsic interest, and it is equally rare for their meaning to be so unequivocal that they can stand alone. Sales (1973), for example, was interested in the number of astrology books published in the 1930s only because of what that number indicated about the relationship between threatening times and authoritarianism. Further, that number, by itself, was and is essentially meaningless. Only within the context of the additional information Sales obtained could the number be used to support the inference that people become more authoritarian when things get tough. Note that by additional information we are not just referring to the other indices that Sales used–the percentage of municipal budgets devoted to police, the lengths of sentences given rapists. The additional information includes all the data Sales had to gather to rule out various alternative explanations for changes in the indices he used. For example, it was not sufficient to show merely that more astrology books were published in the 1930s as opposed to the 1920s. Maybe people had more time for reading all kinds of books in the 1930s. There were a lot of people out of work, with time on their hands. But Sales wanted to know if the demand for this particular type of book increased in the 1930s. Thus, he obtained the total numbers of books published on all subjects in the 1920s and 1930s and calculated the proportions of those two numbers that were astrology books. Sure enough, a significantly greater proportion of the books published in the 1930s were about astrology.

Note that in Sales's (1973) and Padgett and Jorgenson's (1982) research a variety of indicators or outcroppings other than the ones actually chosen might have been used. Sales, for example, might have used numbers of reported UFO citings per year as an index of interest in things mystical, instead of counting articles on astrology. The only thing that limits the choice of indicators is your ability to make a plausible case that the chosen indicator reflects the phenomenon of interest.

As you can see, there are no general indices for use in archival research. The particular ones chosen are usually highly idiosyncratic to the research you are doing. There are, however, a couple of general principles to follow. First, you should have a specific research purpose, or question, or hypothesis clearly in mind. There are some exceptions to this (see page 112), but in general, random searches through records are unlikely to yield anything of value. Your hypothesis, of course, serves as a guide, suggesting

Issues and Discussions ━━━━━━━━━━━━━━━━━━━━━━━━━━━━━━━━━━━━━

SEARCHING FOR THAT NEEDLE

Epidemiology is the study of how diseases originate and spread through human populations. Its purposes are to identify environmental agents, and other factors, that may cause disease and to identify people who may be at high risk of developing a disease. Although not generally considered to be one of the most glamorous fields of medicine, in the last few years the fruits of epidemiological research have received a great deal of coverage in the popular press. Hardly a week goes by without an article appearing in the newspapers or a magazine in which you are given an opportunity to score yourself on risk factors for developing heart disease or cancer or some other dreaded malady.

Much of the research substantiating the potential lethalness of those risk factors was archival research, carried out by combing through medical records (trying to decipher the handwriting of all those physicians). It usually works like this. An epidemiologist will collect reports of a number of people who have, or who had, a particular disease or disorder, the origin of which is unknown. The medical records of those people are then obtained and searched for anything that they all have in common. It can be a wild goose chase, of course, but it can also pay off handsomely. Gordis and Gold (1980) listed a few of the things that have been uncovered in this way: (1) an increased risk of cancer among those exposed to asbestos and vinyl chloride in their work; (2) an increased risk of cancer after exposure to radiation; (3) an increased risk of developing vaginal cancer among the daughters of women who received a particular hormone during pregnancy; (4) German measles contracted by the mother during pregnancy can produce congenital malformation in the child. The list goes on and is indeed an impressive yield.

Note that this kind of archival research is not, however, a purely random search through medical records for whatever will turn up. The investigator starts out with a well-defined group of people, people who have X. The investigator also starts out with the conviction that these people must have something else in common, that is, they must all have made contact with the cause of X. The task, of course, is to find that something else.

which records are pertinent, where you should look. Consider two examples:

1. Miller (1927) was interested in the relationship between economic prosperity and political stability. In an agricultural country, such as the United States in the 1800s, prosperity is closely tied to the weather. When there is plenty of rain, crops grow, the farmers are better off, and whatever party is in power is likely to stay in power. Thus, Miller chose as his index of "good times" the amount of rainfall in the four years preceding presiden-

tial elections. His index of political stability was simply whether or not the party in power was voted out or returned for another term. Between 1825 and 1924, whenever the four years preceding a presidential election were wetter than normal in the major agricultural areas of the nation, the party in power was likely to be given another term. When the preceding four years were drier than normal, the party in power was given the old heave-ho.

2. Phillips and Feldman (1973) examined the possibility that seriously ill people could postpone dying and, thus, exert some degree of control over the timing of their death. By extracting the birth dates and death dates of the worthies listed in *Four Hundred Notable Americans*, they found the number of people dying in the month preceding their birth month was significantly lower than expected. The number of people dying in the three-month period after their birth month was significantly higher than expected. These two findings have become known as the death-dip and death-rise effects, respectively. The data seemed to indicate that people could put off dying until sometime after their birthdays. Schulz and Bazerman (1980), however, have found a number of flaws in the original research and question the reality of these effects. For example, instead of looking at death rates in the *month* preceding and *months* following the birth *month*, if you look at the 31 days before and 31 days after each individual's birthday, the death-dip and death-rise effects vanish.

That brings me to the second general principle about how to proceed in selecting an index to suit your needs. You should begin a sort of trial-and-revision process in which a possible index is proposed and then subjected to critical scrutiny. The scrutiny should be aimed at discovering what plausible interpretations will be allowed by this index in addition to the one intended by the hypothesis. In other words, the problem of index construction is one of operationalizing your research questions in such a way that the measure you extract from the archives reflects the concept of interest and as little else as possible.

An example should help clarify this point. Suppose you are interested in the effect on crime rate of introducing a home-cruiser program, that is, allowing police officers to take their patrol cars home with them and use them when not on duty. The idea behind such a program is that it makes the police more visible in neighborhoods and at shopping centers and that this increased visibility serves as a deterrent to crime. The data you will want to look at to check this hypothesis are contained in police archives – records of crimes reported, arrests made, convictions, and so forth. The point here is that whatever index you finally select, it could not be a simple before–after measure of number of crimes reported. At the very least, your index would have to take into account population changes. Suppose the population is increasing rapidly. The home-cruiser program is instituted and next year crime is up. Would you conclude that the home-cruiser program led to an increase in crime? Another thing you would need to worry about is seasonal variations in crime. If the home-cruiser program were instituted on June 1, and you compared the number of crimes reported in the previous three months with the numbers reported in the following three months, you might again be tempted to draw an invalid conclusion about the effects of the program. In general, crime increases in the summer.

The distinction between the index you use to reflect the phenomenon of interest (such as crime rate reflecting the effectiveness of the home-cruiser program) and the additional information you need to rule out alternative interpretations (such as an increase in crime due to an increase in population) is sometimes a little fuzzy. You could take care of the increased population possibility by using a simple ratio as your index, that is, number of crimes per 10,000 people instead of just the number of crimes. Possible seasonal variations might be a little more difficult to incorporate into a single number. However, you could get the data from the preceding year and set up a comparison of the two years similar to that shown in Figure 2. What you would expect, of course, is that the number of crimes per 10,000 people would be roughly the same in the two March 1–May 31 periods,

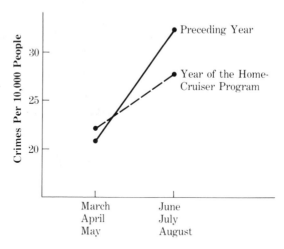

Figure 2 HYPOTHETICAL DATA on a home-cruiser program. If off-duty police officers are allowed to use their police cars, will this be effective in reducing crime? In both the year that the program is instituted and in the preceding years crime increases in the summer months. However, following the introduction of the home-cruiser program on June 1, there was less of an increase than there had been in the preceding summer.

but that the ratio for the June 1–August 31 period would be smaller after instituting the program than in preceding years–even though it might be larger than the ratios in either of the March–April–May periods.

All I really want to convince you of at this point is that you need to keep questioning yourself about the index you want to extract from the archives. Does it really reflect your hypothesis? What additional information is needed? Would you really expect all categories of crime to decrease following the introduction of a home-cruiser program? It is doubtful that such a program would influence white-collar crime, so maybe you need to refine your index. Instead of all crimes per 10,000 people, maybe you should use only certain types of crime. As Webb, Campbell, Schwartz, Sechrest, and Grove (1981) have noted, to assess whether your hypothesis accounts for something you have to be able to rule out all the alternatives that might have produced that same result.

Some Things to Remember about Records and Record Keepers

There is something about archival research that makes it very appealing to many people. It has a quality that research using interviews, questionnaires, experiments, and simulations lack. That something is that there is a realism about the data that grabs you. As Tom Wolfe (1974) once said about good reporting, what makes it fascinating is that you know all this actually happened.

Unfortunately for the use of archives in research, there is a problem. Even though all this may have happened, there may be a lot more that happened that never got recorded. The official name for this difficulty is SELECTIVE DEPOSIT, and it can be a real annoyance. The information you are after may never have been filed away. Someone may have considered it too trivial to bother with, or too much trouble. There is also the possibility that the information of interest to you was incriminating to someone or, at least, would have made them look bad. As a consequence, it was intentionally destroyed. Rathje's (1979) widely publicized Garbage Project, in which he collects and analyzes samples of the garbage of Tucson, Arizona, is unlikely to turn up many letters from secret lovers. Such letters are more likely to be burned than thrown out with the trash. However, some years ago a group of industrial spies was exposed, and it was found that their principal source of data had been the contents of a rival firm's trash bins. Since then, many companies have installed paper shredders. More mundane motives may also influence selective deposit, of course. Even such genuine public documents as the *Congressional Record*, a transcript of the words spoken on the floors of the U.S. Senate and the House of Representatives, are subject to selective deposit. Senators and representatives are allowed to edit the record.

SELECTIVE SURVIVAL is a closely related problem. It is no accident that archeologists tend to be pottery and burial experts. Pottery is durable and tends to survive the onslaught of the elements, and the ancients often took great care to preserve the bones of their departed. Paper, in contrast, is not so hardy, and ink fades. As Webb, Campbell, Schwartz, and Sechrest (1966) have noted, when you cannot find the data you need, there are a number of questions you should consider. Why are those particular records missing? Is there reason to believe they might have been purposefully destroyed? Is it likely they would have reflected poorly on someone? Who was responsible for keeping those records anyway?

That last one is quite an important question, but you need to ask it even–maybe especially–when you find the records you need. Cochran, Gordon, and Krause (1980) have described records as being PROACTIVE to call attention to the fact that the record keeper's desires and beliefs about why the records are being kept precede and, thus, shape the record. If the records are going to be used to evaluate the record keeper's performance, there is always the possibility that the record keeper will simply fake it. But it is usually more subtle than that. Cochran et al. cite an example of some research by McCleary in which it was found that parole officers quite often failed to report parole violations of the people for whom they were responsible. The parole officers' desire to maintain some freedom of action in handling cases turned out to be crucial in determining which violations were and which were not entered into a parolee's record. Not entering particular violations, for example, helped the parole officer on occasion to avoid scrutiny by superiors. Conversely, entering a violation was sometimes used to threaten parolees–better straighten up, that's strike one! Exercising a little discretion about what was entered into the record allowed parole officers to use the record for a variety of purposes. Not entering a violation and letting the parolee know that it had not been entered might help establish or maintain a relationship with the parolee. From the parole officer's point of view, maintaining that relationship might be the means of doing his job well, that is, trying to keep the parolee from slipping back into a life of crime. As Cochran (1978) noted, the records that you view as static descriptions of what happened may have been part of a dynamic system. They may have been tools used by record keepers for accomplishing their own goals.

That does not mean, of course, that records are useless for research. It does mean that you should learn as much as possible about the situation in which the records you want to use were generated. As Cochran et al. (1980) put it, you need to get thoroughly familiar with the dynamic pressures affecting what record keepers write down. Take suicide rates, for example. It is commonly believed that the rates are biased, that suicides are underreported among the middle and upper classes. Why should that be so? Or, take worker productivity. Unless you have taken the trouble to find out the basis for worker compensation in the data being used, you may get several unexplainable peaks in productivity. Piece-rate workers may turn out more work just prior to Christmas and vacation in order to make some extra money. That would not be particularly surprising, but you need to be aware that the extra emphasis on productivity during such periods may lead to neglect of routine maintenance. That, in turn, might result in more equipment breakdown and production decline in subsequent periods. Again, the point is simply the more you know about the situation in which the records you want to use were produced, the more intelligently you can use those records.

In spite of the potential difficulties posed by selective deposit, selective survival, and all-too-human record keepers, I am enthusiastic about the largely untapped potential for research represented by the use of archival data. It is something of a paradox that, in a time when many are demanding answers, pertinent, unused data are lying around gathering dust. And, one of the prime advantages of archival research is that it is generally quite inexpensive. In fact, it is downright cheap. Old newspaper files, public archives, information almanacs are filled with data, waiting for you to put them to use.

Another major advantage of archival research has already been noted. It is generally the most unobtrusive and nonreactive research method available. The interpersonal biases inherent in participant observation and survey research are absent, for example. It is also true that for some research problems, there is no alternative to archival research. But, in order to really make clear the advantages of archival research – and to alert you to a few more of its inherent difficulties – the discussion needs to be broadened to include content analysis. As you will see, content analysis and archival research are very closely related.

Content Analysis

Several years ago I read a book about life in the working class family, a book entitled *Worlds of Pain* by Lilian Rubin (1976). The book was based on intensive interviews with 50 intact families in which neither husband nor wife had more than a high school education and in which the husband was working at what is traditionally referred to as a blue-collar job. The blurbs on a book's cover are usually not to be trusted. They are carefully selected by publishers to help promote sales. But, after reading this particular book, I was convinced that the blurbs on its cover were accurate. It was indeed "a sensitive and compassionate portrayal of childhood, marriage, and adult life among the hard-working not-quite poor . . . (a) devastating critique of contemporary American life." It was a profoundly moving book.

Imagine my surprise, then, when a few weeks later I happened across a review of *Worlds of Pain* in which it was panned as being one of the worst books on the family since *The Happy Hooker*. I could not believe it. My first reaction was that maybe the reviewer read a different book that just happened to have the same title. But, no, all the essential details matched. Same author, same publisher, same price, same number of pages. It was the same book. I then reread the review and it became clear that the reviewer and I applied totally different sets of criteria in evaluating the book. The reviewer attacked the author for not demonstrating that her sample of families was representative. Okay, but. . . . The reviewer seemed to choke with rage over the fact that all the interviews had been done by one person. Well, yes, that can be a problem, but even so. . . .

It is not unusual, of course, for two people to differ in their evaluations of a book. Each person brings different experiences and expectations to the book, which means each may read into the book different things. Each person may also apply different criteria. The result can be one of those protracted, unresolvable arguments about what the book really says. Content analysis differs from such casual evaluations and descriptions of textual material primarily in that it forces you to be explicit about the criteria you have applied and the rules by which you have applied them. As Krippendorff (1980) said, if someone else applied the same criteria in the same manner, they should arrive at the same conclusions about the text in question. Content analysis, then, is a research technique by which certain characteristics of printed or spoken material are systematically identified (Stone, Dunphy, Smith, & Ogilvie, 1966). Consider this example.

An Illustration: Pre-to-Postelection Shifts in Presidential Rhetoric

Have you ever noticed how many politicians seem to have solutions for all the major problems of the world when they are running for election? Things always seem so simple then. All we need to do is (take your pick): Cut taxes! Get government off the back of business! Create jobs! Stimulate the economy! Crack down on criminals! But after taking office, things seem a little different. Those drastically needed reforms turn out to have ramifications that were never mentioned before and that now—after the election—must be carefully examined.

The cynics among us assume they never intended to keep those campaign promises to work wonders anyway. They were just saying whatever they thought would get them elected, whatever would make them look good. Of course, there is another possibility. It may be that the issues really are more complex than an outsider realizes. Something that seems so simple and easy to pull off from an outsider's point of view may indeed have a string of implications that need to be examined before taking action. Cutting taxes should give people more money to spend and, thus, stimulate the economy. But, cutting taxes may also increase deficits, which will lead to increased interest rates, which will give people less money to spend and, thus, depress the economy. Thus, there are two possibilities. The first is that campaign promises are a form of impression management – simple solutions that make the politician look and sound good. The second is that campaign promises reflect a genuine navieté, and after some time in office the erstwhile reformer will learn that things are a little more complex than he or she had imagined.

Tetlock (1981) obtained some evidence on this by applying content analytic techniques to pre- and postelection speeches of twentieth century American presidents. His reasoning was that if the preelection rhetoric was simply impression management, that is, if the candidates were offering quick and easy solutions in order to look appealing to the voters, then you might expect their public utterances to change pretty quickly after the election. They no longer need the votes, so now they can tell the voters that the problems are really somewhat more complex and they will all have to work together toward a solution. On the other hand, if their preelection slogans reflected a real lack of understanding of the complexities involved, then it might take some time – even a year or two – before their public statements began to reflect those greater complexities. It would take some time to learn the system and the interdependencies involved. Thus, Tetlock collected samples of presidential speeches made during four different time periods: (1) the five months prior to election, (2) the first five months in office, (3) the second year in office, and (4) the third year in office. The task of analyzing everything they said would, of course, have been monumental – presidents are a rather talkative lot. So, ten paragraphs were randomly selected for each president in each time period. That makes a total of 40 paragraphs for each president.

The analysis made use of a set of categories devised by Schroder and his colleagues (cf. Schroder, Driver, & Streufert, 1967, Appendix 2) to assess complexity of thought as revealed in language. The categories are based on two concepts: differentiation and integration. DIFFERENTIATION refers to your ability to see different aspects of a problem and to take those various factors into account in making a decision. If you believe the only solution to crime is to lock up criminals and throw away the key, you have a relatively undifferentiated view of the causes of crime. A more differentiated view would recognize that crime has mulitple causes, many of which would be totally unaffected by treating criminals more harshly. INTEGRATION, in Schroder's system, refers to the perception of links or connections among the differentiated aspects of a problem. As you can see, differentiation precedes integration. You have to be aware of the pieces before you can conceive of ways in which they might fit together. Utilizing these ideas about differentiation and integration, Schroder et al. defined the seven-step scale of integrative complexity of thought depicted in Table 1. Inspection of the scale and the examples reveals that higher scores reflect a greater understanding of the issue and a greater subtlety of thought.

Using this scale, Tetlock had two people read each of the 40 paragraphs for each president and assign it a score. The two scorers were unaware of the purpose of the study, and they were also unaware of the source of any given statement. The purpose of keeping the scorers in the dark about these things was, of course, to cut down on the possibilities of bias. If a scorer had known that a particular statement was made by John F. Kennedy and the scorer was a great fan of Kennedy's, a little more profundity might have been read into the statement than was actually there. In the jargon, the scorers were kept blind with respect to the hypothesis and the sources of the statements. Even with these precautions, the scorers achieved fairly good agreement on the assignment of statements to categories. Their reliability was .86 and any disagreements were subsequently resolved by discussion.

Before looking at the results, a brief summary might be useful. Samples of presidential speeches were obtained from four points in time: preelection, immediately after taking office, the second year in office, and the third year in office. Each sample was then read and assigned to one category of Schroder's system for scoring the integrative complexity of thought, a content analysis scheme that has been widely used in recent years. The purpose of all this, of course, was to examine changes in complexity of presidential pronouncements in relation to amount of time in office.

The results are depicted in Figure 3, where it can be seen that, in general, the largest change occurs between the campaign (preelection) and the first month of office. Presidents' preelection statements, as predicted by the impression management hypothesis, were significantly less complex than their early postelection comments. Further, there was no overall trend for complexity to continue to increase after the first month of office. It appears that the cynics were right after all. During the campaign, candidates present the issues in a relatively simple manner and offer relatively simple solutions. Once they are safely in office, they present things differently. One additional bit of evidence on that point. Tetlock did another content analysis, using Schroder's categories (Table 1), of the speeches of presidents who decided to run for reelection. He found that the complexity level of the policy statements of these presidents fell significantly between the next-to-last and last years of their first term in office. In other words, as the next election approached, they reverted back to offering simple solutions.

Table 1 Integrative Complexity Categories[a]

Level of integrative complexity	Category (score)	Definition	Examples
Low	1	Low differentiation, low integration	The country faces a great crisis that threatens us all and requires decisive action. Constantly rising inflation rates are eroding the economic security of our people, yet our government leaders seem impotent in the face of this threat. What shall we do? There is clearly only one solution to this critical problem: immediate drastic cuts in government expenditures.
	2		
Medium low	3	Moderate or high differentiation, low integration	The country faces serious economic problems: high inflation and high unemployment. To control inflation, we need major cuts in government spending; to reduce unemployment, we need to encourage new investment.
	4	Moderate or high differentiation,	
Medium high	5	Moderate or high differentiation, moderate integration	The country faces two interrelated economic problems: high inflation and high unemployment. We confront a painful trade-off here. To reduce inflation, we need to reduce economic growth, thus risking greater unemployment. To reduce unemployment, we need to stimulate the economy, thus risking greater inflation.
	6		
High	7	High differentiation, high integration	The country faces both high unemployment and high inflation rates. To decrease government spending or increase taxes in an attack on inflation will exacerbate unemployment, unless we combine a tough antiinflationary policy with efforts to increase productivity and end regulatory excess. This combined policy will curb inflation and boost economic growth, thus increasing and creating new jobs.

Source: Tetlock (1981).

[a]These integrative complexity categories were used by Tetlock in assessing changes in the speeches of presidents from before to after election. A scorer read a particular paragraph and decided to which category of thought it was most similar; this process is referred to as coding. Note that only Categories 1, 3, 5, and 7 are defined. If a scorer had trouble deciding whether a paragraph represented Category 1 or Category 3, for example, it would be assigned to Category 2.

121

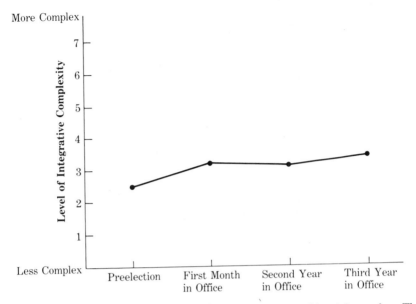

Figure 3 MEAN INTEGRATIVE COMPLEXITY of presidential speeches. The largest increase in speech complexity occurs between the preelection period and the first month in office. (From Tetlock, 1981.)

Some related research has been done by Suedfeld and Rank (1976), who made use of the same content analytic scheme (Table 1) that Tetlock used. Suedfeld and Rank used the categories to analyze pre- and post-takeover writings of 19 revolutionary leaders. Their idea was that the singleminded-ness that seems to characterize revolutionary leaders might turn into a liability if the revolution is successful. As they put it, the pre-takeover revolutionist may often be characterized as a fanatic, a person with a one-track mind who sees everything in strict moralistic terms and who has the idea that all that is evil about society flows from *them*—his opponents, the current power structure, the military-industrial complex, whatever. On the other hand, once the revolution has been accomplished "generally, there is no longer a single overriding enemy, various factions must be reconciled . . . , policies must be based on diverse considerations . . . , ideolgy and practice must be flexible." In short, pre-takeover revolutionaries may be characterized as low in integrative complexity. If they are going to survive politically after the revolution, they need to develop a more complex world view.

To check on this line of reasoning, Suedfeld and Rank obtained samples of pre- and post-takeover writings of 19 revolutionary leaders—from Oliver

Cromwell to Che Guevara. Of the 19, 11 were judged successful on the basis of their having held important public office in the post-takeover government until their natural death or voluntary retirement. The others were judged unsuccessful. The samples of pre- and post-takeover writings of the 19 were then scored using the same categories for integrative complexity that Tetlock used to analyze presidential speeches. Identifying material such as names, dates, and places had been removed from the writing samples. As expected, the successful post-takeover revolutionaries—people such as Patrick Henry, John Jay, V.I. Lenin, Mao Tse-tung—exhibited significantly more complex thought in their postrevolutionary periods. In contrast, the failures—people such as Alexander Hamilton, Leon Trotsky, Lin Piao—did not seem to change following their respective revolutions. Their writings revealed approximately the same low levels of complexity both before and after the revolution.

With these two examples of content analysis in mind, let us look at what is involved a little more closely.

Categories and Coding

As noted earlier, content analysis is a general procedure for objectively identifying the characteristics of textual material. The key, then, the *sine qua non*, is specifying which characteristics you want to identify. Tetlock (1981) and Suedfeld and Rank (1976), for example, wanted to identify different levels of integrative complexity in the speeches and writings of politicians. They were lucky in that Schroder and his colleagues had already constructed a category system (Table 1) that could be used for just that purpose. All that had to be done was thoroughly familiarize coders with the category definitions so that they could read the excerpts of speeches and writings and assign each excerpt to the appropriate category—1 if it reflected low differentiation and integration, 5 if it reflected high differentiation and moderate integration, and so on (Figure 4).

Chances are, you will not be so lucky. You will probably have to construct a category system to reflect those characteristics of text you want to identify. Your set of categories will be determined by your hypothesis, of course, by what it is you are interested in. For example, suppose you were interested in comparing the relative occupational status of males and females depicted on prime time television. You had come across some research by McArthur and Eisen (1976) in which it was found that little girls are more likely to imitate achievement behaviors they hear about in storybooks when the storybook character is female. That started you to thinking about where little boys and girls get their ideas about what they would like to do when they get older. If it is true that children watch as much television as surveys suggest (Murray and Kippax, 1979), then the

"I have reread all my diaries for the past 45 years
and I can't find a clue as to where we went wrong."

Figure 4 CONTENT ANALYSIS involves more than just forming an impression of the material analyzed.

apparent occupations of males and females on TV could be a major source of their ideas about what is appropriate for them. So, you decide to draw up a list of occupations, lay in a supply of junk food, and get set for some heavy TV watching, ahem, research. You might begin with a list like this:

	Males	Females
Professional		
Technical		
Farmers		
Managers/Administrators		
Clerical Workers		
Laborers		
Sales Workers		
Private Household Workers		

You probably would not make it to the first commercial before you became aware of a number of problems with your categories. What precisely, is the distinction between professional and technical? Are you going to put ranch owners with farm laborers? What are you going to do when you come across somebody who will not fit into any of your categories?

Holsti (1969) gives five general guides for constructing a set of content analysis categories that would help out in revising that initial set above. The first is that the categories should reflect the purposes of the research. That seems obvious. But think about the list of occupations for a moment. Hidden away in your reasons for doing the research was the idea that the occupations of males, as depicted on TV, are probably somewhat more glamorous or prestigious. If so, you need to incorporate that into your category system by subdividing the categories into groups: High, Medium, and Low Prestige. Touhey (1974) has obtained some ratings of the relative prestige of various occupations that you could use to do this. Then your refined hypothesis would be that the occupations of women on TV will tend to be lower in prestige than those of men.

The second rule for constructing a set of categories is that they be exhaustive. All that means is that there must be a category into which each relevant item can be placed. Thus, you would need to expand your list of occupation types a little. You would probably also have to add a category entitled Other or Unclassifiable. Many people finesse this exhaustiveness criterion with some such Miscellaneous category, but you need to be a little careful about it. Coding too many items into Other or Miscellaneous might indicate that your category system is missing something.

Mutually exclusive categories, the third guideline, means that each item to be coded—each person on TV in this case—should only be capable of being placed in one category. You might have a little trouble, for example, if you came across a TV character who was a physician and a farmer. You would have to draw up some special coding rules for such cases, such as "classify the person according to the way he or she was first depicted."

According to the fourth rule, the assignment of one item to a given category should not affect the assignment of other items. This is referred to as independence of categories. It should give you no trouble with occupations of characters on TV because each character is a separate person.

Finally, categories should be derived from a single classification principle. That sounds a little heavy, but all it means is that you cannot mix different levels of analysis in the categories. You cannot have one category for oranges and another for fruit because oranges and fruit are at different levels in the system of edible foods; the former is a subcategory of the latter. Physicians are a subcategory of professionals. Hence, you could not have both in your occupational categories. That would not keep you from having physicians, lawyers, nurses, teachers, and other professionals as separate categories, however. Physicians are not a subcategory of Other Professionals.

To summarize briefly, there are five general guidelines to follow in constructing a set of content analysis categories. The categories should reflect the purpose of the research, be exhaustive, be independent, be mutually exclusive, and be derived from a single classification principle.

The categories that were used to illustrate those principles, occupations of TV characters, are relatively clear and concrete. There is widespread consensus about what constitutes an occupation and which occupations are highest in prestige. Quite often, however, the thing of interest is somewhat more nebulous – like the expression of utopian ideas by English and American novelists, or progressivism in Tibetan literature. When you are interested in something like that, you are going to have to put a little more thought and effort into constructing your categories. Some of the flavor of the process involved is illustrated by Stone et al. (1966):

> Suppose we want to identify the extent to which "conservatism" is expressed in writing or speech. Investigators would undoubtedly differ in their intuitive interpretations of the meaning of this concept. Their lack of agreement would be evident if they were asked, without any prior discussion, to make overall ratings of the presence of conservatism in particular speeches. However, by thinking about and discussing the different aspects of the concept, they might well agree on characteristics they would consider signs of conservatism, and if given an explicit set of scoring directions, they would identify them as such. In examining the concepts in detail, they may find it necessary to distinguish between two or more forms of conservatism. They will also need to be specific in distinguishing it from related concepts.
>
> At the simplest level, the characteristics that are considered signs of conservatism might consist of lists of words and idioms. For example, one list might be a category of signs indicating RESTRAINT: careful, caution, cautious, restrained, with care, and so on. Similarly, another list might consist of alternative ways of expressing OBLIGATION: conscience, duties, obliged, ought, proper, and so on. The specification for scoring might then require a co-occurrence of entries from the lists, and in some cases a noun–modifier relationship, as in the larger concept OBLIGATION OF RESTRAINT: "obligation to carefully", "duties to be cautious about", "conscience to be restrained in", "use proper caution in."
>
> Conservatism can, of course, be expressed in many different ways other than a simple concern of OBLIGATION OF RESTRAINT. We might, for example, reason that a conservative person tends to express concern for matters getting out of hand, especially economic matters, and thus we might want to identify references to EXCESSIVE ECONOMIC COSTS. This category might signify a co-occurrence between ECONOMIC QUANTITY, such as beyond . . . means, costly, excessive, exorbitant, expensive, and so on, to produce such combinations as "deficit is too costly", "budget becomes excessive", "exorbitant tax on", "at a price beyond our measure", "costs too much."

There would probably be a number of additional categories needed for a good measure of conservatism. Even with the additional categories, of course, you could never be sure that you had included all of the indices of the concept—conservatism, in this case. But research is a continuous process. The errors and omissions, the ambiguities found when a set of categories is employed, can be used to improve and refine the next set. The whole process can be recycled.

Once your categories are well defined, you simply read the text (or watch the movie) and record the frequency of category appearance. This process must be checked for reliability, and the usual technique is to have two or more coders independently code the same portions of the text. As was noted in the examples by Tetlock (1981) and Suedfeld and Rank (1976), it is best to keep the coders unaware of your hypothesis and of the sources of the material they are coding, if at all possible. If the degree of agreement about the relative frequency of occurrence of the various categories is high, you can have some faith that the coding scheme and categories are well defined. What you conclude from any given content analysis depends, of course, on the hypothesis you started with, the category system you constructed, how the text fits into the categories and last, but certainly not least, the texts you decided to sample.

Sampling

The notion of sampling will be discussed in some detail in Chapter Six (Survey Research) and in Chapter Nine (The Experiment). The purpose here is just to call your attention to the fact that sampling the texts or materials to be analyzed is a major part of most content analysis research. To see why, consider the following examples.

Suppose you were interested in the extent to which newspaper editorial support for a political candidate is reflected in biased news coverage. That would define the texts: You would look at editorials and news stories about candidates; you would not look at the candidates' campaign literature or television commercials or political billboards. Given that you would examine only newspaper editorials and news stories, however, there would still be a sampling problem. You could not possibly content analyze all newspaper editorials and news items about all political candidates at all times and in all places. So, you would be forced to set up some rules for selecting a sample. You might decide to look only at coverage of the presidential candidates of the two major parties in the 1960, 1972, and 1984 elections. Further, you might (arbitrarily) decide to use editorials and news items from a random sample of 10 daily papers from the population of those with circulations of 100,000 or more. That is, for each candidate in each election, you would need to find 10 such papers that supported the candidate editorially. You would *then* have to decide a time period within which to sample. Would you examine news items in each paper every day for three months preceding the election? Two months? Six months? Every third day for three months? Every fourth day for five months? The point is that even with a relatively clear-cut research question, as in the example[1], a series of important sampling decisions have to be made in the process of selecting the texts to be compared.

As Krippendorff (1980) has said, however, you should never lose sight of the ultimate aim of these sampling decisions. That aim is to yield samples that are representative of the phenomenon of interest. In the example of editorials and news coverage, the decisions outlined might not, in fact, do that. Using only presidential elections, elections in which a variety of newspapers and other media have numerous reporters observing the candidates' every move, there might be relatively little misrepresentation of what the candidates actually said or did. There would simply be too many alternative sources against which readers could check the facts and, thus, expose the bias. The phenomenon of interest, editorial support leading to biased coverage, might only show up in campaigns where there is less public scrutiny of the candidates or in local elections in cities where one newspaper has a monopoly on the printed word. Another way of saying this is that you can only generalize the results of your content analysis to the population of texts from which you have sampled. And you had better be able to demonstrate that you have an unbiased sample. Thus, when you want to establish the generality of a finding on the basis of content analysis of only a portion of the pertinent materials, appropriate sampling of those materials is crucial.

There are uses of content analysis, however, for which sampling is less of a problem. If you have the time and energy, or if the amount of material bearing on your hypothesis is relatively small, you can content analyze everything that is relevant. Schmidt (1972), for example, was interested in the explanations given in the popular press for the riots that occurred during the summer of 1967. He first selected 22 newspapers and magazines that he believed would cover the political–ideological spectrum from right to left – *National Review* to *The New Republic*. The selection of those 22 was, of course, a sampling decision, and you might want to quibble about whether they really covered the range of political opinion. But, that was the only sampling involved. Two coders then examined every editorial and feature on the riots that appeared during the entire summer in all 22 newspapers and magazines. All statements suggesting a cause for the riots were extracted, not just a sample. You might be interested in knowing that as that long, hot summer wore on, there was an increasing tendency

[1]Maybe not so clear-cut. How would you set up a system of categories for coding "biased news"?

for the riots to be seen as due to external causes and as being more legitimate expressions of intolerable conditions.

In general, sampling is also less of a concern when you want to use content analysis to learn something about a specific event or a specific person, that is, when you are interested in what Allport (1942) referred to as idiographic research (see page 130). Rosenberg and Jones (1972), for example, extracted all personality descriptions from a single work of fiction by Theodore Dreiser. Their purpose was to see if the way in which Dreiser portrayed his fictional characters was related to what was known about his own personal conflicts and life stresses. It was. All his life Dreiser considered himself to be a nonconformist, fighting for realism in literature and against the forces of convention in society. He was also quite a womanizer—"indefatigably, compulsively promiscuous" as his biographer put it (Swanberg, 1965). These two features of his own life turned out to be the most salient characteristics of his fictional characters. Take another example. Neisser (1981) compared the transcripts of the tape recordings of two meetings between Richard Nixon and John Dean to see if Dean's testimony about what was said at those meetings had been accurate. In terms of the details of the conversations, Dean was almost completely inaccurate, which is why Nixon claimed the transcripts would vindicate him when they were released. However, at a deeper level—in terms of Nixon's knowledge of the Watergate cover-up and being in on the effort to secure hush-money for some of the burglars—Dean was right. But, note that Neisser was not concerned with the issue of whether these two conversations were representative of all those between Nixon and Dean. About other conversations, Dean may well have been wrong. Rather, Neisser was interested in analyzing the two conversations and comparing them to Dean's testimony about them in order to explore some aspects of the nature of memory. Dean, for example, consistently recalled himself as having been more at the center of things than he actually was.

Sampling, then, may or may not be problematic for content analysis. It depends on your hypothesis and the focus of your research. The same thing could be said, of course, about archival research. In fact, it should be clear by now that content analysis and archival research are, in general, variations on a theme. One simply deals with text, one with other kinds of records. It has probably also occurred to you that content analysis has a lot in common with the systematic observational methods discussed in Chapter Three. For both, the development of a set of categories for coding material is the key. Content analysis, however, focuses on behavior once removed, that is, on recorded speech and writing. Thus, it has some problems and some promises that the observational methods lack, and they need to be noted.

NOMOTHETIC AND IDIOGRAPHIC RESEARCH

A little over 40 years ago, Havard psychologist Gordon Allport (1942) called attention to two basic forms of knowledge. The first he referred to as *nomothetic*; it involves the ordering of experience in such a way that some general principle may be extracted. This, of course, is what most people think scientific research is all about. Whether it is blood or bacteria or newspaper editorials that are being sampled and analyzed, the purpose—according to the nomothetic view—is to extract what features the samples have in common. One can then formulate some abstraction about blood composition or bacterial types or editorial orneriness. Allport referred to the second basic form of knowledge as *idiographic*; it involves the detailed analysis of individual events (and/or people). Most people think of this as the province of history or biography and see it as being basically different from scientific research.

In a scholarly review of the use of personal documents such as diaries, letters, and autobiographies in research, Allport rejected the view that idiographic research is nonscientific. He pointed out that acquaintance with particulars, detailed knowledge about individual cases, is the beginning of all scientific research on behavior and social processes. When you start too soon with abstract analysis and classification, you run the risk of coming up with false cleavages, with dichotomies that misrepresent the salient organizations and integrations of personal life. Your first step in any research, then, is to immerse yourself in as much pertinent data and experience as possible. If you are interested in personality or growth and development, for example, read biographies and autobiographies. Look at the collected letters of the famous. Do not apologize for reading fiction. You can learn a lot about sociology or psychology or political science from a good novel.

Keep in mind, however, that different types of personal documents are likely to have different types of built-in biases (Wrightsman, 1981). Diaries, for example, are excellent sources of information about continuities of personal development, but they are likely to be preoccupied with conflict and to gloss over (or leave out altogether) the smooth and pleasant periods of life. Autobiographies are likely to make everything fit too neatly with one or two themes. They are also particularly weak in dealing subjectively with what went on in childhood and adolescence. But, for all aspects of human behavior, personal documents should be considered essential source materials, and content analysis is often the key to unlocking their treasures.

Uses and Abuses of Content Analysis

Focusing on text, on recorded speech and writing, has some of the same problems mentioned in connection with archival research—selective deposit and selective survival, for example. The really crucial documents needed for testing a certain idea may have been destroyed, or altered, or never written, or unattainable for a variety of reasons. Further, as Holsti (1969) has pointed out, even when the documents of interest are available, content analysis can usually tell us nothing about the truth of assertions in the text or about such nebulous qualities as the aesthetic appeal of the text. Similarly, like archival research, content analysis is literally blind to some aspects of human behavior, such as nonverbal communication. As an example, read the minutes of the next meeting you go to and then compare their Spartan quality to your memory of what actually went on—who sat next to whom, the innuendo and sarcasm that occurred, the angry glances, the flirtations, the audible sighs when the more long-winded began to speak.

Unfortunately, content analysis also has something of a bad reputation. It has, in truth, been much abused. As Stone et al. (1966) put it, "a large proportion of studies bearing the label of content analysis have been mechanical, superficial tabulations of who says how much of what to whom." Or as Cartwright (1953) put it, "One of the most serious criticisms that can be made of much of the research employing content analysis is that the 'findings' have no clear significance for either theory or practice. In reviewing the work in this field, one is struck by the number of studies which have apparently been guided by a sheer fascination with counting." This fascination with counting is likely to get worse instead of better as researchers learn to use computers to do their so-called content analysis for them.

On the other hand, it is clear that when appropriately employed, content analysis can be genuinely helpful. Often the only information you have about a particular issue or research question is in documentary form. With such data, content analysis forces you to make explicit the categories and coding rules on which your conclusions about such documents are based. In the absence of an explicit set of categories and detailed coding rules and the established reliability of coders, issues about documentary evidence are, unfortunately, likely to be decided by claims of expertise (or, by who can shout the loudest).

Another advantage that content analysis shares with archival research is a relative lack of obtrusiveness into the processes or phenomena of interest. Both are generally considered to be among the most unobtrusive, nonreactive methods available (Webb et al., 1981). They are usually not confounded by the sorts of biases that are introduced when someone is aware of being a participant in research.

The pioneers of content analysis, in journalism and political science, used it almost exclusively with preexisting documentary materials, such as the materials employed by Tetlock (1981) and Suedfeld and Rank (1976) in the examples cited earlier. However, in recent years it has become increasingly common to use content analysis with textual material that subjects are asked to generate specifically for the research at hand. This is an especially appropriate use when something about the subject's own language or thought is crucial. Much of the psychological research on self-descriptions, for example, has required people to check those adjectives on a list that seem to be descriptive of themselves or to sort previously prepared statements about their behavior in certain types of situations. One of the major problems with such procedures is that they restrict you to a fixed format and a preselected vocabulary. Thus, they may fail to provide you with categories that are relevant or meaningful with respect to your particular perceptions. Allowing people to describe themselves (and others) with terms of their own choosing and then employing content analysis on the resulting descriptions avoids the problem. If you think so-and-so is a jerk, you can say so and not have to resort to some less expressive substitute. And if the coders do not have a category for that one, the system will just have to be revised.

Summary

In his research, Sales used a variety of archival data to test the hypothesis that perceived threat leads to an increase in authoritarianism. The evidence seems to indicate that in the 1930s, compared to the 1920s, cities devoted greater proportions of their budgets to the police; the proportion of books published on astrology increased; rapists were given more severe sentences; more states passed laws requiring loyalty oaths; and the proportion of books published on psychotherapy declined. An odd assortment of findings, indeed, but all predicted by the hypothesis that threatening times bring out authoritarian tendencies. Sales's use of this variety of indicators is an excellent example of triangulation of measurement, as well as a model for archival research. Sales's example also illustrates that the indicators used in archival research are analogous to outcroppings in geology – and although one small outcropping may hint at subterranean treasures, that inference must be shored up with additional data.

Construction (or selection) of indices for archival research is highly idiosyncratic to the problem at hand. Even so, it helps (1) to have a specific hypothesis clearly in mind and (2) to subject all possible indicators to a process of careful scrutiny and revision if they turn out to allow too many alternative explanations. Problems accompany the use of records in research. Selective deposit and selective survival are among the most generally troublesome. It must be kept in mind that record keepers use records for purposes of their own. Thus, you should become thoroughly familiar (if possible) with the situation of the record keeper whose records you want to employ.

Research by Tetlock provides an example of content analysis. Presidential speeches before and at three points after election were examined for evidence of integrative complexity of thought. Samples of the speeches were read and coded into a set of categories devised by Schroder to reflect different levels of differentiation and integration. The results indicated that the largest shift in complexity occurred between the campaign speeches and those of the first month in office, a finding suggesting that the campaign rhetoric had been deliberately simplified in an attempt to win votes.

The key to content analysis is the category system that is devised by the researcher and into which the texts of interest must be coded. General guidelines for construction of the categories can be illustrated in the context of a hypothetical example about the depiction of the occupations of males and females in television scripts. The categories must reflect the purposes of the research and be independent, exhaustive, mutually exclusive, and derived from a single classification principle.

A series of sampling decisions are usually, but not always, involved in content analysis. The nature of those decisions, of course, determines the extent to which you can generalize your results.

Both archival research and content analysis are among the most unobtrusive research methods. Although they each have their limitations, they are both important tools and they deserve to be utilized more than they have been in the past.

Recommended Reading

These four books and one article are all worthy of your individual attention. They are informative and at least three of them are also entertaining. You will have to read all five, however, to find out which three, but you probably can guess from the titles. As a clue to one, you might be interested in knowing that in the Preface to the first edition of the book by Webb et al., the authors say they thought about naming the book *The Bullfighters' Beard*. Apparently, on the day of a big fight, bullfighters' whiskers grow more rapidly than at other times – or else they do not stand quite so close to the razor. That is a rather arcane thing to be aware of, but it gives you a flavor for the sorts of unusual measures and esoteric information sources that the authors claim can be of use in research.

Holsti, O. *Content analysis for the social sciences and humanities.* Reading, MA: Addison-Wesley, 1969.

There are several reasons for recommending this book. First, it is a readable overview of content analysis that remains hard to beat in terms of its avoidance of jargon and clarity of presentation of the main issues. Second, it provides a balanced discussion of the use of computers in content analysis; they are neither always desirable nor possible to use. Most important, however, Holsti provides an interesting review of the variety of ways in which content analysis has been used in the past. Many of the illustrations are sufficiently intriguing that you may be tempted to seek out the original sources and read them in their entirety. For example, on pages 86 and 87, Holsti describes some research by Morton in which content analysis was used to investigate whether or not Paul had really written all of the biblical Epistles that had been attributed to him. The idea was that different authors have identifiably different styles – their sentences vary in length, some use more third person pronouns than others, and so on. On the basis of his analyses, Morton concluded that the Epistles had actually been written by no fewer than six different authors. Fascinating detective work! But, there is more to the story. Questions were raised about the validity of Morton's procedures when someone else applied Morton's analytic technique to Morton's own article. Unfortunately, the results appeared to indicate that the article had been written by several different people.

Roueché, B. *The medical detectives.* New York: Washington Square Press, 1982.

The 22 stories in this book originally appeared in *The New Yorker* between 1947 and 1979. They are all true, and each is about one or more persons who fall prey to some mysterious malady. The plots of these scientific detective thrillers vary. For some, the problem is to find the source of an outbreak of infectious disease. For others, the question is simply to discover what disease a particular patient has. But from the first – about 11 old men who were poisoned by oatmeal in a sleazy cafe – to the last – about a woman whose genetic disease is misdiagnosed as psychiatric – the stories read like thrillers. The tales are often told in the words of the physicians, epidemiologists, and patients who experienced them. There are fascinating accounts of tracking down leads, piecing together evidence, encountering blind alleys, and the gradual ruling out of alternative possibilities to arrive at the answer (usually). In addition to the excellent first-hand accounts of the process and progress of research in each case, you will learn some interesting things about medicine and its history from the book. You also may end up worrying a little more about where and what you eat.

Runyan, W. M. Why did Van Gogh cut off his ear? The problem of alternative explanations in psychobiography. *Journal of Personality and Social Psychology 40:* 1070–1077, 1981.

Two days before Christmas in 1888, Vincent Van Gogh cut off the lower half of his left ear and presented it to a prostitute. Runyon uses this unusual event to explore the issue of explanation in psychobiography. How can one account for events in individual lives? Usually many explanations can be dreamed up that will fit the facts. At least 13 have appeared in the literature to account for Van Gogh's cutting off his ear. But, how do you decide which is correct? Are they all true? Are none of them true? Runyon offers a number of guidelines for evaluating such explanations. Of course, you must realize at the outset that you may never really know why a certain event occurred. But, that does not mean you can hide behind slogans such as "anything is possible." By critically evaluating alternative explanations for the event in light of all available evidence, you may be able to rule out a few of the possibilities. That may seem like a small step, but it is better than standing still.

Todd, A. *Finding facts fast: How to find out what you want and need to know* (2nd ed.). Berkeley, CA: Ten Speed Press, 1979.

This book can be a valuable resource if you are interested in testing ideas about social and behavioral processes via content analysis and archival research. The data you need may simply be sitting on a shelf somewhere. Your problem is to find that shelf, and there are an incredible number of directories, reference guides, indexes, dictionaries, registers, pamphlets, and card catalogs available to help you. Not only does Todd describe the contents of scores of these directories—he even gives you addresses, telephone numbers, prices, and recommendations about what is worth getting a copy of for yourself and what is so expensive that you are better off to use the library copy. There is a *Directory of Special Libraries and Information Centers*, for example, that lists names, addresses, and contents of thousands of special collections throughout the United States. There are even reference books about what reference books are available. One that Todd recommends buying, by the way, is a paperback called *Reference Books: A Brief Guide*. Scattered through Todd's descriptions of resources available to the researcher are practical hints about how to proceed. If you need to contact the Library of Congress, for example, your letter of inquiry should make it clear that you have exhausted the local and regional resources available to you.

Webb, E. J., Campbell, D. T., Schwartz, R. D., Sechrest, L., & Grove, J. B. *Nonreactive measures in the social sciences* (2nd ed.) Boston: Houghton Mifflin, 1981.

Although this book was referred to a few times in the preceding pages, I purposefully tried to avoid relying on it too much so you could have the pleasure of reading it on your own. It is a fascinating review of the variety of unusual—one might, on occasion, say oddball—measures that have been used in research on human behavior and social processes. Its purpose is to expand your consciousness about what is possible. After reading this book, when you start thinking about doing some research you will not immediately fall into the old "construct an interview, design an experiment" trap. There may be better ways to find out what you want to know. Take a couple of random (of course, they are not) examples. Using archives to extract such indices as the number of women in managerial positions, Welch (1978) was able to show that the best places in the country for women are Washington, D.C., San Jose, and Denver. Denver? Wilson and Mather (1974) measured the lifelines on the palms of corpses and found that contrary to what the palmists say, there is no relationship between age at death and the length of the line. Read the book. It will expand your thinking about what can be done.

5

The Interview

Being interviewed appears to have become a normal part of the modern citizen's repertoire of roles. Trained as question answerers from childhood – "me two years old" – we enter adult years responding more or less helpfully to the physician's inquiries, the television reporter's microphone, and the personnel manager's attempts to reconstruct our schooling and work experience. We almost expect to be asked questions whose purpose is not always clear, but which, we assume, will serve a useful function for somebody, somewhere. Benney and Hughes (1956) noted with some amazement the ideological and social shifts that have made so many individuals willing to "populate the statistician's cells" by providing to strangers information about themselves; in their view, this shift in behavior is as worthy of study as the spread of literacy.

The role of interviewer is less widely held. Nonetheless, you have also acquired, over all those years of talking with your fellows, many skills that will carry over (and a few that will have to be unlearned) in making the leap from general tête-à-têtes into the research-oriented interview.

What Is an Interview?

The interview is not generally considered a complete research method by itself. Rather, the various forms of question-asking are essential research tools, the picks and shovels with which information is accumulated. Much if not most, of the data on human behavior is either generated or obtained by interview (or the interview's half-sibling, the paper-and-pencil questionnaire). Whether you are in the laboratory with human subjects or in the field as an observer, your skill in the formulation and asking of questions is usually a necessary (obviously, not sufficient) element in the success of the research venture.

In its broadest sense, an interview is a social interaction between two people, one of whom wants to get information from the other. That interaction, whether face-to-face or only voice-to-voice as over the telephone, is what differentiates the interview from the questionnaire, even when the questions and the possible answers are identical.

The society editor interviewing this week's bride-to-be in order to write about her trousseau and travel plans fits as easily into such a definition of interviewing as does the psychologist asking subjects their reactions to experimentally induced pain or inquiring in depth as to the beliefs and values of extroverts and introverts. Both editor and researcher may get the information each needs. The difference between a general interview and the research-oriented interview is that the latter never loses track of its research objectives. The RESEARCH INTERVIEW, then, is (1) a *social interaction* between two people (2) in which the *interviewer initiates and varyingly controls* the exchange with the respondent (3) for the purpose of obtaining *quantifiable and comparable information* (4) relevant to an emerging or stated *hypothesis*.

These emphases are the ones that dictate much of the planning and decision-making involved in interviewing. The first topic to be discussed, then, is the construction of an interview blueprint, called a schedule, designed to assure that relevant information gets collected. The second concerns ways to assure that any differences in the responses obtained actually reflect differences between respondents in the amount of whatever is being measured and are not errors or distortions caused by the wording or sequence of the questions or by the very human ways in which the interviewer and respondent perceive each other and interact. Before turning to those two topics, however, let us examine the basic assumptions underlying the insistence on quantifiable and comparable data to be obtained in research interviews.

The basic assumption underlying QUANTIFICATION is that if something exists, it can be measured. The simplest form of measurement, of course, is just yes/no: Is that something present? Or is it absent? The process of quantifying – of determining how much of something is present – seems quite natural when the units for measuring are a familiar part of our culture. For example, not only are we taught height as a concept, but also we are taught to think in terms of inches and feet. The question "How tall is he?" includes the concept of height and the way in which to measure it.

But, the assumption underlying quantification is more daring than that; it involves faith that entities can be measured for which the units of measurement have not yet been so clearly spelled out. Most of us would agree that romantic love exists. Many of us would admit to having experienced it. (Cynics or the recently betrayed can substitute some other emotion in which they do believe, such as cynicism.) One way to quantify the amount of love would be to set up some units of measurement, perhaps a simple scale of (1) love-a-lot, (2) love-somewhat, (3) love-a-little, or (4) that-was-last-week. Having set these up on a rather intuitive basis, we could then ask people where they fit concerning their feeling toward their most significant other.

But what do they know? Love is not just blind, it is different for everyone. The trickier part of measuring something for which the units of measurement are not spelled out is in the CONCEPTUALIZATION – the process by which the researcher defines specifically and exactly what it is he or she is talking about. Then we are more certain what it is we are measuring. A specification of love espoused in a book and its film version would suggest asking respondents how many times in a relationship they felt they had to say they were sorry. The higher the score, the lower the amount of love.

The insistence on obtaining COMPARABLE INFORMATION as part of the research interview is because measurement makes sense, or has meaning, only in relationship to similar measures. Our grammar is a distinctively comparative one: good, better, best; fast, faster, fastest. When we ask, "How tall is he?", we are simultaneously asking about his height in a comparative fashion, albeit in the most general way. It becomes more specific once we specify the context: "How tall is he now (compared to the last time I saw him)?" or "How tall is the student playing with blocks in the corner (that is, by how many inches does she deviate from the mean height of other children in the class)?" In short, the measurement of your height does not stand alone – one simple fact in its absolute splendor – but rather makes sense only in the convention of comparability that makes measurement meaningful.

Whatever is measurable is comparable. That is, the attitude of Mr. Brown concerning the mowing of lawns can be compared to the attitude of Mr. Smith on the mowing of lawns in the same sense and, given a proper instrument, with the same assuredness that the number of inches of grass standing in Brown's yard can be compared with the number of inches of grass standing in the yard of Smith. In fact, the height of the grass might well be used as one indicator of attitude toward cutting it.

As Benney and Hughes (1956) said, the convention of comparability distinguishes the research interview from that of the mass-communications industry, which invented the interview to begin with. "As an encounter between (the interviewer and respondent), the typical interview has no meaning; it is conceived in a framework of other, comparable, meetings between other couples, each recorded in such a fashion that elements of communication in common can be easily isolated from more idiosyncratic qualities."

The interview has its own peculiar sources of error, as you will see, but the attention paid to quantification and comparability means that, as a research technique, it is also subject to the laws of measurement and can be judged by those standards. In the interview, as in any other research approach, there is a trade-off between validity and reliability, with precision most often the currency of exchange. Interview questions that separate respondents into those who love, feel neutral about, or despise their mates may be both valid – in that they actually measure what they purport to measure, (in this case, the degree of affection) – and reliable – in that the questions consistently evoke the same responses when asked at different times or by different interviewers. Other questions – say, ones that differentiate people's feelings toward their mates along a continuum of 10 levels – will be far more sensitive to differences (thus, they are more valid), but this same precision may decrease reliability. Collapsing that 10-unit scale will likely increase reliability again – but at the expense of validity.

It is true, of course, that both the reliability and validity of interviews are dependent on the language used by the participants, and all languages are notorious for the ease with which miscommunication is possible. One way to improve the exchange of information that takes place in the interview would be to make language more precise, a technique illustrated in the Issues and Discussions below. The suggestions for improvement in the pages that follow, however, are considerably less drastic than those illustrated in the box.

Variations on a Theme

Making up questions and asking them occur almost simultaneously in conversation—and in some research as well. But, as Cannell and Kahn (1968)

Issues and Discussions

YOU MUST BE ABLE TO THINK IT IN ORDER TO SAY IT

In George Orwell's frightening portrait of a totalitarian society, *1984*, the task that the Party in power had set for itself was the complete control of consciousness. This was to be accomplished by continually rewriting history (so that no evidence of anything contrary to the Party's current doctrine would exist) and by maintaining absolute control of all sources of information available to the public, such as newspapers, books, television, and radio. The primary method by which consciousness control was to be achieved, however, was the construction of a new language, Newspeak. As for the purpose of Newspeak, it was supposed to make it impossible for people to have thoughts antagonistic to the will of the government in power. Its vocabulary was constructed to exclude such "subversive" meanings.

Newspeak was designed, then, not to extend but to diminish the range of thought. For example, the names of all organizations, counties, institutions, and doctrines were cut down into compound, easily pronounced, single words. Thus, "English Socialism" became "Ingsoc." The idea was that abbreviating names in this way narrowed their meaning and excluded old associations. A similar technique was to simply do away with shades of meaning by throwing out many words that referred to variations on a theme and retaining only one word for the core meaning. Thus, *magnificent, excellent, splendid,* and the like were cast out of the dictionary. The whole range of goodness and badness was covered by compounds of good: *doubleplusgood, plusgood, good, ungood, plusungood, doubleplusungood.* By these and other techniques for purging words of ambiguities and secondary meanings, the range of consciousness was to be gradually restricted and made more amenable to control.

have said, it is characteristic of research interviews that the two are conspicuously separated in time and space and often by the division of labor. Such interviews may be conducted in the laboratory or the respondent's living room or on the corner of the street, but they have often been constructed on the researcher's desk in an atmosphere thick with concern about hypothesis formation or testing on the one hand and about the respondent's understanding of and reaction to the questions to be asked on the other.

Certainly there are many exceptions to this dichotomy of question-making and question-asking (particularly in exploratory studies and in many field situations). Typically, however, the interviewer meets with the respondent with the interview itself already firmly planned – and with little latitude to make changes.

The written plan for the interview is known as an INTERVIEW SCHEDULE. It always includes the first item in the following list, but often includes the other items as well.

1. A list of questions to be asked more or less verbatim.
2. Instructions on when and what probes to use, probes being additional questions and procedures designed to encourage the respondent to provide a missing answer or to clarify and enlarge on a given one.
3. Directions for recording responses. In more open interviews, the interviewer may be directed – and perhaps given space on the interview schedule itself – to get down significant phrases in the respondent's own language, note meaningful body language such as sighs or embarrassed shrugs, and note what part of all this was evoked and what seemed to arise spontaneously. In more closed interviews, the interviewer must restrict possible answers of the respondent to categories of response provided by the schedule, for example, Age: 20–29, 30–39, 40–49, and so forth.
4. SPECIFICATIONS (guidelines) for dealing with anticipated problems in fitting respondents' answers into categories. What, for example, do you record when Mr. Jones says "Age? Well, I'm 49 right now, but day after tomorrow I'll turn 50. I think that's right."

Scheduled Interviews

The issue of unvarying presentation of interview questions is such a key one in research that interviews generally are classified as to how scheduled they are.

In the completely SCHEDULED INTERVIEW, the entire script is written ahead of time, with an eye to almost total standardization of the interview from one respondent to the next, regardless of who is doing the interview.

The interview is introduced with standardized greeting and explanation of its purpose. The wording and sequence of questions are fixed and unalterable. If a respondent seems puzzled by any question, the interviewer's instructions are to repeat the question as written without rephrasing. Answers are recorded verbatim or are marked in predetermined categories. (This sounds more rigid than it may actually seem to the respondent, as you can see from the excerpt of a social psychiatry interview in Figure 1.)

This heavy emphasis on standardization of the interview presentation is based on a premise as familiar as gospel to anyone who has ever done experimental research: To produce a response that validly differentiates one respondent from another, the stimulus must be identical. In other words, when you set out to measure something, you do not use a rubber yardstick.

Instead, the meaning of each question must be the same for each respondent, which means, for proponents of highly scheduled interviews, the same wording, the same presentation by the interviewer, and the same probes. The context too must be identical, including the reasons given or implied for asking the questions and the encouragement or reinforcement given for answering them. And because preceding questions help shape the context for the respondent, the sequence of topics and questions must be identical.

Thus, with the instrument for measuring having been built as solid and unbending as possible, the researcher can assume that any variations in responses are attributable to the actual differences between respondents and not to some change in the interview questions themselves.

Of course, the use of an interview schedule with its standardized text does not ensure the presentation of a perfectly equivalent stimulus to each respondent. As will be discussed later, each interviewer, by dint of his or her personality, background, appearance, even his or her very presence, changes the impact of the interview. So do factors outside the control of the schedule, such as temperature of the room, time of day, noise level in the hall. But, in the words of Cannell and Kahn (1968), "this is a minor problem compared to the uncontrolled and almost unknowable variance of interviewing ad lib."

The standardization provided by an interview schedule is believed to aid comparability of interviews, to return to an emphasis provided by our earlier definition. Obviously no single, isolated interview is necessarily any better for being so carefully scheduled. Perhaps the contrary—for even though the schedule as an instrument helps the interviewer by organizing thought, by making certain all topics are covered, by aiding in the household chores of recording and coding, and so forth, it also limits. The interviewer can neither explain the meaning of some word used in a question to a respondent befuddled by it nor take advantage of an unusually responsive

(Instructions to interviewer: If the respondent has never stayed for an extended period of time in any other place besides this community, skip to Question 49.)

44. Why did you move (or return) here?

45. Do you ever wish that you lived
     back in one of the other places
     you've lived?
     (If yes) Were is that?

1. Yes, very much
2. Yes, some
3. No, not at all

46. Were the people in _____
     easy or hard to get to know when
     you first moved here (or last
     returned)?

1. Very easy
2. Medium
3. Hard to get to know
4. Other (specify)

47. How did you feel about the way
     people received you when you came
     (or returned) to _____?

1. Very good
2. Quite good
3. Didn't make much
    difference
4. Bothered you some
5. Bothered you a lot

48. Has moving made much difference in
     your life?

     (If very much or some): What
     kind of difference has it made?

1. Very much
2. Some
3. Very little
4. Not at all

Figure 1 EXCERPT FROM AN INTERVIEW SCHEDULE. In this sequence of questions the interviewer modifies not only the order (by skipping irrelevant questions) but inserts interviewee-dependent information into some (Questions 46 and 47). When these modifications are done smoothly the interview seems less formal than it appears on paper. (From Richardson, Dohrenwend, & Klein, 1965.)

and knowledgeable respondent who could, if asked, provide useful information not allowable within the strict boundaries of the scheduled interview.

49. Have you ever wanted to move away from here very much, but didn't?

   1. No (Skip to Question 51)
   2. Yes

50. List periods of wanting to move away.

I	II
When was it? (R's age and frequency of wish)	Why did you want to go?

III	IV	V
Why didn't you go?	At the time, how did you feel about staying here?	How do you feel now about staying here?

(Say to respondents: "That's all about moving around; now I'd like to ask you about other kinds of changes you've seen.")

Unscheduled Interviews

The UNSCHEDULED INTERVIEW is one in which the interviewer does *not* follow a script with instructions for presentation, wording, and sequence of questions. Instead, there is freedom to fit the questions to the respondent and to the situation.

An UNSCHEDULED STANDARDIZED INTERVIEW is conducted with the same objectives and on the same premise as a scheduled one; that is, to achieve validity of measures and comparability of responses, the interview must act as an identical stimulus to all respondents. But the scheduled interview seeks the necessary standardization by scheduling, so that interview questions themselves are, literally, identical. In contrast, the nonscheduled interview seeks standardization by asking each respondent questions in an appropriate vocabulary, order, and manner so that the interview will mean the identical thing to all respondents.

By definition, the nonscheduled interview is not based on an interview schedule. But the interviewer may use a more or less well developed IN-TERVIEW GUIDE. This guide specifies the classes of information needed. It may be as simple as a reminder of the topics and subtopics that the respondent should cover during the interview, either spontaneously or with some probing and prodding. Or it may be as specific as a list of questions. But whereas the interviewer using an interview schedule was bound to ask questions in the same sequence and to use the same wording, the interviewer using an interview guide is free to make decisions about how and when to ask questions, based on what is already known or can be judged about the respondent (such as age or educational background) and the feedback obtained during the interview as to the respondent's knowledge and ease in discussing various subjects.

Rubber yardstick? Or a more precise measure? Every physician knows that an average sized blood pressure cuff distorts the blood pressure readings for chunkier patients because their flesh interferes. Consequently a conscientious physician sizes up the girth of his or her patient, reaches for an average or large-sized cuff, and then gets a reading that is comparable to others and not in part a reflection of arm size. In the same sense, proponents of the nonscheduled standardized interview argue that it is simply not possible to formulate questions that have identical meaning for extremely heterogeneous respondents. People have markedly different vocabularies, levels of comprehension, word associations, and emotional responses.

This was dramatically noted by the Kinsey interviewers studying sexual behavior (Kinsey, Pomeroy, & Martin, 1948). They found that different subgroups had evolved such different words and phrases to refer to things sexual as to be almost incomprehensible to others. To approach each and all respondents, no matter what their status and affiliation, with a list of questions prepared by a white, middle-class, college-educated researcher was to invite some cognitive confusion, at the least. Furthermore, different words and topics were ego-threatening to different persons, depending on their age, sex, social background, and educational level. For example, males who had never gone beyond the tenth grade felt much more comfortable discussing and admitting to premarital sex or intercourse with prostitutes than they did to masturbation. For college-educated males, however, the reverse was true. The interviewer who was aware of these differences in attitudes then approached those topics in a different sequence. There was also a need for on-the-spot freedom to drop a topic and return to it later if any respondent grew too uncomfortable or reticent (and thus more likely to give incomplete or false answers or perhaps to terminate the interview).

Doubtless sex was a more private and sensitive area in the late 1940s when the famous Kinsey et al. studies (1948) were conducted, although other sources of bias may exist today, with college-educated males more reluctant to admit various lacks of experience or knowledge, for example. Supporters of nonscheduled interviews would consider this possibility and many others.

In general, the nonscheduled standardized interview is most frequently and advantageously used when (1) the topics are sensitive, (2) the respondents to be interviewed come from very different groups, and (3) the researcher is able to do his or her own interviewing or can find and afford interviewers who have sufficient interviewing skills and an understanding of the objectives of nonscheduled interviewing.

If the sensitivity of topics included in the interview is not self-evident, the pretesting of any interview schedule or interview guide should indicate it.

Decisions concerning differences between respondents might be based on the following considerations:

1. How different are the persons to be interviewed likely to be? When interviewing students in the same college, it is probably safe to assume comparable levels of comprehension and emotional significance to questions unless they involve highly specific information, for example, words that engineering students are more likely to understand than are fine arts students, or activities that are likely to be more familiar to fraternity members than to nonmembers.
2. If the groups are clearly different in regard to your questions (if, say, you are interviewing everyone in the building, from the janitorial staff to the dean), how certain is it that you can find out the equivalent meanings for each of the persons or subgroups? Nothing is more damaging to rapport than using last year's slang to a teenager or confusing the in-group terminology of two competing groups or, more likely, simply talking down.
3. Can you even recognize who is who? Are the characteristics that place the respondent in a particular category in which meanings are likely to be different identifiable? If you are adjusting the wording of questions for education level, cues may be available in the respondent's first answers to questions (especially if one of them is, "What was the last grade of school you completed?"). But if you are adjusting your approach

Speaker's Variables

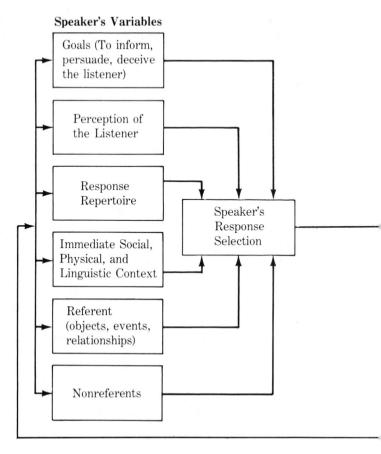

Figure 2 DO YOU HEAR WHAT I AM SAYING? Many things determine whether the message a speaker intends to convey is actually the same as the one received by the listener. The diagram illustrates variables that make a difference in the clarity of speaker–listener understanding. (From Rosenberg & Cohen, 1967.)

to people on the basis of psychological differences, people with father fixations are generally somewhat hard to spot. Rosenberg and Cohen (1967) constructed a diagram of the variables that influence face-to-face communications (Figure 2). Note that the speaker's response and the listener's goal are only two of several variables that affect the listener's interpretation.

All this trouble has centered around the need for standardization to enable comparison of fairly specific responses of the people being interviewed. But the purpose of some research interviews has little or nothing

Listener's Variables

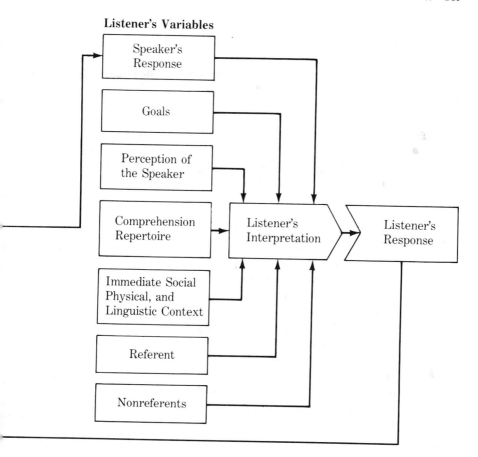

to do with comparability of responses and more to do with collecting information, perhaps in order to understand some phenomenon not yet fully understood, perhaps in order to construct a hypothesis concerning it. The UNSCHEDULED UNSTANDARDIZED INTERVIEW is one in which the interviewer, unhampered by the constructions of an interview schedule or the need to ask all informants the same classes of information, instead asks different respondents different questions to discover what and how much they can contribute to the general concept being explored. Not only questions, but time spent, topics covered, and approaches taken vary with each respondent. Because question formulation and question asking are virtually simultaneous, nonstandardized interviewing is usually done by the researcher himself.

Merton, Fiske, and Kendall's (1956) FOCUSED INTERVIEW is probably the best-known description of an interview in which the investigator defines the situation and maps out what is wanted but allows the respondent considerable latitude to express his or her own definition of the situation, not simply to answer the interviewer's questions about it. A focused interview has the following characteristics: (1) It takes place with persons known to have been involved in a particular situation or experience, for example, those who have read a particular book or who were present during a hotel fire. (2) It refers to situations that have been analyzed prior to the interview. (3) It proceeds on the basis of an interview guide that outlines both the major areas of inquiry and the topics relevant to the research hypothesis. (4) It focuses on the subject's experiences, that is, the reactions, emotions, and attitudes of the respondent concerning the situation under study.

Researchers may capitulate even this amount of control and focus, especially when they are not certain what exactly is needed and who is best able to teach it. ELITE INTERVIEWING is the term used by Dexter (1970) to describe interviews in which the respondent is encouraged to define the situation, to structure his or her own account of it without being guided as to what topic or subtopics to discuss, and to introduce his or her own notions of what is relevant, instead of relying upon the investigator's notions of relevance. Of necessity, such an approach may be used with people who do indeed regard themselves as elite–the influential, famous, and rich. Such people may be unwilling to accept the assumptions with which the investigator starts, and the interviewer may be less likely to insist that such a prominent and well-informed person conform to a standardized line of discussion.

But the research endeavor takes place in ponds of many sizes, and the smart researcher looks for whatever frog best knows its way around. In exploratory studies, in particular, the most humble informants may be regarded less as respondents than as co-workers who help shape the investigator's viewpoint. Nonstandardized interviewing enables the researcher to acquire a feeling for the situation and the people to study and to do so without unnecessarily or prematurely setting boundaries to the study by the hypotheses and presumptions basic to standardized question-asking.

In describing participant observation research earlier, interviews were discussed as a way to build theory. Now consider some of the ways that very open and nonstandardized interviews provide information in the earlier stages of research that can be translated into more structured or standardized interviews later on:

• What should I ask? What specific questions would obtain relevant information?

- Who, in this or comparable groups, would be most likely to have this information?
- What strategy, techniques, and tactics would be most effective in obtaining information? For example, in some parts of the country, an interviewer who was not willing to have a glass of tea before rushing into business would not be well received. Early interviews can determine special vocabularies, areas of sensitivity, the best sequence of questions, and behaviors that inhibit or make easier communication and rapport.
- What are the categories of answers and the range of responses?

Note well, however, that even open and nonstandardized interviews require that you do your homework ahead of time. Find out all that you can about the topic so you know what to ask. In the excerpts given on page 152, the interviewer's questions reveal that a great deal of time has been spent boning up on each interviewee's life and work prior to the interview.

Making Up Questions

Probably the most widely debated issue in question-making actually concerns how the question is to be answered. The alternatives are simple.

Open-Ended versus Closed-Ended Questions

OPEN-ENDED QUESTIONS are those to which the respondent answers as he or she wishes, perhaps with some probing on the part of the interviewer: "What have you learned from this research methods course?"

CLOSED-ENDED QUESTIONS are those to which the respondent must choose between fixed alternative answers, such as ( ) nothing, ( ) very little, ( ) some, ( ) more than usual, ( ) very much.

The answers provided for closed-ended questions must meet three criteria:

1. They must be exhaustive, providing categories into which all possible responses can be fitted. This may require a category called "Other."
2. They must be mutually exclusive, so that either only one answer is right or the instructions specifically state that the respondent is to choose the one best answer or the answer closest to his or her own opinion [This means there can be no grab bags, such as "What have you learned from this course?" ( ) how to read, ( ) how to do cross-tabulations, ( ) how to. . . .]
3. They must be adequately divided. When asked whether they belong to the lower, middle, or upper classes, for example, roughly 9 out of 10

Issues and Discussions ━━━━━━━━━━━━━━━━━━━━━━━━━━━━━━━━━━━━

DO YOUR HOMEWORK!

To avoid wasting your own time as well as that of the people you inter-view, prepare for the interviews by learning all you can about the topics and people of interest. An interviewee who does not have anything to say is bad, but an interviewer who does not have any ideas about what questions to ask is even worse. Below are some questions Richard Evans (1976) asked in his interviews with famous psychologists. Note how much preparation had to go into knowing enough to ask each of the questions:

Evans: Dr. Rhine, I notice in your background that you actually have a Ph.D. in plant physiology from the University of Chicago. Now with this, how did you happen to get into the field of extrasensory perception?

Evans: Dr. Krech, your background seems to show an evolution in think-ing that I think might be interesting to students in psychology. As a student, you were influenced by the very early radical behaviorism of John Watson (1924). Later, you moved away from this and began to consider the importance of ex-perience to the organism. Could you tell us a little about the evolution of your career?

Evans: Dr. Rogers, I'd like to relate some of your views to three of the important dimensions that are almost always dealt with in psychology – motivation, perception, and learning. Beginning with motivation, in psychology we have tended to define this as all conditions which arouse, direct, and sus-tain the organism. This generally is interpreted as a homeostatic model, taken from biology – that the organism seeks to reduce tension and maintain a state of equilibrium. I gather your theory is not developed out of this particular ap-proach to motivation. Is that correct?

Evans: (Dr. Skinner) Humanists often accuse behaviorists of having no con-cern for human values or human good because behaviorists view man as being merely a machine. How do you react to this criticism of behaviorism?

---

persons will answer middle. But if the list is broadened to read lower, working, middle, and upper, then less than half will choose middle.

The closed-ended question has some distinct advantages. The answers are simple to record and to analyze. In fact, many closed-ended questions can be marked directly on topical sensing sheets, which can be read and tabulated by computer.

The ease with which closed-ended questions can be answered also con-stitutes their chief disadvantage. The very availability of answers not only may make it impossible for respondents to offer other, unlisted, answers but also may make it more likely that the listed ones seem correct. The alternatives provided may suggest answers to respondents that they themselves would not have thought of, thus preventing them from thinking the question through. This is particularly true with respondents who are not highly motivated or who are eager to please the interviewer and do the interview right.

The alternatives provided may suggest answers to respondents that they could never have thought of if they tried. With an open-ended question, it is easy to tell whether or not a respondent has much knowledge or interest in a subject—that is one of the reasons open-ended questions are more ego-threatening and must be written with care to minimize such threat. But with fixed alternatives available, any respondent can have a learned-sounding opinion on the political situation in Albania. The closed-ended question requires the respondent only to recognize an answer; but in at least one study, a sizable number of respondents (1 out of every 11) recognized a purely fictitious personality thrown in among the names of real celebrities. Many of the respondents so erring reported having seen the person on television recently.

Some categories seem more desirable than others. Consider age, surely one of the more straightforward questions. But, as can be seen in large surveys, an unlikely number of people report being 20, 30, 40, and other round numbers, suggesting a tendency to round off. The structured question with fixed alternatives—under 21, 21–30, 31–40, 41–50, and so forth—may heighten this tendency (especially when rounding to 30 instead of 31 places a respondent in the company of 21-year-olds rather than that of 40-year-olds).

Open-ended questions have as an obvious advantage the freedom of the respondent to express an opinion. Furthermore, the interviewer can probe, that is, encourage the respondent to amplify or clarify any answer. But even with such probing, the disadvantages of the open-ended question lie in the difficulty of coding and comparing answers. Because the respondent has more freedom to interpret the question, some of the answers may be irrelevant to the researcher's concerns. Other answers may be ambiguous despite the interviewer's efforts. The person doing the interviewing, if not the researcher himself or herself, must be more highly trained and aware of the research objectives and the way the responses will be coded. Although tape recording of responses is always desirable (to capture exact wording or possible nuances of expression), it is time-consuming and expensive (anywhere from 3 to 12 hours of transcription and checking time is required for every hour of interview time; Gorden, 1969).

In general, the two types of questions are best suited for opposite ends of the spectrum of research objectives. Open-ended questions serve best for exploratory research in which hypotheses are being developed or for situations in which the investigator is not certain of the nature, range, and diversity of possible responses. Open-ended questions are also most useful for learning how a respondent arrived at a particular point of view or for those situations in which the respondent may not yet have solidified his or her own views on a topic. Closed-ended questions serve best for much of hypothesis-testing research, in which the objective is to find out whether the respondent agrees or disagrees with some given view so that a specific hypothesis can be confirmed or refuted by highly comparable responses.

One of the difficulties in using open-ended questions is that the answer may be too divergent to be easily comparable. But it is the responsibility – and the art – of the investigator to make the meaning of questions (and alternative answers, if provided) as clear as possible, to ensure that different individuals understand the question in the same way and answer it in the same context. Thus, one of the researcher's main concerns is standardization, whether achieved through identically worded questions or through meaning equivalency. Fortunately, there are yet other ways in which the interviewer can help establish the meaning of questions, even for the most highly scheduled interviews.

Pretesting. After the interview has been designed, a random sample of respondents or a group of respondents representative of those who will be interviewed can be asked the various questions – and then additional questions designed to determine how they understood the original questions. One good technique is to ask the respondent to repeat the question in his or her own words. At the same time, the interviewer can watch for uncomfortableness with or defensiveness about any topic or the wording of any question. Pretesting has its costs – in money, in time, in subjects – because the responses of those in the testing group cannot be included in the final analysis. (After all, the questions asked them were hardly contextually identical, and, in fact – thanks to their reactions – may be changed for the final interviews.) But, as a part of development, pretesting more than pays its way by increasing the validity and reliability of the final measures.

Probes. A probe is some action on the part of the interviewer to encourage the respondent to clarify or amplify an answer or continue with a flow of thought.

As Cannell and Kahn (1968) noted, the use of probing at any given moment will depend on the interviewer's assessment of response adequacy. If the respondent is giving relevant answers in the detail and depth intended by the interviewer, there is no need to elaborate on the original questions or to do more than look interested and take notes. But if the respondent seems to lose interest, grows uncomfortable, or begins to give inadequate answers, then the interviewer can turn to one of a variety of probes:

• Direct questions: Perhaps the single most useful probe is the word *why*. Other direct questions might be, How do you mean that? Can you tell me more about that? Is there anything else?

• Requests for specific additional information: When did you do that? Exactly what did he say?

• Repetition of the original question: for example, Interviewer: "What kind of work do you do?" Respondent: "Work up at the University." Interviewer: "I see. What kind of work do you do there?"

• Echo or repetition of the respondent's last words: for example, Respondent: "Well, I tried studying for finals, but it didn't work." Interviewer: "It didn't work?"

• Silence: When the interviewer looks expectant, pencil at the ready, that itself can be taken as a signal that the respondent is doing fine and the interviewer wants to hear more. However, its value quickly diminishes. Gorden (1969) found that as silences extended from two seconds toward nine, it became increasingly less likely that the respondent would be the one to break the silence, and even less likely that he or she would do so to give a longer and more useful response. Silences of 15 seconds or more often disrupted the interview.

Probes and expressions of understanding and interest such as "I see" or "I understand" have been found effective in lengthening responses. They are also useful in their absence when the interviewer wishes to move on to the next question. They may even be replaced by what Richardson, Dohrenwend, and Klein (1965) called guggles, usually staccato sounds—*uh, ah,* or the beginning of some unfinished word—made by the interviewer to indicate he or she wants to say something. The guggle puts the respondent on notice that the interviewer is eager to say something, and thus, it has the effect of shortening responses. Old-fashioned interrupts, tactfully handled, also serve the healthy purpose of ending an irrelevant answer or refocusing it.

The usage of probes will vary according to the degree of scheduling and the number of closed-ended questions in the interview. With closed-ended questions in a highly scheduled interview, the interviewer may be restricted to probes that repeat the questions, urging a respondent to choose a given alternative, such as "( ) Strongly approve," "( ) Approve somewhat," "( ) No opinion," "( ) Disapprove," "( ) Strongly disapprove," rather than some answer such as "No, people shouldn't do that." And in highly scheduled interviews with open-ended questions, standardized probes may be included for certain questions expected to need clarification for some respondents. Finally, in interviews in which the interviewer is given more freedom to elicit information from the respondent, spontaneous probes are often the aspect that makes interviewing a true challenge to ingenuity and tact.

There are three basic guidelines for the careful, planned construction – or the spontaneous creation – of probes:

1. The interviewer must be sensitive to the effect of any probe on the individual respondent. Some people will need more encouragement and probes than others. Occasionally respondents may be alarmed by silences and jump into irrelevant answers simply to fill time. Others may misinterpret *uh-hum*-type encouragements, feeling that the interviewer is trying to hurry them along.

2. Probes should always be neutral. Although probes act to selectively lengthen responses, they should not also bias the direction of answers. Hildum and Brown (1956) noted that the encouragement "Good," made after selected opinions, influenced the number of opinions expressed in that direction. "Uh-hum" as an encouragement lengthened responses but did not change direction. These results suggest that too obvious encouragements, such as "Good." or "Right." may lead to invalid answers.

3. Probes should be recorded. A good, written interview should record not only what the respondent said but the way in which it was said and the context in which the answer was given – which clearly includes the probes necessary to evoke it.

Sequence

Another way in which the investigator can help establish the meaning of questions is by the order of presentation.

The sequence of questions should make sense to the respondent. Questions should fit with one's experience and order of things, chronologically perhaps, or moving among naturally associated topics. New topics should be marked by clear transition statements, such as "Now I'd like to ask some questions about your own experiences with armadillos," so that the respondent does not spend time and energy trying to answer a new question in the context of the old ones.

The sequence of questions also should work to help establish and maintain rapport and good feeling between the interviewer and the respondent. Experienced interviewers recommend that interviews begin with questions that are both easy to answer and enjoyable. Thus, they recommend

NOT beginning with age, marital status, and occupation, because these are hardly topics of amusement for most of us. When the respondent has become more confident, the interview can shift to more personal or difficult questions.

The most common ordering of questions is called the FUNNEL SEQUENCE, in which general questions are asked first, with each successive question related to the previous question but in a more specific way. Gorden (1969) has outlined succinctly the advantages of this sequence:

1. If the objective is to obtain detailed description and the respondent is motivated to give a spontaneous account, then introducing a topic with the broadest question often will eliminate the need for myriad, small, detailed questions.
2. The funnel approach helps the respondent recall details more efficiently because he or she is allowed to follow personal connections among thought associations.
3. By asking the broadest question first, the interviewer is less likely to close off possible alternative responses. In other words, the respondent's perspective is given before the interviewer imposes another perspective or frame of reference.

The INVERTED FUNNEL SEQUENCE, described by Kahn and Cannell (1957), reverses this order and moves from specific to more general questions.

1. Specific questions at the beginning of the discussion of a topic can help a respondent gain access to forgotten information, forgotten either because the subject is not very meaningful or is too distant in time to be very clear or is too ego-threatening. (For example, a student may report a satisfactory semester, having partially erased from memory the poor start during fraternity rush and the midsemester panic that caught him up.)
2. Having once committed themselves to some generalization, people are likely to answer specific and related questions in light of that generalization (Shweder & D'Andrade, 1980). The man who has just proclaimed himself basically an outdoors type is much more likely to rate fishing as a favorite pastime and to give lower ratings to activities that are not as consistent with his earlier generalization. Beginning with specific questions avoids such bias.
3. Perhaps the respondent has not yet made a generalization about a topic or a judgment about some event, not having previously given the matter any thought. The use of narrower questions first can help him or her organize thoughts and feelings in order to form such an overall opinion.

Avoiding Sources of Error

Clarity: Helping the Respondent Understand the Question

1. Avoid long questions.
2. Avoid words with double meanings or ambiguous usage. Such words are beloved by American humorists ("Do you believe in infant baptism?" "Believe in it, hell, I've seen it!"), but to the researcher interested in validity, they are no laughing matter. The question "Do you usually work alone?" needs to specify what usually means and whether working alone refers to who helps or who is in the room.
3. Avoid negatives. They are hard to understand. Quick now, how would you answer this: "Do you not favor the sale of beer in the cafeteria?" The contortion of "do you not" also implies that the interviewer would prefer a yes answer ("Yes, I do.").
4. Avoid two-part questions. If you ask "Do you favor smaller classes in larger rooms?" and the answer is "Yes," you cannot be certain the respondent is not simply answering whichever part of the question registered loudest or that the opinion on one part of the question was influenced by the opinion on the other. That is, the respondent may feel strongly about larger rooms but does not really have an opinion about the size of the class in them.

Precision: Enabling the Respondent to Answer

5. Specify exactly the time and place of the information you want. A question about "when you were young" can mean almost anything. (A newspaper column recently proclaimed the good news from a study of college girls: they thought "older men" were the most attractive. And now for the bad news, added the well-seasoned columnist: the girls defined "older men" as being about 30. If you fail to see the humor in this, do not worry—you will.) Because of the possibility of different perspectives, it is necessary for the reseacher to provide the one he or she wants. Ask instead, "When you were still in high school, . . ." or "When you were about 10 years old, . . ." or whatever is relevant to the question.
6. Specify exactly the context of the information you want. Lazarsfeld (1944) calls this the PRINCIPLE OF SPECIFICATION. When a professor asks why a given assignment has not been completed, only the most ingenious student begins by explaining he or she became a psychology major in 1984—even though that fact may be a key one in the narrative that leads, eventually, to the undone assignment. Most likely you would pick out the reason you hoped would contribute especially to a mutual understanding of the present unfortunate situation: The book was out of the library; I was sick; My roommate's hamster died, and so forth.

Figure 3 A QUESTION WITHOUT A CONTEXT. Questions for which the context has not been specified, either in the stem of the question or by the preceding questions, are unlikely to turn up useful information. (Cartoon © Sydney Harris.)

In ordinary social intercourse, we can count on the fact that most of the time what is important to the person with whom we are talking is also important to us. In research, it is not wise to make this assumption, or in any circumstance where there is a cultural, social, or educational difference. When one of Chesterton's detectives asked the lady of the manor who was staying with her in the country, she replied that no one was. In her assessment of what was important, she ignored the maid, butler, cook, and a few others (see Figure 3).

7. Word your questions so that the attributes in which you are interested

are the ones that the respondent will address. If you were asked what you liked best about your new blazer, you would be extremely unlikely to answer how pleased you were by the fact that it only has two sleeves, although you certainly would not have bought a three-sleeved one, no matter what other glowing attributes it possessed. But there is a tacit assumption between you and your questioner that coats only have two sleeves and that therefore the fact is inconsequential, in spite of its predominant importance to you as a coat buyer. Again, Lazarsfeld's (1944) examples from market research make clear the error of what he calls the PRINCIPLE OF TACIT ASSUMPTION. If you ask your respondent why he drinks tea, the answers will all pertain to tea, understandably, and probably in unspoken comparison to coffee or cola: It's quick to make; doesn't upset my stomach; won't keep me awake. On the other hand, if you ask why someone drinks Mother Lola's sanquine tea, the responses will be more specific, in unspoken comparison to other brands of tea: It's cheaper, redder, sweeter, more available. The qualities of tea itself, in comparison with other beverages, are not mentioned.

8. Ask questions, if possible, in terms of the respondent's own experiences rather than generalities: not "How much television do you watch on an average day?"; instead, ask "What television shows have you watched in the past two days?"

Lack of Bias: Not Leading Your Respondent into Error

BIAS is "a systematic or persistent tendency to make errors in the same direction, that is, to overstate or understate the 'true value' of an attribute" (Cannell and Kahn, 1968).

9. Do not use biasing or loaded words or questions. "Do you agree with the President's proposal that . . . ?" is a very different question from "Do you agree with the recent proposal that . . . ?" and even more different from "Do you agree with the Minority Caucus proposal that . . . ?" even when what follows is identical.

An exception must be made to injunctions against biased questions and that is when the investigator specifically wants to divide the population into two groups: those who hold an extreme view and those who hold a view somewhere below that. The classic example is "Would you favor sending food overseas to feed the starving people of India?" This question once quite effectively identified the number of people who were so opposed to shipping food overseas that their opinion held up against the strongly biased notion of starving people (Kahn & Cannell, 1957).

10. Avoid leading questions, that is, questions so worded as to suggest the most appropriate answers.

a. Do not reveal your expectations. "You are generally happy with this class so far, aren't you?"

b. Do not suggest the range of normal answers. Loftus (1975) asked a random sample of patients about headaches. But half were asked, "Do you get headaches frequently, and if so, how often?" Respondents reported an average of 2.2 headaches per week. The other half, who were asked, "Do you get headaches occasionally, and if so, how often?" reported only 0.7 headaches per week. She then asked about headache products used. Half the subjects were asked, "In terms of the total number of products, how many have you tried? 1? 2? 3?" The other half were asked the identical question except for the suggestions at the end which were, "1? 5? 10?" As expected, the group primed with the largest numbers were led toward larger estimates, an average of 5.2 compared to 3.3 for the first group.

c. Do not plant premises or information. That, of course, is what a lawyer means by the leading question. "How short was the robber?" will usually bring forth a shorter estimate—having suggested the idea of shorter than normal—than the customary question "How tall was he?" The question "How fast were the cars going when they smashed into each other?" got higher estimated speeds than a question about the same two cars that merely "hit" each other, although subjects had seen the same collision on videotape. On retest a week later, Loftus (1975) found that the subjects who had been asked about the "smashing" cars were more likely to remember broken glass lying around. There was none.

11. Alternate questions likely to have yes and no answers. There is evidence some people tend to agree with whatever is being asked, whereas others go out of their way to disagree (Richardson, Dohrenwend, & Klein, 1965). Persons with lower educational and socioeconomic status have been found to have a greater tendency toward yea-saying than do respondents with a college education.

Tact: Protecting the Respondent's Self-Esteem

Questions are ego-threatening if they make the respondents feel poorly informed or that their opinions and behaviors are socially unacceptable. The essential process of protecting self-esteem is what Cannell and Kahn (1968) have called SANCTIONING, building into the question the implication that one answer is as acceptable as another throughout a range that easily includes the respondent.

12. Do not ask unnecessarily awkward questions. "Did you finish high school?" may require an admission of failing to do so. "What was the last grade you completed?" permits a positive answer. You can make

possibly offending questions less so by making the simple statement that people's opinions differ and that such factors sometimes help us to understand the differences.

13. Use face-saving phrases. "Do you happen to know who the congressman is from this district?" "As you know, more than half the registered voters in this county were not able to get to the polls last May. Were you able to vote?"

14. Make it easier to express what might be considered unacceptable opinions or behaviors. "Some people feel it's important to report all income for taxes; other people feel this isn't necessary in all circumstances. What would your feeling be?" In fact, the Kinsey et al. (1948) interviewers often made it more difficult to express acceptable behaviors. People were not asked "Did you ever . . . ?" but rather "When did you first . . . ?" Such questions place the burden of denial on the respondent but also sanction the behavior in question. Venereal disease clinics use this approach matter-of-factly, referring to one's sexual partners, thus not making the patient responsible for correcting an erroneous singular.

The Interview as a Social Occasion

Both interviewer and respondent arrive at the moment of the interview with different histories, personalities, attitudes, and values, all of which can color how the two perceive and interact with each other. In general, the more unlike the two participants in the interview, the more likely there will be errors and impaired interaction. Part of this lies in the increased chance for misunderstanding, part in the ease with which people who are similar can talk, and part—a large part—in the almost inevitable societal patterns of what is sometimes called caste and class.

Skin Deep: Age, Face, and Sex. Differences count, particularly when the topics are sensitive ones. There are things you do not want to tell your mother. Benney, Riesman, and Star (1956) found, not surprisingly, that when interview questions turned to sexual habits the least inhibited communication occurred when both interviewer and respondent were young people of the same sex. The most inhibited? People of the same age but opposite sex. Erlich and Riesman (1961) also found that adolescents tended to tell older interviewers what they assumed they wanted to hear: They reported fewer instances of behavior considered undesirable by middle-class adult standards and greater adherence to parental instructions. Still other studies have reported that the age and sex of interviewers affect the flow and kind of information from respondents.

Much of the early literature on interviewer effect looked at race and ethnic memberships. Hyman's (1954) classic studies of interviews showed that black interviewers obtained significantly more reports of resentment and dissatisfaction with various American institutions from blacks than did white interviewers. These results are likely indicative of the sensitive social climate of the times and the possibly threatening nature of the questions. But another early study conducted by Robinson and Rohde (1946) suggested that respondents tried to avoid making statements that might cause the interviewer discomfort or invoke disapproval. In this experiment selected interviewers were assigned to ask New Yorkers about their attitudes toward Jews. One group of interviewers was chosen on the basis of both looking Semitic and having a Semitic-sounding name. The second group was judged to look Semitic but to have a non-Semitic-sounding name. And the third group had neither the appearance nor name to suggest they were Jewish. The three groups of interviewers obtained significantly different responses. The more likely the respondents were to believe that their interviewer was Jewish, the less likely they were to make statements that could be considered anti-Semitic.

Caste and Class. There are several sources of misunderstanding and possible tension between the middle-class, college-educated interviewer and the respondent with a lower socioeconomic and educational status. A greater tendency toward acquiescence or deference was well illustrated in a study by Lenski and Leggett (1960) in which low-status respondents questioned by middle-class interviewers agreed with two mutually contradictory positions used at widely separated points in the interview. Another source of invalid data was suggested by Katz (1942): working-class respondents felt freer to express more radical social and political opinions when their interviewer was also of working-class origins. The relationship between class and other characteristics can be seen in Williams's (1964) study of race and class. Ten years after the Hyman study, which suggested that blacks were reluctant to express race-related opinions to white interviewers, William looked at the difference in status among black respondents. Higher-status blacks were far less affected by the skin color of their interviewer when reporting what black newspapers they read, whether or not they would consider sending their children to white schools, what aspirations they had for themselves and their families, and other questions believed to be threatening.

Erasing the Differences. How is the interviewer to counteract these effects? For age, race, sex, and obvious class characteristics such as accent, there is little he or she can do. Fortunately, interviewer sensitivity itself can have an effect, as has been shown in various training experiments.

In fact, interview training often consists largely of alerting the interviewer to the kind of social inequalities interviewees are likely to perceive and to techniques for minimizing these. One way is simply to behave as if both parties were of equal status, whether or not this is actually so. Interviewing may be one of the few social transactions in which this occurs for some respondents. Another way is to dress in an approximation of the style of the respondents – within reason. Newly purchased bib overalls will not fool members of a farming community, but they are likely to be annoyed and/or amused by jeans, long hair, and a vasectomy pin or a pin-striped suit and diamond pinky ring. Perhaps the right level could be reached by dressing like students and teachers in the local junior college.

Of course, despite their education, middle-class interviewers will sometimes meet more than their match. When respondents feel superior, whether in terms of money, power, or intellect, the interviewer can only respect that feeling and be aware of possible acquiescence and deference on his or her own equally socialized part. Benney and Hughes (1956) said that in their experience such high-status respondents try to reestablish equality in the interview by addressing themselves subjectively to the investigator who, although invisible, is likely to more nearly equal their self-perceived status, or to the sponsoring institution itself (anyone can talk to the Rockefeller Foundation).

But in some instances characteristics of age, race, sex, and class may not be overcome. If the interview is to deal with areas for which such characteristics are likely to have a strong impact – if the questions are on racial problems or labor relations or sexual behavior – consideration should be given to matching the interviewer and respondent as closely as possible along the key dimensions.

Interviewer expectations. Face to face with the respondent, the interviewer is given immediate cues as to the person's social status and level of sophistication – not to mention age, race, and sex. As an experienced social creature (with an inevitable number of biases and prejudices accumulated and varyingly suppressed throughout life), the interviewer may have unconscious expectations as to how any respondent is likely to be and feel – or more exactly, to answer the questions with which the interviewer is so familiar. An unwary interviewer may allow his or her perception of the respondent to effect both what is asked and how the answers are interpreted (see UNSHARED ASSUMPTIONS on the next page).

The interviewer's own values and attitudes also can affect his or her findings. This can be seen in one of the earliest studies of interview effects, an experiment conducted in 1929 by Rice. Different interviewers talked to transients in flophouses and cheap hotels. Much of the data they obtained were similar from one interviewer to the next, but this similar-

UNSHARED ASSUMPTIONS

One aspect of the interview context involves the assumptions that each participant makes about the knowledge, experiences, and personal situation of the other participant. Schegloff (1972) noted that in selecting terms to refer to physical locations, for example, a speaker must be sensitive not only to his or her and the listener's present location, but to the listener's knowledge of the place referred to. Giving directions to someone who is familiar with the local terrain is much easier than giving directions to someone who is not. Often, however, we assume that the person to whom we are speaking shares our geographical perspective and/or knowledge, and we may discover that this assumption was unwarranted. Schegloff (1972) gave the following example from a collection of calls to the police department of a midwestern city.

C: Uh, this is Mrs. Lodge calling from 121 Sierra Drive.
D: 121 Sierra.
C: Yes.
D: Ma'am, where's Sierra located?
C: It's on the corner of Sierra and uh-hh Smith Drive.
D: Sierra and Smith.
C: Yes . . .
D2: Uh, where is this Sierra and Smith located? We gotta know about this.
C: 121 Sierra Drive. It's right on the corner . .
D2: Right on the corner of Si-uh of what? Sierra and Smith. Where is Smith?
C: Sierra Drive. Sierra and Smith.
D2: I wanna know where Smith is located.
C: Well, it's uh right off Flint Ridge.
D2: Off Flint Ridge.
C: Yeah.
D2: Where're you at ma'am, are you in the County? You're—you're in [nearby community].

Both the caller and the police assumed a shared geographical perspective, and they were both wrong. The result was a lot of fumbling and repetition before communication begins to take place, in the last line of the quote.

ity ended when it came to asking about the causes of the men's destitution. One interviewer consistently found the path to the flophouse lined with whiskey bottles, whereas another interviewer found his subjects reporting themselves as the victims of social and industrial conditions. Clearly, the interviewers were honest and well-intended, but one was a prohibitionist and the other a socialist. Later experiments in which interviewers were explicitly trained to avoid the intrusion of their own expectations into the collection of data seem to indicate that it is possible to guard against this particular error (Cannell, cited in Cannell & Kahn, 1968).

Perhaps the most difficult task for an interviewer is maintaining neutrality that ensures that the answers obtained are valid measures of the attribute being measured – and not responses to the quirks and charms of the interviewer. To err on the side of the cool automaton is to lose the respondent entirely. To overly enchant the respondent is to set such a mood of good will and rapport that he or she would be reluctant to mar it with negative responses or answers that such a new friend might not appreciate or share. It is a difficult line, but one well worth walking.

Discussions of interviews, such as this one, necessarily spend many pages on the dangers with which this research tool is fraught. But, interviewing also has its delights. First, there is no other way to so efficiently gather data, especially when you think of the respondent's answers as telescoping hours of behavior or even years of experience and attitude formation.

Second, it is clearly the most sociable of all the research tools. Benney and Hughes (1956) have described the interview as "not merely one of the many ways in which two people talk to each other," but also as "the game which we play for the pleasure of savoring its subtleties. It is our flirtation with life, our eternal affair, played hard and to win, but played with that detachment and amusement which give us, win or lose, the spirit to rise up and interview again and again."

And last of all, it is a process of infinite variety and intrinsic interest. Students of human behavior are primarily interested in people and the way they interact. Consequently the interview is not only a way of obtaining information, but a part of its subject matter.

Interviewer: "And you do agree with that statement, do you not?"

Summary

The major thrust of a research interview is that the interviewer takes control over the exchange in order to get from respondents information that he or she can quantify and compare in order to measure differences between peoples' attitudes, knowledge, or behavior. The researcher's biggest fear in interviewing is that he or she will actually be measuring only differences in the interviewees' responses to the interview process itself: not differences in what various subjects know or feel, for example, but differences in how they understood or responded to the questions in the interview.

Because measurement and comparison are the objectives of the research interview, the interview itself (and the behavior and demeanor of the interviewer) is usually STANDARDIZED (made comparable for all interviewees) in one of two ways.

The scheduled interview is based on the assumption that to produce a response that validly differentiates one respondent from another, the stimulus itself must be identical. Consequently scheduled interviews are ones in which the wording, sequence, and delivery of questions are spelled out in a carefully prepared interview schedule or written plan.

An unscheduled interview can also be standardized, however, using an interview guide that directs the interviewer to seek the same kinds of information from subjects but gives him or her latitude to vary question wording, sequence, and delivery, so that the interview will have the equivalent meaning and impact for all respondents.

Of course, some research-oriented interviewing is less concerned about quantifiable and comparable data and more concerned about obtaining as much and as widely varying information as possible. Consequently, the interviewer will ask different respondents different questions, depending on what he or she wants to know and how much knowledge and willingness to talk any given interviewee seems to show. Such interviews usually involve neither a schedule nor a guide but rather a combination researcher-interviewer flying by the seat of his or her pants–in this case, a working hypothesis. Such interviews are referred to as being both unscheduled (no plan) and unstandardized (no effort to get the same or comparable information from all subjects).

Questions can be answered by leaving the question open (allowing the respondent to respond as he or she wishes) or by making it closed (providing fixed alternative answers between which the interviewee must choose). Open-ended questions give the interviewee more opportunity to express real answers but are harder to code and analyze; closed-ended questions are easily comparable but are likely to suggest or obscure answers. Questions can be asked in a funnel sequence, in which general questions are asked first, with each successive question becoming more specific, or in an inverted funnel sequence, in which specific questions at the beginning help the respondent move to broader generalizations.

These are decisions to be made in the planning of the interview. The errors to be avoided include poor clarity or precision; not biasing the response by leading questions or loaded words; and not threatening or damaging the interviewee's self-esteem. The interviewer–respondent interaction also provides sources of error because people respond to each other on the basis of such factors as age, race, sex, and social status. The job of the interviewer is to minimize these as much as possible and to be aware of his or her own expectations of how any respondent is likely to answer questions.

And lest it sound like too many apples and oranges to juggle, remember that you are somewhat experienced in the underlying social interactions, that the research questions that send us into the interview area in the first place help shape many of the decisions made as to the form of the interview. This chapter and the next give you some of the nuts and bolts to obtain those answers.

Recommended Reading

Evans, R. I. *The making of psychology: Discussions with creative contributors.* New York: Knopf, 1976.

Richard Evans is a social psychologist at the University of Houston. Beginning in the early 1960s, he conducted a series of in-depth interviews with many of the most creative and famous psychologists of the century. This book, the eleventh in the series, contains interviews with 28, many of whom you will recognize immediately: Erich Fromm, C. G. Jung, R. D. Laing, B. F. Skinner. The discussions make fascinating reading and illustrate some of the pleasures and pitfalls of interviewing such an elite group. On the pleasure side, it is clear that an articulate, intelligent interviewee can make the interviewer's life easy by providing full, detailed, interesting answers to questions. On the pitfall side, it is equally clear that such people are likely to redefine your questions (or ignore them altogether) when they believe you have missed a point or are headed in the wrong direction. The interviews also highlight how much the interviewer must know ahead of time to know what questions to ask. Evans had to do a lot of homework before going to talk to these people.

Farb, P. *Word play: What happens when people talk.* London: Hodder and Stroughton, 1977.

Interviews depend on language and language is a fascinating subject, to which this delightful book by Peter Farb bears testimony. Treating social interaction as a game, governed by a variety of implicit and explicit rules, Farb brings in a vast array of anecdotes, observations, data, and ideas to illustrate the nature of the game itself. The range of topics discussed is amazingly broad: from an amusing analysis of how the Marx Brothers' comedy routines confirm the existence of language rules (by breaking them), to why artificial languages (like Esperanto) will probably never be popular. Of particular interest for the would-be interviewer is the chapter "Verbal Duelling." As Farb has pointed out, we typically expect speakers to alternate in conversation, A speaks, then B speaks, then A, and so on. This is usually referred to as the ABAB pattern. This anticipated pattern of a typical interaction can lead to some unanticipated results when pushed to its limit. Farb gave this example from Jewish folklore of a conversation that supposedly took place on a train in Poland:

> A young man asked a merchant, "Can you tell me the time?"
> The merchant looked at him and replied: "Go to hell."

"What? Why, what's the matter with you! I ask you a civil question in a properly civil way, and you give me such an outrageous answer! What's the idea?"

The merchant looked at him, sighed wearily, and said, "Very well. Sit down and I'll tell you. You ask me a question. I have to give an answer, no? You start a conversation with me – about the weather, politics, business. One thing leads to another. It turns out you're a Jew – I'm a Jew, I live in Lublin – you're a stranger. Out of hospitality, I ask you to my home for dinner. You meet my daughter. She's a beautiful girl – you're a handsome young man. So you go out together a few times – and you fall in love. Finally you come to ask for my daughter's hand in marriage. So why go to all that trouble? Let me tell you right now, young man, I won't let my daughter marry anyone who doesn't even own a watch."

As Farb noted, the humor comes from our implicit expectations about the ABAB pattern in conversations. The merchant understood that pattern so well he could anticipate the entire course of events and chose to short-circuit it at the outset.

Jourard, S. M. *The transparent self* (rev. ed.). New York: Van Nostrand, 1971.

One of the things you are likely to discover if you conduct many interviews is that people differ in how much they are willing to disclose about themselves. Some people seem to want to tell you everything there is to know and others seem to volunteer nothing. Jourard and his colleagues have found that there are reliable differences among people in this respect. For example, women generally disclose much more about themselves to others than do men. Further, it seems to be the case that people are much more willing to disclose their likes and dislikes to someone who is, in turn, open and honest with them. Jourard saw the inability to be open about oneself to others, an inability that may stem from a variety of sources such as anticipated social rejection, as a major factor in much personal unhappiness. Because the interview is first and foremost an interpersonal situation, the quantity and quality of information obtained is bound to be a function of both the interviewer's and the interviewee's openness to each other. This book, however, is not intended as a guide to how you can manipulate others into telling you more. As Jourard put it, his idea is that you can attain your fullest potential only by being brave enough to be yourself with others and by not hiding behind the masks of various roles and assumed identities.

Levine, M. Investigative reporting as a research method: An analysis of Bernstein and Woodward's *All the President's Men. American Psychologist 35*, 626–638, 1980.

Investigative reporting, like much of the qualitative research in the clinical and social sciences, begins with a more or less explicit working theory in order to make sense of a mass of disconnected pieces of information and to guide subsequent investigation. And, not so very differently from other kinds of research, investigative reporting looks for enough data to justify publication. Results must be grounded in evidence, the reliability of which is probed and checked in a number of ways. Not all the information sought by reporters Bernstein and Woodward was about the events of Watergate; much concerned the social network in which the participants were involved and their varying reliability as informants. The need for hard evidence brought about an ongoing search for and imaginative use of public and not-so-public documents. The reporters varied their interview approaches according to what information different respondents might be expected to have and how cooperative or reluctant they might be in imparting it. In dealing with sensitive subjects, they had to sell themselves as human beings before asking questions. They evaluated the language of respondents carefully. When various White House spokespersons used similar words refuting a story, they took that as an indication that the counterattacks had been orchestrated by the President. Conflicting stories, on the other hand, became a different kind of evidence. And they watched their subjects for anger, discomfort, refusal to confirm or deny statements made by the interviewer, and other nonverbal clues. The major controls came from the reporters themselves, who each had veto power on the other's enthusiasm; from the work of other reporters on other papers; and from their own editor at the *Washington Post*, who constantly cross-examined them and pressured for more documentation and confirmation of information from more than one source. Both Levine's article and the book he explores in it are well worth reading. They contain many hints about the flexible and adaptive use of interviewing.

Terkel, S. *Working.* New York: Avon, 1975.

In social science research, interview questions are usually formulated so specific hypotheses may be addressed. Often, however, the interview is used in a more exploratory manner. What is termed unscheduled interviews can be used to find common themes that spontaneously emerge in discussions with different people. One of the most effective ways to present such themes is direct quotation—just letting people speak for themselves. Studs Terkel has spent many years interviewing people from all walks of life. His method of operation is quite simple—he just turns on a tape recorder and gets people talking. This books contains over 700 pages of what people have told him about their jobs, how they feel about what they do for a living. The people doing the talking range from a washroom attendant at the Palmer House in Chicago to an internationally known film critic. They all have something to say and Terkel rarely intrudes into their comments. The subject of the interviews—work—is fascinating, but be sure to note how the presentations are organized to enhance their impact. Often Terkel quotes someone for a couple of paragraphs before inserting a little descriptive information about the speaker. The descriptive data, of course, are then seen in a somewhat different light.

6

Survey Research

The Nature and Varieties of Surveys

From Abstract Concepts to Specific Questions

ISSUES AND DISCUSSIONS:
    ONE PERSON'S CONSTANTLY IS ANOTHER'S HARDLY EVER

Types of Surveys

ISSUES AND DISCUSSIONS:
    SELF-SELECTION AND BIASED SAMPLES

ISSUES AND DISCUSSIONS:
    SOME UNINTENDED EFFECTS OF ASKING QUESTIONS

Explanatory Analysis

Sampling

An Illustration: Television Viewing and Fear of Crime

Respondents Are Only Human

Summary

Recommended Readings

For the average person, survey research is probably the most visible and pervasive form of research in the social and behavioral sciences. Even if you escape the dubious honor of being personally interviewed by academic opinion gatherers, it is hard to get through a day without having information about your opinions and behaviors solicited on items that range from trivial to tragic. Restaurant managers want to know how they are doing, and they stick a little card between the salt and pepper shakers for you to fill out. How was the service? How would you rate the food? Comments? Telephone pollsters want to know if you think the President is doing a good job and if the election were held tomorrow, for whom would you vote? Census takers want to know how many people live in your house and how many bathrooms you have. Magazines print questionnaires they want you to answer, tear out, and mail in. Market researchers want to know if you prefer brand X or brand Y, and why? The Internal Revenue Service wants to know how much money you made last year and whether or not you gave anything to charity.

Except for the requests from the Census Bureau and the IRS, you could, of course, refuse to participate. Many people do. But, you would find it more difficult to avoid being exposed to and affected by the results of survey reseach. The results of the latest poll appear in the news with ever-increasing frequency, especially during election years. Political careers are aborted because of the polls. New products are marketed. Policies are changed. Thus, to the general public, survey research is not only the most frequently encountered social science method, it may well be the most influential. The descriptive information obtained from surveys is useful for a variety of practical purposes, from predicting election outcomes to marketing attractive products. But, as you will see, survey research is also used to gather information bearing on basic social and behavioral questions.

The image that usually comes to mind when survey research is mentioned is of someone standing on a doorstep, clipboard in hand, earnestly taking notes on what the scowling occupant has to say. Survey research does often involve interviewing: The members of a selected group of people – the sample – are each asked the same series of questions. But a preprinted questionnaire that each person, or respondent, fills out on his or her own may also be used, and it can be mailed instead of being delivered in person. Surveys can also be conducted over the telephone. Each of these variations has certain advantages and these will be covered in this chapter.

The Nature and Varieties of Surveys

As Babbie (1973) has noted, there are three general objectives that may be achieved with survey research. The first, and most familiar, is DESCRIP-

TION. This is what the U.S. Census Bureau is charged with, that is, to provide a profile of the distribution of ages, living arrangements, incomes, and other attributes of the population of the United States every 10 years. Of course, most surveys are not focused on the entire U.S. population. That would be too time-consuming and expensive. Rather, some smaller, more specific population and purpose are defined. Wallace, Wallechinsky, and Wallace (1982), for example, were interested in finding out the least favorite household task of American women. Hence, they hired the Gallup Organization of Princeton, New Jersey to contact a sample of 1352 women and ask them. The least favorite task, by the way, was washing the dishes, followed by cleaning the bathroom and ironing.

The second general objective that may be achieved with survey research is EXPLANATION. This is the objective that is of greatest interest in most social and behavioral research; researchers try to construct surveys in such a way that the data obtained will help explain why certain things are related to each other. Of course, it is necessary to establish that these particular things are related before bothering to explain why. So, descriptive and explanatory research are in many instances inseparable. For example, in a study of a massive 1-day teachers' strike that occurred in New York City on April 11, 1962, Cole (1969) found that Jewish teachers were much more likely to have walked out than were Christian teachers. That, of course, is a piece of purely descriptive information. But, the question of interest was why? There is nothing inherent in the Jewish religion that would predispose one to strike. However, Cole (1969, 1972) also found that Jewish teachers were more likely to be liberal and that liberal teachers were more likely to strike than were conservative teachers. Thus, the relationship between being Jewish and striking was explained.

The third objective for which survey research is sometimes used is EXPLORATION, exploratory analysis of an issue or problem area. Here there is a great deal more flexibility both in the sample of people you contact and in the nature and ordering of the questions you ask. The goal is to find out as much as you can about the issue and the subissues, the dimensions and the ramifications of the problem area. Thus, the more different perspectives and the more freedom you allow people in giving their points of view on the issue the better. For example, Terkel (1975) conducted a series of unscheduled interviews on the general topic of work with people from all walks of life. The structure and direction of each interview varied, as each person was simply encouraged to talk about what he or she did for a living and how they felt about it.

In the pages that follow, the focus will be on the descriptive and explanatory uses of survey research. They are the ones that require the greatest attention to detail and the most thorough preparation in order to be done well. That assumes, of course, that you already have at least a general idea about what it is you want to describe or explain or both. If not, an exploratory survey (talking to people who know something about the area of interest) may help. But, even if you have some hypotheses in mind and have decided that a survey is called for to test them, you still have a long way to go. To begin, you have to convert the conceptual elements of those hypotheses into specific, carefully worded questions.

From Abstract Concepts to Specific Questions

Converting the conceptual elements of your hypotheses into specific items on a questionnaire is an example of the process of OPERATIONALIZA-TION. You should already be somewhat familiar with this process from Chapters 1 and 4. But, just to refresh your memory, a concept is operationalized by specifying instances of it, by saying what you would have to see or hear or touch or smell in order to be convinced that the thing referred to by the concept was present. In the discussion of archival research in Chapter Four, for example, considerable time was devoted to a discussion of selecting those items of information to be extracted from the archives, that is, the indicators of the phenomena of interest. Some research by Sales (1973) was described in which he had to choose, from among multiple possibilities, those things that he would be willing to accept as indicators of increased authoritarianism. One indicator that he selected was increased allocation of funds to police departments, but he might have used some other marker. This process of choosing, of saying what it is you are going to take as indicators of your concepts, is referred to as operationalization.

In survey research, those choices revolve around deciding which questions to ask and how to word them. Those choices are important, because there is a great deal of evidence that the way in which a question is worded influences how respondents answer. For example, Bradburn (1982) has pointed out that wording changes in a question can focus attention on particular meanings. He cited an example of questions taken from a Gallup Poll in 1945. When asked whether they thought the government should give money to the unemployed until they could find a job, 63 percent of the respondents said, "Yes." But, when asked if they would be willing to pay higher taxes so the government could give money to the unemployed until they could find a job, only 34 percent said, "Yes." The second question, of course, made explicit a consideration (taxes) that many of the respondents did not think about when they were answering the first question. Ideally, what you would like to do is to write questions so that they mean exactly the same thing to all respondents. You want to avoid questions with ambiguities that allow some respondents to focus on one possible meaning and other respondents to focus on a different meaning.

Unfortunately, as illustrated in the Discussion below, even when people use the same words, they may mean different things. But, the goal is still for the questions, and answers, to be interpreted in the same way by everyone, and there are some things that will help. Sudman and Bradburn (1982) have offered three rules:

Issues and Discussions

ONE PERSON'S CONSTANTLY IS ANOTHER'S HARDLY EVER

In one of Woody Allen's movies, there is a couple who are having problems with their relationship and each is seeing a psychiatrist. When asked about the frequency with which they have sexual intercourse, the female tells her psychiatrist, "Constantly, about three times a week." When asked the same question, Woody tells his psychiatrist "Hardly ever, only about three times a week." In the movie, it is hilarious. For the survey researcher, it is not so funny. Indeed, all too many people seem to have adopted the attitude that "when I use a word it means just what I choose it to mean, neither more/nor less."

Frequency expressions such as *always, frequently, very often, sometimes, seldom,* and *never* are pervasive response categories to questionnaire and interview items. But, as Pepper (1981) has noted, only for a few such expressions is there agreement on exactly what they mean. How often is *often*? Or, how rare is *seldom*? As you might expect, the ones on which there is agreement are the ones that define the ends of the scales. Ratings from several studies indicate that *always* is generally perceived to mean 99 or 100 percent of the time. *Never* is generally perceived to mean 1 or 0 percent of the time. For other such words, the definitions appear to vary from study to study. *Sometimes,* for example, is perceived to mean somewhere between 20 and 46 percent of the time. The definition of *seldom* varies between 9 and 22 percent of the time.

To some extent, the definitions attributed to frequency expressions depend on the context. If you are discussing rain in Seattle, *very often* will have a meaning different from the one it has when you are discussing earthquakes in California. It also may depend on whom you ask. If you go to movies every week, then you may believe that the behavior of someone who only goes once a month could be appropriately described as *seldom* going. But to a person who never goes to the movies, going once a month may be perceived as going *very often.*

One possible solution to the ambiguities introduced by such varied definitions is to avoid frequency expressions altogether. That is, instead of providing response categories such as *frequently, sometimes, seldom,* and *never,* be specific. Provide response categories that require respondents to define their terms:

a. More than once a day   d. Two or three times a week
b. Once each day   e. Once a week
c. Four to six times a week f. Less than once a week

1. Restrain the impulse to write specific questions until you have thought through your research questions.
2. Write down your research questions and keep them handy while you are working on your questionnaire.
3. Every time you write a question, ask yourself, "Why do I want to know this?" Answer it in terms of the way it will help you to answer your research questions. "It would be interesting to know" is not an acceptable answer.

If everyone adhered to those simple rules, the world would be a better place, for respondents at least. Questionnaires and interview schedules would not be so long and cluttered.

One thing that may help in thinking through your research questions is to take each area of interest, or concern, and make a list of exactly what you think is involved. Start with the general topic and then get more and more specific. At each level, write down all the issues that come to mind and any implications or implicit meanings you can think of.

Try an example, one that will be developed in a little more detail than usual in order to use it to illustrate a number of points in the sections that follow. Suppose you were interested in attitudes toward the use of the insanity defense in criminal cases. Based on newspaper editorials and public reactions to several well-known cases in recent years, one might have developed the impression that people, generally, are quite negative about the use of that defense. There is something that seems to rub many people the wrong way about the practice of finding defendants "not guilty by reason of insanity," especially when they (the defendants) clearly committed the dastardly deed in question. What you want to know is why that upsets people so, why are people so negative toward that particular legal maneuver? The first thing to remember is that an impression that people are negative does not count as evidence. The first step, then, would be to get some data on the validity of that impression. That means the survey would need one or more questions assessing peoples' attitudes, pro or con, about the insanity defense. As was mentioned earlier, you do not need to explain why something is so until you have established that it is.

The next thing to ask is why. What are some possible reasons why people would support the use of the insanity defense? What are some reasons why people might oppose its use? It could be that people are simply uninformed, that is, that they do not know the legal definition of insanity. Perhaps some are negative because they believe that those who are found not guilty by reason of insanity will be set free, put back out on the street to do others harm. Or, perhaps, it has more to do with a general philosophy of life that people should always be held responsible for their actions. On the other hand, maybe it is really due to a fear of the unpredictable, a belief that the truly insane are capricious people who lash out randomly at those around them. Maybe people want to deny that there is such a thing as insanity because they find the very idea threatening to their sense of safety and invulnerability. Maybe those who favor the use of the insanity defense believe that human nature is basically uncontrollable and that the threat of punishment is not really a deterrent to crime. Maybe . . . , and so on.

As you see, it can get complicated very quickly. Indeed, you could probably come up with a number of additional reasons why someone might be positive or negative toward the use of the insanity defense. What happens as you go through this process, however, is that you realize you could not possibly test *all* of those ideas in a single survey and the questions of greatest interest will become clearer. In no time at all you end up with a list that includes the phenomenon of interest, two or three possible explanations you want to test, and notes about additional information that might be pertinent and, hence, worth asking about. It might look something like this:

Research Questions
    I. Attitudes toward the insanity defense
       A. Negative?
          1. Believe it lets the guilty go free
          2. Know the legal definition of insanity?
          3. Belief in individual accountability
          4. Believe that punishment deters crime
       B. Positive?
          1. A general trust-others attitude
          2. Member of the helping professions
   II. Relevant additional demographic information
       A. Educational level: more highly educated, less negative?
       B. Sex: females less negative?
       C. Religious orientation: Hindus less negative?

Suppose that your ruminations about the topic had produced this brief outline of the research questions thought to be most interesting. There are several things to note. First, one of the nice features of survey research is that you can obtain evidence of a number of possible explanations for the phenomenon of interest simultaneously, that is, in the same questionnaire or interview schedule. All you have to do is include appropriate questions about each. Second, in constructing those questions, one of the best sources of inspiration is previous research on the topic. For example, in a telephone interview, Hans and Slater (1983) asked respondents the following question, which you might be able to use:

> How strongly do you agree or disagree with the following statement: "The insanity defense is a loophole that allows too many people to go free." Do you strongly agree, agree, disagree, strongly disagree, or neither agree nor disagree with that statement?

On second thought, you probably cannot use it. The question is loaded. The word *loophole* has a clear negative connotation. This sounds better: "How do you feel about allowing defendants accused of crimes to plead 'not guilty by reason of insanity'? Would you say you are strongly in favor, in favor, undecided, opposed, or strongly opposed?" Using other people's questions for inspiration, you see, does not mean you have to copy exactly, although that is perfectly acceptable. Sudman and Bradburn (1982) say it is not only acceptable, but preferable. If you can find a question that has been used previously and that suits your purpose, use it. It will enable you to compare your results with those obtained in prior research. The third thing to note about the preceding outline is that there is (or should be) a reason behind each entry. If you cannot think of a reason why a person's age might be related to his or her attitude toward the insanity defense, then do not ask people how old they are. It will only take up time and the answers you obtain will never be used. Finally, note that the outline indicates that you are going to have to ask respondents several different *types* of questions: questions about their attitudes toward the insanity defense, questions about their knowledge (what is the definition of insanity?), questions about specific beliefs (does punishment deter crime?), questions about demographic characteristics (what was the highest grade in school you completed?), and questions about their general orientation to life. That mixture of question types is actually a good thing. It will help keep the respondents' interest and attention throughout the interview.

Having decided on the research issue of greatest interest, you can start writing questions. In Figure 1, there is a first draft of an interview schedule derived from the outline. Note that it begins with an introductory statement telling the respondents the general topic you will be asking them about and also telling them approximately how long the interview will take. In this particular case, it should not take long at all. If you think it will be obvious whether the respondent is male or female, then you do not need to ask about that. You can simply note it on the interview schedule. If you were planning to conduct the interview over the telephone, that might not be safe. Then you would need to ask. Note also that it is better not to start off with the other demographic questions (educational level, religious preference, and occupation) because those might be items about which some respondents are a little sensitive. With such items, it is better to put them later in the interview, after the respondent has relaxed and some rapport with the interviewer has developed. Remember, every item on the interview schedule or questionnaire should be directly traceable to one of the entries on the outline of research questions. In Figure 1, the numbers and letters in the right margin indicate the research question to which each item pertains.

Before proceeding, take a moment and look at the items in Figure 1

Date of Interview: _____

Time Interview Started: _____

HELLO! I'M _____ FROM FAR OUT STATE COL-
LEGE. WE ARE CONDUCTING A BRIEF OPINION POLL AND WOULD
VERY MUCH APPRECIATE IT IF YOU WOULD ANSWER A FEW QUES-
TIONS. WE ARE INTERESTED IN FINDING OUT HOW PEOPLE FEEL
ABOUT THE USE OF THE INSANITY DEFENSE IN CRIMINAL TRIALS
AND ALSO A LITTLE ABOUT THEIR GENERAL BELIEFS ABOUT
OTHERS. THE QUESTIONS I WOULD LIKE TO ASK YOU WILL ONLY
TAKE ABOUT 5 OR 10 MINUTES OF YOUR TIME AND YOUR ANSWERS
WILL REMAIN COMPLETELY ANONYMOUS. DO YOU HAVE ANY
QUESTIONS?

1. How do you feel about allowing defendants accused of crimes to plead   (I)
"not guilty by reason of insanity?" Would you say you are:
____ strongly in favor   ____ strongly opposed
____ in favor   ____ undecided
____ opposed

2. It has been suggested that a person's mental state at the time a crime   (I)
is committed is irrelevant to the question of whether or not the person is
guilty of committing the crime. Do you
____ strongly agree   ____ strongly disagree
____ agree   ____ neither agree nor disagree
____ disagree

3. In a few words, what do you think is the legal definition of insanity?   (IA2)

4. Currently, when a person is found "not guilty by reason of insanity,"   (IA1)
which of the following do you think is most likely to happen to that
person?
____ set free (A)   IF C OR D, ASK:
____ put on probation (B)   How long do you think they would be
____ confined in a mental   kept there?
institution (C)
____ sent to jail (D)   _____

Figure 1 AN INTERVIEW SCHEDULE. This schedule was prepared for the
collection of data on attitudes toward defendants' use of the insanity plea in criminal
proceedings.

5. Do you believe that punishment, or the threat of punishment, serves as   (IA4)
a deterrent to crime?

_____ yes   _____ no   _____ undecided

NOW I WOULD LIKE TO READ YOU FOUR STATEMENTS. YOU
TELL ME WHETHER YOU STRONGLY AGREE, AGREE,
DISAGREE, STRONGLY DISAGREE, OR ARE UNDECIDED AFTER
EACH.

6. An individual's worth often passes unrecognized no matter how hard he   (IA3)
or she tries.

_____ strongly agree   _____ disagree
_____ agree   _____ strongly disagree
_____ undecided

7. The average person is largely the master of his or her own fate.   (IA3)

_____ strongly agree   _____ disagree
_____ agree   _____ strongly disagree
_____ undecided

8. If you act in good faith toward people, almost all of them will recipro-   (IB1)
cate with fairness toward you.

_____ strongly agree   _____ disagree
_____ agree   _____ strongly disagree
_____ undecided

9. If you give the average person a job and leave him to do it, he will   (IB1)
finish it successfully.

_____ strongly agree   _____ disagree
_____ agree   _____ strongly disagree
_____ undecided

Figure 1   *(Continued)*

a little more closely. You will see that in addition to variations in question
focus, that is, attitudes, beliefs, knowledge, and demographics, there are
also several variations in question form. There are two open-ended questions (3 and 11). There are STATEMENTS[1] to which respondents will be asked
to respond with one of five alternatives ranging from "strongly agree" to
"strongly disagree." There are also a couple of CONTINGENCY QUESTIONS (4
and 12), questions that are asked only when the respondent answers the

[1]When several items of this type concern the same topic, as items 6 and 7 or 8 and 9 in Figure
1, the responses to those items may be combined to form what is referred to as a LIKERT
SCALE. More about this later in this chapter.

FINALLY I WOULD LIKE TO ASK YOU A COUPLE OF QUESTIONS ABOUT YOURSELF.

10. Are you currently employed, either full or part time?   (IB2)

_____ yes   _____ no

11. What kind of work do you do (did you do on your last regular job)?   (IB2)

_____

12. What is your religious preference? Is it Protestant, Catholic, Jewish,   (IIC)
some other religion, or no religion?

_____ Protestant   _____ none
_____ Catholic   _____ other (ASK WHAT.)
_____ Jewish   _____

IF PROTESTANT, ASK WHAT DENOMINATION.

_____ Baptist   _____ Presbyterian
_____ Methodist   _____ Episcopalian
_____ Lutheran   _____ other (ASK WHAT.)
                                    _____

13. What was the highest grade in school you completed?   (IIA)

_____

(NOTE RESPONDENTS SEX) _____ male   _____ female   (IIB)

THAT'S ALL. THANKS VERY MUCH FOR YOUR HELP.

Time Interview Ended: _____

Figure 1 *(Concluded)*

preceeding question in a certain way. As with question focus, a little variety in question form helps keep the respondent, and the interviewer, from getting bored.

Once you have a rough draft of your interview schedule in hand, complete with instructions to the interviewer, the next step is to try it out on a few people. Technically, this is referred to as PRETESTING. The point is to find out whether those questions, which may seem crystal clear and letter perfect to you, are intelligible to others (see Figure 2). If the first few people you try the questions on end up asking a lot of questions in return about what you really mean, chances are you need to rewrite the

Figure 2 WHY ARE YOU HERE AND WHAT DO YOU WANT? The introductory comments to a respondent are very important. To avoid misunderstandings introductory comments should convey, clearly and concisely, exactly why you are there and what will be expected from the respondent. (Cartoon © Clarence Brown.)

questions. Babbie (1973) has noted that many "no answer" or "undecided" responses is another clue to problems with a particular question. For example, it might be that question 5 in Figure 1 will produce a lot of "undecided" responses because some people do not know the meaning of *deterrent*. Babbie also noted that qualified answers and spontaneous unsolicited comments about questions and response alternatives are sure signs of trouble. However, one thing you do *not* want is for everybody to answer the questions in precisely the same way. That may sound a little surprising. But think about it for a moment. If you are interested in explaining why people are negative toward the use of the insanity defense, what you are really interested in is explaining how people who are negative *differ from* people who are positive. So, you have to have data from some people who are positive in order to see what they are like (and how they differ from those who are negative). What you want, then, is for your questions to produce some *variability* in responses, and a pretest can tell you if they are doing that. There will be more on this point under "Explanatory Analysis," but first let us examine some of the options available for collecting information about attitudes toward the insanity defense.

Types of Surveys

Once you have decided on the questions you are going to ask and if your questions have survived, or been revised in light of, pretesting, you still have several decisions to make. Actually, the decisions would probably have been made—implicitly, at least—while you were in the process of thinking through your research questions. But for purposes of exposition, pretend that you have not yet given any thought to them. As you will see, if you were really doing a survey, that would mean you would be in for a lot of revisions on your questionnaire at this point.

The first decision involves the form your survey will take. There are basically three options: face-to-face interviews, a self-administered questionnaire, and a telephone survey. For a long time, when someone mentioned survey, it was assumed they were referring to a series of face-to-face interviews with each of a number of people, the respondents. In the last few years, however, questionnaires received through the mail or found in magazines and places of business have become so commonplace that they may be replacing the face-to-face interview as the typical example of surveys. In any event, each of the three options has certain advantages and disadvantages. To help you remember them, they are organized below under three headings: expense, nature of the questions that can be asked, and potential biases.

Expense. In terms of expense, the questionnaire that you mail, or hand out to a group of people, is clearly superior to, that is, cheaper than, a series of face-to-face interviews. It is also usually less expensive than telephone interviews, unless you plan on doing all the telephone interviews yourself and call only people in your local dialing area. Not too long ago, some friends of mine and I (Jones, Wekstein, & Morris, 1985) sent a brief, two-page questionnaire to 180 people. Our total costs were a box of envelopes, a ream of paper, two mimeo stencils, $72 in postage, a little time licking stamps, and a couple of paper cuts. To have gone out into the community and tracked each of those people down would have been much more time-consuming and strenuous. There are exceptions, of course, but when they are feasible, self-administered questionnaires are the cheapest source of survey data, even if you have to pay postage both ways.

Questions. Why not just call up those 180 people and interview them over the telephone? That would have saved envelopes and stamps. Good question, and it brings me to my second point. The decision about whether to use questionnaires or face-to-face interviews or telephone interviews depends in part on the kinds of questions you plan to ask. In our study, we asked the respondents to rate each of 73 different items on a seven-point scale. That would have been a very tedious telephone conversation, not to mention the problem the respondents would have had keeping the seven-point rating scale in mind. Chances are we would have heard a lot of receivers slam down on about item 28 or so. Thus, we opted for a questionnaire in which respondents could see the scale right there in front of them as they were rating each item.

Generally, the face-to-face interview is the most flexible in terms of the types of questions that can be asked. Open-ended questions are no problem at all, of course. With a well-trained, relaxed interviewer, they often sound like spontaneous conversation. With closed-ended questions having several response alternatives, the interviewer can hand the respondent a card with the answer options printed on it, as in Figure 3A. It is also best to ask knowledge questions in face-to-face interviews. Filling out a questionnaire in the privacy of his or her home, a respondent might be tempted to look up the answer before proceeding. A variety of props can be used to test knowledge or preferences or both in the interview. To test geographical knowledge, the respondents can be shown a map and asked to label the parts (Figure 3B). To test musical knowledge, they can be played a tape and asked to name the composer. Pictures and products can be displayed and preferences, esthetic and otherwise, solicited. In contrast to this high level of flexibility, the mail or self-administered questionnaire is rather constrained in terms of question format. There, open-ended questions have to be kept to a minimum because people do not like to write out long answers. Complex contingency questions should be avoided, if possible, because they are likely to be skipped or misunderstood. And the appearance of the questionnaire itself is *very* important. An attractive, brief, well laid out questionnaire with lots of white space that looks like it would be a snap to answer is, in fact, much more likely to be answered.

It should be clear by now why you cannot wait until your questions are completely formulated to decide what type of survey to conduct. Question form and survey type are intimately related. What might work well in an interview could be a disaster in a self-administered questionnaire. The ordering of questions also needs to be considered in light of the type of survey you plan to conduct. For an interview, the questions should start

STRONGLY IN FAVOR

MODERATELY IN FAVOR

DON'T CARE

MODERATELY OPPOSED

STRONGLY OPPOSED

DON'T KNOW

(A)

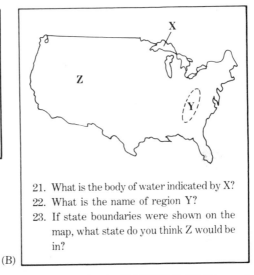

21. What is the body of water indicated by X?
22. What is the name of region Y?
23. If state boundaries were shown on the map, what state do you think Z would be in?

(B)

Figure 3 PROPS USED IN THE FACE-TO-FACE INTERVIEW. (A) The card with the response options is handed to the respondent to help him or her keep all options in mind when making a choice. (B) The outline map is shown to the respondent who then is asked a series of questions about it.

off nonthreatening, interesting, and, perhaps, open-ended. For a self-administered questionnaire, the initial questions should be brief, closed-ended, and easy to answer.

Biases. Although the self-administered questionnaire is usually the least expensive form for collecting survey data and the face-to-face interview is the most flexible, they each have their biases. With the interview, most of the problems stem from the fact that the interview is a social occasion, as was discussed in Chapter Five. The advantages of having a live, intelligent (presumably) interviewer on the scene are great, however. He or she can note things that are difficult to ask, such as the respondent's apparent mood and the condition of his or her clothes and surroundings. With a mail questionnaire, the greatest problem, in addition to the constraints on question format already discussed, is the fact that many people will not return the questionnaire. Then you are faced with the issue of whether those who did return it are different in some way from those who did not. If they are, you will have an unrepresentative group of respondents and any conclusions based on such a group would be suspect because of a NONRESPONSE BIAS (see page 186). With both face-to-face and telephone interviews, the problem of nonresponse is somewhat less than

Issues and Discussions ━━━━━━━━━━━━━━━━━━━━━━━━━━━━

SELF-SELECTION AND BIASED SAMPLES

A SELF-SELECTED SAMPLE is one in which the respondents themselves decide who will and who will not be in the sample. Such samples might arise by the respondents seeking out the opportunity to be included or by their refusing to be included. Many magazines, for example, include questionnaires on various subjects from time to time and ask their readers to take a few minutes to fill out the questionnaire and mail it in. For several reasons, the results from such surveys should be regarded with suspicion, First, most magazines appeal only to particular types of readers. *Cosmopolitan* and *Fortune* are not oriented to the same audiences, neither are *Time* and *Rolling Stone*. Thus, the people who see a questionnaire in a magazine are already unrepresentative of the general population. They are only representative of people who seek out exposure to that particular magazine. Second, it is very doubtful that the results of such surveys are even representative of the opinions and attitudes of the readers of the magazine in question. Most people who buy the magazine will not bother to fill out the questionnaire. Further, chances are that at least some of those who go to the trouble of filling out the questionnaire will never get around to mailing it. Thus, when the results of the survey appear in a later issue of the magazine, they are likely to consist of the opinions and attitudes of those readers of the magazine who (1) are most interested in the topic, (2) have the least to do, and (3) happened to have a stamp handy.

Usually, it is difficult to know *exactly* how much bias is introduced by self-selection. That that bias can be quite dramatic, however, is illustrated by the following. Three days before the November 1983 elections, a Lexington, Kentucky television station broadcast a viewer call-in poll. Viewers were invited to call the station and vote for their favorite candidate for lieutenant governor. The three candidates were Steven Beshear, Don Wiggins, and Eugene Stuart. When the telephone vote was tabulated that evening, it looked as if Wiggins would be the next lieutenant governor; he had 50.6 percent of the vote. Three days later, when the real vote was tabulated, there was indeed a landslide – 63.4 percent for the winner, Steven Beshear. Wiggins got less than 1 percent of the vote.

Ultimately, of course, no one can or should be coerced into responding to a survey or questionnaire. So, there is always the chance that response rates of less than 100 percent reflect some degree of self-selection of the sample into responders and non responders.

with a mail questionnaire. People apparently find it much more difficult to say no to an interviewer than to throw a questionnaire in the trash.

In addition to the issue of survey format, that is, questionnaire versus interviews, there is another design decision that is intimately related to the research questions providing the motivation for a survey. That is, do you want to trace changes over time in the variables of interest? If not, you will be conducting what is referred to as a CROSS-SECTIONAL SURVEY in which data are collected at one point in time to describe and/or explain something at that time. For example, in November 1983 the *New York Times* conducted a telephone survey of 1309 adult men and women (Dowd, 1983). Respondents were asked questions about whether or not they worked outside the home, how much they liked their jobs, if they had ever been discriminated against in the workplace, and other items such as how working affected their parental roles and responsibilities. In connection with the latter issue, the poll found that 59 percent of the females thought that women employed outside the home were just as good, or better, mothers than women not employed outside the home. Only 44 percent of the males interviewed held that view. Another example of a cross-sectional survey is the study, mentioned earlier, by Hans and Slater (1983). Between June 28 and July 1, 1982, they conducted telephone interviews with 434 men and women from New Castle County, Delaware. Only a week prior to that John Hinckley, Jr. had been found not guilty by reason of insanity of the attempted assassination of President Reagan. Hans and Slater were interested in reactions to that particular trial and verdict. They found that 65.7 percent of the respondents did not think Hinckley was insane, 87.1 percent thought the insanity defense was a loophole, but only one respondent (out of 434) knew the legal definition of insanity. The cross-sectional survey is by far the most frequently encountered variety, and, as Babbie (1973) has noted, if your goal is one-time description, it is for you. It provides a snapshot in time, a capsule of information about what the respondents have to say right now, today.

However, there are many research questions for which a LONGITUDINAL STUDY is required, a study that gives you information about changes over time. For example, suppose you were interested in how getting married affects social relationships with same-sex peers. The popular stereotype is that when people get married they gradually, or abruptly, quit going out with the boys (and the girls). You could try examining the issue with a cross-sectional survey by selecting some respondents who were married and some who were not and asking them all about how frequently they see their friends. If you did and if you found that those who are married had fewer friends or saw their friends less often or both, you still would not be able to say that their getting married was the reason for that. Someone would quickly point out that the married people may have had fewer friends before they got married. In fact, it is entirely possible they got married because they were lonely.

You need to do a PANEL STUDY (Markus, 1979) to answer questions involving changes over time. Select a group of respondents, all of whom are single, and interview them about their friends: "How many friends do you have?" "How often do you see them?" "Do you enjoy being around them?" Then, at some later point in time, you interview *exactly the same people* again. Presumably, in the interval some of them will have gotten married. If the newlyweds now see their friends less often, you will be in a much better position to argue that getting married produced the decrease. Of course, if it turns out that on the second round of interviews even the confirmed singles are seeing less of their friends, you are going to have to look for another cause for the general decrease in sociability. Maybe everyone is working overtime to keep their standard of living up. Panel studies tend to be quite time-consuming, as you probably can guess from this example. You might have to wait a long time for any sizable number of the initial group to get married. There is also the danger that you might not be able to reinterview all the initial group: Some may move and leave no forwarding address; some may die; some may simply refuse to be interviewed a second time. The problem is referred to as panel ATTRITION, that is, loss of part of the original group of respondents at the second or third round of interviewing. If there is some systematic reason for panel attrition, you end up with a biased sample. Another potential problem with panel studies, especially when the waves of interviews are fairly close together, is that answers the second time may be affected by the fact that the respondents just answered all those questions not too long ago. Unfortunately, a great deal more than just their answers may be affected, as you can see from the Discussion on the next page.

Given the expense and effort involved in keeping track of all the members of a panel, it is sometimes possible to employ a substitute design that will still let you examine issues of change over time. In a panel study, the *same* sample of respondents from a given population is contacted repeatedly. In a COHORT STUDY, *different* samples from a given population are contacted (Glenn, 1977). For example, using the questionnaire in Figure 1, you might want to examine how attitudes toward the use of the insanity defense change with increasing education. You could interview a sample of tenth graders, wait two years, and interview those same people again. If you did that, you would have conducted a panel study. However, it would be easier to interview, simultaneously, a sample of tenth and twelfth graders from the same schools. If you did the latter, you would have conducted a cohort study. But, be sure to note the hidden assumption. That is, you have to assume that in the two years since the current twelfth graders were tenth graders, there have been no changes in the general population of tenth graders. You have to assume that the tenth graders of today are just like the tenth graders of two years ago. It is because subtle changes may occur in the total population over time that cohort studies can be a little tricky. The tenth graders of today may not be like

SOME UNINTENDED EFFECTS OF ASKING QUESTIONS

An assumption that seems to be shared by most survey researchers is that survey research itself has no impact on the life of the typical respondent. At most, there may be a small inconvenience due to the time taken up answering questions. Aside from that, there is usually very little, if any, concern about what taking part in a survey will do to the respondent.

Some research by Rubin and Mitchell (1976) has suggested that this assumption about lack of impact needs to be examined more closely. Rubin and Mitchell reported some research on the development of relationships between dating couples. The research began in 1972. Several hundred couples were recruited and asked, individually, to fill out lengthy questionnaires about a wide range of experiences, attitudes, sex, and other events bearing on their relationships. The couples were then contacted again a year to 18 months later and asked a number of additional questions about how their relationships had changed since the initial participation.

At the time of the initial contact, in 1972, all of the couples described themselves as dating or going together. By 1974, 20 percent of the couples were married, 45 percent had broken up, and 35 percent were still dating. When asked about whether participation in the initial questionnaire session had had any impact on their relationship, 46 percent of the females and 47 percent of the males said that taking part in the survey had indeed had an effect. Rubin and Mitchell suggested that there are two ways in which this occurred, via processes of definition and processes of disclosure. Processes of definition occur on an individual level. As a result of taking part in the study, questions were raised in each person's own mind about exactly how they felt about the other person and the relationship. Processes of disclosure occur on a dyadic level. That is, after taking part in the initial study couples discussed the questions and their answers with each other. In fact, on the follow-up questionnaire, 89 percent of the females and 86 percent of the males reported that they had discussed their answers to the earlier questionnaire with their partners. Thus, areas of potential conflict were more likely to be brought to the surface than they would have been had the couples not taken part in the study.

Rubin and Mitchell also noted that by setting in motion the processes of definition and disclosure, the study pushed participants toward outcomes, such as breaking up, that would otherwise have taken much longer or, perhaps, never occurred at all. They questioned whether letting subjects know at the outset that such effects *might* occur would have been appropriate. The problem with such an informed consent procedure, of course, is that emphasizing the potential impact of the study in advance could well have had a self-fulfilling prophecy effect. But, it is clear that you need to consider the possibility that simply being asked certain questions may have a long-term effect on people.

the tenth graders of two, or twenty, years ago. If the population has changed, any comparison between cohorts will be confounded with those changes.

There are other ways to approximate the kinds of longitudinal information that you can obtain with a panel study without going to all the time and effort required to conduct a long-term study. You might, for example, be able to find an earlier study that asked questions similar to the ones you are interested in. You can then compare your results with those earlier results. In her discussion of the *New York Times* survey mentioned earlier, Dowd (1983) did just that. She compared the results obtained in November 1983 with the results from a 1970 survey sponsored by Virginia Slims. In 1970, 53 percent of the women surveyed cited motherhood as "one of the best parts of being a woman." In 1983, only 26 percent of the women said that. When you do try to use previously collected data to compare to your own, ask yourself the following questions: Are the samples of respondents really similar for the two surveys? Are the questions they were asked sufficiently similar to allow comparison? If the answer to either of these is no, the comparison will not be very informative.

To summarize, then, there are two basic design decisions to be made when contemplating a survey. First, will you interview each respondent in person or use a questionnaire or interview the respondents over the telephone? Second, will you try to trace changes over time or not? The answers to both of these questions, of course, are determined to a large extent by your purpose in conducting the survey, that is, by what you hope to learn. And, unless you are interested in simply describing the attributes of a sample, what you hope to learn by conducting a survey usually revolves around how to explain the relationship between two or more variables. Thus, a few words are in order about explanatory analysis. Data do many things, but they rarely speak for themselves.

Explanatory Analysis

To explain a phenomenon means to give a reason for it, to make it comprehensible. It is something people do, or try to do, all the time; and there is nothing particularly esoteric about the process of explanatory analysis in survey research. To get a feel for what is involved, let us work through a simple example.

Suppose that you had administered the interview schedule in Figure 1 to a sample of 50 male and 50 female respondents and found that 78 percent of them were indeed opposed or strongly opposed to allowing those accused of crimes to plead not guilty by reason of insanity. That, of course, is a purely descriptive piece of information. It tells you something about an attribute of your respondents, that is, the majority of them have a negative attitude toward the use of the insanity defense. Your first thought might be to see if that is true for both males and females. To do that, you can construct a CONTINGENCY TABLE, which is simply a format that allows you to inspect the relationships among variables. Like this:

Attitude	Males (%)	Females (%)
Opposed	80	76
In favor	16	18
Undecided	4	6

What this particular contingency table does is let you see the relationship between sex of the respondent and attitude toward the insanity defense. In other words, it lets you see the extent to which attitude toward the insanity defense is *contingent upon* or *depends on* the sex of the respondent. As you can see, sex does not appear to make much difference. Both males and females are predominantly opposed. If you consider the 50 males and 50 females to be one sample of 100, the technical term for what has been done in the above table is a SUBGROUP ANALYSIS. That is, you have examined the relationship between being a member of a particular subgroup of the sample (males versus females) and the variable of interest (attitude toward the insanity defense). Another way of saying this is that the sample has been STRATIFIED by sex.

In the preceding case, the subgroup analysis yielded some additional descriptive information. Now you know that the vast majority of *both* males and females in the sample are opposed to the use of the insanity defense. But, you still do not have an inkling as to why. As you might have guessed, however, subgroup analysis is the key to that question, why? As Babbie (1973) has pointed out, subgroup analysis is typically motivated by the expectation that the stratification variable will provide an explanation for the phenomenon of interest. Try it. Think back to the early discussion of formulating the research questions to be addressed in the schedule depicted in Figure 1. Someone apparently had a hunch that people who oppose the use of the insanity defense might erroneously believe that those found not guilty by reason of insanity would be set free. The specific question written to get some data on this hypothesis is Question 4 in Figure 1. Now that the results are in, you can check on the fate of the hunch. To do so, collapse the four response alternatives to Question 4 into two by combining those that indicate a belief that the guilty will go free ("set free" and "put on probation") and those that indicate a belief that the guilty will spend some time off the streets ("confined to a mental institution" and "sent to jail"). Then you array the data in a contingency table with, possibly, this result:

Attitude Toward Insanity Defense	Belief About Disposition	
	SET FREE/PROBATION (%)	JAIL/MENTAL HOSPITAL (%)
Oppose	89.2	25.0
Favor	10.8	62.5
Undecided	0.0	12.5

It appears that there was something to the hypothesis. About 90 percent of those who believe the insanity defense lets the guilty go free oppose its use. In contrast, of those who believe defendants found not guilty by reason of insanity will be incarcerated, 62.5 percent favor use of the insanity defense. Of course, these data are hypothetical. But should the results actually have turned out as depicted in the table, you would have gone a long way toward explaining why so many people are opposed to the insanity defense. At least part of the *reason* for their opposition seems to be that they believe that it lets the guilty go free.

There may well be other reasons why someone would oppose the use of the insanity defense. As noted previously, one of the nice things about doing survey research is that you can check on several different explanations for a phenomenon at one time. For example, in the interview schedule in Figure 1, there are two items (6 and 7) that were included in order to explore the possibility that those most opposed to the insanity defense might be staunch believers in individual responsibility. The hypothesis in this case was that their strong belief in individual responsibility causes them to oppose the use of the insanity defense. But the real purpose in including these items was to illustrate the notion of an INDEX. To create an index you simply combine the answers to two or more related questions. With the answers to Questions 6 and 7 in Figure 1, you can create an index of belief in individual responsibility. First, note that the items are *reversed*, that is, someone with a strong belief in individual responsibility is likely to disagree with Question 6 and agree with Question 7. The purpose of reversing items on a questionnaire or on an interview schedule is not to trick the respondents but to help prevent them from falling into a tendency to agree, or disagree, with questions that they have not listened to carefully. So, in constructing the index, you must be sure to reverse the scoring on some of the items. Here, for the answers to Question 6, you would assign a 1 to "strongly agree," a 2 to "agree," a 3 to "undecided," and so on. For the answers to Question 7, you would assign a 1 to "strongly disagree," a 2 to "disagree," and . . . ; you get the picture. Then, for each respondent, you simply add their two numbers together.

Someone who strongly disagrees with Question 6 and strongly agrees with Question 7 is a firm believer in individual responsibility and will receive a score of 10 on the index. Someone who strongly agrees with Question 6 and strongly disagrees with Question 7 does not believe in individual responsibility and will receive a score of 2 on the index.

There are basically two reasons why you might want to create a single index out of the responses to two or more items. First, an index often helps create variability. Earlier it was mentioned that to relate differences on some attribute to the phenomenon of interest, you first have to establish that people do differ on that attribute. An index can help you do that. For example, suppose that instead of Questions 6 and 7 in Figure 1, you had simply asked 100 people, "Do you believe in individual responsibility? Yes or no?" At best, you would then have been able to separate the 100 people into two categories, believers and nonbelievers. But, by asking two questions, each with five response options, and then combining the answers, you can spread those people out along a scale that runs from 2 (definite nonbelievers) to 10 (definite believers) and make finer distinctions among them. I would expect that persons scoring 10 on this scale would differ considerably in the firmness or certainty of their belief about individual responsibility from persons scoring 6. But, both subgroups would have been lumped into the Yes category with the one question–two alternatives approach. As a result, any differences in the consequences of their differing beliefs would have been obscured.

The second reason for constructing an index is that many concepts are simply too complex to be captured with a single question. You may need several questions, each worded somewhat differently, but all attempting to assess the variable of interest. For example, one of the problems that plagues survey researchers and personnel officers alike is the tendency of some people to be so concerned about winning the approval of others that they are not as honest as they should be in answering questions. The bias that this produces is referred to as the SOCIAL DESIRABILITY BIAS, and Crowne and Marlowe (1964) constructed a 33-item questionnaire to measure it. Some of their questions, each of which is to be answered "true" or "false," are listed below. The letter in parentheses beside each one indicates the socially desirable answer.

(T) I have never intensely disliked anyone.
(F) I like to gossip at times.
(T) I always try to practice what I preach.
(T) I never hesitate to go out of my way to help someone in trouble.
(F) On occasion I have had doubts about my ability to succeed in life.

To arrive at the index, one point is scored for each response in the socially desirable direction. Thus, a person's score can vary from 0 (a real shoot-from-the-hip-type) to 33 (Goody Two-Shoes). One thing to note in this, and in the earlier example, is that each of the items to be combined into the index was given equal weight. There are procedures for constructing and analyzing scales with items that differ in relative strength or extremity, but such procedures are seldom used and would probably not be of much use to you. However, if you are interested, a good source on the topic is Dawes (1972).

Regardless of whether you construct an index or simply divide your sample on the basis of their answers to the single question, subgroup analysis is the key to explaining relationships among variables. The presence of negative attitudes toward the insanity defense was explained by showing that they stemmed, at least in part, from a belief that the insanity defense lets the guilty go free. People without this belief tended to have a more positive attitude. Note that it would not have worked the other way. It would be very hard to argue that the negative attitude produced the specific belief that the insanity defense lets the guilty go free. But it is entirely plausible that that belief could have produced a negative attitude.

Thus, the final point to be made here is the following. Any time you plan on stratifying a sample for the purpose of explanation, you need to think carefully about which variable is the cause (the INDEPENDENT VARIABLE) and which the effect (the DEPENDENT VARIABLE). That determination, in the example, was based purely on logic and quite often that is all you will have to go on. You will have to make a case that A could plausibly cause B, and, unless your logic is sound, people will argue with you about it. There are some instances in which the time relationship between the two variables will help you decide which is the independent and which the dependent variable. That is, if the values of one variable occur prior to or are determined before the values of the second variable, then the one whose values are determined first can only be the independent variable. For example, although there may be some controversy about the clarity of the evidence that smoking causes cancer (Eysenck, 1980), *nobody* would believe that cancer causes smoking because smoking comes first, cancer later. Similarly, good high school grades *may* lead to acceptance at the college of your choice. But acceptance at the college of your choice usually comes too late to produce good high school grades. However, even when there is a clear time order to the variables of interest, you still have to be able to make a reasonable argument for how the first causes the second.

Sampling

It is always nice to find a way of doing things that will save you time and energy, provided that you do not sacrifice quality in the process. In survey research, sampling is just such a time and energy saver. Furthermore, when done properly, it not only does not sacrifice quality, it may actually improve the quality of the data obtained. To show you why this is so, the first order of business is to define a few terms.

In any survey, the focal group about which we want to learn something is referred to as the POPULATION OF INTEREST. Suppose the population is composed of individual people, in which case each person is considered to be an ELEMENT of the population. An element of the population is also referred to as the UNIT OF ANALYSIS, the unit about which information is to be obtained and conclusions drawn. For example, the National Park Service conducts periodic surveys to help them plan changes in the facilities that they provide for the public (New York Times News Service, 1984). The population of interest in this case consists of all potential users of the National Park System. The elements, or units of analysis, of course, are individual persons. But it is not always the case that individuals are the units of analysis. You might be interested in the relationship between family composition and socioeconomic status, in which case families would be the units of analysis – even though you might obtain all your information about each family from only one family member.

Now, if the population of interest to you is fairly small, you are in luck. You simply administer your questionnaire, or interview schedule, to all of them. If you want to know how the people on your block feel about that proposal to route an interstate through the neighborhood, you can make up your questions and poll everybody on the block. Usually, however, the populations of interest in survey research are somewhat larger and more geographically dispersed. Thus, it is very difficult to contact each and every member of the population. So, what is typically done is that a relatively small portion, a SAMPLE, of the population is contacted. That National Park Service survey mentioned a moment ago did not contact *all* potential users of the National Park System. That would have meant interviewing tens of millions of people. They probably would have had to close down all the parks to get the necessary workers to do that many interviews, and then it would have taken years. They did not do that. What they did was to interview a national sample of 5757 people between September 1982 and June 1983. Thus, sampling can save you time and energy by decreasing the number of people you have to interview. That means fewer interviewers to be trained and monitored, assuming you were not planning to do it all yourself. It also means that money is saved and the study can be completed in a more reasonable period of time.

The danger, of course, is that the preferences of those 5757 people – 26 percent of whom liked to jog – may differ from the preferences of the population of potential park users. The Park Service would not want to spend a lot of time and money putting in jogging trails if only 2 or 3 percent of the park-goers use them.[2] More generally the question is, how representative is your sample of the population as a whole? Is the distribution of attributes, opinions, and beliefs in the sample the same as their distribution in the population? Are the relationships among variables in the sample the same as in the population? Representativeness is *the* major issue in sampling, and the reason for its importance is simple. You want to be able to make inferences about the population as a whole based on what you find to be true of the sample. If the sample is biased in some way, then your conclusions about the population are likely to be incorrect.

In the Discussions on page 186 it was pointed out that one way in which unrepresentative samples can arise is via self-selection – members of the potential sample separating themselves into responders and nonresponders. Instead of the sample that you wanted, you get those people most interested in the topic, those who had time to fill out the questionnaire, and those who happened to have a stamp with which to mail it. And do not be awed by sheer numbers of responders. Recently, *Playboy* magazine published the results of a survey of current sexual practices and attitudes in the United States (Petersen, 1983). It was announced that over 100,000 respondents had taken part in the survey, that is, they filled out a questionnaire that appeared in the January 1982 issue of *Playboy* and mailed it in. By way of comparison, it was pointed out that in Kinsey's famous studies in the 1940s only 5940 women (Kinsey, Pomeroy, & Martin, 1948; Kinsey, Pomeroy, Martin, & Gebhard, 1953) and 5300 men participated and that Shere Hite's reports on female and male sexuality (Hite, 1976, 1981) were based on only 3019 females and 7239 males. But, the fact remains that, despite 100,000-plus respondents, the readers of *Playboy* are an unrepresentative sample of the adult population of the United States; and, quite likely, the 100,000 respondents are even an unrepresentative sample of the readers of *Playboy*. Similarly, the 90,000-plus women who responded to Ann Landers's sex survey in January 1985 were hardly a representative sample. The fact that 72 percent of the respondents preferred affection and cuddling to *the act* is interesting but not very informative about the preferences of the population of American Women.

So, how are you to obtain a representative sample? The first thing to do, of course, is to decide on the population of interest. Then, one way to proceed is to construct what is referred to as a SAMPLING FRAME, a list of each element in the population. If the population of interest to you consists of students enrolled at your college, then the sampling frame is a list

---

[2]There is another danger here, even if the preferences of the population were accurately reflected in the preferences of the sample. That is, there is quite a difference between saying you like to jog and actually getting out and pounding the pavement. The problem is that of the discrepancy between words and deeds (Deutscher, 1966; Dillehay, 1973), and it is one that you need to be especially sensitive to in survey research.

of the names of all students currently enrolled. That sampling frame would be fairly easy to construct because, presumably, somewhere in the bowels of the registrar's computer, there are all the ingredients. With a little updating – additions for late enrollments, deletions for drops – you could fairly quickly come up with a list in which you had confidence. Other populations are not so easily listed, of course. No one keeps a list of shade tree mechanics or part-time poets or joggers. If such esoteric populations are of interest to you, you may be tempted to settle for what is referred to as a CONVENIENCE SAMPLE: those shade tree mechanics you can find easily, joggers you happen to know. You can often learn a great deal from a convenience sample. Just be sure you keep in mind that the sample may be completely unrepresentative (Kruskal & Mosteller, 1981). That means you should always preface any comments about it with something like, "The four joggers I was able to talk to one Saturday over in Middleton Park said . . . ."

But, suppose you are able to construct a sampling frame fairly directly. You have a list of all the registered voters in your county or all Mercedes owners in the state or all soccer players in your school district who drive green mopeds or whatever other peculiar population has piqued your interest. Now what? You select your sample from that list, of course, but you have to select it in such a way that every name on the list has an equal chance of being included in the sample. Your sample will then be a RANDOM SAMPLE of the population. If there are 2000 names on your list, for example, and you want a sample of 200, you might select every tenth name. In this case, you would refer to the sample as a SYSTEMATIC RANDOM SAMPLE with a SAMPLING INTERVAL of 10 because you selected every tenth name. Or, you might write each of the numbers from 1 through 2000 on little slips of paper, put them all in a box, and draw out 200. You then take the names from your list that correspond to the numbers as your sample. In this case, you would have a SIMPLE RANDOM SAMPLE. You could also use a table of random numbers, which will be described in Chapter 9, to select your sample.

For scientific purposes, convenience samples are not usually acceptable because they usually are unrepresentative. But it is also true that it is often an almost impossible task to construct a sampling frame that lists every element in the population. Fortunately, sampling frames can be devised that do not require you to list every single element in the population. This method is referred to as MULTISTAGE CLUSTER SAMPLING. Essentially what you do is divide the population into segments, or clusters, of elements. Then you take a sample of clusters. That means you only have to list the elements in the clusters that are in your sample, not every element in the entire population. You then take a sample of the elements from each cluster included in your initial (cluster sampling) stage. For example, if you were interested in the population of a particular city, you might first divide the city into blocks or groups of blocks that have approximately the same number of residences in each. Next you would take a sample of blocks. Then you would select ten residences, say, from each of the blocks included in your initial sample and interview someone from each of those.

You might even get a little more sophisticated and create what is referred to as a STRATIFIED SAMPLE. For example, suppose that in that population of 2000 that was mentioned earlier there are 800 females and 1200 males and you have reason to believe that sex is an important variable with respect to whatever it is you are interested in–it often is. So, you want to make sure that males and females are included in your sample in appropriate numbers, that is, in proportions that correspond to their presence in the population. You could treat males and females as separate populations and take a 10 percent sample from each. Or, you could just rearrange your sampling frame so that the females are all listed first and then take every 10th name. Either way you would end up with 80 females and 120 males in your sample. When taking a systematic sample like this from your sampling frame, there is one thing to beware of. That is, you need to make sure that your list does not have some sort of periodic ordering that corresponds to your sampling interval or to some multiple of your sampling interval. For example, Mosteller (Kruskal & Mosteller, 1981) revealed that he once found himself sampling every 32nd soldier from roster lists of bunkhouses, each of which contained 32 men. The problem was that the roster lists had been arranged in order by rank. So, taking every thirty-second soldier gave a sample in which everyone had the same rank. The bunkhouse population, however, had a variety of ranks and, hence, the sample was unrepresentative.

There will be more to say about sampling in the chapter on experimentation, where you will be introduced to the notion of quota sampling. But, it is important at this point to have a feel for why the variations on random sampling usually produce a representative sample. The basic notion is really quite simple. The assumption is that when all the elements in a population have an equal chance of being included in the sample, the characteristics of the elements included in the sample should turn out to be about the same–on the average–as the characteristics of all the elements. With a sample of only one or two, of course, that is not a safe assumption; but with larger numbers, it usually is. For now, let us give the preceding discussions of operationalization, explanatory analysis, and sampling a little more focus with an example.

An Illustration: Television Viewing and Fear of Crime

In 1925 a Scotsman named John Baird successfully transmitted a few fuzzy human images via a device that has subsequently come to be known as television. Although not widely available in the United States until the 1950s, the impact of Baird's invention on subsequent generations has been phenomenal. Gerbner and Gross (1976) noted that by the mid-1970s, nearly half of the 12-year-olds in America spent as much time watching TV each day as they did in school.

Of course, there is nothing necessarily wrong with that. Television is a medium for transmitting information, just as books, magazines, teachers, and newspapers are. But there is reason to believe that the picture of reality television presents is a distorted one. As Gerbner and Gross (1976) pointed out:

> Unlike the real world, where personalities are complex, motives unclear, and outcomes ambiguous, television presents a world of clarity and simplicity. In show after show, rewards and punishments follow quickly. Crises are resolved, problems are solved, and justice, or at least authority, always triumphs. . . . In order to complete a story entertainingly in only an hour or even a half hour, conflicts on TV are usually personal and solved by action. Since violence is dramatic, and relatively simple to produce, much of the action tends to be violent. As a result, the stars of primetime network TV have for years been cowboys, detectives, and others whose lives permit unrestrained action.

In fact, a content analysis (Chapter Four) revealed the following about programming on primetime TV. About 20 percent of the males featured were occupied in some form of law enforcement. Care to guess how many adult males are so occupied in real life? Less than 1 percent. There is other evidence that television depicts the world as a more violent place than it really is (Murray & Kippax, 1979). But just think about it from the point of view of your own experience for a moment. How many murders have you, personally, witnessed? And how many have you seen on TV?

It occurred to Gerbner and Gross (1976) that the steady diet of excessive violence that the typical viewer sees on TV might well have an impact on his or her perception of reality. Thus, they asked people about their television viewing habits and a variety of other questions, including how safe they felt and how likely they thought it was that they would be a victim of violence. Television viewers were divided into "light" and "heavy" on the basis of their answers to questions about how much TV they watched each day (not their weight). Heavy viewers were those who watched four or more hours a day; light viewers were glued to the tube for two or fewer hours a day. As anticipated, heavy viewers were not only more distrustful of others, they were much more likely to believe that their chances were higher of being involved in some sort of violent incident in any given week. Gerbner and Gross conclude from this that the relationship between TV watching and fear of violence is direct and causal. As they put it, "We have found that violence on prime-time network television cultivates exaggerated assumptions about the threat of danger in the real world."

Well, maybe. Doob and MacDonald (1979) were not so sure. They pointed out that there was something Gerbner and Gross neglected to consider, something that might account for their result without invoking the notion of a distorted sense of reality among heavy TV viewers. That is, there is evidence that heavy TV watching is inversely related to social class. (You, of course, are an exception.) Generally, the lower the socioeconomic status, the more TV watched. But, there is also evidence that the lower one's socioeconomic status, the more likely you are to live in a neighborhood with a high crime rate. So, it follows that people who watch a lot of television might have a heightened fear of being victimized because, in fact, they live in more dangerous neighborhoods.

While that sounds quite reasonable, some data are required to help decide the issue. To obtain those data, Doob and MacDonald contacted the Metropolitan Toronto Police and found that they have divided the city of Toronto into 210 patrol areas. The patrol areas vary in size, depending, in part, on the number of calls received by the police from the area in question. At the request of Doob and MacDonald, the police identified the 10 patrol areas with the highest number of reported assaults and woundings and the 14 patrol areas with the lowest number of such reports. From these two sets, four geographic areas of approximately equal size were chosen: two from the 10 high-crime areas and two from the 14 low-crime areas. The high-crime areas had a mean rate of assaults of approximately 400 per 100,000 population. The low-crime areas had a mean rate of about 7 per 100,000. Next, within the two high-crime areas 119 and 85 households, respectively, were randomly selected. Similarly, within the low-crime areas, 118 and 86 households, respectively, were randomly selected.

The study took the form of a door-to-door survey. The person answering the door at one of the randomly selected households was asked to list all the persons over 18 years of age living there. One of those persons was then randomly selected—right there, on the spot—and interviewed, or an appointment was made with that person for a later interview. Note that what you have here, then, is a three-stage sampling procedure. In the first stage, areas of the city were purposefully, *not* randomly, selected to represent high- and low-crime areas of approximately equal size. Then, households within those areas were *randomly* selected. Finally, adult individuals within the selected households were *randomly* selected. Thus, the only enumeration of elements necessary was a listing of households in the two high-crime areas and the two low-crime areas. That sort of information can often be obtained from a city directory, a commercially produced book that lists all of the places of residence and mailing addresses in a city. Although the listing of all places of residence in four police patrol areas may seem a little tedious to you, it is a whole lot easier than listing all the places of residence or all the people in a city the size of Toronto.

The individual interviews conducted by Doob and MacDonald took about 45 minutes each to complete. Respondents were first asked to identify all the television programs they had watched during the preceding week. Then they were given a 37-item, fixed-alternatives questionnaire, which included questions tapping their perception of the likelihood that they would be the victims of a crime. They were asked, for example:

> What do you think the chances are that if you were to walk alone at night on the residential streets of your neighborhood each night for a month that you would be the victim of a serious crime?

and

> How likely do you think it is that you or one of your close friends will have their house broken into during the next year?

Taking the data from *all* respondents together, the results replicated the earlier findings by Gerbner and Gross. That is, the more television people watched, the more likely they were to be afraid for their own safety. But, it was indeed the people in the high-crime areas who watched more television – well over 30 hours a week. When the data were examined within each crime area, there was no relationship between the amount of television watched and fear of violence in the low-crime areas. Thus, as Doob and MacDonald (1979) pointed out, it appears that television itself is not the cause of the exaggerated fear of victimization that Gerbner and Gross found earlier. The source of that fear seems to be quite realistic. The people who are most afraid are the ones who live in high-crime areas. They also happen to watch a lot of TV. After all, that is a whole lot safer than walking the streets.

What Doob and MacDonald did, in effect, was a form of subgroup analysis. They demonstrated that the relationship between television viewing and fear of victimization is not causal. The relationship is produced by the fact that those who watch the most television live in high-crime areas. At least, that appears to be so at this point. Doob and MacDonald neglected to provide some vital information, that is, how many people in each of the four patrol areas refused to be interviewed. If differential numbers of people refused in the high- and low-crime areas, Doob and MacDonald may have based their conclusions on biased and, hence, unrepresentative samples of the residents of those areas. They do point out that not everyone interviewed completed the 37-item questionnaire. For example, in one of the high-crime patrol areas, only 83 of 119 respondents (i.e., 70 percent) did so. Further, the fear of victimization index that Doob and MacDonald used was based only on those respondents who completed the entire questionnaire. So again, there is the possibility of bias. One other item: Over 70 percent of all respondents were female. The point is that while the Doob and MacDonald study seems to enhance our understanding, it may not be the final word on the issue. There is the distinct possibility that their results were distorted in unknown ways by those people who refused to be interviewed, by those who did not complete the questionnaire, and by those who were not at home when the interviewer knocked. These three categories of people, of course, are nonresponders. Unfortunately, there are also a variety of ways in which respondents can distort the results of a survey (see Figure 4).

Respondents Are Only Human

More than any other research method, survey research relies on what people say – on SELF-REPORTED CHARACTERISTICS (attitudes, behaviors, feelings, and thoughts). The problem with that is that a great deal of the information thus obtained is impossible to verify and, for a variety of reasons, it cannot always be taken at face value. As Fiske (1980) put it, when independent evidence against which to validate is not available, you can never be sure when verbal reports are veridical. What can be done, then, to help ensure that the answers obtained to your questions are valid?

One solution to the problem created by the absence of external criteria is to trick the respondents, that is, convince them that you really do have a way of checking on their answers. Evans, Hanson, and Mittelmark (1977), for example, were interested in the prevalence of cigarette smoking among preadolescents. Smoking for this group is taboo, of course, and Evans et al. were concerned that it would be underreported. Thus, they employed a version of a technique known as the BOGUS PIPELINE. They convinced the subjects that their self-reports could be independently verified by a physiological measuring device that was, in fact, bogus. Prior to filling out a questionnaire about how much they smoked, some children saw a videotape about a new saliva test that could detect the presence of nicotine. They were then asked to give a saliva specimen themselves, told that it would be analyzed by the lab test they had just seen described, and, finally, they filled out the questionnaire about their smoking habits. As you can imagine, many more youngsters admitted to smoking under these conditions than among comparison groups who had not seen the videotape or been asked to give a saliva specimen. Others have used variations of the bogus pipeline technique to assess such socially undesirable characteristics as negative attitudes and prejudices toward ethnic groups. Sigall and Page (1971), for example, convinced subjects that their gross positive or negative feelings toward various groups could be detected by a physiological device similar to a lie detector. As expected, they found

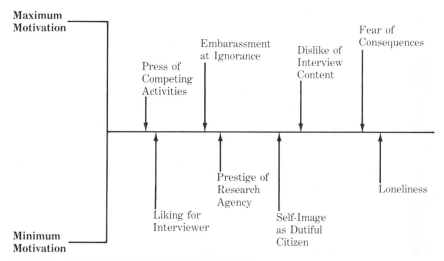

Figure 4 FACTORS AFFECTING RESPONDENT MOTIVATION. If a respondent likes the interviewer or feels duty-bound to respond as a good citizen, the inclination to give accurate answers increases. A respondent busy with other activities or embarrassed about not knowing how or what to answer has diminished motivation to take part in the interview. (From Cannell & Kahn, 1968.)

more prejudice and derogatory opinions expressed when subjects thought their true feelings would be registered by the machine.

However, for most survey reseach, such bogus pipeline devices are simply not feasible. Even if they were, if widely used, word would get around that they were phony and, hence, they would no longer be effective. Of course, the assumption behind the bogus pipeline is that respondents will be trying to hide something. What is more likely is that there are certain things that respondents will be a little uncomfortable about discussing. Topics that they consider sensitive, or personal. They may hold certain unpopular or socially undesirable attitudes, and they may be concerned that you will think less of them if they tell you how they really feel or what they really did. For such threatening topics, there are several ways of asking questions that will help you obtain more valid information without resorting to the elaborate deception necessary for the bogus pipeline approach. For example, Sudman and Bradburn (1983) suggested that for questions about potentially threatening topics, such as sexual behavior or alcohol use, it is best to use open-ended, long questions, with familiar words. It is also best to embed those questions in a list of more and less threatening topics, so that their perceived importance will be reduced.

Even when the information you are seeking is relatively innocuous and nonthreatening, there are two general, and very human, problems that can keep you from your goal of obtaining accurate and precise information: the respondent's lack of motivation and fallible memory. It should be obvious that a key requirement for a successful interview is that the person being interviewed be motivated and willing to provide the information you are seeking. There are, of course, many things that determine the level of the respondent's motivation to help you out by answering questions; some of the relevant forces are summarized in Figure 4. One partial solution to the motivation problem is to pay respondents for the time they spend being interviewed, but that can get quite expensive. Another, more general, approach is to try to make the interview a pleasant experience. That means keeping it relatively short and treating the respondent with courtesy and respect. You will find that many people are quite pleased to have someone take their opinions seriously and listen to what they have to say.

Motivation is important, but there are limits to what even the most highly motivated and well-meaning respondent can do. For example, in early research on child development, the most frequently used technique for gathering information was to interview mothers. It was assumed that mothers, being around their children constantly, would be the most aware of progress and skill development in all areas. However, efforts to check on the reliability and validity of mothers' reports proved sobering. Illness episodes, for example, were often forgotten, and not reported later, unless they had been very severe. The realization gradually dawned that mothers' reconstructions of children's pasts were often, even usually, distorted. Thus, in the early 1960s the question was raised, "what would the Ideal Research Mother be like?" Wenar (1961) suggested that she would (1) faithfully record events, feelings, impressions and observations as they happened; (2) remember with perfect fidelity; and (3) have the power of total recall upon request.

But, mothers—and other survey respondents—are just not like that. The fallibility of memory is, in fact, the most serious problem with non-threatening questions about past behaviors. To help respondents answer such questions accurately, however, there are several things you can do. You can make your question as specific as possible. You can, also, encourage respondents to consult any records they might have that would help them answer. A related technique is the use of diaries. Respondents can be asked to make notes about the occurrences of certain behaviors and then use those notes to answer your questions at a later date. You can also build memory cues into your questions. Instead of just asking what recreational activities they engaged in during the past month, you read them a whole list of such activities and ask which they engaged in.

What, then, would the Ideal Respondent be like? In addition to the attributes of Wenar's Ideal Research Mother, the general, all-purpose Ideal Respondent would have to have a few additional qualities. First of all, he or she must be motivated to provide complete and accurate information to the research worker. This means, of course, that the Ideal Respondent would immediately see the necessity for putting aside whatever he or she is doing when the interviewer knocks. He or she should also be somewhat impressed by the prestige of the agency sponsoring the research, should like the interviewer, understand perfectly what is being asked – even when the interviewer mumbles – and should have no fear of the consequences of revealing the most intimate details of his or her sex life, tax return, criminal records, or current communicable diseases.

There is no evidence that an Ideal Respondent has ever existed. Rumors that one was once observed trying to break into the National Opinion Research Center to fill out some more questionnaires were never substantiated.

Summary

Survey research is probably the most visible and influential variety of research in the social and behavioral sciences. The descriptive information obtained from surveys is useful for a variety of practical purposes, including the marketing of consumer goods and getting the attention of recalcitrant politicians. Three purposes can be served by surveys: description, explanation, and exploration of a topic area. The descriptive use of surveys is the most familiar, that is, the use of surveys to obtain information on the attributes of the population of interest. Of greater interest in social science circles, however, is the use of surveys to gather information that will help explain relationships among variables.

When planning a survey, the first step is to get clearly in mind exactly what you want to find out. One way to do that is to make a list of the issues you want to be able to address with the results of the survey. You then use that list to write out the specific questions you want to ask each respondent. Formulating those questions, of course, is the process of operationalization. An interview schedule can comprise several different types of questions: open-ended, closed-ended, contingency, and Likert-scale items. Once you have a draft of the questions you would like to ask, it is a good idea to pretest it on a few people. If they do not understand what you are asking or if they all give the same answers, it is time to redo your questions.

Data can be collected in one or more of three basic ways: face-to-face interviews, self-administered questionnaires, or telephone interviews. Each format has certain advantages. The questionnaire approach is cheaper, usually, but is fairly constraining in the types of questions you can ask. The face-to-face interview is the most flexible in terms of the types of questions that can be asked. But, unfortunately, conducting a number of face-to-face interviews can be quite time-consuming and expensive. Personal interviews also tend to be subject to a number of potential biases stemming from the fact that they are social occasions. On the other hand, they tend to result in lower nonresponse rates than mailed questionnaires or telephone interviews. Another basic design decision involves the choice of a one-time, or cross-sectional, survey versus the use of survey data collected at several points in time in order to trace longitudinal changes in the variables of interest. With longitudinal surveys, you might select a panel study, in which the same people are repeatedly contacted, or a cohort study, in which different samples from the same population are contacted.

The basic logic of explanation in survey research can be seen with the use of contingency tables and subgroup analysis. The variable used to split your sample into subgroups is referred to as the stratification variable. Subgroup analysis is typically motivated by the expectation that the stratification variable will provide an explanation for the phenomenon of interest. Subgroup analysis can be illustrated by research by Doob and MacDonald. Using high- versus low-crime areas as the stratification variable, they found that the relationship between television viewing and fear of crime held only in the high-crime areas. Thus, the relationship was explained by the fact that people who watch the most television happened to live in areas with the highest crime rates. That is why they are the most fearful.

Respondents are, after all, only human. To get high-quality information from them, you have to provide some motivation for them to help you and you have to be aware of the fact that memory is extremely unreliable.

Recommended Reading

These four books and one chapter will help you improve your skills in conducting and evaluating survey research. I suggest that you start with *The art of asking questions* and follow that with *Conversations at random*.

Brady, J. *The craft of interviewing.* Cincinnati: Writer's Digest Books, 1976.

Addressed primarily to journalists, Brady's book offers scores of helpful hints about interviewing. Although you may miss the scholarly references, their absence is more than made up for by examples culled from popular magazines, newspapers, and memoirs of both the famous and the infamous. There are chapters on how to ask questions, on doing your homework (so you will know what questions to ask), on establishing rapport, on taking notes, and even on interviewing over the telephone. Brady offers very sensible advice on almost every issue the novice interviewer might worry about. Clothing? Physical appearance? Opening line? The value of playing dumb? It is all there. There is even a list of six ploys to use when you have to ask some tough questions, questions that may make people uncomfortable.

1. *Blame someone else for the question.* "Some of your critics have said . . ."
2. *Imply that the question is a playful one.* "Let me play the devil's advocate for a moment . . ."
3. *Preface the question with some praise.* "Now that you are recognized as one of the finest actresses in the world, I wonder if you would comment on some of those nasty little stories about your first years in Hollywood?"
4. *Use separate, apparently disconnected questions.* "At what age do you think people should be allowed to purchase alcoholic beverages? This is followed sometime later by, "How old were you when you started drinking?"
5. *Use jargon, when it is available, for sensitive targets.* Personally, I am not too sure about this little bit of advice. You should use jargon only if it is very clear that both you and the person being interviewed are comfortable with it. Besides, this seems to conflict with Brady's next point.
6. *Your best bet is to ask the question in a matter-of-fact manner, no matter how sensitive the area.*

You will, no doubt, find other things to disagree with in this book, but it is both entertaining and informative.

Payne, S. L. *The art of asking questions.* Princeton, NJ: Princeton University Press, 1951.

This is an unusual book. First published in 1951, it has since been reprinted many times – a sure sign that people are still buying it and, presumably, finding it useful. It focuses, almost exclusively, on how to word individual questions in a survey. There are chapters on problem words, loaded questions, the dangers of taking too much (or too little) for granted – all profusely laced with examples. Consider this example: "How do you feel about your income tax – that is, the amount you have to pay the government on the money you take in during the year?" As Payne pointed out, this question would insult 9 out of 10 people by telling them that you have assumed they do not understand what income tax is. But, simply reversing its internal order makes the question much more acceptable. Then it reads, "How do you feel about the amount you have to pay the government on the money you take in during the year – your income tax?" Now the explanation does not sound like an explanation. Payne's advice on question wording is thorough, detailed, and well-documented. But, best of all, it is conveyed in a pleasant, entertaining style that makes the book very easy and enjoyable to read.

Wheeler, M. *Lies, damn lies, and statistics: The manipulation of public opinion in America.* New York: Dell, 1976.

If you have read the material in the preceding chapter carefully, you will not learn a great deal that is new about how to do survey research from Wheeler's book. But, what will make it worth your while to read *Lies* is Wheeler's documentation of the day-by-day misuse of survey research. He has painted a genuinely disturbing picture of the ways in which the polls that appear, almost daily, in your local newspaper intentionally and unintentionally misrepresent the facts. He also has given an interesting historical analysis of the ways in which polls have become important politically and socially. I must confess that I found the book to be a little unsettling. I am ashamed to admit it, but when I used to read the latest Gallup (or Harris or Roper or Yankelovich) poll, I usually took it at face value. My assumption was that these were professional people, that is, they were objective and scientific. According to Wheeler, that is not a safe assumption. In fact, if half the things Wheeler has said about some of the nationally known poll takers are true, the best thing to do with the next poll you see reported in a newspaper is wad it up and throw it away. On a more positive note, Wheeler has provided a series of questions you should ask yourself about the polls you see reported on TV or in newspapers and magazines. For example, what was the precise wording of the question(s) asked? How was the sample obtained? Who paid for the poll to be taken? Could you answer the question(s) asked?

Converse, J. M., & Schuman, H. *Conversations at random: Survey research as interviewers see it.* New York: Wiley, 1974.

For several years, groups of graduate students at the University of Michigan were each required to conduct a set of a dozen or so interviews in a project called the Detroit Area Study. The study was conducted by the Survey Research Center, and the students' participation was in connection with a year-long research practicum. Following a period of training and pretesting, they spent a week in Detroit tracking down their assigned respondents, calling back for the not-at-homes, and listening (for hours) to people who often seemed to be from a different world. After collecting their interviews, the students were required to write a paper outlining the insights gained about the processes of interviewing and carrying out survey research in the field. With liberal use of quotations from those papers, Converse and Schuman have presented a revealing look at the everyday triumphs and tragedies of survey research from the perspective of those actually doing the interviewing. It is both entertaining and enlightening. As an added benefit, there is an annotated bibliography describing many of the classic papers and books on interviewing and survey research. Given all this in fewer than 115 pages, how can you miss?

Dean, J. P., & Whyte, W. F. How do you know if the informant is telling the truth? In L. A. Dexter (Ed.), *Elite and specialized interviewing.* Evanston, IL: Northwestern University Press, 1970.

Is it possible to tell what people really believe on the basis of a few questions put to them in an interview? As Dean and Whyte have pointed out, the question itself implies that some basic and true attitude or opinion lies beneath the surface, like a vein of gold that the interviewer can uncover if he or she is skilled enough. But, in fact, respondents' statements can never be taken for more than their own, *very* personal perceptions, filtered and modified by cognitive and emotional reactions. Your job, as interviewer, is to recognize and avoid possible influences of the interview situation on the respondent's perception, interpretation, and reporting of subjective data such as emotions, opinions, attitudes, and values. Even supposedly objective data cannot be taken as the real truth—the reporting of it in an interview may reflect a unique perspective and personality. Major sources of distortion include a respondent's efforts to answer questions about some event not actually observed or remembered, the selective perception of certain aspects of situations and not others, and emotional needs to make situations fit his or her own perspective. Think, for example, of the differing but honest and angry accounts of how your last romance ended. There is also the possibility that a respondent may simply be lying, perhaps to protect a friend's reputation or his or her own self-image. Thus, trying to understand the informant's situation and outlook helps the interviewer detect distorted reports. Other things the interviewer can do include being alert for implausible answers, checking on the reliability of informants, and comparing the accounts of different informants.

7

Quasi-Experiments and Field Experiments

To many people, the notion of experimentation implies activity and excitement. To experiment is to be alive, to try new things, to change something, to grab the world–or, at least, your corner of it–and shake it in order to see what will happen. The world is constantly changing. New laws are passed, new products are marketed, new programs are introduced, new drugs and medical procedures are made available. As Toffler (1971) has so eloquently pointed out, modern civilization seems at times to overwhelm us with change, but it is unclear how much of that change is real progress. Progress, of course, is a wonderful thing. But, change and progress are not always identical, and it behooves us to be able to distinguish the two.

Consider an example. The Discussion on page 5 described a well-known reform that turned out to be a dud, even though the politicians who introduced it claimed it to be a genuine winner. The reason it was mentioned in Chapter One was simply to point out that just because Y follows X, you cannot conclude that Y was caused by X. Of course, you know that by this time. Now, a little more detail about the reform in question (Campbell, 1969b) will introduce the subject matter of this and the next chapter. The year was 1956, and following an unusually high number of traffic fatalities in 1955, the state of Connecticut instituted a severe crackdown on speeders. At the end of the year 40 fewer people had been killed on the highways of Connecticut than in the preceding year. Accordingly, the Governor (Abraham Ribicoff) issued the following statement: "With the saving of 40 lives in 1956, a reduction of 12.3 percent from the 1955 motor vehicle death toll, we can say that the program is definitely worthwhile" (Campbell, 1969b).

Think about that for a moment. Would you be willing to conclude that the crackdown on speeders was the *cause* of the decrease in traffic deaths? I hope not. You need more information first. Suppose 1956 had less rain and snow and consequently cleaner and dryer roads than 1955? Suppose that surrounding states, which did not institute a crackdown on speeders, had also experienced a decrease in traffic fatalities? Suppose that the Department of Transportation in Washington had instituted a nationwide Fasten-Your-Seatbelt campaign in 1956. If so, the decreased death toll in Connecticut might have been due to the decreased likelihood of fatal injuries in accidents, not to the crackdown on speeders. You could probably generate a number of other hypotheses to explain why Governor Ribicoff's proclamation of the success of his quasi-experiment in highway safety was somewhat incautious. That, by the way, is what the crackdown was, a QUASI-EXPERIMENT, although the Governor did not know it. He had all the elements: a change in the existing state of affairs (the crackdown), an outcome measure to evaluate the effectiveness of the change (the number of highway fatalities), and a number of comparisons that he could have made (but did not) to help him decide if it was indeed the crackdown that reduced the number of traffic fatalities in 1956.

The major purpose of this chapter is to alert you to the sorts of comparisons you need to make and the kinds of questions you need to ask yourself whenever you are trying to determine the results of a given change in the existing state of affairs. And it does not matter if it is you, or Congress, or the brute force of nature that introduces the change, the questions are the same.

Interventions and Naturally Occurring Changes

At first blush, the task sounds simple. If you have reason to believe that a change in the existing state of affairs will be followed by certain consequences, then after the change has occured, you look to see if those consequences are present or absent. That, of course, is exactly what Governor Ribicoff did. The reason that he concluded more than he should have was that in his situation there were a number of PLAUSIBLE ALTERNATIVE EXPLANATIONS for the consequence he was interested in, that is, a decrease in traffic fatalities. Unfortunately, Governor Ribicoff's predicament seems to be the rule rather than the exception. That is, the apparent consequences of planned interventions and naturally occurring changes often can be attributed to a variety of more or less plausible causes other than the intervention or change in question. That means your task is not just to look and see if the anticipated consequences are present, but to think of ways—preferably, ahead of time—for eliminating all of those additional plausible explanations for the consequences of interest. This thinking of ways to eliminate plausible alternative hypotheses is what is meant by DESIGNING RESEARCH.

That task can be quite tricky because most interventions and naturally occurring changes are relatively complex phenomena. Consider this example. Mount Saint Helens erupted on May 18, 1980. The effects of the eruption were disastrous for a number of nearby communities and a pair of alert investigators thought that it might be an excellent opportunity to study naturally occurring reactions to such circumstances. Thus, in the months following the eruption, Pennebaker and Newtson (1983) conducted telephone and face-to-face interviews with area residents, collected information about calls to the police and letters to the editors of local newspapers, and, generally, tried to assess how people were coping with the aftermath of the volcano. Surprisingly, they found that people in different communities were not reacting in similar ways. Forty-four percent of the people contacted in Longview, Washington even refused to be interviewed. The refusal rate in other communities was only about 12 percent. Further investigation revealed that the reason Longview residents were responding in atypical ways was because the volcano had had a different effect on their community. By the time Pennebaker and Newston did their interviews, the crisis had passed for most towns in the area. But, Longview was located on a river and was threatened by flooding for several months after the eruption. Thus, many of the residents of Longview were still in a state of acute anxiety. The point here is that interventions and naturally occurring changes are often complex and may interact with components of the preexisting situation in peculiar ways. That means you need to develop a thorough knowledge of both the change itself and the situation in which the change is introduced (see opposite page). You will recall from Chapter Two that developing intimate familiarity with the situation was a crucial component of participant observation. It is also critical for well-conducted quasi-experiments.

Nonequivalent Groups

There is another thing that makes the task of understanding the effects produced by interventions and naturally occurring changes quite difficult. That is, they usually happen only once, and to one group. Quite often, because of the cost or logistics involved, even planned interventions cannot be duplicated—much less volcanos. For example, on July 6, 1972 the state of Nebraska enacted a no-fault divorce law (Mazur-Hart & Berman, 1977). For purposes of evaluating the effect of that law on the divorce rate, it would have been nice if it could have been made to apply only to a randomly selected sample of married couples living in Nebraska. Then one could compare the subsequent divorce rate among those couples to the rate of another randomly selected sample to whom the law did not apply. That legal arrangement, of course, was impossible. The law had to apply to everybody or it would have been laughed out of court. As you will see in Chapter Nine, when you can randomly assign subjects to treatment and no-treatment groups, it solves a lot of problems.

But, if all you can do is make some observations or measurements after an intervention or change has occurred, you will have what is referred to as a ONE-SHOT CASE STUDY and, for purposes of inferring whether or not an intervention made a difference, the one-shot case study is useless. To help you see why that is so, a couple of symbols will be useful. Following Donald Campbell and his colleagues (Campbell & Stanley, 1966; Cook & Campbell, 1979), let X stand for an intervention (or change or treatment or manipulation) of some sort and O stand for the observation (or assessment) of effects. Then, the one-shot case study looks like this:

$$\overrightarrow{\text{X} \qquad \text{O}}$$
$$\text{(Time)}$$

THINGS ARE DIFFERENT IN THE FIELD

It is important to remember that the results of research are determined, at least partially, by the setting in which the research is conducted. For example, examination of the results of laboratory studies of attitude change leaves the clear impression that attitudes are easily changeable. Subjects exposed to brief persuasive communications often show massive shifts in attitudes, sometimes changing completely from one side of an issue to the other (Cooper & Jones, 1970). On the other hand, field experiments on the effectiveness of mass media leave one with the impression that attitude change is genuinely rare. Millions of dollars spent in prolonged election campaigns, for example, often appear to change the attitudes of only a very small percentage of the voters.

In an analysis of the differences between the two types of research, Hovland (1959) suggested a number of variables that may account for this. First, there is a difference in *discrepancy*. In laboratory studies of attitude change, subjects are usually exposed to communcations arguing for positions quite different from their own. In field settings, however, a great deal of self-selection takes place. That is, those people who show up to hear candidate X are likely to agree already with most of what he or she has to say. Hence, not much change is possible. A second difference concerns the *nature of the issues*. Laboratory studies of attitude change quite frequently use noninvolving issues, issues of no great import. In contrast, field research is typically concerned with socially and politically significant issues—issues deeply rooted in the respondents' world views, life-styles, and reference groups. A third difference is the *timing of measurement*. In laboratory research, measurements of attitude are often made within minutes after exposure to the persuasive communication. In field research, attitude assessment may not take place for days, or even weeks, following exposure to the communications or events intended to change attitudes.

There are other differences in the two settings, but the point here is simply that the circumstances into which you introduce an intervention or treatment can make a tremendous difference in its apparent effectiveness. That is why it pays to develop a thorough understanding of the situation into which you plan to introduce the manipulation of interest.

The reason it is useless for the purpose of inferring whether or not the intervention has an effect is that you have nothing to compare the O to.

Suppose that Mazur-Hart and Berman (1977) had done a one-shot case study of the effects of the Nebraska no-fault divorce law. What they would have been able to say would have been something like: "In July 1972 the Nebraska no-fault divorce law was enacted, and in September 1972 there were 350 divorces in Nebraska." You see the problem. For all you know there might have been 350 divorces in Nebraska every month for the last century. The one-shot case study gives you no explicit data to which you can compare your observations. When people conduct one-shot case studies, there is often an implicit comparison to their expectations about what their observations would have been like if X had not occurred, but that is not acceptable. Their expectations may be cockeyed. You need data! Are those 350 divorces per month an increase or a decrease? (We'll return to the Mazur-Hart and Berman study later—they really had a better plan for determining the results of the Nebraska no-fault divorce law.)

Consider some of the things you would have to add to the one-shot case study to make it into a more respectable design for purposes of inferring cause-and-effect relationships. The following sections will discuss what additions help increase confidence about causal inferences that X, whatever it may be, really made a difference.

Think about the one-shot case study for a moment. A change has occurred, and you have some observations made after the change. The simplest step toward building a better design would be to secure observations both before and after the change. That seems to presume that the change is planned, but it does not have to be. It depends on what you select as your indicator(s) of the effects of the change. There are archives full of records that might have an appropriate pretest index. In any event, if you can obtain some information about the state of affairs prior to the change, the one-shot case study becomes the ONE-GROUP PRETEST-POSTTEST DESIGN and looks like this:

$$O \qquad X \qquad O$$

(Time)

That is an improvement, but not much of one. To understand why, think about that Nebraska no-fault divorce law again. It was enacted in July 1972 (the X above). Assume that in May 1972 there were 325 divorces in Nebraska (the first O). Then in September 1972 there were 349 (the second O). Would you be willing to conclude that the divorce law had had an effect? You should not be because the number of divorces in Nebraska might have been increasing at a steady rate of six per month for a long time. That means that between May and September there would have been an increase of 24 divorces regardless of any new law: 331 in June, 337 in July, 343 in August, and 349 in September.

Try another improvement. The one-shot case study lacks a basis of comparison; if you can find another group that was not exposed to the intervention (or treatment or volcano), that would help. Then the design could be diagrammed like this:

Group 1	X	O
Group 2		O

(Time) →

That is certainly an improvement. The problem, of course, is that if Groups 1 and 2 turn out to differ at the time of observation, there will still be the nagging suspicion that they may have differed before Group 1 was exposed to the intervention. If they did, then it will be very difficult to argue that exposure to X is what produced the difference at the time your observations, the O's, were made. Of course, the more evidence you can summon to support the argument that Groups 1 and 2 were indeed equivalent before the occurrence of X, the stronger this design will be for discovering whether or not X has made a difference for Group 1. This design has two names: Campbell and Stanley (1966) referred to it as the STATIC GROUP COMPARISON. Cook and Campbell (1979) preferred the more descriptive POSTTEST-ONLY DESIGN WITH NONEQUIVALENT GROUPS.

Many naturally occurring changes are, of course, unanticipated. The eruption of Mount Saint Helens, for example, was certainly not planned by the powers-that-be in Washington State. With such events, the posttest-only design with nonequivalent groups can give you useful information about the consequences of the change. But remember, the key to its usefulness is your ability to convince yourself (and others) that the groups were similar on the measures of interest prior to the occurrence of the intervention. However, with planned interventions, there is a better way. If you know when and to whom an intervention is going to occur, you can go in before its occurrence and document the standing of the two groups on the measures of interest. Then, one of the groups is exposed to the intervention; and, subsequently, you observe both groups a second time. If you do all this, the design you will be using is referred to as the UN-TREATED CONTROL GROUP DESIGN WITH PRETEST AND POSTTEST. It is diagrammed below:

Group 1	O	X	O
Group 2	O		O[1]

According to Cook and Campbell, (1979), this may be the most frequently used research design in the social sciences. As an example of a situation in which it might be employed, suppose you were interested in the effec-

---

[1]You will note that the time line has been dropped. Just remember that it is implicit in all of the designs in this chapter. The farther a symbol is to the right, the later that operation is in time.

tiveness of handing out samples of food – say, pizza – on sales of that food in supermarkets. You might record pizza sales in two different supermarkets for a week, hand out free samples in one of them for a second week, and then record sales in both supermarkets again for the third week. If sales were up during the third week in the supermarket in which you had handed out pizza, but not in the other one, you might be able to conclude that free samples do enhance sales.

But then again, you might not. Now that you have been introduced to a few quasi-experimental designs, let us focus a little more closely on some of their shortcomings. Earlier it was mentioned that the major purpose of this chapter was to acquaint you with the sort of questions you should ask yourself when trying to determine the results of a given change or manipulation. That is the topic to be discussed before describing any additional designs. As you will see, there are a few things you would need to worry about before you could conclude that handing out of pizza slices enhances sales. The mere fact that sales are up in the store in which you did hand out pizza, but not in the other one, is not enough (see page 219).

Problems in Making Causal Inferences

Mark Twain once said that we should be careful to get out of an experience only the wisdom that is in it. He had probably never heard the phrase INTERNAL VALIDITY, but he seemed to have a feel for what it means. Simply stated, the question of internal validity is the question of whether an intervention or change does, indeed, make a difference. Did handing out those hot slices of pizza really cause pizza sales to increase in Store A? Or was it the fact that a nearby pizzeria went out of business that third week? Did that crackdown on speeders really reduce traffic fatalities? Or had traffic deaths been steadily declining over the years as cars became safer and highways wider (see Figure 1)?

The concept of internal validity was formulated by Donald Campbell almost 30 years ago, in 1957, and has been extensively developed by Campbell and Stanley (1966) and Cook and Campbell (1979). Fortunately for you, Campbell and his colleagues have made explicit a number of general threats to internal validity, possible contaminating factors you must be able to rule out before concluding that the intervention or change of interest to you really made a difference. At last count (Cook & Campbell, 1979), there were 13 threats to internal validity – 13 potential problems that might keep you from inferring that your intervention really had a causal effect on the subsequent state of affairs. Those 13 are defined and briefly illustrated below. Following the definitions, you will see how some of those quasi-experimental designs introduced in the last section measure up. There is

GETTING THE RESULTS YOU EXPECT IS NOT ENOUGH

When a field experiment turns out as you anticipate it will, you should be especially careful in your attempts to evaluate alternative explanations. There is a real danger that because the study seemed to work, you will be less than thorough in your efforts to think up plausible alternative hypotheses that could predict the same result.

Eysenck (1965) has reported an interesting historical example that illustrates the potential for being misled about a causal explanation when two hypotheses predict the same result. It concerns the famous Broad Street Pump in London, England. The pump was one of the main water sources for an area of London that was beset by an epidemic of cholera. An epidemiological study by Snow found that, for the most part, members of households for which the water supply was not obtained at the Broad Street Pump did not get cholera. Thus, he arrived at the hypothesis that cholera was being transmitted via the polluted water from the Broad Street Pump. He removed the handle from the pump so that it could not be used and ended the cholera epidemic. However, a man named Farr also had conducted a series of studies that had led him to a different conclusion. He had become convinced that the most important factor in the transmission of cholera was elevation above sea level. Thus, his recommendation was that people be moved away from the low-lying areas, which included the area served by the Broad Street Pump, to higher inland regions. The point is that if Farr's suggestion had been followed and the population of London had been evacuated to the higher inland districts, the cholera epidemic would have ended—just as it ended when the handle was removed from the Broad Street Pump. If the population was out of reach of the Broad Street Pump, they would no longer have been obtaining their water there. Thus, as Eysenck has noted, the success of an intervention is not necessarily evidence for the hypothesis on which the intervention was based. You have to be able to rule out any and all plausible alternatives first.

a related concept, called external validity, which will be discussed at the end of Chapter Nine.

The first threat to internal validity is HISTORY, all the events going on in the world at the time of your study, other than your intervention. If any of those events could plausibly have produced the same change that you were hoping your intervention would, you are in trouble. If there really had been a nearby pizza place that closed down in the same week you were trying to assess the effects of giving free samples of pizza in the supermarket, that would provide a plausible explanation for the rise in pizza sales at the supermarket.

*"Lately I've been very happy, but I don't
know if it's me or vitamins."*

Figure 1 INTERNAL VALIDITY is basically an attributional issue. Has the intervention (treatment) made a difference, or did something else cause the change? (Drawing by Wm. Hamilton © 1978 The New Yorker Magazine, Inc.)

The second threat to internal validity is MATURATION. People are constantly changing. They get older, wiser, heavier—all on their own, that is, without regard to your research. If the effect you are looking for could plausibly be attributed to normal maturation processes, no one is going to believe it was produced by your intervention. Maturation can be a genuine problem if your research is in an educational setting or with children or both. For example, if you were interested in whether taking a year of Latin—yes, some of us actually did that—improved vocabulary, you could not simply give a vocabulary test to students before and after their year of Latin classes. Chances are their vocabularies would have increased in size over the year even without the Latin classes.

The third and fourth threats to internal validity are referred to as TESTING and INSTRUMENTATION. Testing is the problem posed by the possibility that if you give the same test or measure to people on more than one occasion, their responses the second and third time may be influenced by the mere fact of having taken the test before. They may remember their previous answers, for example, or they may try consciously to change their answers. Thus, testing refers to the possibility of a change due to repeated test-taking or observation. In contrast, instrumentation refers to the possibility of a change in the test or observations themselves. For example, suppose that as part of your research you were having observers code classroom interactions between teachers and students. After a couple of weeks of that, the observers may become bored and begin missing things because of inattention. Thus, the results would look as if teachers were interacting less with students as the semester progressed, but, in fact, it was the observers who had changed. They were simply missing more interactions as the semester dragged on.

STATISTICAL REGRESSION is the fifth threat to internal validity. It stems from the fact that people tend to vary somewhat in their performance from time to time. Thus, if you score really well on a test, chances are you may not do so well the next time. Or, if you really blow it, chances are you will do a little better next time. What this means for research is that you have to be very careful when you select people for participation in the research because they had either a very high or a very low score on some measure. For example, suppose you select people for a compensatory reading program because they did extremely poorly on a test of reading comprehension. You then administer the program and retest them. If they do better the second time, at least part of the improvement may be due to statistical regression and you will have to be able to rule that out before skeptics will believe your program is effective.

The sixth and seventh threats to internal validity are SELECTION and MORTALITY. As noted earlier, many interventions and changes can be administered to—or happen to—only one group. That means the group you use as a comparison group may not be equivalent. Selection simply refers to this notion that people in different groups are, indeed, often different. In many instances they select themselves into certain groups. Those who take Latin in high school, for example, are different from those who take shop. They have different interests and career plans and, hence, could not be considered equivalent groups for most research purposes. Mortality refers to another kind of self selection. It refers to the fact that some people may drop out of a group during the course of your research. Suppose you have two groups at the outset that are roughly equivalent, but, during the course of research, some people drop out of the group that was not exposed to the intervention. At the end you will not know if the intervention made a difference. It could be that any difference between the two groups on the posttest is just due to the fact that some people dropped out of the comparison group and left a biased sample of the original comparison group.

The eighth threat to internal validity is actually a cluster of threats—all the things that can produce an INTERACTION WITH SELECTION: history, testing, maturation, instrumentation. For example, suppose you administered an educational program to a group of 11-year-old girls and used as a comparison group 11-year-old boys. At the pretest, the two groups had been equivalent in terms of their scores on standard tests and achievement, but at the posttest, a year later, the girls did significantly better than the boys. Would you be willing to conclude that the educational program had made the difference? That would be questionable, because at the 11-year-old to 12-year-old stage girls and boys are maturing at different rates and girls are, generally, doing better in school at that age than are boys. Not only would there be the possibility of a selection–maturation interaction in this case, there is also the possibility of a selection–history interaction. Different things are happening to 11-year-old girls and boys outside of the classroom. Hence, you could not necessarily attribute the girls' greater achivement at age 12 solely to your educational program. As for the possibility of a selection–testing interaction, you might anticipate that if the girls in your study are really doing better in school and maturing at a faster rate than boys, they will also benefit more from taking the same test twice. They will be more likely to have developed good test-taking habits and, possibly, will be more likely to remember their answers from the previous test. Again this will make them look better than the boys on the posttest, but it will not be due to your educational program. Selection–instrumentation interactions can also be a problem, and they refer to differential assessments of your groups that are due to the nature of the measuring instruments you use. For example, suppose you were using classroom observers in the study just mentioned to assess the quality of answers given in class by girls and by boys. The observers might quickly come to expect that the girls generally will give better answers. Once that expectation develops, the observers are no longer unbiased. From then on, they may very well see what they expect to see (Jones, 1977).

The ninth threat to internal validity is AMBIGUITY ABOUT THE DIRECTION OF CAUSALITY. Fortunately, it is not usually a problem in quasi-experiments and field experiments because a cause always has to precede an effect; and in quasi-experiments there is usually a clear temporal relationship between the intervention or change of interest and the assessment of its consequences. Ambiguity about the direction of causality is more likely to be a problem in survey research in which all the variables of interest are assessed at the same time by self-report.

The tenth and eleventh threats to internal validity are closely related: DIFFUSION OR IMITATION OF TREATMENTS and COMPENSATORY EQUALIZATION OF TREATMENTS. If you have set up a quasi-experimental design in which one or more of the groups get to do something neat, there is a danger that members of the groups not exposed to that intervention will hear about it and do it on their own. For example, if you were trying to assess different weight-loss plans and started one group of overweight volunteers on a regimen of daily aerobic dancing and another group on a bland diet, you might end up with some members of the latter group taking up aerobics. It is much more fun than dieting. Similarly, compensatory equalization of treatments may occur if one or more of the treatments appear to be better than the others. If people with the power to do so become aware of this, they may feel obligated to do something for those not receiving the better treatment.

The final two threats to internal validity are also closely related: COMPENSATORY RIVALRY by those who find out they are receiving less desirable treatments and RESENTFUL DEMORALIZATION by those receiving less desirable treatments. In the former, those who find out they are receiving less desirable treatments may try harder just to show they can do it on their own, that is, without the advantage of your treatment, whatever it may be. This, of course, will spuriously reduce differences between groups at posttest time. In the case of resentful demoralization, those receiving the less desirable treatment may simply quit trying all together, out of spite. This, in turn may spuriously increase differences between the groups at posttest time. In either case, you will not be able to get an accurate assessment of just how much difference your treatments have made.

The 13 threats to internal validity are summarized in Table 1. It is a good idea to commit them to memory and check them off each time you think you have a foolproof design. Remember they are all potential alternative explanations that can be troublesome whenever you are trying to determine whether the intervention or treatment of interest to you really made a difference. If the apparent effect of the intervention can plausibly be attributed to one or more of the threats to internal validity, you will not be able to tell whether or not the intervention really did anything. That can be very frustrating, especially if you have invested a lot of time, effort, and possibly, money—not to mention ego—in the research. Thus, what you want to do is avoid getting yourself into that state of attributional ambiguity, of not knowing whether it was the treatment or selection or maturation or something else that made the difference. That means you have to try to anticipate which threats to internal validity are likely to be operating in the circumstances under which you will be doing the research. You then design the research, as best you can, to obtain the evidence necessary to rule out the influence of those threats to internal validity.

Ruling Out Alternative Explanations by Design

Remember the one-shot case study? It should be clearer by now why it is scientifically useless. Not only does it provide you no explicit basis for comparison, it provides no means of controlling for any of the relevant threats to internal validity. Cook and Campbell (1979) have noted that there are several different ways in which the word *control* is used. So, let me be clear about exactly what is meant here. *Control* is sometimes used to refer to your ability to hold constant all extraneous factors in the situation in which the research is conducted. That is often feasible in laboratory research, as you will see in Chapter Nine. Unfortunately, it is usually not feasible in quasi-experiments and field experiments. But simply because it is impossible to hold those extraneous factors constant does not mean you can ignore them, or just wish them away. They may crop up in one or more of the threats to internal validity, for example, as a part of *history*.

Because you cannot hold extraneous factors constant, you have to find a way to demonstrate that they did not have a determining influence on the observations of interest to you. That usually means adding another condition or two to your design, for example, another group of people who experience the same extraneous events, but not the intervention. These other groups, or conditions, are referred to, of course, as control groups. Thus, if you add a control group to the one-shot case study, it becomes

Group 1   X   O

Group 2   O

which is the posttest-only design with nonequivalent groups. In this design when you obtain a difference between the two groups at the time of your observations, you can feel fairly confident in ruling out history, testing, and instrumentation as having produced that difference. Both groups presumably experienced the same historical events and both were tested with the same instruments at the same time. (But do not forget that you have nonequivalent groups, so selection might still be a threat to internal validity.) The point here is that in quasi-experiments and field experiments the notion of control has to do with particular threats to internal validity and how you try to eliminate those threats by the way you design your study and carry it out. The result of this approach to control is often what Campbell and Stanley (1966) referred to as PATCHED-UP DESIGNS. In such

Table 1 Thirteen Threats to Internal Validity

History Events other than the intervention that occur during the course of the research.

Maturation Changes in respondents that may occur during the research, such as growing older and (one hopes) wiser.

Testing Repeated testing can produce apparent changes in performance level. That is one reason so many eleventh graders take the Practice Scholastic Aptitude Test.

Instrumentation Your measuring instrument itself may change over time. If you use observers, for example, they may get bored after a few days and be less careful.

Statistical Regression If you select respondents on the basis of extreme scores on a pretest, then chances are the next time you test them their scores will be less extreme.

Selection If the respondents in the various conditions differ at the outset, then you may have problems interpreting the effects of your intervention.

Mortality If respondents drop out of some of your conditions, you may end up with different kinds of people in different conditions, depending on why the drop-outs occurred. Attrition is actually a better word for this because the respondents do not usually die off.

Interactions With Selection Maturation, history, and instrumentation may all interact with selection. For example, if you test all treatment subjects in one group and control subjects in another, whatever unique events occur during those testing sessions may confound your comparisons. A higher noise level during their session may cause control subjects to perform less well.

Ambiguity About Direction of Causality This is usually not a problem in quasi-experimentation because the intervention precedes the observation of its effects. However, if your intervention initiates a cycle involving feedback (warm instructor, pleased students, warmer instructor, even happier students) and you do not make your observations until sometime later, there could be a problem.

Diffusion or Imitation of Treatments Communication between subjects in various conditions of your research can be a problem.

Compensatory Equalization of Treatments If the respondents in one condition find out that those in another condition are getting some desirable treatment, then they may find a way to get the desirable treatment for themselves outside of the research setting.

Compensatory Rivalry by Those Receiving Less Desirable Treatments If one group receives better treatment (such as improved working conditions) and those in another group find out about it, they could decide to demonstrate that they can do better even without the piped-in music and carpet on the floor.

Resentful Demoralization by Those Receiving Less Desirable Treatments On the other hand, they may get annoyed and quit working at their normal level.

Source: Cook and Campbell (1979).

designs, features are added to control specific factors that you think might be operating in the situation in which the research is to be carried out.

But how, exactly, do you go about it? It is very difficult to give specific advice in answer to that question. So much depends on the intervention, or change, of interest to you, on what you anticipate will be the effect of the intervention, on the situation into which the intervention is introduced, on the people who will be affected by the intervention, and so on. However, there are a couple of general guidelines that may help. Ellsworth (1977) has suggested that one way to proceed is to imagine that intervention producing exactly the effect you hypothesize that it will. Then ask yourself this question: What are the most likely alternative explanations that people could offer for that effect if I told them about it? Make a list and figure out what information you would need to counter each item on the list. It might be that you will need an extra condition or two to get some of the information. In other cases, it might be as simple as a few additional questions that need to be asked the participants in the study. For example, in the Mazur-Hart and Berman study of the Nebraska no-fault divorce law, they decided they needed long-term data about the number of divorces in Nebraska. They used that to rule out the alternative hypothesis that the increase in divorces from the months immediately before to the months immediately after the enactment of the law was no larger than the typical month-to-month increase. Similarly, in regard to that Connecticut speed crackdown mentioned earlier, it would be nice to know if traffic fatalities decreased an equivalent amount in 1956 in surrounding states, which, presumably, had had similar weather, but had not toughened up on speeders.

Ellsworth (1977) also has pointed out that if you are able to choose the setting (i.e., the situation into which the intervention is introduced) the availability of appropriate control groups should be one of the major considerations in your choice. As she put it:

> It is my hunch that many investigators devote a great deal of effort and creativity to finding a setting or population that provides a good embodiment of the treatment variable and that they then cast about hurriedly at the last minute for some sort of control group. The control group is exactly as important as the treatment group in research, and in fact it is impossible to separate the value of one from the value of the other.

She cautioned that quasi-experimental designs require particular attention to the question of appropriate control groups because there will usually be a number of ways in which the control and treatment groups are not equivalent. Each of those differences may pose a threat to internal validity.

Consider an example illustrating this notion of patching together the information and control groups needed in a particular setting. Imagine that you are employed in a college of medicine and are a member of the curriculum committee. One of the problems facing the committee is how to handle a stream of student complaints that too much material is being covered in lectures in their physiology course. Sound familiar? Because of the tremendous amount of material to be learned in physiology, the faculty (naturally) say they cannot cut down on what is presented. Thus, if any change is to be made, it must somehow be in the area of increasing what the students absorb from the lectures. It occurs to you that one possibility is to have the audiovisual department record all physiology lectures, make multiple copies of the cassettes, and allow students to check out those cassettes so that they can listen to the lectures again – and again and again and again, if necessary, until every last detail has found a home in their heads.

The committee is quite willing to try out your suggestion, but the dean says that if he is going to be asked to find the money to pay for all those cassettes he wants some evidence that the scheme is either useful or not useful. Deans tend to be a little conservative about anything concerning money. So, having taken a course in research design some years ago, you propose that a pretest–posttest design with a control group is needed. (In case it has slipped your mind, this is the design:

$$\begin{array}{lccc} \text{Group 1} & \text{O} & \text{X} & \text{O} \\ \text{Group 2} & \text{O} & & \text{O.)} \end{array}$$

Your idea is that this year's freshmen medical students will serve as Group 1 – the complaints were from last year's class and the committee is meeting in late August, before the semester begins. Someone then suggests that next year's class could serve as Group 2, but that is rejected by the committee because, if the taping appeared to be beneficial for students, they would want to continue it. After all, you want all those future doctors to know as much as is humanly possible. So, that means you will have to go back and use last year's class as Group 2.

The next problem is how can you establish that this year's class and last year's class are really equivalent. Everybody is always talking about raising standards, and if the admissions committee were a little tougher in admitting students to this year's class, that could be a problem. It might be that what last year's students thought was a real crusher of a course, this year's students will take in stride. Well, it so happens that there is a standardized test that all applicants to medical school have to take. It is called the MCAT (for Medical College Admissions Test). There are national norms available on the MCAT, and it is a good measure of general scientific knowledge for college seniors. So, you decide to use the average MCAT scores of the two classes as the pretest. If the average MCAT scores turn out to be about the same for the two classes, you will be willing to assume that on entering their first year of medical school the students in the two classes were about the same in terms of academic preparation and such relevant skills as study habits. That is probably a safe assumption. Note that as you are making this decision, the data for the pretest are already in. They are in the files, with the applications that each student for this year's and last year's classes submitted. All that is going to be required is to go through the files and extract the numbers—a version of archival research that you should remember well from Chapter Four.

What is next? Probably the next decision would be what to use for the posttest. You might use grades in the physiology course; but grades often reflect things other than knowledge, and besides, the physiology faculty may just throw tests together the day before the exam, that is, the tests may not be particularly well constructed. However, at the end of their second year, all medical students are required to take an exam referred to as National Boards, Part One, which tests their knowledge of the basic sciences relevant to medicine: biochemistry, anatomy, behavioral science, pharmacology, pathology, and, yes, physiology. So you decide to use performance of the two classes on the first part of National Boards as the posttest. This means, of course, that you are going to have to wait two years before the data for this year's entering class will be in. One other thing, so that the pretest and posttest will be directly comparable, you are going to have to convert the average scores of the classes on each to a percentage of the maximum possible score.

Pretend that everything goes according to plan. There are no missing MCAT scores in the files, the dean agrees to foot the bill for the tapes and the taping, no students drop out of either class, the college librarians are willing to dispense and collect the tapes, and everybody takes the National Boards on schedule.[2] Two years later, you eagerly tabulate the results and they look like Figure 2A. Elated, you take this graph down to the Dean and proudly announce that your idea was a success. He takes one look at the figure and says, "Don't be silly! So, the average performance of the two classes on the MCAT was about the same. How do you know that it was really the tapes that made a difference? Maybe the students in the class for whom the tapes were available simply thought that the faculty was more interested in them and, hence, were inspired to put forth a little more effort? Haven't you ever heard of the Hawthorne effect? I suggest you try reading about it in the original, which, I believe, is Roethlisberger and Dickson (1939)." The Dean, it appears, is no slouch (see page 230).

(see page 230).

[2]You realize, of course, that this is ridiculous. Nothing ever goes completely according to plan. Several of Murphy's Laws (Dickson, 1978) apply here, including: (1) If anything can go wrong, it will; (2) Nothing is ever as simple as it seems, and (3) Everything takes longer than you expect.

(A)

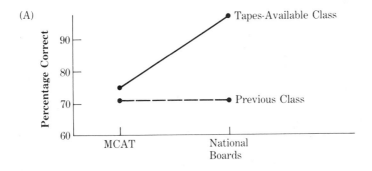

(B)

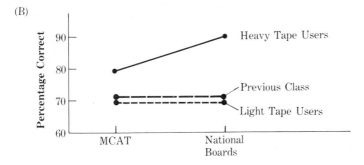

Figure 2 TWO HYPOTHETICAL OUTCOMES for the quasi-experiment in which one class of medical students are provided tape recordings of lectures. In (A), members of that class appear to do better on their National Board Exams than do members of the preceding class, who did not have the tapes available. However, (B) shows that only the students who actually used the tapes did better.

Thoroughly chagrined, you go back to your office and ponder this for awhile. Then it occurs to you that the librarians, bless their souls, have records of who checked the tapes out and how often. If you could get those data, then you could take the class for whom the tapes were available and break it down into two groups: Heavy and Light Tape Users. Another day or two of digging around in the librarian's files and your design has become a little more complex. Now it looks like this:

	MCAT SCORES	TAPES	NATIONAL BOARDS
HEAVY TAPE USERS	O	X	O
LIGHT TAPE USERS	O	X	O
PREVIOUS CLASS	O		O

When you graph the results, you find that tape use seemed to make a difference, even though those who used the tapes the most had higher scores

Issues and Discussions ━━━━━━━━━━━━━━━━━━━━━━━━

THE HAWTHORNE EFFECT

In the 1920s, a series of studies that were destined to become quite famous were conducted at the Hawthorne Western Electric plant in Chicago. In what is perhaps the best known of the studies, a group of women whose job was to assemble electrical relays for telephones were separated from other workers and put into a special room. There the people conducting the research (Roethlisberger & Dickson, 1939) made a number of changes in the conditions of work. For example, the workers in the Relay Assembly Test Room, as it was called, were given free lunches, rest pauses, shortened work hours, and were allowed to participate in a small group incentive payment plan. In addition, there was a change in the nature of the supervision to which they were subjected. The new style of managerial discipline was unusually friendly and free-and-easy and was designed to get the workers to relax and be more open about the things that bothered them. The purpose behind this new managerial style was to allow the evaluation of changes in the work environment, such as changes in lighting, hours of work, and length of rest pauses, without contamination. It was thought that if supervisors were open and willing to listen, for example, workers would be more honest and straightforward in reporting what they liked and did not like and a better assessment could be made of the optimal working conditions.

It turned out, however, that the only thing that really seemed to matter was this new attitude on the part of the supervisors. Now they appeared to be interested in the workers, and, in return, the workers seemed to work harder no matter what physical changes were introduced into the work setting. The Hawthorne Effect, as it came to be known, refers to this serendipitous finding that workers, and, presumably, subjects in research, are very responsive to the mere fact that someone has taken an interest in them. This can be a real problem in trying to evaluate the effects of an intervention, or treatment. You will need to be able to rule out the Hawthorne Effect before you can conclude that it was the specific nature of the intervention of interest that made a difference.

---

on both the pretest and posttest. The graph turns out like Figure 2B.

In pondering the graph, it occurs to you that the dean is still not going to be convinced that it was the tapes that made the difference. What he is going to say this time is something to the effect that you have identified an interaction between selection and maturation. (He once took a course in research design also.) "The good students were the ones who made use of the tapes. They were better prepared to start with–note their higher MCAT average–and they were maturing, academically, at a faster rate.

So they end up with even higher scores on the National Board Exam. The tapes were a waste of money."

How can you counter that argument? Well, you will need to show that even though the Heavy Tape-Users may, in general, have been better students all along than the Light Tape-Users, the tapes produced an additional increment in performance for them. You need a time series design.

Interrupted Time Series

Remember the Mazur-Hart and Berman study of the Nebraska no-fault divorce law? The design they actually employed is referred to as an IN-TERRUPTED TIME SERIES. It is an elegantly simple design and is very similar to the one-group pretest–posttest design described earlier. The difference is that in the interrupted time series, instead of one set of observations before the intervention and one set of observations after, you have multiple observations before the intervention and multiple observations afterward. It looks like this:

$$O \quad O \quad O \quad O \quad O \quad O \quad O \quad X \quad O \quad O \quad O \quad O \quad O \quad O \quad O$$

It is a vast improvement over the one-group pretest–posttest design, in which all you know is the size of the change, if any, from pretest to posttest. But, you do not have anything to which you can compare that change. In the interrupted time series design, you can tell whether the magnitude of the change from just before to just after the treatment is any different from the changes between the other adjacent pairs of observations. You can also tell whether there is an overall trend in the data, that is, an increase or decrease over time. But, if the intervention really does have an effect, you can expect some sort of sharp change in that overall trend in the observations immediately following the intervention. Using data on divorces per month from 1969 through 1974, Mazur-Hart and Berman found that there was, indeed, an increasing number of divorces per month in Nebraska over that six-year period. However, they also found that the 1972 enactment of the no-fault law had no discernible effects on that increase. They then did separate time series analyses for blacks and whites. That revealed that the law did have an effect for black couples, but not for whites. Divorces for both groups were increasing over the entire period (1969–1974); but after the law was enacted, there was an even greater increase among blacks. Similarly, separate time series analyses for couples under 30 years old, between 30 and 50 years old, and over 50 years old revealed that only for the latter group did the law increase the rate of divorce.

Campbell (1969b) was able to show that an interrupted time series design was of great help in interpreting the results of that Connecticut speed crackdown we mentioned earlier. The data he employed are plotted in Figure 3. As you can see, the change from before to after the crackdown was actually smaller than some of the other year-to-year changes. The decreases in fatalities from 1951 to 1952 and from 1953 to 1954 are actually larger than the decrease that appeared to result from the crackdown in 1956. The chart in Figure 3B also illustrates the notion of statistical regression. That is, if you move along the chart from left to right, when you reach any point that is the highest so far, the next point is lower, that

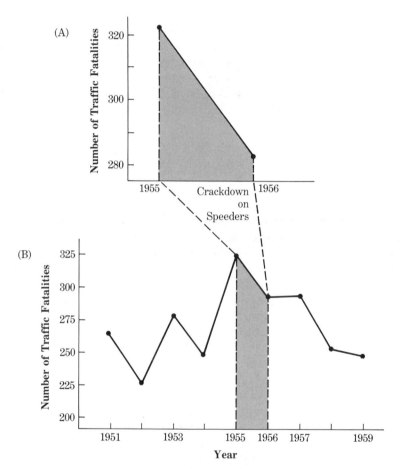

Figure 3 THE APPEARANCE OF EFFECTIVENESS. The Connecticut speed crackdown of 1956 was instituted because of the record high number of traffic fatalities in 1955. (A) Viewed alone the data for 1955 and 1956 show a sharp decline in traffic deaths and appear to lead to the conclusion that the crackdown was effective. (B) When those same data appear as part of a time series the previous conclusion is clearly premature. (From Campbell, 1969b.)

is, closer to the average of the series as a whole. Similarly, when you reach any point that is the lowest so far, the next point is higher. Thus, time series data give you a better idea of the context into which an intervention or treatment is introduced. Compare A and B, in Figure 3 for example. They convey completely different impressions of the efficacy of the crackdown.

With the addition of an untreated control group, the interrupted time series design becomes considerably more informative. With such an addition, the design becomes

Group 1   O   O   O   O   O   O   X   O   O   O   O   O   O

Group 2   O   O   O   O   O   O   O   O   O   O   O   O

Now you can see whether the trend in the data for Group 1 differs from the trend for Group 2. The key, of course, is that there should be an abrupt discontinuity in the trend for Group 1 immediately following the intervention, but no such abrupt change for Group 2 should occur at that particular time. Note that this design enables you to rule out the effects of history and instrumentation as threats to internal validity, but the simple one-group time series does not. The reason for that is that both groups are presumably experiencing the same extraneous external events and the observations being made are the same for both groups. It also enables you to assess whether there is an interaction of selection and maturation, which the simple pretest–posttest with nonequivalent groups cannot do. To see what makes the difference, look at Figure 4. The point here is not for you to memorize which designs take care of which threats to internal validity. Rather, the point is to show that if you understand the basic nature of the threats to internal validity, a little carefully applied logic and common sense will help you piece together the best design possible under your particular circumstances.

For example, Doob, Carlsmith, Freedman, Landauer, and Soleng (1969) reported an imaginative use of a time series design. They noted that there are several psychological reasons why an introductory low price for an article might have an effect opposite to that intended. Dissonance theory (Wicklund & Brehm, 1976), for example, predicts that the higher the price you have to pay for something, the more you will come to like it. You have to justify to yourself why you were willing to pay the higher price, and you can do that by convincing yourself that it really is a swell product. Another possibility is that when a product is introduced at a low price it becomes defined as a cheap product. When the price is later raised to the normal selling price, it is not seen as worth it. In a series of five time series field studies (using mouthwash, toothpaste, aluminum foil, light bulbs, and cookies), Doob et al. examined the effect of introducing a product at a lower than normal price and then later raising the price to its correct level. They selected pairs of supermarkets and introduced the product – say,

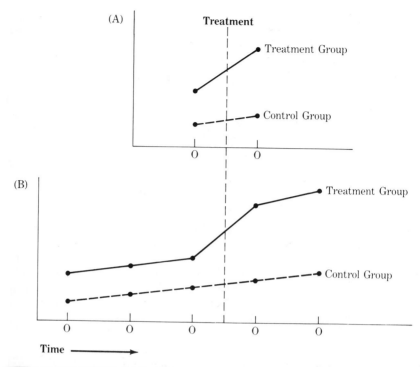

Figure 4 PRETEST-POSTTEST CHART does not rule out the possibility of an interaction between group selection and maturation. (A) It is possible that the treatment group had been improving at a faster rate than the controls, even before the treatment was administered. (B) The interrupted time series design allows you to assess the improvement rates of the two groups prior to treatment. In the case above, it looks as though the two groups had been maturing at similar rates before the treatment, but the treatment increased the rate of improvement of the group exposed to it.

mouthwash—into one member of each pair at a price of $0.25 per quart bottle and kept the price there for nine days. In the other member of each pair, the identical mouthwash was introduced at $0.39 a bottle. After nine days, the price was put at $0.39 per bottle in both supermarkets of all pairs. Sales were recorded continuously by the sundries buyer as he replenished stock in each store. Three weeks after the beginning of the study, stores where the initial selling price was $0.39 were selling more of the mouthwash than stores where the initial selling price—for exactly the same mouthwash—was $0.25.

Note that there is no reason why the number of observations before and after the treatment should be the same. It simply looks better that way in a diagram. But, if your initial observations were simply to establish the comparability of the two groups, you might have a design that looks like this:

$$\text{Group 1} \quad O \quad X \quad O \quad O$$
$$\text{Group 2} \quad O \qquad\quad O \quad O$$

This is very similar to the design used by Baum, Fleming, and Singer (1982) to examine the reactions to the decontamination procedures used following the nuclear reactor accident at Three Mile Island. Group 1 in that case consisted of residents of Three Mile Island. Group 2 consisted of residents of Frederick, Maryland, a town some distance away from the reactor. The treatment was the venting of the radioactive gases from the contaminated building into the atmosphere and the observations were a variety of performance, self-report, and biochemical measures taken before and after the venting took place.

There are other variations on the interrupted time series that can enhance its value for establishing a cause and effect relationship between the treatment and what follows. One that is particularly good is referred to (Cook & Campbell, 1979) as the INTERRUPTED TIME SERIES WITH SWITCHING REPLICATIONS. The idea is that the intervention is introduced to both groups but at different points in time. It looks like this:

$$\text{Group 1} \quad O \quad O \quad O \quad X \quad O \quad O \quad O \quad O \quad O \quad O$$
$$\text{Group 2} \quad O \quad O \quad O \quad O \quad O \quad O \quad X \quad O \quad O \quad O$$

The nice thing about this design is that it gives you the opportunity to see if the treatment works in each of two different groups at two different points in time. If it does, that should increase your confidence that it really is the treatment that is making the difference. If it works for one group, but not the other, you will have a puzzle on your hands. It could be that the time of introduction is crucial or that there is some characteristic peculiar to the group in which the treatment worked that is crucial.

There are a number of other variations on the basic interrupted time series design. But with each, the key is to decide what data you would need to make a case that it was, indeed, the intervention of interest that changed the nature of the series and to rule out each of the threats to internal validity. As Cook and Campbell (1979) point out, your best tools in this endeavor are logic, common sense, and a clear understanding of the nature of the intervention and its anticipated effects. A word of caution is in order on this last point. For the greatest interpretability in any of the time series designs, the intervention (or treatment) should produce its effects quickly. For interventions that are implemented slowly, over a long period of time, or for interventions that have delayed effects, the data from the time series are likely to be ambiguous. The effects may not show up in the observations immediately following the onset of the intervention. That means it is going to be more difficult for you to establish that it was the intervention that produced the effects. People will look at the data from the observations immediately following the intervention and say, "See, nothing has changed." There are several things that will help in such situations. One is to have a strong, plausible, theoretical explanation for why the effects of interest should be delayed. Another, that Cook and Campbell (1979) recommend, is to try the two-group time series with switching replications. When you can demonstrate similar delayed effects in both groups, it becomes more believable that they were produced by the intervention.

An Illustration: The British Breathalyser

On October 9, 1967, Her Majesty's government began enforcing a new law aimed at reducing traffic accidents and fatalities. At the time, there had been a continuous annual rise in automobile-related deaths and serious injuries in Britain stretching back into the early 1950s. But the specific impetus for the new law was a series of studies that implicated alcohol use as a factor in the production of a large percentage of those automobile accidents. In the preceding year, for example, a report by the Automobile Manufacturer's Association (1966) had cited three studies of fatal accidents in each of which over 50 percent of the drivers had been found to have alcohol in their bloodstreams. Thus, as Ross, Campbell, and Glass (1970) pointed out, the British government had a good, sound basis for believing that getting drunk drivers off the roads would decrease the carnage on the highways.

Officially referred to as the British Road Safety Act of 1967, the new law had four essential points. First, the legal limit was set at 0.08 percent alcohol in the blood. That means that anyone who was found to have a higher concentration of alcohol in the bloodstream was considered to be intoxicated and, thus, breaking the law if he or she happened to be driving an automobile. To give you an idea of what that 0.08 percent means, it is the level of intoxication a person weighing 160 pounds would reach if they had four drinks, each containing 1 oz of 86-proof alcohol, within one hour. The second feature of the law was that police were authorized to give an on-the-scene breath test if they had reason to believe that a driver had been drinking or had committed a traffic offense. The breath test was referred to as the Breathalyser and involves exhaling into a device that registers the amount of alcohol present in the exhaled breath. It is not particularly accurate; but if the driver failed this test, he or she could then be taken to a police station for a more accurate blood test. If the blood test revealed a concentration of more than 0.08 percent alcohol, the driver was then charged with driving under the influence of alcohol. Third, the law instituted a mandatory punishment for drunken driving: suspension of the driver's license for one year and a fine of 100 pounds sterling or imprisonment for up to four months or both. There were also penalties for failure to submit to the breath test or the blood test or both. Finally, the law was given a great deal of advance publicity, so that the public was well aware—in advance—of both the date on which it would take effect and the penalties involved. Ross et al. (1970) noted that this latter feature is important for purposes of doing a time series analysis of the effects of the law. The publicity helps to produce an abrupt change in the series. If it turned out that there was only a gradual change over time as people became aware of the new law, it would be difficult to distinguish such a gradual change from long-term trends. To determine whether the new law really reduced traffic fatalities, Ross et al. decided that some sort of control series was needed. They considered using data from Ireland and/or Belgium, but those countries differed from Britain in a variety of ways, including the hours that drinking establishments were open, rates of automobile ownership, and highway construction. Because it was anticipated that the new Breathalyser law would have its effect primarily during and immediately following the hours that pubs were open on weekends, it occurred to them that it should be possible to use casualties at other times of the week as a control. That is, the casualty rates between 7:00 a.m. and 10:00 a.m. Monday through Friday, when the pubs are closed and people are on their way to work—and, presumably, not drinking—should not be affected by the new law. On the other hand, the casualty rate on weekend evenings and the wee hours of Saturday and Sunday mornings, when the pubs are open and people are winding their way home from a night on the town, should indeed be influenced by the new law.

The data are presented in Figure 5 for the three-year period beginning in January 1966 and ending in December 1968. The Breathalyser law went into effect just a little past the middle of this period, in early October 1967. As you can see in the figure, the law had essentially no effect on the control series, that is, the fatalities and serious casualties occurring during commuting hours. However, in the months immediately following implementation of the law, there was a precipitous drop in the numbers of fatalities and serious casualties occurring on weekend nights. Ross et al. (1970) reported that the drop in fatalities on weekend nights that occurred between September and October of 1967 is the largest one-month shift for the entire three years plotted in the figure. It was also the largest one-month shift since January 1961, which was the farthest point back in time for which data on monthly casualty rates by seriousness of casualty were available. The odds against the September to October 1967 shift being the largest, by chance alone, are 93 to 1.

It appears that the British Road Safety Act of 1967 really had the intended effect of reducing traffic fatalities and serious casualties. But, before

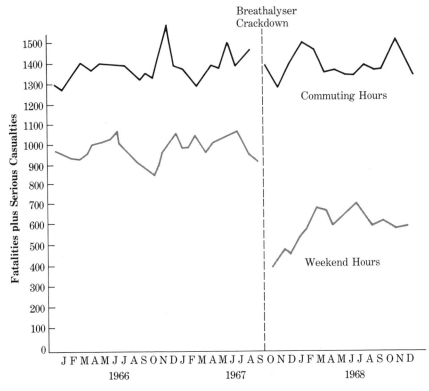

Figure 5   TRAFFIC FATALITIES drop during weekend hours with Breathalyser crackdown (October 1967) but not during commuting hours. (From Ross, Campbell, & Glass, 1970.)

Ross et al. could feel confident about that conclusion, they had to consider a number of threats to its validity. First, inspection of Figure 5 seems to indicate that maturation is not a factor. The data for October 1967 and the ensuing months do not appear to be a continuation of a trend that had started prior to the implementation of the law. Also, there is no reason to believe that testing or instrumentation are relevant threats here. The procedures for recording traffic accidents and casualties were well established and the data from the control series (commuting hours) – seem to indicate that they did not change with the beginning enforcement of the new law. Neither is regression a plausible alternative to the finding that the new law produced the drop in fatalities and serious casualties. You will recall that regression was a confounding factor in the Connecticut speed crackdown because that crackdown was instituted as a result of a record-high number of traffic deaths in 1955. In contrast, the figure shows that the months preceding October 1967 were not particularly unusual in terms of the number of deaths on British highways. Also, the data following the Breathalyser crackdown are more, rather than less, extreme, considering the preceding series as a whole. Regression effects produce subsequent data that are closer to the mean of the preceding series, not farther from the mean.

Ross et al. went on to consider a number of specific situational factors that might conceivably have been related to the drop in fatalities and serious casualties on weekend nights following the crackdown. These included general improvements in traffic control that were occurring in Britain at the time, newly introduced standards for tires and tire safety inspections, fewer two-wheeled vehicles on the road, and insurance discounts for safe driving. There are at least two reasons why none of these seem to be plausible explanations for the precipitous drop in fatalities that occurred in October 1967. First, these were all gradual or continuing changes or both. The new tire standards, for example, would have shown an effect only very slowly as new cars with the improved tires were put on the road and replacement tires were purchased for older cars. Similarly, the improvement of roadways and traffic control was an ongoing project, and insurance companies did not suddenly begin giving discounts for safe driving on October 9, 1967. The second reason why these are not plausible alternative explanations is that they did not make a difference in the control series (the number of fatalities and casualties during commuting hours). If highway improvements had suddenly reached the critical point of perfection in September 1967, the sharp decrease in accidents would have been noticeable during commuting hours as well as on weekend nights. It was not.

One of the nice things about the British Breathalyser study was that the data necessary to evaluate the effects of the new law were routinely collected and had been for years. They were sitting there in the archives waiting for Ross et al. to make use of them, and the British Ministry of Transport was good enough to furnish the data on request. No one was inconvenienced, no one's routine was interrupted, and no one was made to feel like a guinea pig. Unfortunately, research in natural settings is not always like that. The interventions and treatments utilized in some quasi-experiments and field experiments do interfere with people's lives, and that poses some ethical problems.

Some Ethical Considerations

Imagine yourself at a Provincial Park in upper Canada. You have spent a long day canoeing and hiking and after dinner at the lodge, you plan to take in the free movie in the recreation room. You show up at 7:55 p.m. and find a seat; and promptly at 8:00 o'clock the movie begins. Surprise!

It is not the movie that was advertised on the bulletin board. Instead, it is a film about alcohol abuse and safety in the national parks. It does have some interesting facts. In 1979, for example, there were 316 drownings, one third of which were related to alcohol use. Even so, you feel puzzled. But, the film is short. It is over in 15 minutes. Then the lights go on again, and the Park Ranger asks everyone to fill out a brief questionnaire. Your puzzlement increases, as do the grumblings in the back of the room, but rather than make a scene, you quickly fill out the questionnaire. Finally, at 8:25 p.m., the lights go off again and the movie you came to see begins. The next day you ask the Ranger and find out you have been in a field study conducted by the Addiction Research Foundation in Toronto. They are interested in changing attitudes toward drinking and are showing the film you saw to some people and simply asking others to fill out the questionnaire without seeing the film.

How would you feel about that? No one asked whether or not you would be willing to participate. No one paid you for the 25 minutes of your time that the film and the questionnaire took. The columnist from the *Toronto Star* to whom this actually happened was more than a little annoyed (Jones, 1984), although he was quite sympathetic to the need for action on alcohol-related accidents. As he put it, he was a "bit short" with park personnel the next day. The issue, of course, is lack of informed consent and, possibly, invasion of privacy – although he could have refused to answer the questions on the questionnaire. There was also some deception involved. If the columnist had not complained and inquired about what was going on, he would never have known who was sponsoring the research or why the research was being done.

The columnist's reaction to his involuntary research participation is, apparently, not an unusual one. Wilson and Donnerstein (1976) described eight field experiments to a variety of people aged 17 to 85 and asked them how they would feel if they found out they had been a subject in such research. Two of the eight field experiments were as follows:

> A female and a confederate experimenter visit shoe stores at times when there are more customers than salesmen. One of them is wearing a shoe with a broken heel. She rejects whatever the salesman shows her. The confederate, posing as a friend of the customer, surreptitiously takes notes on the salesman's behavior (Schaps, 1972).

> People sitting alone on park benches are asked to be interviewed by an experimenter who gives the name of a fictitious survey research organization that he claims to represent. At the beginning of the interview, the experimenter asks a person sitting nearby, who is actually a confederate, if he would mind answering the questions at the same time. The confederate responds with opinions that are clearly opposite those of the subject and makes demeaning remarks about the subject's answers; for example, "that's ridiculous"; "that's just the sort of thing you'd expect to hear in this park." (Abelson & Miller, 1967)

These field experiments had actually been done, and they represent a strategy of accosting individual subjects (Bochner, 1979) to secure their participation in the research. (For another strategy, see the discussion of STREET THEATER below.) Wilson and Donnerstein found that a large percentage of the people to whom such research was described did not believe it was justified. Many also reported that they, personally, would have felt harassed if they had been singled out for participation.

One of the major reasons that investigators attempt such unobtrusive research, of course, is that it avoids many biases that are present when subjects know they are taking part in an investigation. For example, if

---

Issues and Discussions

STREET THEATER

In an effort to enhance the meaningfulness and generalizability of their research, many social and behavioral scientists took to the streets in the 1960s and 1970s. Their intent, usually, was to test hypotheses about social behavior in natural settings: street corners, subways, park benches, shops, libraries, any of a variety of places in which people would not be conscious of being participants in research. One of the basic techniques for recruiting subjects in such situations is what Bochner (1979) referred to as the STREET THEATER STRATEGY. That is, you stage an incident of some sort that is sufficiently salient so that everybody in the immediate vicinity will notice it. You then record the reactions to the incident.

Consider a few examples. Piliavin, Rodin, Piliavin (1969) were interested in helping behavior and had a confederate stagger and fall to the floor of a subway car. In some cases the confederate appeared to be sick, in other cases he appeared to be intoxicated. The measures of interest were how many people attempted to help and how quickly they did so. Latané and Elman (1970) repeatedly staged a theft in which one or two robbers walked out of a Beverage Center with a case of beer, in plain sight of other customers. The measure of interest here was how many people reported the theft.

Bochner (1979) said that the street theater strategy should only be used when it is not "so intrusive as to injure, alarm, or affront members of the public." Think about the two situations just described. Would you have been alarmed or affronted by them? I would, especially if I later found out it was all just research that some cute folks down at the college were conducting. The study by Wilson and Donnerstein, which is described in the text, indicated that my reaction is not unusual. Many people find it very arousing and distressful to see others apparently suffering in public places or to be witnesses to apparent crimes. Because of these sorts of concerns and the lack of informed consent procedures in such field experiments, the enthusiasm for the street theater strategy in research seems to be on the wane.

they do not know they are taking part in research, they are less likely to respond in a socially desirable manner or to be concerned about what the investigator will think of them. But, as Cook and Campbell (1979) pointed out, "from ethical and perhaps legal perspectives, much technically feasible unobtrusive experimentation is not desirable since it violates the ethical requirement of 'informed consent'." However, Campbell (1969a) and others have argued that if what the subjects are asked to do in such research is innocuous, takes very little time or effort, and is within the range of the subject's normal experience, then it can be ethically justified. For example, placing apparently lost letters in different locations to see whether the people who find them will mail them (Milgram, 1969) is probably not an objectionable procedure.

A problem with such innocuous treatments, however, is that they are not likely to deal with anything of real significance in the respondents' lives. When the treatment is something that will make a difference in the subject's life, a new set of ethical concerns arise. As you know by now, untreated control groups are usually essential for establishing that a treatment does have a certain effect. But if the treatment is a beneficial one – or even a potentially beneficial one – it may be difficult to justify withholding it from some people while giving it to others (Diener & Crandall, 1978). In fact, some people would argue that withholding a known beneficial treatment cannot be justified. But, there are exceptions, and there is at least one way around the problem. One exception consists of those circumstances in which available resources are simply not sufficient to treat everyone in need. For example, if you were interested in the issue of whether or not admission to a home for the aged was beneficial or harmful for the elderly, you will have to work within the capacity of the homes that are willing to cooperate in your study. One possibility is that while people are on the waiting lists, they can serve as the untreated control group. That is, you could compare the health and well-being of those admitted to the health and well-being of similar people on the waiting list. Lieberman (1961) used such a design in his examination of mortality rates among people admitted to the Orthodox Jewish Home for the Aged in Chicago. During the period between 1947 and 1959, 860 applicants were placed on the home's waiting list after an initial physical and mental screening. Of these 860, 700 were later admitted to the home, 78 withdrew their applications, and 82 died while still on the waiting list. The waiting period for the 700 actually admitted averaged 6.4 months following completion of the screening tests and interviews. Lieberman computed the mortality rate for those admitted to the home for the first year following admission and found a 24.7 percent first-year mortality rate. The comparable rate for those who died while still on the waiting list was only 10.4 percent. Those are surprising figures, and they may say something about the expectations that many people have about homes for the aged, that is, that they are places where one goes to die. But, the point here is simply that Lieberman could not have done the study if the home in question could have accommodated everyone who applied as soon as they applied. There would have been no people who died while still on the waiting list to whom to compare the people admitted to the home.

The Lieberman study suggests a way around the ethical problem posed by the necessity of withholding beneficial treatments from some in order to evaluate the effects of the treatment, although in Lieberman's study it appears that withholding what people sought was beneficial. In any event, the idea is that treatment can be temporarily withheld from one group of subjects. Patients applying for psychotherapy, for example, often are put on a waiting list until the therapist has a free slot in his or her schedule. The patients on the waiting list could conceivably be used as controls for those currently in therapy, and the relative improvement in the two groups over the ensuing weeks could be compared. It may have occurred to you that what is being advocated here is a version of a time series design we discussed earlier, the interrupted time series with switching replications.

Note that the ethical problem posed by an untreated control group is only a problem when you have reason to believe that the treatment will indeed be beneficial. As Diener and Crandall (1978) have noted, when the treatment is of unknown efficacy, there is no problem with having an untreated control group. In fact, you may find that you have done the members of that group a favor if the treatment turns out to be harmful.

Summary

To establish whether or not a given intervention has certain effects, it is usually necessary to have some basis of comparison. That is, you need some information about what the situation would have been like without the intervention. The problem is that many interventions and naturally occurring changes occur only one time and to only one group of people. Thus, to establish a basis of comparison, it is often necessary to use another, nonequivalent group to whom the intervention did not occur. That can result in some ambiguity because every way in which the two groups differ is a possible threat to the validity of any inference concerning the effects of the intervention. But, a design such as the untreated control group design with pretest and posttest can be quite helpful in this regard because the data from the pretest enable you to establish the preintervention similarity of the two groups.

There are at least thirteen threats to internal validity, that is, thirteen possible contaminating factors that you must be able to rule out before concluding that the intervention or change of interest to you really made a difference. These threats are history, maturation, testing, instrumentation, statistical regression, selection, mortality, all the things that can interact with selection, ambiguity about the direction of causality, diffusion or imitation of treatments, compensatory equalization of treatments, rivalry, and demoralization. That is the standard list of things to watch out for. But, in addition, there may be specific factors in the setting in which you plan to do research or specific aspects of your procedure that can cause problems. You have to imagine the intervention producing exactly the change you expect, then ask yourself; "What are the most likely alternative explanations that people could offer for that effect, if I told them about it?" Then you decide what additional data you will need to rule out those alternatives.

Several variations of the interrupted time series design can be used. Interrupted time series designs, especially those with an untreated control group and those with switching replications can be excellent ways of ruling out most of the threats to internal validity. In addition to enabling you to establish the effects of an intervention more clearly than the designs discussed earlier, the interrupted time series designs also enable you to see trends over time and changes in those trends. They enable you to rule out such threats to internal validity as interactions between selection and maturation which you cannot do with the simpler untreated control group design with pretest and posttest. As an added benefit, the interrupted time series design with switching replications avoids the ethical problems of withholding a possibly beneficial treatment from the control group. In the interrupted time series with switching replications, both groups are exposed to the treatment, just at different points in time.

The usefulness of quasi-experiments and field experiments have been illustrated by the analyses of the Connecticut speed crackdown, the Nebraska no-fault divorce law, a hypothetical example concerning taped lectures, and, finally, the British Breathalyser. In each of these examples, the emphasis was on establishing the data or additional information or both needed to rule out all plausible threats to internal validity, that is, threats to the inference that it was the intervention in question that made a difference. With the Connecticut speed crackdown, the threats to internal validity apparently could not be ruled out. With the British Breathalyser, in contrast, all the plausible threats could be ruled out.

Finally, ethical problems arise in quasi-experiments and field experiments. These include lack of informed consent, invasion of privacy, and withholding of beneficial treatments from people who could profit from them. More will be said about these issues in Chapter Eight.

Recommended Reading

Like this chapter, these five readings present an assortment of ideas and concepts that may prove useful in designing and evaluating field research. If forced to extract a common theme from the five, I would have to say it is the notion of flexibility, of trying an idea or design to see if it is useful and of being willing to discard it if it is not.

Kidder, L. H. Qualitative research and quasi-experimental frameworks. In M. B. Brewer and B. E. Collins (Eds.), *Scientific inquiry and the social sciences.* San Francisco: Jossey Bass, 1981.

Many people think of qualitative research as purely descriptive and unconcerned with causal analysis. But, as Kidder noted in this chapter, reports of qualitative research often contain numerous propositions about the causal relationships among the events observed. How are you to assess the validity of those propositions? According to Kidder, one possibility is to take the threats to internal validity that were identified in the preceding chapter and try to apply them, one by one, to the events observed. *History:* Was there something about the particular period(s) observed that would have influenced the events? *Testing:* Did the observer's presence influence what happened in a way that changed the course of events? *Mortality:* Did some members of the group being observed drop out or refuse to go on and, if so, how did that change what happened? If you do this systematically you may find that you can place more (or less) confidence in the causal propositions contained in reports of qualitative research. It is a good exercise in the logic of research, and Kidder works through several examples to show you how it can be done.

Medawar, P. B. *Advice to a young scientist.* New York: Harper & Row, 1979.

Sir Peter Medawar's *Advice* is one in a series, sponsored by the Alfred P. Sloan Foundation, in which certain accomplished and articulate scientists have been encouraged to write about their own scientific lives. The sponsor's hope was that the series would help inform a general public understanding of the scientific enterprise. It is difficult to tell how well they have succeeded, but the two books from the series that I have read (*Advice* and Lewis Thomas's *The Youngest Science*) are both worth your time and effort. *Advice,* after all, is only about a hundred pages long. Yet, in it Medawar managed to comment on everything from how to present a scientific paper (do not read and be brief) to the life-style most conducive to creativity (quiet and untroublesome). The tone is amazingly patronizing at times, but there are some interesting observations about research. For example, Medawar pointed out that the beginner must, of course, know the literature, that is, he or she must read "but intently and choosily and not too much . . . by far the best way to become proficient in research is to get on with it." You cannot wait until you know everything that has been written on the subject. You will never get around to collecting your own data if you try, and Medawar rightly has noted that getting some results of your own is, psychologically, most important.

Merbaum, M., & Lowe, M. R. Serendipity in research in clinical psychology. In P. C. Kendall & J. N. Butcher (Eds.), *Handbook of research methods in clinical psychology*. New York: Wiley, 1982.

Many people have called attention to the role of accidental discoveries, or serendipity, in research. Unfortunately, they all seem to cite the same two or three well-known examples, such as Fleming's discovery of penicillin in 1928. They then quote Pasteur—"Chance favors the prepared mind," admonish you to prepare your mind, and go on to another topic. After seeing the same two or three examples over and over, you begin to wonder if the role of serendipity is overstated. That is, if there are only two or three examples, it is hardly worth learning to spell the word. Thus, Merbaum and Lowe have done us all a service by searching the literature for examples of serendipity. The list they have compiled is quite an impressive one and includes, for example, Pavlov's work on conditioned reflexes, Skinner's discovery of the effects of certain reinforcement schedules, and Olds and Milner's discovery of pleasure centers in the brain (they put an electrode in the wrong place). Merbaum and Lowe also discussed why it is often, even usually, difficult to recognize the implications of unanticipated results in research. As they put it, most researchers approach their work with a strong confirmatory stance, that is, they seem to be looking only for data that will support their hypothesis. They seem not to see the data that support other ideas. The lesson is that you need an open, as well as a prepared, mind.

Swingle, P. G. (Ed.). *Social psychology in natural settings: A reader in field experimentation*. Chicago: Aldine, 1973.

The 24 chapters in this book will provide you with a good sample of the imaginative use of field experimentation to investigate a variety of topics. Consider the following examples. In Chapter 11, Knox and Inkster have reported a study carried out at a race track in which they questioned some bettors immediately before and others immediately after they had placed their bets. The latter were significantly more confident that their horse would win. In Chapter 1, Smith and Curnow have described a study in which they varied the volume of background music in eight supermarkets and found that the louder the music, the less time shoppers spent in the stores. (Personally, I wish the results of that study could be distributed to all store managers.) In Chapter 3, Heussenstamm reported that students who had had no traffic violations in over a year suddenly began receiving more than their share of tickets when they put Black Panther bumper stickers on their cars. In Chapter 7, Doob and Gross found that the higher the status your car implies, the less likely the person behind you will be to blow their horn when you sit too long at a traffic light. These and the remaining chapters make interesting reading, and they are sure to give you some ideas about field settings and techniques for testing the hypotheses of interest to you.

Ricken, H. W., & Boruch, R. F. (Eds.) *Social experimentation: A method for planning and evaluating social intervention*. New York: Academic press, 1974.

This is a book that will give you a good review of the material we have covered in this chapter, as well as an introduction to the issues that we shall cover in the following two. It contains discussions of why and when to experiment, experimental design and analysis, quasi-experimental designs, and problems in the execution and management of research. The book was commissioned by the Social Science Research Council and written by a panel of distinguished methodologists, which included Donald T. Campbell. It is written in nontechnical language, so do not be afraid. After all, one of its avowed purposes is "to interest younger social scientists who may not yet have fixed their career objectives or who wish to expand the range of their capabilities to include the use of experimental methods for analyzing, planning, and evaluating solutions to current and future social problems." The book also contains a lengthy appendix of annotated references to research that has employed quasi-experimental and experimental designs in the field. It is well worth reading.

8

Evaluation Research

To evaluate something means to ascertain its value or worth, to examine and judge it. It is something that you do all the time. You evaluate people, places, courses, restaurants, almost everything you come in contact with, and you do it so quickly and automatically sometimes that you are not even conscious of its occurrence. In fact, it seems to be unusual to withhold judgment about anything. Once you have formulated an opinion about something, of course, you are likely to act on that opinion as if it were the truth. You have a bad meal in a restaurant and never go back. You meet someone who seems unpleasant and abrasive and you avoid them in the future.

The danger, of course, is that your initial evaluations may not be based on good evidence. You might have visited the restaurant on the chief cook's night off. The person who seemed abrasive might have been under a lot of stress that particular day. The consequences of these faulty judgments are usually benign. There are many other restaurants, and people, around and the absence of the ones that you misjudged is unlikely to create a great deficit in your life. Usually, you are even protected from regretting their absence because you never find out that you misjudged them. But if you could afford to eat out only once in a great while, you might be a little more careful. You might call the restaurant and find out ahead of time what night the chef was off. You might ask around to see if anyone else had eaten there and what their opinion was of the place. The point, of course, is that when your resources are scarce, you have to be more careful about how you use them.

On a societal level, resources usually are scarce, so you do indeed have to be careful about how they are allocated. Support of a program like Medicare may mean that there are other worthy programs that cannot be funded. Providing free school lunches for poor children sounds like a great idea, but what will that mean about the availability of funds for Aid to Families with Dependent Children? Even when funds for a particular program are available, you want to know whether or not they are being used properly. Because funds are limited, you are particularly sensitive about waste and inefficiency. If those free school lunches are being served, are they going to the neediest kids? Are they nutritious? Are the supplies for them being purchased at economical prices? In 1984 there was a public uproar when it was revealed that the Department of Defense was paying outrageous prices for simple tools and supplies for the armed forces. A hammer that you or I could purchase for $7 at the local hardware store cost the government $436 (Figure 1). When things like that occur, taxpayers feel that they are being taken for a ride, and rightly so. With increasing government expenditures on social, educational, and medical programs, there has been increasing pressure from the taxpayers – via Congress – to

HOW TO CHARGE $436 FOR A $7 HAMMER

From the Congressional Record, May 15. When Iowa Representative Berkley Bedell asked the Department of Defense how it could justify paying $436 for a hammer that retails for $7.66, the Navy furnished him with this breakdown of costs from the contractor, Gould Electronics.

Purchased Item		Amount
ITEM–HAMMER. QUANTITY–1.		
Direct Material		$7.00
Material Packaging		1.00
Material Handling		
Overhead (19.8%)		2.00
Engineering Support:		
Spares/Repair Dept.	1.0 hr.	
Program Support/		
Admin.	0.4	
Program Management	1.0	
Secretarial	0.2	
	2.6 hrs.	37.00
Engineering Overhead (110%)		41.00
Manufacturing Support:		
Mechanical Sub-assembly	0.3 hr.	
Quality Control	0.9	
Operations Program		
Management	1.5	
Program Planning	4.0	
Manufacturing Project		
Engineering	1.0	
Quality Assurance	0.1	
	7.8 hrs.	93.00
Manufacturing Overhead (110%)		102.00
		283.00
General & Administrative		
Expenses (31.8%)		90.00
Negotiation Fee		56.00
Interest Charge		7.00
TOTAL PRICE		$436.00

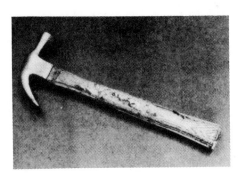

Figure 1 REVELATION OF GOVERNMENT WASTE has been a major force behind the growing demand for evaluation research. (From *Harper's*, October, 1984.)

see that the money is being well spent, to see that the public at large is getting its money's worth.

The growth and spread of evaluation research are the direct result of this mounting pressure for accountability and sanity in the allocation of the nation's resources. As research methods go, however, evaluation research is still relatively young. And, like many adolescents, its identity is somewhat diffuse. EVALUATION RESEARCH can best be characterized as a heterogeneous assortment of techniques, procedures, and methods for "collecting, analyzing, and interpreting information on the need, implementation, and impact of intervention efforts to better the lot of humankind and improve social conditions and community life" (Rossi, Freeman, & Wright, 1979). That takes in a lot of ground. Translated, what it means for you is that all of the methods discussed in the preceding chapters are relevant to evaluation research. Participation observation, archival research, interviewing, quasi-experimentation – the whole kit and caboodle.

But there is more. There is an element in evaluation research that is largely absent from any of those methods taken individually, although it was briefly touched on in the discussion of participant observation. That is, evaluation research is often, even usually, a political undertaking (Cronbach, Ambron, Dornbush, Hess, Hornik, Phillips, Walker & Weiner 1981; Weiss, 1972). Programs compete for funds and attention. They have constituencies, people who profit from their continuation and suffer when they are terminated. There are conflicts of interest that have to be negotiated. The people in charge of running a program may see it in a completely different light from those charged with evaluating it. There is institutional inertia to be overcome, both to get new programs started and to end programs that are ineffective or too costly for the benefits derived. All of this makes evaluation research tremendously exciting, of course; but it can also make it tremendously frustrating. To top it all off, the evaluation researcher is usually attempting to get some evidence about a program that he or she had no part in setting in motion. But, let us take these things one at a time.

Policies, Programs, and the Need to Check Things Out

It is important to note at the outset that policy and program are not the same thing. A POLICY is a general, usually somewhat abstract, statement of principle. It is designed to influence decisions and determine actions by pointing out the desired end result. Congress, for example, may decide that it is bad for the nation for small businessmen to be driven out of business. The reasoning might be that with fewer small businesses, there would be a growth of monopolies, a decrease in competition, gradually rising prices, and lessened pressure for innovation. Thus, the Small Business Administration (SBA) might be charged by Congress with finding ways to encourage and sustain small businesses. One thing the Administration might do is loan money at low interest rates to people with an idea for starting a new business. This money-lending scheme would be a program by which the SBA hoped to realize the Congressional policy of encouraging small-scale entrepreneurship. Note that the SBA could have come up with other programs to achieve the same aim. They might have started a series of workshops on management techniques designed to help those already in business run their establishments more efficiently and more profitably. A PROGRAM, then, is simply a specific procedure, or plan, for attempting to reach the goal spelled out in the policy. And, a given policy might be realized by any of several different programs.

Congress, of course, is not the only policy-setting body. Your local city council might become concerned about the number of injuries and deaths due to drunk driving and charge the police department with finding ways – that is, programs – for getting drunk drivers off the highways and streets. But – and this is one of the reasons why some people have shied away from evaluation research – policy is often set without the advice and consent of those who are later asked to evaluate the programs intended to operationalize the policy. In the preceding chapters, it has been assumed that you would have complete control over your research, all the way from problem definition to final report. Evaluation research involves relinquishing some of that autonomy and, quite often, working on problems that others have defined for you. The trade-off, however, is that your research may have more of an impact on the real world, but there is no guarantee. As Ford (1977) put it, you are not under any obligation to do policy-action research; but if you do, you need to be aware that your "contribution will not be the only or even the major determinant of the ultimate decision." Policy-making – and policy revision – is, and is likely to remain, a political process, at least for the foreseeable future. But, well-conducted program evaluations can and do help shape the evolution of policy by producing pertinent and important information about which programs are worthy of continued support and which are not.

That is indeed important to know because it appears that many programs that may have looked great on the drawing board turn out not to accomplish what they were intended to accomplish. They just do not fly. For example, Mosteller (1981) and his colleagues collected a number of reports of social, sociomedical, and medical innovations that had been subjected to careful evaluations. The programs were quite diverse, ranging from an attempt to reduce delinquency among girls to a treatment for cancer of the bronchus. After studying the evaluation reports, each innovation was scored on a five-point scale, from +2 to −2. If the evidence indicated that the program (or treatment) appeared to work really well, it was given a +2. If it had no effect, it was given a 0. If it was much worse than the treatment it replaced, it was assigned a −2. Unfortunately, of 28 different innovations found in the literature, fewer than half were beneficial. Fifteen of the 28 received a score of 0 or less. That is cause for concern. It is also an excellent justification for evaluation research. As Mosteller (1981) has noted, if we are going to enjoy the benefits of social, educational, medical, and technological innovations, we need to weed out the bad from the good. If we do not, we end up paying double for things that do not work. They will cost us both in dollars and by blocking the introduction of more effective programs. The way to begin that sorting process is by being very clear about exactly what the program is supposed to do.

What Is Supposed to Be Accomplished?

From a practical point of view, the major problem with policy is that it is so abstract. Even though "to do the greatest good for the greatest number" may be an admirable goal, how would you know when it was being done? Statements of policy are usually not quite that lofty, but they are often close. Wholey, Nay, Scanlon, and Schmidt (1975), for example, noted that one of the goals of the National Institute of Mental Health in setting up the Community Mental Health Centers (CMHC) program was to "develop a community mental health science." How would one know when that had occurred? At exactly what point do the snippets of data and scattered ideas pertinent to a topic coalesce into a science? What is a science, anyway? The point, of course, is that policy has to be translated into clearly stated, measurable objectives before evaluation proper can even begin. As Shortell and Richardson (1978) put it, "There is no more important task for program administrators, providers of care, policy-makers, and evaluators than to specify in clear, precise, and measurable terms the program objectives to be accomplished." In other words, if you do not know where it is you are trying to go, you will not know when you get there. You also will not know if you do not get there.

Specifying those objectives is the first stage of the evaluation process. If you are in on the setting of policy, that is clearly an advantage, because then you are likely to have a firmer grasp of the intentions behind the policy. But, even if you are called in after the policy has been chiseled in stone, your first task as an evaluation researcher is to get the interested parties to agree about the objectives of the program. Securing that agreement is important—one might even say, crucial. Without it, you might put in a lot of time and effort, only to find out that half of the people concerned think you measured the wrong things. They were hoping that summer program for teenagers would reduce the rate of high school dropouts, not increase their average reading scores. Lack of prior agreement about objectives will give everybody ammunition to shoot the program down—and your efforts along with it. Of course, if they do not like what you find, they will manufacture some ammunition of their own—but, more about that later.

Given the importance of clearly stated, and agreed upon objectives, how do you go about writing them? Shortell and Richardson (1978) have made some suggestions that may help. First, they pointed out that there are a number of issues relevant to the program that you should think about. These are

1. CONTENT Is the program intended to change behavior? Or is it intended to change more subjective things such as knowledge, opinions, or attitudes?
2. LEVEL OF ABSTRACTION Are there objectives that differ in their concreteness and order of hoped-for achievement? For example, you may plan to provide educational outings and trips for underprivileged children (a concrete objective) so that their interest in school will be maintained (a more abstract objective that may be realized later). Beware of objectives that are too abstract, however. (See the Discussion on page 256 for one reason why.)
3. TARGET For whom, precisely, is the program intended?
4. SHORT-TERM OR LONG-TERM EFFECTS Will the effects of the program show up immediately, or will you have to wait until next year to see if it made any difference?
5. MAGNITUDE OF EFFECT How big a change do you expect?
6. STABILITY OF EFFECT How long is the effect supposed to last?
7. CONFLICTING EFFECTS If there is more than one objective (which there usually is), do any of them conflict with each other?
8. SIMILARITY OF OBJECTIVES If there is more than one objective, are they basically similar or will you be looking for effects in different domains?
9. IMPORTANCE If there is more than one objective, which are the most important?
10. SECOND-ORDER CONSEQUENCES Are there likely to be any unintended side effects of the program?

That is quite a list, but if you go through it systematically, you will find that you have sharpened your thinking about what the program is supposed to accomplish. That, in turn, will help you communicate the objectives to others and, possibly, make agreement—or, at least, negotiation—easier.

Shortell and Richardson had a couple of other suggestions about objectives. They noted that in your final list, each objective should state only a single aim or purpose. Sound familiar? It should. That is the same advice I gave you earlier about writing questions for interviews and questionnaires—no double-barreled questions (or objectives) allowed. It is also best to state your objectives with strong verbs, verbs that are action-oriented and describe an observable behavior. *To increase, to write,* and *to go* are examples of strong verbs. *To encourage, to promote,* and *to understand* are considerably weaker. They do not imply a specific action that you can see with the naked eye.

Once the objectives have been clearly stated, the next step is to get

DOES PSYCHOTHERAPY WORK?

The *American Heritage Dictionary* defines psychotherapy as the psychological treatment of mental, emotional, and nervous disorders. That takes in a lot of territory. In fact, some say that psychotherapy is such a broad collection of techniques, procedures, schools, and approaches that the question "Does psychotherapy work?" is meaningless. Gary VanderBos, an official of the American Psychological Association, goes even further. He has said, "It is a stupid question. It's like asking, 'Does surgery work?' " (Marshall, 1980). The only answer you can give to questions like that is, "Well, it depends."

Even so, in the last few years there has been increasing pressure from the U.S. Congress for some clear evidence on the effectiveness or ineffectiveness of psychotherapy. The pressure is generated, as pressure so often is, by people debating the issue of how best to allocate scarce economic resources. About 20 percent of the money spent in the United States on mental health care is used to pay for some form of the 100 or so different kinds of psychotherapy. Congress, being at least partly from Missouri, wants proof of effectiveness before agreeing to finance that 20 percent under Medicare. Consequently, in 1980 the National Institute of Mental Health began a $3.4 million trial comparing drugs to two forms of psychotherapy in the treatment of depression (Kolata, 1981). The two forms of psychotherapy to be evaluated are cognitive behavioral therapy and interpersonal therapy. The aim of the former is to show patients that they are reacting too negatively to ordinary events. In contrast, the aim of interpersonal therapy is to help the depressed get along better with others. The idea is that if their social relations improve, their depression will go away.

Critics of the study are quick to point out that it will still not answer the general question of whether psychotherapy works. But, the general question is unanswerable. The study will provide some evidence on the effectiveness of two specific versions of psychotherapy, and that is a step in the right direction. The point here, of course, is that in evaluation research you have to make your questions specific before you can begin to address them. Overly general questions may produce debate, but they are not likely to produce useful answers.

everyone to agree on what will serve as an index, or indicator, of each. This, of course, is the key step in operationalizing the objectives, a process you should be familiar with by now. At first glance, however, it might seem that if you have followed all of the above suggestions in writing your objectives, they would have been, *ipso facto*, operationalized. Not so! Consider the following example to see why.

Suppose that you are asked to conduct an evaluation of a psychiatric in-patient clinic and that one of the agreed upon objectives (Willer, 1977) is to provide frequent feedback to treatment staff about each patient. That is a reasonable objective, but it can be operationalized in several different ways. There could be weekly staff meetings at which each patient's behavior for the last week is discussed. You could arrange for the ward nurse to call each member of the treatment staff daily and report on their patients. You could station observers on the ward to code patient behavior into a 25-category coding system (see Chapters 3 and 4, if you have forgotten what that is). The observers might then report to you and you would give feedback to the treatment staff. You could station observers on the ward to code patient behavior into a 17-category coding scheme. . . . You see the point, no doubt. Clearly stated, measurable objectives still have to be operationalized, and usually, there are several ways in which that could be done. Thus, not only do you need agreement on the objectives themselves, you also need agreement on exactly how each will be achieved.

Once you have the objectives and they have been operationalized to everyone's satisfaction, there are still three steps to the overall evaluation process: (1) the implementation of the program, (2) the assessment of its impact, and (3) an analysis of the costs of the program relative to its benefits and effectiveness. For example, once the National Institute of Mental Health had decided what the Community Mental Health Centers program was supposed to accomplish (vague though it may have been), there remained the tasks of funding, staffing, building (or renting) Community Mental Health Centers around the nation (implementation), then finding ways to determine whether their presence made any difference (impact assessment), and, finally, calculating the costs of the program relative to benefits and effectiveness. (Impact assessment and cost benefit/effectiveness analysis will be discussed in the following section.)

What is implementation? Suppose that you have a beautifully designed program, with clear objectives that are well operationalized and that you are all geared up to do an impact assessment and cost-benefit analysis. All that will be wasted if the program is never implemented properly. It would be like a new car getting to the end of the assembly line without an engine. Just because the program is carefully designed, you cannot assume that everything will fall into place as planned. As the old saying goes, "There is many a slip 'twixt the cup and the lip." If the guy who was supposed to bolt the engine in was out to lunch when that new car rolled by, somebody is going to get a lemon. Not really, of course, because there is somebody a little farther down the assembly line who checks that the engine is really there. Similarly, in evaluation research, it is necessary to conduct what are referred to as FORMATIVE EVALUATIONS (Williams, 1975); that is, evaluations that address the question of whether the program has been implemented as planned. Before the overall impact of the program can be assessed, as Shortell and Richardson (1978) put it, ". . . the first question that must be asked is whether the program is operational." The objectives that deal with formative evaluation are usually the lower-order, more concrete ones: "Select three demonstration schools and three similar comparison schools." "Select a program coordinator." "Lease or buy six television monitors and video recorders." All those things have to be done to get the program in place and running smoothly. Then, and only then, can the impact of the program be determined. Determining the overall program impact is referred to as SUMMATIVE EVALUATION.

Using All the Tools You Have

If this were a typical evaluation research text, you would be in for some heavy methodological discussions at this point. But most of the methods used in evaluation research have already been covered in the preceding chapters. Participant observation, interviewing, archival research, content analysis, quasi-experimentation – everything that has been covered can be and has been tailored for use in specific evaluation projects. The key to carrying out high-quality evaluation research is to choose the best single method or blend of methods for the research that you want to do. It is a task that deserves some thought and planning after you have developed a thorough familiarity with the policy that is to be implemented via the program and the resources available for doing so. What is being advocated, of course, is the same general research strategy spelled out in Chapter One, that is, an open-minded exploration of the best method(s) available for finding out what is wanted about the program of interest.

Lest I be accused of avoiding an issue, however, I must point out that there is a controversy among evaluation pundits about the relative merits of quantitative versus qualitative research. There are some who say that all the problems of evaluation research can be traced to a lack of "rigor." But I do not believe it. It seems to me that Cronbach's (1977) position is the most reasonable one. He has argued that the primary concern should be with the utility of the data obtained, not with the method by which it is obtained. If you can find out something useful about a program by talking to a few disgruntled employees, then talk to them. If the only way you can get the data you need is by participant observation, then participate and observe (and do not forget to take good notes). If you need a time series design with switching replications, then set it up and switch when the time comes. If you need archival data, then locate the necessary records and extract whatever you require. Use whatever you have in your toolbox that will get the job done, that is, whatever you have that will help you determine whether the program's objectives are being achieved.

Actually, you are already familiar with the essential components of the most useful, and most rigorous, evaluation designs that you could employ, although you may not have put the pieces together yet. The designs are referred to, generally, as RANDOMIZED TRIALS and involve combining some of the quasi-experimental designs from the preceding chapter with random assignment of subjects to treatment and nontreatment groups. Consider this notion of RANDOM ASSIGNMENT first. Think back to the chapter on survey research for a moment. There, randomly selecting subjects to be interviewed was discussed and several ways in which that could be done were pointed out. The point, of course, was to obtain a representative, unbiased sample, one whose characteristics were similar to those of the population as a whole. If you selected such a sample, you could then feel fairly confident about inferring that what they had to say in answer to your questions was representative of the attitudes and opinions of the population. With random assignment of subjects to treatment and nontreatment groups, the goal is essentially the same. You want subjects in each group (a sample) to be similar to the population of subjects as a whole and, hence, similar to the subjects in the other groups (i.e., the other samples).

Random assignment of subjects to conditions is not always feasible. But, when it is, you overcome–at one fell swoop–all the ambiguities discussed in Chapter 7 that result from the use of nonequivalent groups for the treatment and control conditions. The reason is that randomly assigning subjects to conditions enables you to assume that the groups were equivalent at the outset. Thus, any differences that appear on the posttest cannot be attributed to preexisting (i.e., pretreatment) differences among the groups. Of course, that is assuming that the groups all experience the same nontreatment events between random assignment and posttest. As Cook and Campbell (1979) put it, random assignment "does not guarantee that the initial comparability between groups will be maintained over the course of an experiment." That is up to you–and fate. But, random assignment does give you that initial comparability to work with, and that is a genuine advantage (see Figure 2).

The internal validity of all of the designs discussed in Chapter Seven (with the exception of the one-group designs, which are hopeless) can be considerably enhanced by randomly assigning subjects to conditions. When we follow the method of Campbell and Stanley (1966) and let R stand for random assignment, the Pretest–Posttest Design with Control Group becomes

Group 1   R   O   X   O
Group 2   R   O   O

With that simple addition, it becomes a true experimental design, nothing quasi about it. For example, Mosteller (1981) mentioned a large-scale evaluation study that used this design. It was carried out by the Blue Cross insurance company in Kansas, and the purpose was to determine whether

"Find out who set up this experiment. It seems that half the patients were given a placebo, and the other half were given a different placebo."

Figure 2 A VERIFIABLE EVALUATION of a new treatment always includes a group of subjects who are given a placebo treatment. In medical research the placebo would be a pill, for example, that looked and tasted like the real drug but which had no pharmacological effect. In education research the placebo group would be treated like the treatment group except that the placebo group would not be exposed to the treatment itself. (Cartoon © Sidney Harris.)

or not the apparently excessive use of hospitalization, which is extremely costly, would decrease if the company started paying for more outpatient care. Five thousand persons were randomly assigned to an added-benefits group, free of charge. What that meant was that for one year the company would pay for much of their outpatient care, that is, things that were not covered under the regular plan unless the patient was hospitalized. These 5000 constituted the treatment group and were compared to a randomly selected group of 10,000 who continued on the old system (hospital costs only) for a year. The random assignment was quite important here because it gives us some confidence that the two groups could be considered initially comparable in terms of their year-to-year medical problems and costs. The results, by the way, were surprising and contrary to expectation. The amount of hospitalization for the group with the added outpatient benefits went up 16 percent, whereas for the control (regular plan) group it went up only 3 percent. It may be that the added outpatient benefits, which were free, induced people to consult their physicians more often and, hence, more problems were found that required treatment. However, the fact that results were in the direction opposite to what was expected again underscores the need to evaluate new programs.

More will be said about both random assignment and experimental design in the following chapter. Here it is necessary to mention one additional type of data that is becoming increasingly important in the evaluation process. As Wortman (1983) has pointed out, it is becoming common in the overall evaluation of program effectiveness for the final step to consist of a determination of whether or not the program is an efficient way to implement the desired policy. And, efficient is defined in terms of economics. Is the program a good use of scarce economic resources? If the program of interest is one of several alternative programs that could achieve the same objectives, a COST-BENEFIT ANALYSIS may be required. That means that all costs and benefits of the program have to be converted to monetary terms. That, in turn, enables you to compare projects or programs by calculating a cost:benefit ratio for each. The one with the lowest ratio wins; it provides the most benefits for the least cost. But, converting everything to a dollar value may force you to make some very arbitrary judgments. Suppose, for example, that one of the innovations of interest is a new treatment for patients dying of cancer and that, on the average, it seems to prolong the life of those treated by six months to a year. How much, precisely, is six more months of life worth? And how do you figure quality of life into the equation (see page 262)? As Rossi et al. (1979) put it, "Social programs do not ordinarily produce results that can be accurately valued by market prices," and when that cannot be done the results of the cost–benefit analyses of those programs are misleading.

COST-EFFECTIVENESS ANALYSIS, in contrast, does not convert everything to dollars. Rather, it uses whatever units you focused on in operationalizing a given program's objectives and tells you what it has cost to achieve those effects. Comparison with different, or alternative, programs is usually not the object here. The results of a cost effectiveness analysis of a preschool flu vaccination program, for example, might be phrased in terms of the cost to reduce the incidence of flu by 500 cases. Or it might be phrased in terms of the cost of reducing absenteeism by 100 percent over the

HEART TRANSPLANTS

Until recently, the American medical community seemed to assume that if a procedure or medication was known to be effective, there was no justification for withholding it from a patient. With advances in medical technology and the spiraling cost of supplying that technology to patients, the assumption that everything possible should be done for every patient has come under fire. The issue is whether or not society as a whole can afford to pay. For example, since 1973, 80 percent of the cost of kidney dialysis and kidney transplants has been paid by Medicare. By December 1980, that was costing U.S. taxpayers about 1.5 billion dollars per year (Kutner, 1982).

Partly because of such costs, in 1980 the Secretary of the Department of Health and Human Services announced that new medical technologies will have to be evaluated on the basis of their social consequences before the government will finance their being made widely available. The particular technology that she singled out for close scrutiny was heart transplantation (Knox, 1980). As part of its assessment, the Department of Health and Human Services plans to collect and analyze data on the 200 plus heart transplants that had taken place in the United States in the 1970s as well as data from new cases. Some of the things they plan to look at are issues such as how much additional life a transplant produces, the total cost per case, the quality of life after having a transplant, and the resources necessary to perform transplants successfully. This latter item is an interesting issue that applies to other new technologies as well. When a new surgical procedure is introduced, it is often introduced at one, or a few, highly specialized centers. Heart transplants were being performed throughout the 1970s by Norman Shumway at Stanford University Medical Center. As Knox put it, Shumway nursed "the controversial operation through its nadir in the early 1970s and gradually improved its dismal early success rates through rigorous patient selection, better diagnosis of the early signs of rejection, and fine-tuning of immunosuppression." In other words, at Stanford in the early 1980s, the procedure has a pretty good success rate, but the conditions there are nearly ideal: a great deal of experience by the chief surgeon, a supportive team, and the ability and willingness to carefully select only those patients most likely to profit from the procedure and stand the strain of the operation.

What the Department of Health and Human Services is worried about, of course, is that under less ideal conditions, the success rate of the procedure will plummet and the government will still be stuck with the bill. The issue is a more general one, however. The conditions under which any new treatment is introduced are often different from what will later be the typical conditions under which the treatment or program will be expected to operate. And it is those typical conditions, when all the enthusiasm of doing something new is gone, that you need to worry about.

previous year. With cost effectiveness analysis, there is no need to convert one day's absence by one child to a dollar value as there would be with a cost–benefit analysis of the same program. There is an important complication of both cost-benefit and cost–effectiveness analysis, however. It has to do with the question of perspective. That is, from whose point of view are the costs, benefits, and effects of the program to be calculated? It can make a tremendous difference.

The Turbulent Setting of Evaluation

Abt (1979) has related that he once heard a surgeon say that if he had a female patient whose mother and sister both had breast cancer, he would recommend an immediate bilateral radical mastectomy as a prophylactic measure. That is a rather drastic preventive step to take. It is not like being told you should brush your teeth three times a day. From the surgeon's point of view, it would, however, maximize the effectiveness:cost ratio for the patient because the only benefit he was focusing on was pure duration of life. Without breasts, the patient's chances of living longer would be increased because even relatively frequent screening is likely to miss some of the most deadly forms of breast cancer, which do seem to have a hereditary component. Needless to say, from the patient's point of view there would be other considerations than pure duration of life. She would want to think about how the operation would influence the quality of her life as well. Besides, in 1979 only about 16 out of every 100,000 women died of breast cancer. That is an item of information that the patient would undoubtedly want to take into account in deciding whether or not to follow the surgeon's recommendation. With odds that slim, and in her favor, she might well decide to take her chances and stay out of the operating room.

The conflicting perspectives between an individual patient and his or her physician about the relative benefits to be derived from a given course of action illustrate only a small part of the more general problem, however. Evaluation is, as was stated earlier, a political undertaking. If the attempted political influence and intrigue stopped once policy had been set and the objectives of a program agreed upon, the evaluation of the program might proceed in a relatively straightforward manner. But it does not work that way. For example, in 1981 the nation's air traffic controllers went out on strike for more pay. There were at the time several studies in the literature that purported to demonstrate how stressful the job was (e.g., Rose, Jenkins, & Hurst, 1978). Air traffic controllers were said to experience disorders such as ulcers and depression much more frequently than did members of the general population. The reason, or so the research seemed to indicate, was the nature of their high-pressure jobs, jobs that required constant alertness and in which a mistake could cost hundreds of lives. Those studies had been in the literature for years and were generally considered noncontroversial. At the time of the strike, however, they were dug out and held up to ridicule. Their results were called into question. It was claimed by those who wanted to end the strike that the studies had been poorly conducted and sloppily done. Now, it appeared, air traffic controllers really had one of the poshest jobs around – short hours, high pay, and only a two-year training period. You did not even have to go to college to qualify.

The point, of course, is that when the stakes are high – as they usually are in evaluation research – different, and more powerful, motives come into play. It is all well and good to think of evaluation research as just another scientific endeavor, but it is not. It, more than any other topic in the preceding chapters, directly touches people's lives and well-being. Thus, high-quality evaluation research requires that you take into account the multiple perspectives that can be brought to bear on the program of interest. Failure to do so can have serious consequences.

Multiple Constituencies

One of the things that evaluation research has in common with participant observation is that they both take place in real-life, action settings. Both are carried out in settings where something else is going on, something other than pure research. And, as Weiss (1972) has noted, the something else takes priority. The research is seen as less important. After all, if you are there to evaluate what is going on, it has to continue to go on in order for the evaluation to take place. Thus, like a good participant observer, the evaluation researcher must be as unobtrusive as possible and not disrupt the normal course of events. But, the extent to which you are able to do that depends very heavily on your relationships with the people running the program.

There are many potential sources of friction between program personnel and someone who has been called in to evaluate "their" program. Because of the nature of most social and educational programs, program personnel are likely to be service oriented. They are teachers, social workers, therapists, probation officers, people whose job it is to deliver services to others. They are oriented toward helping others, toward doing whatever is necessary to see that those in their charge learn, or get a job, or stay out of trouble. Thus, program personnel and evaluators are likely to have completely different orientations at the outset. To the program personnel, it does not matter what it is about the program that makes it work, just so it works. To the evaluators, it is important to document everything – gut feelings and testimonials are not considered high-quality evidence. As Weiss (1972) pointed out, program personnel are likely to be irritated by the skeptical attitude of evaluation researchers. Program personnel have to believe in what they are doing in order to be effective, and they are likely to find the researcher's questioning and nit-picking to be a depressing and unnecessary intrusion. The effects of this supportive versus questioning orientation toward the program are likely to be magnified by personality differences between program personnel and researchers. The program personnel are more likely to be action oriented, concerned about people, and wanting to deal with specific, individual cases. Researchers, in general, are likely to be somewhat more detached, concerned about theoretical and methodological issues, and to have little or no loyalty to the particular program being evaluated.

On the basis of different orientations, Weiss (1972) has called attention to several specific issues that are likely to provoke conflict between program personnel and evaluation researchers. The first has to do with selection of program participants and assignment of some participants to control groups. Program personnel are likely to have a number of implicit criteria for selecting participants. They usually want persons they believe they can help or those most in need. Thus, they are likely to get agitated when evaluation researchers start talking about random selection of clients and random assignment of some to a control (no-treatment) condition. They may view the latter as unethical because it means withholding services from people who need them. Evaluation, of course, requires data, and often that means new questionnaires that the program's clients must fill out and/or records that program personnel have to maintain. Program personnel view such things as intrusions, paper-shuffling exercises that keep them from doing what they do best. There is also an element of rivalry between evaluation researchers and program personnel, rivalry compounded by a sense of threat that program personnel may feel at being evaluated in the first place. Program personnel are likely to see themselves as doing the real work of the agency, often on a tight budget and under less than optimal conditions. They may see evaluation researchers, with the clipboards and the questionnaires and the turned-up noses, as just another hassle they have to put up with. But, the problem is that those clipboard carriers seem to have the boss's attention and what they tell him or her about the program may well have serious implications.

Many of these potential sources of conflict can be short-circuited with a little common sense, of course. Involving program personnel in the evaluation from the outset will help. Making them a part of the process can lessen the likelihood of a we–they relationship developing. It also helps if it is made clear that the evaluation is focusing on the program and not on how well or how poorly individual program personnel are doing their jobs. Weiss

MORE EFFECTIVE SCHOOLS, OR NICER WORKING CONDITIONS?

In the mid-1960s, the City of New York instituted a new educational program in about 20 ghetto-area schools. It was referred to as the More Effective School Program, and the idea was that the quality of education in those schools could be greatly improved if the schools simply had more resources available. Hence, the resources were made available—in the form of money. In the 1966–1967 school year, for example, the average cost per pupil in the schools in the More Effective School Program was about $900, compared to half that per pupil in other schools. That meant that the schools in the program could have luxuries such as psychological counseling, specialized instruction, smaller classes, new equipment, and lower teacher–pupil ratios.

The Center for Urban Education in New York set up a design to evaluate the impact of the More Effective School Program. For comparison purposes, they selected some ghetto-area schools not participating in the program. On everything known to affect academic performance, the students in the two sets of schools were initially similar (Fox, 1967; Cole, 1972). The evaluation that ensued involved observation of classrooms, interviews with teachers, and testing of the students at various points in time after the program began. As you might expect, teachers in the schools participating in the More Effective School Program were predominantly positive and enthusiastic about the program and observers rated the quality of teaching as being higher in the schools in the program. But, on the crucial measures of student performance, the More Effective School Program was an out-and-out failure. As Fox (1967) put it, the program "made no significant difference in the functioning of the children, whether this was measured by observers rating what the children did in class, and how they do it, or whether it was measured by children's ability in mathematics or reading on standardized tests." And, as Cole (1972) has pointed out, questionnaire data indicated that the program did not even yield the psychological benefit of giving the students a more positive attitude toward school.

Another experiment that did not work and was abandoned? Not on your life. Not only was the More Effective School Program not abandoned, in 1967 the United Federation of Teachers made expansion of the program a key demand in a strike. Why? Although it was true that the program failed the kids, it was great for the teachers: smaller classes, new equipment, nicer working conditions. Who could ask for anything more? The United Federation of Teachers had also been a moving force behind the program in the first place; and people involved in getting a program going may be the last to admit that it has failed.

(1972) has noted also that management incentives for program personnel to facilitate, rather than hinder, the evaluation process can be a real boon. And, as always, a little simple, straightforward communication about what is going on at each step of the process is a big help. There is a danger here, however. If the feedback given to program personnel indicates that some parts of the program are working better than others or that certain things are simply not working at all, they may try to change the project in midstream. After all, they see their job as doing the most they can for each individual client that the agency is supposed to serve. If you tell them that something they have been doing is a waste of time—assuming you can convince them of that fact—they will try something new tomorrow. If they do, then you may have a different program on your hands. But, more about that in the next section.

Although the potential for conflict does seem to be greatest with those actually doing the day-to-day work of implementing the program of interest, there are other vested interests in any program that can make life difficult. (For an example, see page 266.) Shortell and Richardson (1978) have said that there are at least five different groups that have a stake in the typical evaluation: (1) the organization in which the evaluation takes place, (2) individual program administrators, (3) the agency that is funding the organization and the evaluation, (4) the public and consumer groups, and (5) the program evaluators themselves. Be sure to note that this is an underestimate of the concerned parties in most instances. For example, the program administrators in many service agencies are different from those who actually deliver services, and it is the latter, as you have just seen, with whom there is the greatest potential for conflict with evaluation researchers. But, even if you take Shortell and Richardson's list as a minimum, look at the variety of different motives that may be seeking a way to express themselves in one lowly little evaluation project:

1. The organization may hope to
   a. show other groups that it is effective
   b. justify past expenditures
   c. justify future requests for more money
   d. determine what should be done next
   e. justify firing program personnel

2. Individual program administrators may hope to
   a. gain a pat on the back or a promotion
   b. gain greater control over subordinates
   c. learn how to serve clients better
   d. show that the program should be redirected
   e. be able to avoid evaluations in the future

3. The funding agency may hope to
   a. spend unspent money so that their allocations will not be decreased in the future
   b. find out whether services are being efficiently delivered
   c. obtain evidence necessary for policy alteration
   d. make themselves look good to Congress
   e. justify terminating the program

4. The public and consumer groups may hope to
   a. find out how tax dollars are being spent
   b. gain more control over the program
   c. obtain the evidence necessary to oust program administrators
   d. redirect the program to other target groups
   e. get the program moved to another neighborhood

5. Program evaluators may hope to
   a. contribute to knowledge
   b. make a name for themselves
   c. see the program improved
   d. see the program terminated
   e. none of the above

It is not just a problem of multiple interest groups, then, each with a different perspective. Rather, as Cochran (1980) has said, each party has multiple motives, and it is important to remember that survival is likely to top each person's list. Evaluation is not an anemic academic exercise. Members of the groups mentioned above may feel quite strongly about what they want a particular evaluation to accomplish. Their very livelihood can depend on the outcome. That means they may do what they can to see that the desired result is obtained. And, do what they can includes everything from foot-dragging and throwing monkey wrenches to facilitating your every move and telling you more than you really wanted to know.

Given this crossfire of motives, there is likely to be constant pressure on the program to change, to do more of this and less of that, and even to stop doing some things altogether. From the point of view of someone trying to evaluate what is going on, that can present real problems.

The Slippery Program

With the objectives agreed upon, the design set up, good relations with the program personnel, what could go wrong? Just about everything. The typical social or educational innovation is part of an open system, and that means there are all sorts of uncontrollable external forces pushing and pulling on the components of the program. As Weiss (1972) put it, just as you get everything under way and the data collection is running smoothly, the program will slither off in a completely new direction. It will not happen overnight. In many respects it would be better if it did because that would get your attention. It is more likely to gradually evolve, for slight changes to be introduced from time to time as the program personnel find better ways to do things and as the internal and external political climates change. This evolutionary process seems to be the rule and not the exception. (See page 270 for a description of the stages in the life of medical innovations.) As Shortell and Richardson (1978) noted, the actual results of new programs often bear little likeness to the original intent. They are usually much more modest than it was anticipated they would be; and, in spite of that, they take longer to accomplish.

Why is that? The major reason seems to be that the setting of the typical program is extremely complex and that that complexity is not taken into account in planning. In many instances it may be impossible to take it into account for the simple reason that it is not sufficiently well understood. Even when the complexity of the environment is appreciated, it may not be predictable. For example, several years ago the Federal Government set up a large-scale field experiment in New Jersey. The object was to evaluate a technique for supporting needy families; the technique is referred to as a negative income tax and works as follows: payments to families are made when their income is below a certain level. But, unlike some welfare programs, payments do not completely stop when family income rises above that level. Rather, as income rises, payments gradually decrease. The question of interest was whether this type of sliding scale would provide more incentive for people on welfare to work. Under the old system, there was little incentive to work because the family was likely to experience a drop in income—their welfare would be cut off completely—when someone got a job outside the home. Unfortunately, while the experiment was under way, there was a shift in the welfare policy of the State of New Jersey. New Jersey had been picked as the site of the experiment partly because state welfare laws covered only households headed by females. Suddenly, New Jersey extended its coverage to households headed by unemployed males. Some of the latter were, in fact, part of the Negative Income Tax Experiment. Not only did that complicate the comparisons that had been planned for the experiment, it got local officials agitated about the possibility that some people were double-dipping, that is, accepting state and federal welfare payments. In an effort to get at the guilty parties, state officials obtained a court order for the records of the experiment (which families were receiving payments and how much). The order was not enforced but the project was required to reimburse local welfare departments for the excess amounts they had given to families receiving both forms of payment (Kershaw & Fair, 1976). The point is that when the Negative Income Tax Experiment was being planned on the

Issues and Discussions ━━━━━━━━━━━━━━━━━━━━━━━━━━━━━━━━━━━━━

SEVEN STAGES IN THE CAREER
OF A MEDICAL INNOVATION

Because health is such a basic essential to everything else that we might want to do, people often seem a little too eager to believe the best about new medical procedures and drugs. Time after time in the last few years, new medications and technologies have been introduced with great fanfare only to fade into oblivion after a few years. McKinlay (1981) has outlined a set of seven stages by which this cycle of approval and opprobrium seems to work itself out.

STAGE 1. *PROMISING REPORT* – The careers of most such innovations seem to be started on their upward trajectories by the appearance of an enthusiastic report in the mass media. These enthusiastic reports are often based on nothing more than the observations of one physician who has tried the new procedure with, at most, a handful of patients.

STAGE 2. *PROFESSIONAL ADOPTION* – Responding to peer pressure and/or wanting to deliver improved care, other physicians adopt the innovation and try it on a few patients.

STAGE 3. *PUBLIC ACCEPTANCE* – Because their physicians are recommending it, the public accepts the new procedure and develops a generalized belief that it is a good thing and ought to be more widely available.

STAGE 4. *STANDARD PROCEDURE* – The innovation achieves the status of acceptance and is the standard procedure for the malady in question. Note that up to this point there is still no controlled evidence for the innovation's effectiveness. Everything so far has been based on a few case studies and the testimonials of those who have tried the new procedure.

STAGE 5. *CONTROLLED TRIALS* – Finally, someone gets around to doing the appropriate research, that is, with conditions to control for the placebo effect, which has confounded everything up to this point.

STAGE 6. *PROFESSIONAL DENUNCIATION* – If the results from the controlled trials are negative, all the professionals whose case reports have supported the, now questionable, procedure are quick to criticize – not the procedure, but the controlled trials.

STAGE 7. *EROSION AND DENUNCIATION* – As better evidence on the ineffectiveness of the procedure continues to accumulate, it gradually fades into oblivion.

The key to short-circuiting this long, drawn-out cycle would be to jump from Stage 1 to Stage 5, but that has its problems also. Controlled research is expensive and time consuming, and a full-scale test of every new idea that came along would use up a lot of resources.

Federal level, there was no way of anticipating what the government of the State of New Jersey was going to do four or five years down the road. That was simply an unknown in the equation.

But, even when you know the specific obstacles to be overcome in order to operate a program smoothly, there is often a tendency to overestimate the ease of doing so. Part of that may be the understandable optimism of those starting out on a new endeavor. But part of it may be a failure to appreciate a very simple statistical fact. For example, suppose you have designed a remedial reading program and plan to evaluate it by using the following experiment. Four schools in your community in which first graders scored below the national average on reading comprehension tests will be used. Two of the schools will be randomly selected to serve as controls and will continue their usual reading instruction for first graders when school opens in the fall. First graders at two other randomly selected schools will be exposed to the new reading program. You have all your materials ready to go, some money from the Board of Education to carry out the study, and the approval of the local school superintendent. There is just one catch. The superintendent says she does not like to make the teachers in her schools participate in research. She leaves it completely up to each teacher and principal whether or not they take part in projects such as yours. That means you have to get the approval of four principals and (assuming three first grade classes in each school) twelve teachers. But, says the superintendent, they are generally a cooperative lot and she is about 90 percent sure that they will agree to help you out. Suppose that that estimate is correct, that is, that the chances are 90 out of a 100 that each of the four principals and twelve teachers will say yes. What is the probability of getting them all to agree? Ready for this? The probability that all 16 will agree is .185, and that is pretty low.[1] It means you probably are not going to be able to implement the program as planned. A smaller sample of schools may be necessary, maybe only one control school and one in which the first graders are exposed to the remedial reading program.

This is one of the reasons why formative evaluation, which was discussed earlier, is so important. Not only do you need to document the form in which the program actually gets under way, but from time to time you will need to see if it is still similar to the way it started. And, all too often, it will not be. Halfway through the fall, one of those nice teachers who agreed to help you out may inform you that he does not like your remedial

[1]The probability of several independent events all occurring is determined by multiplying the probabilities of each together. That is, the probability of A, B, and C occurring is calculated by multiplying the probability of A by the probability of B and then multiplying that result by the probability of C.

reading program; and, furthermore, a couple of weeks ago he discovered a way of doing it better and has been trying that out on his first graders.

What do you do in a situation like that? The first rule is; Stay calm! You may still be able to salvage some useful information. Weiss (1972) suggested that in those situations in which programs shift unexpectedly, you may be able to rethink your model of the program itself. That is, instead of considering the program as a static entity that is put in place and evaluated, you may be able to develop a more dynamic conception of the program. For example, if the teacher mentioned above were sufficiently clear about how he had changed your remedial reading instruction, you might be able to consider his idea as a new, two-stage version of your treatment. If so, you would be able to compare it with the controls (no remedial reading) and with those first graders exposed only to the remedial reading program as you designed it. You never know, his idea might be better than yours.

The key to being able to take advantage of such shifts in programs is staying flexible, and Cronbach et al. (1981) have offered a few suggestions about how you can do that. One thing to avoid is committing every dollar you have to spend and every hour you have available to obtaining the data described in the initial evaluation plan. You will need a little slack to regroup when something unexpected occurs. In other words, you should expect the unexpected – and be prepared to take advantage of it. Another thing that may help is to think of the overall evaluation as taking place in stages, with some analysis and rethinking occurring in the gaps between stages. Surprise results and program changes that are identified in the early stages may help sharpen your thinking about exactly what kinds of data you should be collecting and you can make it a point to get those data in the later stages. But, if the program is completely overwhelmed by internal and external changes, your best bet may be to forget the evaluation altogether and prepare a careful, well-documented treatise on why and how things went wrong. That, in fact, might be just as useful to the interested parties as your evaluation would have been. Perhaps an example will clarify a few of these points.

An Illustration: Decreasing the Stress of Hospitalization

Ideally, a hospital should provide a restful environment for patients, an environment that will help speed their recovery by providing for them a temporary respite from the stresses and strains of daily life. Unfortunately, it does not always work that way, especially in the larger, major hospitals around the country. Like other large institutions, hospitals often are forced into bureaucratic routines. Things are to be done in a certain way, at a certain time, with no exceptions. There is usually no malevolent intention behind these routines; it is simply a matter of getting the jobs done that need to be done while keeping chaos at some tolerable level. Take food service, for example. A five hundred-bed hospital has an enormous food preparation task. Not only must all the patients be fed several times a day, many of them are likely to be on special diets. Add to that the medical and nursing and housekeeping staff members, who are going to want breakfast, lunch, and dinner when they are working. And visitors will want to eat, too. Well, you see the problem. Imagine how that would be complicated by allowing each patient to call down to the kitchen whenever he or she awoke and to order whatever he or she happened to want for breakfast. The solution is to retreat into routine: breakfast trays are taken to patients' rooms between 7 and 8 a.m. and everybody gets the same thing, except, of course, for those on special diets.

That is certainly a rational solution, at least from the hospital's point of view. But, consider it from the patient's point of view. Suppose the patient is a late sleeper, that is, he or she does not usually get up until 8:30 or 9:00 a.m. What then? Well, they either change the habits of a lifetime or miss breakfast. But, missing breakfast is not a good idea for someone recovering from surgery or disease. They need all the nutrition they can get to help them get their strength back. But they also need their sleep, and being rudely awakened at some ungodly hour just to eat breakfast is not a good way to start the day. Of course, breakfast at a certain hour is just one of many ways in which hospital routines can unintentionally increase the amount of discomfort and distress that patients must endure. Tests are scheduled at specific times; but when patients arrive at the designated locations, they have to wait. Doctors, nurses, technicians, phlebotomists, Pink Ladies pop into the patients' rooms unannounced at all hours of the day and night. There is absolutely no privacy. Rooms have to be shared with complete strangers, who, needless to say, are not up to par themselves. People may get better in self-defense, just so they can go home and rest up.

Several years ago, in an effort to see if some of this unnecessary stress could be avoided, the University of Kentucky Hospital set up a model patient-care wing (Moore, 1981). It was referred to as 3-North, a not-very-imaginative title reflecting the simple fact that it was in the north wing on the third floor. It was to be a general medical–surgical treatment unit. The 20-bed unit was completely remodeled, with six private rooms and seven semiprivate rooms, that is rooms with two beds. Other units of the hospital had four-bed wards. The remodeling of 3-North was even more extensive: a kitchen was put in so that patients and/or staff could prepare food; the nurses' station was moved to a central location so that nurses would always be closer to patients; a patient lounge and solarium were installed and equipped with television, games, and reading material, which patients were encouraged to use; comfortable furniture was put into the rooms; and the entire wing was redecorated in bright, cheerful colors instead of the institutional grays and greens that dominated the rest of the hospital. In the model unit the pattern of nursing care was also changed to what is referred to as primary care nursing. That is, one nurse was assigned responsibility for all of a given patient's nursing care for the duration of his or her stay in the hospital. In the other units of the hospital, a team nursing approach was more common, with different nurses doing different things for the patient. Even the composition of the staff on 3-North was changed. Compared to the other units of the hospital, fewer nursing assistants were used, that is, nearly all of the providers of care on 3-North were registered nurses. There were some other changes, but you get the picture. All of the changes were geared toward reducing the disruptive, unnecessarily unpleasant aspects of hospitalization.

The question, of course, was whether any of this would really make any difference to the patients. Would they get well more quickly? Could they be discharged more rapidly? Did they really experience less stress in the hospital? To answer these questions, Moore (1981) set up a very simple time series design with a control group. His plan was to randomly select patients from those admitted to 3-North between March 1979 and February 1980 and assess their physical and psychological status on the first, fourth, and tenth days after their admission. For a comparison group, he randomly selected patients from among those admitted to other general medical–surgical units of the hospital during the same time period and, similarly, assessed their status on days 1, 4, and 10 after admission. The design looks like this:

		3-North Admission	Day 1	Day 4	Day 10
Group 1	R	X	O	O	O
Group 2	R		O	O	O

Just in case you have forgotten, R stands for random assignment. In this case, the assumption was that patients would be randomly assigned to appropriate units in the hospital on a space-available basis.

To measure experienced stress, Moore constructed a scale that he named the University of Kentucky Hospital Stress Checklist (UKHSC). He did that by drawing up a list of things that might happen to a hospital patient that could, possibly, be considered stressful. Patients were then asked to rate each of the 40 items in terms of how bothered they would be if the thing described by the item happened to them. Some examples of items in the UKHSC are:

"I was told something would happen at a certain time, but it didn't."
"I called for a nurse and had to wait over 5 minutes for her to come."
"I had difficulty getting an explanation of my illness."
"Someone made several unsuccessful attempts to perform an uncomfortable procedure on me."

From the ratings, the 40 items could be ordered in terms of bothersomeness. It turned out that having a roommate discharged was the least bothersome and needing pain medication, but not getting it, was the most bothersome. Patients in the study proper were then asked on days 1, 4, and 10 of their hospitalization to check each of the items that applied to them. A number of other measures were also employed to assess the patients' physical and mental status. These included a Mood Adjective Rating list, on which patients were asked to indicate how they were feeling at the time (happy, depressed, helpless, angry). Patients were also administered a Physical Recovery Inventory on which they were asked to rate their physical well-being in a number of different categories such as appetite, ability to move around, strength, and stomach condition. Finally, patients were asked to rate the amount of pain they were experiencing (Volicer, 1978). Another crucial measure, the number of days from admission to discharge, was simply taken from hospital records.

It turned out that patients assigned to the model unit did experience less overall stress, at least as indicated by the frequency with which things on the stress checklist happened to them. That, of course, is a good thing. Unfortunately, it also turned out that patients were not randomly assigned to the model unit and other units of the hospital. The 3-North unit quickly gained a reputation among hospital physicians and nurses as being a VIP ward, the best that the University had to offer. It was no secret that it was really a posh place; all you had to do was to stick your head in the door to see that. But, instead of random assignment, what had happened was that almost as soon as the unit had opened, hospital physicians had started selecting those of their patients whom they wanted to be admitted to that particular wing. As Moore (1981) put it, they put the well-insured, higher status, university-affiliated patients on 3-North, especially if those patients were somehow connected with the medical professions themselves. A sample of the occupations of patients assigned to the two groups in Moore's design is given in Table 1. It can be seen that there is almost no overlap in the socioeconomic status of the two groups.

Needless to say, that was not supposed to happen. But, it is important to recognize that it was not a conscious plot on the part of the hospital's

Table 1 A sample of the occupations of patients assigned to the experimental and comparison groups in Moore's study of the innovative patient care unit at the University of Kentucky Hospital.

3-North	Other Units
Owns large farm, insurance adjuster, & school board member	Construction worker
Retired from public service	Unemployed
University teacher	Disabled coal miner
Factory manager	Housewife; spouse of an electrician
Physician	Beautician
Student; son of a lawyer	Housewife, spouse of disabled coal miner
Nurse	Part-time waitress
School bus driver	Unemployed
Housewife; spouse of a physician	Housewife; spouse of a repairman
Wife of university faculty member	Widow of a tenant farmer

Source: Moore (1981).

physicians to ruin the design. Rather, it was the cumulative result of a large number of independent, individual decisions made by those physicians in requesting assignments for their patients. Occasionally, for patients whom they happened to know personally or with whom they had the best rapport, a bed on the model unit was requested. After all, as hospital wards go, it really is nice. (It is no accident that the Governor of the state was assigned to the 3-North unit when he had the misfortune to be hospitalized.) Over the course of a year, however, those occasional requests resulted in a highly unusual and unrepresentative sample of patients being assigned to the unit – patients who were better educated, wealthier, and probably not as sick to begin with. The net result, of course, was that any comparisons of the recovery rates of patients assigned to the model unit and other units of the hospital were completely meaningless because of preexisting differences among the two samples of patients.

It was an unfortunate result. Now it will probably never be known whether the patient care innovations introduced on 3-North really make a difference in the speed and ease of recovery. Methodologically, however, the study is a valuable reminder of the importance of formative evaluations – to see that a program is in place as planned. Moore (1981) took a great deal of time and effort to track down the ways in which random assignment of patients to units in the hospital went awry. And, always remember, it could happen to you.

Summary

Evaluation research is a little different from the other topics that have been discussed in preceding chapters. It is an assortment of techniques, procedures, and methods for analyzing the implementation and impact of social, educational, and medical innovations. It is also a fairly recent development, traceable directly to increased government expenditures on such innovations and the accompanying pressure for accountability and sanity in allocating the nation's scarce economic resources. For the practitioner, evaluation research is likely to differ in another way from other methods. That is, it involves relinquishing some autonomy in picking and choosing the problems to be pursued and working on research problems that have been defined by those who have established policy or set programs in motion or both. The *quid pro quo* for this, however, is that the work of evaluation researchers has a chance of having a greater impact on society.

Given that the typical evaluation researcher is not a member of the policy-making body, the first step is to translate that received policy into clearly stated, measureable objectives. You need to ask yourself a series of questions about what the program is really intended to do. For example, is it intended to change behavior? Whose behavior? Will the effects show up immediately? How long will they last? Once you have the objectives clearly in mind, you have to operationalize each. What, precisely, are you going to use as an indicator that each objective has been achieved? But, the problem is even more difficult, because once you have stated the objectives of the program as best you can and selected an indicator of each, you have only just begun. Next, you have to get all the interested parties to agree that your version of the objectives is really what the program is all about and that the measures you propose are valid indicators of those objectives. That, of course, is likely to require some diplomatic skill, not to mention extended negotiations.

Once you have the objectives operationalized to everyone's satisfaction, the next step is to implement the program. Some of the objectives should be concerned with seeing that the program is indeed implemented as planned, and this process is referred to as formative evaluation. If you neglect it, you may find that the program you had in mind never made the transition from the drawing board to reality. But, assuming you get the program in place and running, you then have to evaluate its impact, a process referred to as summative evaluation. This is the payoff, of course, the information that everyone is awaiting with bated breath. To do it well, you should not be shy about using every tool you have, from participant observation to randomized control trials. The primary concern is with the utility of the information you obtain, not the method by which you obtain it.

Evaluation often takes place in a turbulent setting. More than any of the other research methods, evaluation research is likely to have a direct effect on people's lives, and they are not likely to behave as disinterested scientific observers while you calmly go about your business. If they have a stake in the outcome of the research, they are likely to let you know about it – forcefully. And, for the typical programs that are subjected to evaluation, there are likely to be multiple interested parties. The greatest potential for conflict seems to be between the people charged with the day-to-day operation of the program of interest and those charged with evaluating it. Making it clear that the evaluation is focused on the program and not on how well, or how poorly, they are doing their jobs may help tone down some of the conflict. A little common sense and being as unobtrusive as possible will also help. In addition to the problems posed by having many different people interested in the program you are trying to evaluate, there is another serious problem in the tendency of programs to evolve and change while the evaluation is in process. They, quite often, just will not stand still long enough for you to get a reading on how things are working out. The problem is inherent in the nature of evaluation research because you are not likely to have the necessary authority and control to keep the program from shifting. The best thing to do is to anticipate that the program will indeed shift and to plan your evaluation in stages. Flexibility and keeping some resources in reserve will also help.

Evaluations can fail even when no one is trying to shoot you down. A study of an innovative medical unit designed to reduce the stress of hospitalization illustrates this point. Occasional requests by hospital physicians that particular patients be assigned to the unit completely undermined the random assignment of patients to the experimental and control units. Eternal vigilance is not only the price of liberty, it is also the price of interpretable comparisons.

Recommended Reading

The two books, two chapters, and monograph series in this list will further your education and enlightenment about evaluation research. Each has something to offer. The Weiss book is probably the best place to start. It is an easily readable, informative overview of evaluation research.

Cronbach, L. J., Ambron, S. R., Dornbusch, S. M., Hess, R. D., Hornik, R. C., Phillips, D. C., Walker, D. F., & Weiner, S. S. *Toward reform of program evaluation.* San Francisco: Jossey-Bass, 1981.

In 1517 Martin Luther posted his 95 theses, attacking various ecclesiastical abuses, and, thus, began the period known as the Reformation. With a somewhat grandiose analogy, Cronbach and his associates begin their book with 95 theses that they hope will hasten the process of reforming program evaluation. Their view is that by not recognizing the political nature of evaluation, evaluation research has often missed the boat. As they put it, "The proper mission of evaluation is not to eliminate the fallibility of authority or to bolster its credibility. Rather, its mission is to facilitate a democratic, pluralistic process by enlightening all the participants." The key word there is *enlightening*. Consider a few of their theses: #26 – What is needed is information that supports negotiation rather than information calculated to point out the correct solution; #77 – Large scale evaluations are not necessarily better than smaller ones; #86 – The best safeguard against prematurely frozen standards for evaluative practice is multiple, independent sources of criticism; and last, but definitely not least, #95 – Scientific quality is not the principal standard – an evaluation should aim to be comprehensible, correct and complete, and credible to partisans on all sides. The theses provide a good summary of the authors' major points, but memorizing them is no substitute for reading the book.

House, E. R., & Woolridge, R. J. (Eds.) *New directions for program evaluation.* San Francisco: Jossey-Bass, 1978-1984.

This is a series of monographs, each addressed to some specific aspect of program evaluation. Recent titles include Philosophy of Evaluation, Measuring Effectiveness, Making Evaluation Research Useful to Congress, Training Program Evaluators, and even Measuring the Hard-to-Measure. If you were convinced of the value of time series analysis in the last chapter, you might be interested in monograph #16; Applications of Time Series Analysis to Evaluation, edited by G. A. Forehand. Actually it might be more useful if you were not convinced. Perhaps Forehand and colleagues can do the job. In any event, the monographs appear four times a year. Each is edited by a recognized expert, who selects a panel of authorities in his or her specialty to prepare original chapters for that issue. They are available in paperback, and you can order the one particular issue you desire or, if you are really feeling well-heeled, you can subscribe to the entire lot. You might also try your neighborhood library.

Seidman, E. Unexamined premises of social problem solving. In E. Seidman (Ed.), *Handbook of social intervention.* Beverly Hills, CA: Sage, 1983.

In this chapter, Seidman described some of the ways that hidden assumptions can result in the misdefinition of problems. He has pointed out how your particular view of the world, the spirit of the times, dominant societal values, and others with vested interests in getting the problem defined in a certain way are all pitfalls for the unwary. For example, the notion of individual responsibility, which is a widely held value in our society, can result in focusing, too exclusively, on the victims of poverty in planning programs of social intervention. The belief that we are all responsible for ourselves may lead us to blame the poor for their plight, when, in fact, there may be multiple external reasons for their situation. Seidman's point, of course, is that careful problem definition may be the most important service that you can render in evaluation and policy research. If you misunderstand the issues, chances are you will end up investigating the wrong problem. That means, of course, that the real problem will go unaltered.

Weiss, C. H. *Evaluation research: Methods of assessing program effectiveness.* Englewood Cliffs, NJ: Prentice-Hall, 1972.

The text of this slim paperback is less than 130 pages, but in those few pages Weiss has provided an excellent introduction to the problems and processes of evaluation research. For you, of course, it will be a review because you have already been introduced to the subject, but it is a review that is well worth your time and effort. My major reason for recommending it, however, is that Weiss provides an extensive bibliography that will be of use if you should decide to pursue some evaluation research on your own. She has divided the bibliography into sections: Conceptual and Methodological Issues; Illustrative Evaluation Studies; and References on Design, Measurement, Sampling, and Analysis. Many of the studies cited are real classics, evaluations that were carried out before there was such a thing as evaluation research.

Wortman, P. M. Evaluation research: A methodological perspective. *Annual Review of Psychology 34*, 223-260, 1983.

The Annual Review of Psychology publishes in-depth reviews of current research in all areas of psychology. The reviews of a particular topic area are scheduled on a rotating basis, usually every three or four years. The first chapter reviewing developments in evaluation research did not appear until 1976, which should tell you something about its relative age, or rather, its relative youth. The chapter by Wortman is the third in the series. He has covered three main developments: (1) social experimentation, which you should be familiar with from the preceding two chapters, (2) meta-analysis, a statistical technique for aggregating the results of many studies, and (3) cost–effectiveness analysis, the determination of whether or not programs are efficient in their use of scarce economic resources. I, of course, have not spent much time on topics 2 and 3. That, in fact, is the major reason for recommending the chapter. It will serve as a good, nontechnical introduction to two important topics that can, unfortunately, get very technical, very quickly.

9

The Experiment

The Essence of the Experiment

Designing What You Need

What Experiments Can and Cannot Do for You

Summary

Recommended Readings

The laboratory experiment is probably the most powerful technique available for demonstrating causal relationships between variables, that is, for demonstrating that a change in one variable produces a change in another. That is a pretty strong statement, even with the hedge "probably" included. But it is true! The only reason for hedging at all is that an experiment, like other research methods, may not be feasible for particular problems or in particular settings. If you are interested in understanding what led to the demise of the Babylonian civilization and the ascendence of the Assyrian one, experimentation is not going to help you very much. For such a question, experimentation is definitely not the most powerful technique available. But, if your problem is one that can be attacked experimentally, you are in luck.

Compared to participant observation, archival research, and interviewing – all of which were familiar to Aristotle – experimentation on psychological, behavioral, and social processes is relatively new. There are, however, occasional reports of attempted experiments scattered throughout history. One story, for example, has it that an ancient king wanted to know whether children raised without exposure to language would develop a language on their own. So, a couple of unlucky babies were selected, isolated, and tended to only by slaves who were unluckier. They had had their tongues cut out so that they could not talk. In spite of such legends, which revealed at least a rudimentary understanding of some of its elements, experimentation remained a seldom-used tool for investigating human behavior.

Things began to change in the 1800s, however. Toward the end of the century, with the mounting successes of the experimental approach in fields such as physiology and physics and medicine, it was almost inevitable that some enterprising spirits would try it out on behavior. One of the first to take the plunge was a psychologist named Triplett at the University of Indiana.

In going over the official bicycle records of the Racing Board of the League of American Wheelmen, Triplett (1897-1898) noticed that bicycle racers seemed to do better when they were paced by a swift multicycle or when they were in competition with others than when they were out on the track by themselves, that is, when they were simply racing against the clock. Apparently others had noticed this phenomenon also because several ideas had been put forward to explain it. One such idea was termed Suction Theory, that is, the notion that the pacing machine created a slight vacuum behind it which drew the huffing and puffing bicycler forward at a little better speed than he could manage on his own. One of the strongest arguments in favor of this theory was the fact that a man named Anderson had been able to exceed 60 miles an hour on a bicycle at Roodhouse, Illinois when paced by a railroad locomotive. Another suggestion was that the strained attention to the revolving wheels of the pacing machine in front produced a sort of hypnotism in the pursuing rider that allowed him to ignore fatigue and pain to push himself beyond his normal limits.

The archival records that Triplett consulted established, very clearly, the fact of better performance under competition and paced conditions than during solitary time trials. However, there was no way to distinguish among the various explanations for that fact. Too many things were happening at once. There was even some evidence of self-selection, that is, that men who were particularly good in competition would not participate in the solitary time trials and vice versa. Thus, Triplett decided to study the issue of competition versus solitary performance in a way that would allow him to rule out some of the possible reasons for the effect. He designed a simple laboratory experiment in which people were asked to wind fishing reels. Again, he found that people did better (reeled faster) when competing with others than they did when alone, but the list of possible explanations for this phenomenon was now greatly reduced. Suction theory, for example, was simply no longer appropriate. Self-selection was ruled out because Triplett had the same people wind reels under both conditions.

Note what Triplett did. First, he observed an aspect of behavior—bicycle riders performing better against others than when alone—for which there were many plausible explanations. Second, he conceptualized this behavior as an instance of a general cause and effect process—competition leads to improved performance. What he wanted to know, of course, was why or how competition leads to improved performance. So, third, he designed a setting in which he could induce competition so that this general process could manifest itself, but a setting in which the plausible explanations for its occurrence would be greatly reduced in comparsion to the number of explanations that could be invoked in the natural setting. In short, he designed an experiment to establish why the presence of one variable (competition) changed something about a second variable (performance).

It sounds simple, and it can be. It can also be fun. But before going into the details, you might be interested in knowing the fate of this once-seldom-used tool for investigating human behavior. By the mid-1960s and early 1970s, the laboratory experiment had become tremendously popular as a research method, particularly among psychologists. For example, in 1972, 83 percent of the articles published in the *Journal of Personality and Social Psychology* involved experimentation (Higbee, Lott, & Graves, 1976). In fact, the laboratory experiment has become so popular, that it has generated a backlash (Ring, 1967; Gergen, 1973). Many people have felt called upon to point out that there are, after all, other research methods available and that there are some issues of importance that cannot be investigated in a laboratory experiment. You, of course, already know that, so you are ahead of the game. But, back to what is involved to see if it can be made clear why the experiment has enjoyed such a surge in popularity since Triplett's time.

The Essence of the Experiment

Basically, an EXPERIMENT is a form of research in which you actively manipulate or change something (the independent variable) in order to see what effect that change has on something else (the dependent variable). There is more involved, but before describing the rest, it is important to realize that there are several ways in which an experiment is simply an extension of the methods discussed in the proceeding chapters. For example, all research methods may be thought of as techniques for insulating your observations and inferences against error (Kaplan, 1964). There is a constant temptation to infer more than you should from your observations and to read into your own experiences lessons that may not really be there (see page 285). Thus, research methods help keep you honest by forcing you to be explicit about (i.e., to acknowledge) the conditions under which your observations have taken place. Similarly, all research methods generally have as their goal the provision of evidence about causal relationships between variables. Whether the variables of interest are as complex as patterns of child rearing and adult personality (Mead, 1949) or as simple as caffeine ingestion and hand tremor, the point of the research is usually to demonstrate that one leads to the other. To do this, of course, all research methods are grounded upon the notion of comparison. In fact, it is probably not going too far to say that the concept of comparison is the single most important concept in research. Again, all research methods help you be explicit about what precisely you are comparing with: the patterns of child rearing in Samoa compared with those in the United States; drinking three cups of coffee compared with drinking one; and so on. The factor that differentiates the laboratory experiment from the other research methods is its ability to provide you with the most unambiguous information about a causal relationship between variables. The question, of course, is, What are the features of an experiment that enable it to do that?

Manipulation

The first such characteristic of experimentation is manipulation, and, as you are no doubt aware, it simply means changing something. If you are interested in improving the look of your living room wall, for example, you might try a nice picture instead of that old STOP sign. If you want people to stand closer when you talk, you might try cutting down on the

DID IT REALLY MAKE THAT MUCH DIFFERENCE?

There is a poem by Robert Frost called "The Road Not Taken," which goes like this:

> Two roads diverged in a yellow wood,
> And sorry I could not travel both
> And be one traveller, long I stood
> And looked down one as far as I could
> To where it bent in the undergrowth;
>
> Then took the other, as just as fair,
> And having perhaps the better claim,
> Because it was grassy and wanted wear;
> Though as for that the passing there
> Had worn them really about the same,
>
> And both that morning equally lay
> In leaves no step had trodden black.
> Oh, I kept the first for another day!
> Yet knowing how way leads on to way,
> I doubted if I should ever come back.
>
> I shall be telling this with a sigh
> Somewhere ages and ages hence:
> Two roads diverged in a wood, and I—
> I took the one less traveled by,
> And that has made all the difference.

Mr. Frost was an excellent poet, but it is clear he could have profited from a quick course in research methods. There is simply no way of knowing whether taking the less-traveled road made any difference at all.

In looking back on their lives, many people identify choice points that, in retrospect, seem to have been quite important. They decided to go to Harvard instead of Yale. They chose the Army instead of the Navy. They spent a year in Europe instead of joining the Peace Corps. And while they were at Harvard or in the Army or in Paris, they met this guy who . . .. And the tale unfolds. They ignore the fact that they have no data on what would have happened had they chosen the other alternative. Their lives might have been even more exciting if they had gone to Yale or joined the Navy or spent a couple of years in the jungle. They have assumed that the foregone alternatives would have led to a dull, uneventful, or impecunious life, a fallacy we might term the UNFOUNDED IMPLICIT BASELINE COMPARISON. So the next time one of your friends starts that sort of smug reminiscing about what smart decisions they have made, you might point out that they are missing some data. Of course, you might want to make sure you have a few spare friends before you do that.

garlic for breakfast. As these examples imply, manipulation is usually done with a purpose in mind. We want to see "what will happen if . . . ." Similarly, in an experiment, the interest is in what happens when some aspect of the setting is changed. Does that change make a difference in how people respond to the setting?

Note that with the exception of a few of the quasi-experimental designs discussed in Chapter Seven, this concept of manipulation is not a part of the other research methods we have described. Quite the contrary! In survey research, participant observation, or archival research, the researcher's usual goal is to leave the research setting or participant or both exactly as he or she found them. Thus, there is a very real sense in which the experiment provides a more active role for the person doing the research. That may, in fact, be part of its appeal. The experimenter gets a chance to get in the lab and tinker—try it and if that does not work try something else.

The concept of control is closely tied to the notion of manipulation. If you change something, you usually will want to know whether the change has any effect. Suppose you switch to super unleaded gas and get your car tuned up in an effort to stop the ping in your engine and that you do both of these things on the same day. If the ping stops, you will not know whether or not the new gasoline had an effect. Similarly, if you stop eating garlic for breakfast, get a new wardrobe, switch to Listerine, and make it a point to be nicer to people, chances are people will indeed seem friendlier, but you will not know whether Listerine had anything to do with it. In other words, when you are interested in whether a given manipulation of some aspect of the environment has any effect, you need to control, or hold constant, other aspects of the environment.

Of course, you cannot hold all other aspects of the environment constant. It is impossible to run the clock back and replay situations at will— once with and once without your manipulation. You can never know exactly what would have happened had you done A instead of B in a particular circumstance. You can only try doing A in the future in similar circumstances. Given that everything except your manipulation cannot be held constant, what things should you attempt to control? You need to hold constant or control those other aspects of the environment that might plausibly be expected to interfere with or obscure observations of the change produced by your manipulation.

For example, suppose you had developed a hunch that attitude change is a gradual process, that people take in some information relevant to an attitude and mull it over for a while before it affects their attitude on the issue. Further, suppose you designed an experiment in which you planned to test this idea by exposing people to a persuasive communication advocating abolition of the death penalty and measuring their attitudes toward the death penalty immediately afterward and again a week later. If you had such a plan, you had better pray for an outbreak of peace and good will during the week between measurements. A sensational murder case breaking into the news that week would very likely confound your results. You might control for this possibility by conducting the experiment at a summer camp in which you had confiscated all the radios or could otherwise censor the news coming into the camp.

The aspect of the environment that is manipulated in an experiment is usually referred to as the INDEPENDENT VARIABLE, and one of the basic decisions facing the would-be experimenter is how to present the independent variable. Aronson and Carlsmith (1968) have pointed out that it usually boils down to the question of manipulation by instruction (i.e., by what you say to the subjects) or manipulation by event (i.e., by something that happens to the subjects). As an example of the instruction type of manipulation, Byrne (1971) has conducted a large number of experiments testing the general hypothesis that similarity leads to attraction. In his experiments, similarity has usually been manipulated by giving subjects information about the attitudes of the stranger. That is, either the stranger had attitudes and opinions very similar to those of subject or the stranger had very dissimilar attitudes and opinions. An example of the event type of manipulation is contained in an experiment by Piliavin, Rodin, and Piliavin (1969) in which subway riders were confronted by an emergency situation in which a man fell to the floor of the car and seemed to be in need of help. One aspect of this situation that was manipulated was the apparent source of the man's difficulty. On some occasions, the man smelled strongly of whiskey and appeared to be drunk, whereas on other occasions there was no odor of whiskey and the man simply appeared to be ill.

As you can see from the two examples above, when you manipulate an independent variable by some event or by something that happens to the subjects, you are likely to have more impact on them. They will sit up and take notice. Think about how you might have felt if you had been in one of the subway cars Piliavin et al. chose to use in their experiment. If you do not live in New York, chances are you might have been a little apprehensive about the subways to begin with; then to have some drunk pass out and fall to the floor right in front of you would have confirmed your worst fears. Beside such a vivid, involving manipulation, the use of instructions or of some printed information to manipulate an independent variable seems to pale by comparison. But there is a trade-off built into this event versus instruction decision about how to manipulate your independent variable. Events are likely to be relatively complex and to introduce some ambiguity about what, precisely, is being manipulated. In the Piliavin et al. study, the intention was to manipulate only the perceived source of the man's problem (alcohol versus some undefined illness), but beliefs about the value of intervening, attributions of responsibility, feelings of disgust, and sympathy were probably all affected by the manipulation. Instructions of the type used by Byrne (1971) to manipulate similarity of another's attitudes usually enable you to be more precise about what is being manipulated, but you may pay for that precision by failing to really capture the subject's attention. (More information about this *event + impact* versus *instruction + control* issue will be presented later.)

When you have an independent variable such as similar or dissimilar attitudes, it is usually said that the independent variable has two levels. But you can have more than two if you like. Bryne, for example, has usually manipulated perceived attitudinal similarity by employing finer gradations than simply similar versus not similar. When you have a variable you want to manipulate, the different levels of degree of the variable are referred to as TREATMENTS, and a common procedure is to expose some subjects to one treatment, some to another treatment, and some to no treatment at all. The latter are usually referred to as NO TREATMENT CONTROL SUBJECTS. For example, suppose you were interested in the effect of varying degrees of food deprivation on the tendency of subjects to see food related items in ambiguous shapes such as those formed by inkblots. You might deprive some subjects of food for 24 hours prior to asking them what they see in the inkblots, some for 48 hours, and some not at all. You would need the data from the undeprived subjects as the control or comparison in order to interpret the data from the two experimental conditions (24 and 48 hours deprivation). If, for example, the undeprived subjects see just as many food-related items as the others, then amount of deprivation would not suffice as an explanation for seeing such items.

The aspect of the environment that you examine or measure to determine whether your change in the independent variable has had any effect is usually referred to as the DEPENDENT VARIABLE. If your hypothesis is correct, changes in the latter will depend upon changes in the independent variable. In the food deprivation example, the dependent variable might be some measure of the total amount of food-related imagery in response to five different inkblots. The independent variable, of course, is the length of deprivation. In Byrne's studies manipulating the similarity of a stranger's attitudes to the subject's attitudes, the dependent variable is usually some measure of attraction: how much the subject thinks he or she will like the the stranger. In the study by Piliavin et al. (1969), the major dependent variable was how many people came to the aid of the man on the floor.

The purpose of any experiment, of course, is to determine whether changes in the independent variable produce changes in the dependent variable. As mentioned earlier, to do that you must hold constant those aspects of the experimental setting (other than the independent variable) that might plausibly be expected to influence the dependent variable. In a typical experiment there are many things that have the potential of producing changes in the dependent variable, but the most recurrently troublesome are preexisting differences among subjects exposed to different levels of the independent variable. Consider a couple of techniques that have been devised for handling this problem.

Assigning Subjects to Conditions

Typically an experiment involves comparisons of the responses of subjects exposed to the independent variable with the responses of subjects not exposed to the independent variable, or it involves comparisions of the responses of subjects exposed to different levels of the independent variable. When the subjects in these various conditions are systematically different to begin with, their responses may very well differ even in the absence of the independent varaible. Take an extreme example. Nobody who was interested in the effects of caffeine on weight-lifting ability would compare the amounts lifted by male college students who had had a cup of coffee with the amounts lifted by female college students who had not had a cup of coffee. The comparison would be worthless, except as an example of how not to do research. The two groups of subjects (coffee drinkers and nondrinkers) differed systematically prior to their exposure to the independent variable.

There are basically two techniques for ruling out, or controlling, the influence of such preexisting group differences. The first is called MATCHING and involves trying to equate the subjects in different conditions on the basis of certain known characteristics. For example, suppose you were interested in various ways of reducing stress and you designed an experiment to compare the relative effectiveness of Transcendental Meditation, jogging, and biofeedback. If you believe that age and sex might be important variables determining how people respond to stress, and to your three stress reduction programs, you would want to match on these variables. For every 50-year-old male assigned to the jogging condition, you would have to assign a 50-year-old male to the TM condition and another to the biofeedback condition. (For a better design you should also have a no-treatment control condition which would mean a fourth 50-year-old male.) On the other hand, you would probably be safe in assuming that hair color is unlikely to be related to stress reduction. Hence, you would not believe it necessary to match subjects in the various conditions on hair color—although stereotypes about redheads suggest that maybe you should (Jones, 1982b).

Table 1 illustrates the use of a QUOTA MATRIX, a device that will help you match subjects. First, you decide what variables you intend to use

Table 1   Matching Subjects to Experimental Conditions by Using a Quota Matrix

A. Subjects available for experiment[a]

Age group (years)	Overweight subjects		Normal subjects	
	Male	Female	Male	Female
20–29	8	7	16	18
30–39	(16)	19	25	29
40–49	21	23	18	/17\
50–59	11	10	8	9
60+	[7]	4	◇5◇	3

B. Distribution of subjects to four experimental conditions[b]

1 No-treatment control	2 Jogging	3 TM	4 Biofeedback
(4)	(4)	(4)	(4)
[1]	[1]	[1]	[1]
/4\	/4\	/4\	/4\
◇1◇	◇1◇	◇1◇	◇1◇

[a]All subjects potentially available for research have been categorized by their age, sex, and weight.
[b]Subjects are assigned to each condition:
○ Male subjects: overweight, 30–39
□ Male subjects: overweight, 60+
◇ Male subjects: normal, 60+
△ Female subjects: normal, 40–49
Not all of the subjects will actually be assigned. For example, because there are only three females of normal weight who are over 60 years old, there are not enough subjects in that category to enable assignment of one such subject to each condition.

in matching. In the stress reduction experiment, suppose you decide that, in addition to age and sex, you want to match subjects on body weight, that is, whether they are overweight or normal. Then you draw up a matrix like that in Table 1, in which you categorize the people potentially available to participate in your experiment. Finally, you assign equal numbers of persons from each category to each condition. If you have 16 overweight males who are between 30 and 40 years old, for example, then 4 of these would be assigned to each of your four conditions.

According to Box, Hunter, and Hunter (1978), we may define a block as a portion of the available subjects (e.g., overweight males between 50 and 59 years of age) who could reasonably be expected to be more similar to each other than to the remaining subjects. Thus, the technical term for what you are doing when you use a quota matrix like that in Table 1 is BLOCKING. There are several statistical advantages to blocking, which we need not go into, but you can see how it would help make comparisons of the various treatments more precise. In the example, age, sex, and weight of the subjects should not contribute to any differences among the conditions.

The problem with blocking and, more generally, with matching is that you can never be sure you have matched subjects in the various conditions on the really important variables. The earlier reference to redheads was not entirely facetious because it seems to be the case that personality type is a more important determinant of reaction to stress than either age or sex (cf. Glass, 1977). Matching can promote a false sense of security by leading you to believe that your experimental and control groups were really equated at the outset, when in fact they were not equated at all on a host of variables.

The second solution to the problem of controlling for or ruling out preexisting differences among experimental groups is a better one. It is the process of randomly assigning subjects to conditions, or RANDOMIZATION. In principle, randomization is simple. If your design called for an experimental condition and a control group, say, you would simply need to ensure that for all potential subjects the probability of being assigned to the control group was equal to the probability of being assigned to the experimental group. With only two conditions, you could use a coin – an unbiased one, of course. For each subject you flip the coin: Heads means that subject is assigned to the experimental group and tails means that subject is assigned to the control group.

When your design has more than two conditions – and most designs do – you can use a TABLE OF RANDOM NUMBERS to help you achieve randomization of subjects to conditions. I have prepared such a table for you, and if you will look at the Appendix to this book you will see that it consists of rows and columns of the digits 0 through 9. The table in the Appendix was generated by a computer that was instructed to print out the numbers in such a manner that for each successive entry in the table any of the digits 0 through 9 was equally likely to be selected. That is, the table is a random arrangement of the digits.

The table is used in the following manner: Suppose you had five conditions and 100 subjects and you wanted to randomly assign the subjects to the five conditions. First, number the subjects 00 through 99. Then pick an arbitrary point in the table—say, the beginning of the sixteenth row on the first page. Reading across that row you look at each successive two-digit number: 01, 92, 93, 21, ... The first 20 subjects whose numbers you see get assigned to Condition 1, the next 20 to Condition 2, and so on. It is a very simple way of randomly assigning subjects to conditions. Just in case you have a little trouble following the example, however, there are a couple of additional examples on how to use the table at the beginning of the Appendix.

In practice, achieving true random assignment can be very difficult, and all sorts of subtle biases may operate in determining which subjects get assigned to which group. To use volunteer subjects in one condition or treatment and paid or coerced subjects in another would be an obvious error because the motivations of the two groups differ sharply. McDavid (1965), for example, has shown that volunteer subjects are much more interested in winning approval than are subjects who are required to participate in research. Similarly, to use an 8 o'clock section of students in the experimental condition of a study and a 10 o'clock section of students enrolled in the same course in the control condition would also be an example of nonrandom assignment to conditions. Students who schedule their classes for 8 o'clock may be quite different from those who schedule their classes for 10 o'clock.

In general, randomization is better than matching for ruling out the possibility that preexisting group differences, and not the different levels of the independent variable, account for any differences you obtain on responses to the dependent variable. Randomization assumes, of course, that, when all subjects have the same likelihood of being assigned to any of the conditions, personal characteristics of subjects in the various conditions should average out about the same. For large numbers of subjects, that is usually a safe assumption. For only a small number of subjects, it may not be so safe. If you only have four or five subjects in each condition, then one weird subject in the control group, say, could throw off your whole experiment. So, you need to be a little skeptical about the effectiveness of randomization when you only have small numbers of subjects. As Campbell and Stanley (1966) have pointed out, randomization may assure unbiased assignment of subjects to groups but it does not always guarantee the equivalence of such groups.

One way in which you can check on the initial equivalence of groups is to give some sort of premeasure or pretest after the groups have been constituted. For example, if you are planning an attitude change experiment, you might want to administer a questionnaire to assess attitudes on the pertinent issues prior to introducing your experimental manipulation—just to make sure that subjects in the various conditions have similar attitudes to begin with. The major problem, of course, is that such a pretest might sensitize subjects to what you are interested in and as a result, they might not respond naturally. Lana (1969) recommended several ways of overcoming this problem, for example, embedding the crucial pretest item in a long questionnaire with a variety of items or separating the pretest in time from the actual experiment or collecting the pretest data in a different setting from that in which the experiment is conducted.

Before going on, take a moment to look at the following list. These are the major concepts that have been discussed since the beginning of the chapter. If you understand them you already have a basic grasp of the experiment. Give yourself a test. See how many of them you can define without peeking at the Glossary.

Manipulation	Matching
Independent variable	Blocking
Levels	Quota matrix
Treatments	Randomization
Manipulation by instruction	Table of random numbers
Manipulation by event	Pretest
No-treatment control	Plausible alternative explanations
Dependent variable	

They are not all new, of course. You probably thought I beat the notion of plausible alternative explanations to death in the last chapter and randomization should at least be familiar from the chapter on Survey Research. To illustrate these concepts, and some others to be mentioned later, I would like to describe an experiment on the way in which stereotypes influence memory.

An Illustration: Memory for Stereotype-Consistent Information

The term STEREOTYPE was originally employed in the printing and newspaper industries. It referred to a one-piece metal sheet that had been cast from a mold taken of a printed surface, such as a page of set type. The stereotype was used to print—over and over and over—whatever figures or words had been cast into its surface. The term was adopted by Walter Lippmann (1922) to refer to the pictures in our heads of various racial, national, religious, and other ethnic groups. The connotation that Lippmann apparently intended was that of an unvarying form or pattern, of fixed and conventional expression, and of having no individuality, as though cast from a mold. To stereotype members of a particular group then, means thinking about and referring to members of that group as though they were all the same (cf. Jones, Hendrick, & Epstein, 1979).

In the last few years there has been some intriguing research on the possibility that the very way we take and process information about others may play a role in perpetuating stereotypes. Cohen (1981), for example, has suggested that we are more likely to remember information about another person that is consistent—as opposed to inconsistent—with our stereotype of the group to which the person belongs. The reasoning behind that idea goes something like this. Whenever we observe another person doing something, there is usually much more information available than we could possibly attend to. So, we are selective. We can only take in (encode) part of what is there. That being the case, it may be that our prior knowledge, our stereotype of the person's group, cues us to attend to, or enables us to encode more easily, those aspects of the person's behavior that are consistent with that prior expectation. Another possibility is that we encode information consistent and inconsistent with our stereotypes equally well, but that later, after some time has passed we find it easier to recall (retrieve) information that is consistent with the stereotype. If such differential retrieval is the key, then when asked to recall aspects of the person's behavior immediately after observing it, you should be able to report both stereotype-consistent and stereotype-inconsistent information. That is, you indeed encoded both. But when asked to make your report a week later (when you would have to retrieve the information from long-term memory), you might find that stereotype-consistent information comes to mind more easily.

To test these ideas, Cohen decided to use the stereotypes that people have of waitresses and librarians. To do that, the first order of business was to find out precisely what behaviors, characteristics, and life-style preferences are seen as differentiating the two. Thus, Cohen had a number of students write out descriptions of an imaginary woman who either worked full time as a waitress or who was employed as a librarian. From these descriptions, she extracted a large number of features, from things such as *has blonde hair* to *likes classical music*. Next, she asked a larger group of students to rate each of these characteristics in terms of how likely it was to be exhibited by a waitress and how likely it was to be exhibited by a librarian. (Note that we have not gotten to the experiment yet; what is being described is how Cohen went about preparing the stimulus materials to use in the experiment. Careful preparation of the stimulus materials is a crucial aspect of any experiment.) Once Cohen had obtained the ratings, she selected two sets of 18 features. In each set, nine features had been rated as being likely to be exhibited by a librarian, but not a waitress; and nine had been rated as being likely to be exhibited by a waitress, but not a librarian. Just in case you want to see how they square with your own stereotypes, the two sets are presented in Table 2. Finally, using the characteristics listed in the table, Cohen made two videotapes of a woman and her husband having dinner and talking in their home. In each videotape, one complete set of 18 features was used. That is, in each videotape, there were nine things consistent with the stereotype of a librarian and nine things consistent with the stereotype of a waitress.

Compared with all this preparation, Cohen's actual experiment is going to seem quite simple. She told subjects that they were going to be asked to look at the videotape and that, after looking at the tape, they would be asked a few questions about the personality of the woman on the tape. Just prior to looking at the tape, half of the subjects were told that the woman on the tape was a librarian. The other subjects were told that the woman they were about to see was a waitress. After looking at the tape,

Table 2 Characteristics differentiating stereotypes of librarians and waitresses

Set 1	Set 2
Librarian features	
Eats roast beef	Eats salad
Plays piano	Drinks wine with dinner
Has fresh flowers in room	Uses formal table setting
Wears glasses	Traveled in Europe
Bookshelves in room	No television
Eats angel food cake	Spends day reading
Plays golf	Artwork on walls
Likes classical music	Receives bestseller as gift
Nonaffectionate with husband	Receives history book as gift
Waitress features	
Eats hamburger	No salad
Plays guitar	Drinks beer
No fresh flowers	Informal table setting
Does not wear glasses	Not traveled in Europe
No bookshelves	Television
Eats chocolate cake	Spends day working
Bowls	No artwork on walls
Likes pop music	Receives nightgown as gift
Affectionate with husband	Receives romantic novel as gift

Source: Cohen (1981).

some subjects were immediately asked to answer a few questions about what they had seen, whereas other subjects were asked to come back either four or seven days later. When they returned, they were asked the same questions about what they had seen on the tape. The questions were, of course, intended to measure the dependent variable, that is, their ability to recall stereotype-consistent and stereotype-inconsistent information from the videotape.

That is the whole experiment. The first thing to notice is that Cohen had, not one, but two independent variables. That is, she manipulated two things: (1) the stereotype invoked by instructions given subjects immediately prior to seeing the videotape and (2) whether they were asked about what they had seen immediately afterwards, four days later, or seven days later. In tabular form, you might depict Cohen's design like this:

Stereotype Invoked by Instructions	Time of Measurement of Dependent Variable		
	Immediately	4 days later	7 days later
Waitress	1	2	3
Librarian	4	5	6

As you can see, there were six conditions (1–6), and subjects were randomly assigned to conditions. Such a design, in which each of the levels of one independent variable appears in conjunction once and only once with each of the levels of the second independent variable is called a FACTORIAL DESIGN. Because there are two levels of the first independent variable (i.e., waitress, librarian) and three levels of the second (i.e., immediately, 4 days, 7 days), the technical name for this particular design is a 2×3 factorial.

Note that if Cohen had only been interested in measuring memory for stereotype-consistent and stereotype-inconsistent information immediately after viewing the videotape, her design would have looked like this:

Stereotype Invoked by Instructions	Immediate Memory Assessment
Waitress	1
Librarian	4

In this case she would only have needed two groups of subjects (the original Groups 1 and 4) and the design would have been called a SINGLE-FACTOR DESIGN. Or, she might have been interested only in memory for information consistent and inconsistent with the waitress stereotype in relation to time. In this case, she could have employed another single-factor design making use of these groups of subjects:

Stereotype Invoked by Instructions	Time of Measurement of Dependent Variable		
	Immediately	4 Days Later	7 Days Later
Waitress	1	2	3

The major advantage of combining two such single-factor designs into one factorial experiment is that you can look at the INTERACTION of your independent variables. Two variables are said to interact if the effect one has depends upon, or changes with, different levels of the other. Perhaps that can be made clearer by first showing you Cohen's actual results and then showing you a couple of other ways in which her results could have turned out. The actual results are depicted in Figure 1. They can be summarized fairly succinctly by saying that (1) at all three measurement points stereotype-consistent information is recalled better than is stereotype-inconsistent information, and (2) memory of both consistent and inconsistent information decays as time passes. These effects occurred regardless of which stereotype (waitress or librarian) had been invoked by the instructions given subjects prior to the videotape.

Note that Cohen really had two separate dependent variables: how well subjects recalled stereotype-consistent information and how well they

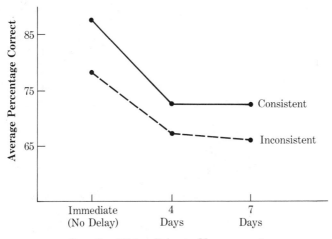

Length of Delay Prior to Measurement

Figure 1 STEREOTYPE CONSISTENT INFORMATION is remembered more accurately. When subjects thought they had watched a waitress or a librarian they were more accurate in remembering behaviors on the videotape that were consistent with their stereotype of the woman's supposed occupation. (From Cohen, 1981.)

recalled stereotype-inconsistent information. Overall subjects did better at remembering stereotype-consistent information or, to use the proper phrase, there was a *main effect* for consistent information. Similarly, there was a *main effect* for time of measurement, but there was no *interaction* between memory for consistent versus inconsistent information and time of measurement. To say that there is a MAIN EFFECT for some variable, such as time of measurement, simply means that overall time of measurement made a difference. To say that there was no interaction between memory for consistent versus inconsistent information and time of measurement means that the difference in memory for consistent and inconsistent information was approximately the same at each time of measurement.

The two graphs in Figure 2 show outcomes that *might* have occurred in Cohen's experiment. Note that both of these graphs still depict a main effect for stereotype-consistent information, that is, overall, consistent information is recalled better than inconsistent information is. However, the graphs also depict interactions between memory of stereotype-consistent versus stereotype-inconsistent information and time of measurement. In A, memory for inconsistent information seems to decline over time whereas memory for consistent information seems to stay about the same. In B, memory for consistent information again seems to stay about the same, but memory for inconsistent information actually seems to improve. When an interaction does occur, you have to be very careful about generalizing your results. For example, based on her data, Cohen can say that stereotype-consistent information is recalled better than stereotype-inconsistent information. However, if the results depicted in B had been obtained, that statement would have to be qualified. In the latter case it is clear that whether stereotype-consistent or stereotype-inconsistent information is recalled better depends on the point in time at which you assess recall, that is, there is an interaction between memory for consistent or inconsistent information and the passage of time. After seven days there is essentially no difference between memory for consistent and inconsistent information.

Before leaving Cohen's experiment, there is one last point to mention and that has to do with her preparation of two equivalent videotapes and her use of two stereotypes. Suppose that she had made only one videotape and invoked only one stereotype by telling subjects that the person that they were about to see was, say, a waitress? Had she done that her results would have been much less convincing because we might have suspected that there was something peculiarly waitress-like about the actress or her behavior on the videotape. By having some subjects believe that the same actress on the same videotape was a librarian and showing that those subjects remember more librarian-consistent aspects of her behavior, Cohen has decreased the plausibility of any argument that her stimulus materials

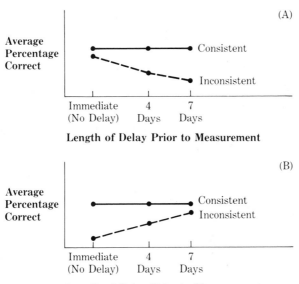

Figure 2 TWO FORMS OF AN INTERACTION between elapsed time and memory for consistent and inconsistent information. (A) Memory for stereotype consistent information stays at about the same level over time, but memory for stereotype inconsistent information gets worse as time passes. (B) Memory for stereotype consistent information again seems not to be affected by the passage of time, but memory for stereotype inconsistent information actually improves as time passes.

were biased. Further, by using two sets of waitress–librarian, consistent–inconsistent features (i.e., by making two different videotapes), Cohen, in effect, conducted an INTERNAL REPLICATION of her experiment.

To REPLICATE something simply means to duplicate or reproduce or repeat it. As can be seen in the Discussion on page 300, there are several varieties of replications; but, unfortunately, none of them are very popular. In fact, replication is one of the most neglected aspects of research in the social and behavioral sciences. It is not too difficult to see why. A full-scale replication of any experiment would be as time-consuming and costly (probably more costly with inflation) as the original experiment, without its advantages. You get very little credit for creativity in the scientific community if you appear to be doing what someone else has already done. But there are many ways of carrying out partial replications, as Cohen did by using two videotapes, without the added time and expense of a complete second study. For example, you might have two different experimenters each run

RELICATE, REPLICATE, REPLICATE!

One of the things that should be very clear by now, after you have plowed through the preceding chapters, is that there are multiple ambiguities surrounding research in the social and behavioral sciences. Because of that, one demonstration of a given cause-and-effect sequence is never sufficient. Any experiment needs to be repeated with different manipulations, experimenters, and measurements (to probe its internal validity); in different settings and with different subjects (to establish its external validity). Replication, in short, is not only the road to progress, it is absolutely essential even if all you want to know is where you are, that is, what you really know, at the moment.

Replications come in several varieties. EXACT REPLICATIONS of research are those in which all aspects of the original research are duplicated precisely. For most of the hard sciences, exact replications are routine. In chemistry, for example, at 10°C under atmospheric pressure with constant humidity, hydrogen and oxygen would be expected to combine in the same manner in Israel as in England. In research on human behavior, however, Israelis and Englishmen would not necessarily be expected to react in the same manner to a given stimulus. You might argue that if we pick a stimulus that has the same meaning to both, we would get the same reaction. If we did that, and assuming there are other differences in setting such as time of day and experimenters, we would have changed the hypothetical Israeli–English study from an exact to a CONCEPTUAL REPLICATION, or to what Campbell (1969a) called a heteromethod replication. According to Jones (1966), a conceptual (or heteromethod) replication involves "(a) tailoring an independent variable to fit the outlook of sub-

half of the subjects in every condition. That is not ideal, but if the results are the same regardless of experimenter, you could place more confidence in those results than in the results of a single experimenter. The plausibility of the argument that two experimenters biased the results in exactly the same way is considerably less than the plausibility of the argument that any given experimenter may have biased the results.

Designing What You Need

The key thing to remember about the process of designing an experiment is that it is an exercise in simple, everyday logic. You do not need a knowledge of esoteric statistical techniques. You do need to be very clear about the hypothesis you want to test. Quite often one of the first things jects in a particular locale, and (b) making arbitrary changes in procedure that should not affect the basic result."

In research on human behavior, exact replications are usually not possible; experimenters, subjects, and settings are almost sure to differ, even when you manipulate and measure your variables in the same way as in the orginal research. Conceptual replications are thus more natural for the social and behavioral sciences, but they can pose problems. If your conceptual replication fails to reproduce the original result, you may not be able to say why. It may be because the new way you chose to manipulate the independent variable was flawed, or it could be because you used male subjects instead of female subjects or it could be because . . ..

Suppose that in reading a research report you notice a flaw in the procedure. It occurs to you that if the author had done something a little differently he or she would have gotten a different result. In short, you are able to suggest a plausible alternative explanation for the findings, and you want to do the research to demonstrate that your explanation is more valid than the author's. The type of replication you need to conduct under these circumstances is called a BALANCED REPLICATION. In a balanced replication, you include the conditions necessary to duplicate the original conditions as precisely as possible and the new condition(s) in which you change or eliminate the flaw that you think is responsible for the original results. Inclusion of the original conditions is necessary to show that with your different setting and subjects you can duplicate the author's findings. Then, when you also demonstrate that the procedural change suggested by your alternative explanation for those findings produced a different set of results, you will have won your case.

that happens when you begin to think about ways of testing a hypothesis is that you realize you are a little fuzzy about exactly what the hypothesis is. Variables that seem clear-cut when you are just toying with them may turn out to be extremely complex when you give them a little serious thought. Group size is a good example. On the surface, it seems very straightforward. But it is really quite complex. If your initial hypothesis was something like "members are less satisfied in large work groups than small work groups," a little analysis might suggest that it is not really size but rather ease of communication that is the important thing. It just happens that in large groups it is usually more difficult to communicate with other group members than it is in small groups. So, your revised hypothesis would be "the greater the ease of communication in groups, the greater the member satisfaction." Of course, I realize that you probably could not care less about group size or communication patterns in groups, but the point is simply that the first step in designing any experiment is to specify your hypothesis as precisely as possible. Only when you have done that can you begin to set up the appropriate conditions to test it.

Some Standard and Not-So-Standard Designs

"Testing the hypothesis" means simply demonstrating that changes in the independent variable produce changes in the dependent variable. An experimental design that allows you to do that is said to be internally valid, or to have internal validity. Campbell and Stanley (1966), the high priests of design, are rather dogmatic on this issue. According to them, achieving internal validity is the *sine qua non* of experimental design. An internally valid design is one that enables you to say that your experimental treatment, your manipulation, did make a difference. Although you may not be banished to outer darkness for constructing a design that lacks internal validity, you will be cursed with uninterpretable results.

It is, of course, impossible to foresee everything that might interfere with your ability to make causal inferences linking the independent and dependent variables in a specific setting. But, as you will recall from Chapter Seven, there are a number of threats to internal validity that can be foreseen and dealt with – with varying degrees of success – by design. Cook and Campbell (1979) listed 13 such threats, which are summarized in Table 1 in Chapter Seven just in case they have slipped your mind. In fact, it would be an excellent idea to memorize them so that you can check them off mentally when you are designing an experiment. I tried to think of a good mnemonic for you by using the first letters of each, but what can you spell with HMTISSMIADCCR? If you want to try it, you can get another vowel by substituting *attrition* for *mortality*.

The basic design that qualifies as a true experiment, the bare minimum so to speak, is one in which you randomly assign subjects to two conditions, expose subjects in one condition to your manipulation, and then have subjects in both conditions respond to your dependent measure. The official title of this design is the posttest-only control group design. Let R stand for random assignment of subjects to conditions and X and O stand for the manipulation and measurement, respectively (which, of course, you remember from Chapter Seven); then the design may be diagrammed like this:

$$R \quad X \quad O_1$$
$$R \qquad\;\; O_2$$

Compare

This is simple, but elegant. The design rests on the assumption that because subjects are randomly assigned to conditions and because measurement occurs at the same point in time for both conditions, any differences at the time of measurement must be due to the manipulation, X, in the experimental condition. There is only one comparison to make.

An example of a study using this design is one by Deci, Betley, Kahle, Abrams, and Porac (1981), in which subjects were asked to solve some interesting puzzles under competitive or noncompetitive conditions. The hypothesis was that when tasks were performed to win a competition it detracts from the intrinsic interest of the tasks themselves. Consequently, people who performed the tasks under competitive conditions were expected to put the tasks aside more quickly after the competition was over than did people who had worked on them for the same amount of time under noncompetitive conditions. Sure enough, they did. Note that subjects in both conditions worked on the same puzzles, and in both conditions another person, who appeared to be a subject also, but was actually an accomplice of the experimenter, was seated across the table and working on the puzzles. The manipulation, the treatment, was simply that subjects in one condition were led to believe they were in competition with this other person. Subjects in the control condition were just asked to work as quickly as possible.

Before commenting on how the posttest-only control group design fares with respect to the threats listed in Table 1 in Chapter Seven, let me introduce you to two more true experimental designs. You will no doubt discern a certain family resemblance among all three. The pretest–posttest control group design is arrived at by simply adding a pretest to each of the conditions in the posttest-only control group plan. Diagrammatically, it looks like this:

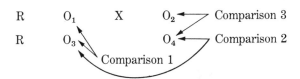

Now, however, there are three comparisons of interest. Comparison 1 will tell you whether or not your random assignment really worked. Comparision 2 will tell you how much effect history, maturation, testing, and statistical regression have had on your posttest. Comparision 3 will tell you whether your manipulation had any effect, and if so, how much. The latter statement assumes that Comparison 1 indicated that randomization did work, that is, that there was no difference between groups on the pretest.

If you take the two preceding diagrams and place one on top of the other, you will have a third experimental design. This one is called the

SOLOMON FOUR-GROUP DESIGN (Solomon, 1949), and it looks like this:

Group 1	R	O_1	X	O_2
Group 2	R	O_3		O_4
Group 3	R		X	O_5
Group 4	R			O_6

As you can see, there are a number of comparisons that could be made here. The basic advantages of this design are that it enables you to estimate (1) the magnitude of the effects due to pretesting and (2) the interaction of pretesting with your independent variable (X). Rearranging the design as a 2×2 factorial design emphasizes the comparisons available:

	No X	X
No pretest	4	3
Pretest	2	1

To determine the main effect of pretesting, you would compare the average response on your dependent measure from Groups 3 and 4 combined with the average response from Groups 1 and 2 combined. To determine the main effect of your manipulation, you would compare the average response of Groups 3 and 1 combined with the average response from Groups 4 and 2 combined. In addition, of course, you would be able to look at the interaction (or lack of interaction) between pretesting and your manipulation. It might turn out that your manipulation is effective only after subjects have been pretested; that is, the average response from Group 1 is greater than that from Group 2, but Group 3 does not differ from Group 4. If that result did occur, it would mean that you could only generalize your results to pretested groups.

Having presented these three basic designs, I must confess that the most common one, the one you are most likely to see and, perhaps, use yourself, is the simplest one – the posttest-only control group design. This bias occurs because pretesting is not too popular. It introduces the possibility of alerting subjects to the research topic. As Silverman (1977) has noted in relation to studies of attitude change, it does not require an IQ that would get you into MENSA to realize what is going on when someone asks you to fill out an attitude scale on nuclear power, listen to a persuasive communication on the benefits of nuclear power, and then fill out another scale on nuclear power. Besides, when you have a fairly good-sized sample and randomly assign subjects to conditions, pretesting is – usually – just not necessary.

However, even more ubiquitous than the posttest-only control group design is what might be called the YACAN[1] Design, a versatile, multipurpose design for which the diagram depends on your hypothesis and the setting in which you choose to test it. Both the hypothesis and the setting may dictate that certain conditions be added to achieve the comparison of interest to you and/or to rule out various alternative explanations. For example, you will recall that Cohen (1981) was interested in memory for stereotype-consistent and stereotype-inconsistent information at various points in time after viewing the behavior of a person who was supposedly an exemplar of the stereotype. Thus, in addition to measuring memory immediately after exposure, she had to add conditions in which measurement did not occur until four or seven days later. Or to take another example, Glass and Singer (1972) were interested in the possibility that noises, such as the noises of traffic and people and machines that one might be exposed to in a large city, are stressful at least in part because they are uncontrollable. You know that you cannot turn them off, that there is nothing you can do to make them go away. To test this idea Glass and Singer needed at least three conditions: (1) controllable noise; (2) uncontrollable noise; and (3) no noise control. Again, the point is simply that the number and nature of conditions necessary when you design an experiment depend on the nature of your hypothesis.

Which brings us back to the threats to internal validity. The three standard designs mentioned earlier—the posttest-only control group, the pretest–posttest control group, and the Solomon four-group—all do a pretty good job of controlling for or ruling out the first eight threats listed in the table (at least, that is what most textbooks on the subject will tell you). For example, when your dependent measure shows a difference between the experimental and control groups, history is said to be ruled out as an explanation for that difference because the same historical events have occurred to both groups, with the exception of your manipulation. Similarly, selection and maturation and statistical regression are ruled out as threats by randomization, which ensures that subjects in all conditions are equivalent to start with (at least, theoretically).

My position on this issue is a little more conservative. I do not think you can really make a judgment at all until you see all the details of the experimental procedure. It is like a football coach drawing X's and O's on a chalkboard. Everyone can see how things are supposed to work and why certain things are supposed to be done, but out on the field it is a different story. The concern switches from why certain things are supposed to be done to how you do them. It is one thing to understand why that guard is supposed to be moved backward and to the left (so the ball carrier can race through the opening thus created), but it is quite another thing to actually move that 265-pound mass of muscle.

Designing an experiment often presents the same sort of problem. It

[1]YACAN, You Add Conditions As Needed.

is easy to see why Glass and Singer (1972) needed one condition in which subjects would be exposed to controllable noise and one in which the noise would be uncontrollable. That was what they were interested in. But how, precisely, were they to set up those two conditions while keeping the amounts of noise constant in the two? If the noise really is controllable in one condition, then what is to keep subjects in that condition from turning it off when it gets unbearable and, thus, experiencing less noise? If they did experience less noise, then you would not be able to tell whether the differences between the controllable-noise and uncontrollable-noise conditions were due to controllability or noise or both.

Setting the Stage

The point, of course, is that once you have decided what conditions you need to test your hypothesis you have to decide on a procedure. Relatively speaking, the decisions about what conditions you need are on a pretty abstract level. If you had reason to believe that the expertise of a communicator was an important variable in his or her effectiveness, then you might decide to have one condition in which a highly expert communicator presents a message, one condition in which someone low in expertise presents the same message, and a no-message control. On the other hand, the decisions about your procedure must be very precise and concrete. You have to decide how you are going to manipulate and measure the variables of interest. Will you use a 5-point scale, a 7-point scale, or a 31-point scale? How will the questions be worded? What do you plan to say to subjects when they arrive at the appointed time and place? What appointed times and places do you plan to use? How will the experimental room be furnished? In short, everything from the first to the last second of your contact with the subjects has to be planned and is a part of the procedure. If it is not, you will be guilty of what Barber (1976) has called the loose-procedure effect, and the results of your experiment may be uninterpretable because of variations in what you said or did to different subjects, variations that may have influenced how they responded to your dependent measures.

This is the point at which experimental design becomes more of an art than a science. You must write, produce, and direct, as well as serve as prop manager and stagehand for a one-act play. Remember the care and detail that went into Cohen's (1981) construction of those videotapes for subjects to watch? First, she had to determine what the stereotypes of waitresses and librarians really were. Then she had to have each feature rated to make sure it was not an aspect of both stereotypes, that is, each item used on the videotape had to be consistent with one of the stereotypes and inconsistent with the other. Finally, she had to write out a script for the woman and her husband to enact while the videotapes were being filmed.

Another example of the things involved in setting the stage for an experiment is provided by the following classic experiment on conformity. Asch (1952) arranged a situation in which naive subjects were confronted with a clear discrepancy between what they saw in front of them and what a group of apparently similar others said was there. The stimulus materials Asch used were simple lines. For a number of different sets of lines, subjects were asked to judge which of three comparison lines on one card was the same length as a standard line on a second card. For every set of cards, each member of a group of seven to nine subjects was to make this judgment aloud and in turn. There was only one catch. In each group there was only one real subject. All of the others were accomplices of the experimenter who had been instructed to make incorrect judgments on certain trials. Thus, the naive subject, who was always maneuvered into a seat so that he or she would make a judgment after most of the other group members, was repeatedly confronted with a discrepancy between what they thought was correct and what the group said was correct. The results were dramatic. Compared with control subjects who simply made the line judgments alone, subjects confronted with the conflict between what they saw and what the group appeared to see made five times as many errors in matching the standard and comparison lines.

You may have noticed that both Cohen's (1981) and Asch's (1952) experiments involved deception. Cohen's was relatively minor. She simply mentioned to subjects before turning on the videotapes that the person they were about to see was a waitress (or a librarian); and, of course, the person was not. Asch's deception was somewhat more elaborate. He recruited a number of accomplices, had them pose as naive subjects, instructed them to give a number of incorrect responses, had them take certain seats in the room so that the real subjects would be in the position of giving a judgment after the accomplices had given theirs, and, finally, administered the whole session with a straight face. The one real subject in each group was led to believe that the experiment was on visual perception. In reality, of course, it was about conformity. But, if Asch had told subjects that he was studying conformity, then chances are he would not have observed a single error on the line judgment task.

The use of deception in experimental research has prompted a number of heated exchanges over the last few years. Some have gone so far as to say that deception should be avoided at all costs (cf. Seeman, 1969), but that seems a little extreme to me. If you can manipulate and measure the variables of interest without using deception, you should, of course, do so. However, if your design can best be realized by a minor, temporary deception that is not in any way harmful to subjects, then I see no problem.

Just be sure you note the key words in that last sentence. *Minor* and *not harmful* should be self-explanatory. *Temporary* means that one of the obligations you incur should you decide to use deception is that you thoroughly explain the entire experiment and the reasons for the deception to all subjects as soon as the experiment is over. The technical name for this procedure is DEBRIEFING, and it is an important part of the experiment. Debriefing usually takes the form of a casual, relaxed, post-experimental discussion. Not only will it give you a chance to find out whether subjects saw through your deception, but also it will enable you to solicit suggestions from them about how the experiment might be improved.

You need to be aware, however, that debriefing can create other problems. As indicated by the last few threats to internal validity in Table 1 of Chapter 7, subjects can and often do inform others about what goes on in an experiment. When the informed subjects participate in the study, their data may thus be worthless. They are not likely to tell you that they knew ahead of time that you were going to deceive them, not after they just deceived you by going through the whole procedure as if they were naïve about it. Newberry (1973), for example, found that many subjects who were informed ahead of time about an experiment by an accomplice (posing as a subject who had just been in the experiment) would not admit that they had any prior knowledge of the study. Campbell (1969a) has pointed up other disadvantages of debriefing. As he noted, "It provides modeling and publicity for deceit . . . . It reduces the credibility of the laboratory and undermines the utility of deceit in future experiments."

Related to this is the fact that debriefing often informs the subject of his or her own gullibility, and for some this could be very damaging to their self-esteem. Thus, one could argue that it might be better not to debrief subjects when the deceptions are minor. The deceptions in Cohen's (1981) experiment, for example, seem to fall into this category.

If it is at all possible to investigate what you are interested in without the use of deception, however, then you might be better off to do so for practical as well as ethical reasons. Parents often tell their children that it is simply easier to be honest because then they do not have to remember the lies they have told. Similarly in an experiment involving deception, you usually cannot get away with one little misrepresentation of what is going on. Cohen (1981) did, but that is really an exception. From the subject's point of view, everything about your procedure has to make sense. That means you have to have an overall, coherent cover story, a pseudo-rationale for everything the subject is asked to do (or put up with). Asch's cover story was that he was studying visual perception. Hence, it made sense that subjects would be asked to make judgments of line lengths. Further, an ideal cover story is so constructed that the manipulation of your independent variable and the measurement of your dependent variable seem natural within the context of the story. If Asch had been studying visual perception, it would have been natural to ask other subjects to state what they were seeing (the independent variable), just as it was to be expected that the real subject would have to state what he was perceiving (the dependent variable). You might note that in terms of our earlier discussion of manipulating independent variables, Asch's manipulation was clearly of the event variety, and it certainly had an impact on the subjects. For another example of an experimental cover story that really had an impact (too much of an impact according to Baumrind, 1964) see the Discussion on page 310.

The major problem with an elaborate cover story is that in adding all the little details of procedure that will make the cover story believable, you are likely to introduce a number of extraneous variables. If one of these supposedly extraneous variables can plausibly be related to changes in your dependent variable, you are in trouble. The internal validity of your experiment would be lost. Of course, the more elaborate the cover story, the greater the number of extraneous variables and the more likely it is that at least one of them will have some effect on your dependent variable.

For example, instead of using that carefully constructed videotape to study memory for stereotype-consistent and stereotype-inconsistent information, Cohen (1981) might have introduced her research to subjects as an investigation of the campus library facilities. The rationale could have been that the university administration had received a number of complaints about the competence and helpfulness of the librarians in several sections of the library and, as a result, the experimenter had been contacted and asked to conduct an inquiry into the matter. At first the experimenter had intended to simply interview the students who had filed the complaints, but it turned out that most of them were no longer on campus (they all flunked out because they could not find the books they needed). So, the experimenter had decided to conduct a little undercover investigation. At this point the subject would be given an index card with a reference to a nonexistent book by an obscure, nineteenth-century, British entomologist. The subject's task would be to go over to the library, find the reference librarian's office, ask for help in finding the book, and come back to report on what happened. As you have probably already guessed, the reference librarian would be an accomplice of the experimenter and his or her behavior, characteristics, and office decorations would have been carefully selected ahead of time. There might be stacks of books and papers scattered about (stereotype-consistent) the desk of the librarian, who sat there smoking a cigar (stereotype-inconsistent).

If the experiment had been done in this way, there is no doubt that it would have had greater impact on subjects than Cohen's videotape. But,

OBEDIENCE AND AUTHORITY IN THE LABORATORY

In one of the few human experiments that has ever been made into a movie for television, Milgram (1963, 1964, 1974) created a situation designed to throw into conflict the apparently legitimate authority of the experimenter in the lab and the moral principle that we should not harm others. Milgram's research involved two subjects, one of whom was a confederate of the experimenter and had been instructed to behave in certain standardized ways. The cover story was that the study was about the effects of aversive stimulation on learning. The naive subject was to teach a list of word pairs to the other subject (the confederate) by administering an electric shock each time the learner made an error. The learner was put in a separate room and, while the real subject watched, had his arms strapped to a chair (supposedly to prevent excessive movement) and an electrode attached to his wrist. The teacher was then taken into an adjoining room and seated in front of an electrical apparatus, a shock generator with a row of switches ranging from 15 to 450 volts. To convince the subject that he would really be administering shocks to the learner, the subject was given a sample shock "just to show how the generator worked." The subject was told to shock the learner after each incorrect response and to move up 15 volts each time.

The electrode attached to the learner was actually a dummy and the learner never really received any shocks at all. But note how much was done to make the cover story hang together. The real subject got a sample shock to convince him that the shock generator really worked. The learner's arms had been strapped down so that he could not just walk out. The two were put in separate rooms so the subject would be less likely to detect that the learner was not really being shocked.

look at what else would have happened! The elaborate deception would have introduced a number of extraneous variables, many of which might have had an effect on what subjects remembered about the librarian. For example, the introductory comment that there had been some complaints about the competence and helpfulness of some of the library personnel might have biased subjects from the outset. It might have alerted them to the possibility that this was not a typical librarian. Hence, they might be overly attentive to stereotype-inconsistent information. Another possibility is that subjects might feel guilty about being a party to the apparent deception of the librarian and that might make their interaction with the librarian strained and unusual, which again would influence what they remembered.

There are a couple of terms used to refer to those extraneous variables

The experiment then began with the subject reading word pairs, via an intercom, to the learner. After reading through a list of pairs, the subject would then read the first word of each pair and four alternatives for the second word. The learner was to select the correct alternative, but, as you may have guessed, he made a number of incorrect responses. With each error, of course, the shock level escalated and at about 75 volts the man supposedly receiving the shocks began to vocalize his discomfort. At 150 volts he demanded to be released from the experiment and by 225 volts, his only response had become an agonized scream. If, at any point, the subject turned to the experimenter and questioned whether he should continue shocking the learner, the experimenter calmly directed him to continue.

The results of Milgram's study are both surprising and distressing. Over 60 percent of the subjects continued to shock the learner until the maximum shock had been delivered—450 volts! This was in spite of the fact that many of the subjects were extremely concerned about the victim and repeatedly called out to him in an attempt to find out whether he was okay. The victim had fallen silent after 330 volts and, for all the subjects knew, was either dead or unconscious.

The elaborate cover story and props used by Milgram were quite effective. Very few subjects became suspicious that the man in the other room was not being shocked. In addition, many subjects showed clear evidence of a great deal of agitation, nervousness, and confusion over what was happening. In terms of creating in the lab the conflict he wanted to study, Milgram was indeed successful. The sad part is that so many subjects resolved the conflict by continuing to shock the victim instead of telling the experimenter to go jump.

that mar the interpretation of results and destroy the internal validity of an experiment. The most common one is the word *confounded*, which Webster defines as "caused to become confused" and "failed to distinguish." Thus, a manipulation would be confounded if it actually changed several different things at once. You would not know which of them produced changes in the dependent variable. In fact, they all might. The more elaborate the scenario you construct for an experiment, the more likely you are to introduce CONFOUNDING VARIABLES. That is why it is best to keep your procedure as simple as possible.

It should be clear by now why you cannot really tell whether an experiment is internally valid until you see both the design and the procedure. With a little imagination you could easily extend our investigation of that cigar-smoking librarian into precisely the same 2×3 factorial design that

Cohen (1981) used. (For three of the conditions, you would have to devise a rationale for subjects to interact with an experimental accomplice posing as a waitress, but that is not too difficult.) You can see, however, that Cohen's procedure is much tighter than the hypothetical variation on it could ever hope to be. It introduced many fewer extraneous variables. It is true, of course, that Cohen's procedure may have been somewhat artificial and her results, thus, somewhat difficult to generalize to other settings. This issue of external validity will be taken up later. For now, the point is simply that you have to be very careful in constructing your procedure. It is incredibly easy to introduce confounding variables and things that will serve as the basis for plausible alternative explanations of your results. As Hendrick and Jones (1972) have pointed out, most sources of alternative explanations will be quite specific to some detail of your procedure or setting. The room was too hot, so subjects got drowsy and inattentive and missed the part where you said they had a chance to win a prize, which was supposed to be the independent variable. Or, the opinion scale you were using as your dependent measure was ambiguously worded, so many subjects just skipped it. However, there are a few general sources of alternative explanations – in addition to those in Table 1 of Chapter Seven – that you can be prepared for.

Chance and Other Alternative Explanations

It may have occurred to you that you are getting fairly close to the end of the chapter on experimentation and there has still been no mention of statistics. For many people, experimental design and statistics do seem always to be uttered in the same breath, like a compound curse. But they are really separate topics. Experimental design is an exercise in logic or common sense. It is a process in which you lay out the conditions necessary to obtain interpretable information bearing on your hypothesis. Statistical analysis is a process that tells you whether you may discount a specific alternative explanation for the results of your experiment, that is, that the results you obtained were due to chance.

There are many excellent statistical texts that will show you how to do the necessary analyses. I just want to make sure you understand why chance has to be ruled out as an explanation for the results of an experiment. Earlier it was mentioned that most data of interest in the social and behavioral sciences have a great deal of built-in variability. You might anticipate, for example, that most of your friends would be in favor of tighter gun control laws. But, if you were to ask them to respond to an attitude scale on the topic, you surely would not expect them all to check the same point on the scale. Some would be more extreme than others and some, unless you have an unusually homogeneous group of friends, would even be opposed to such laws. Similarly, the people assigned to the various conditions in an experiment can usually be expected to vary in how they repond to the dependent measure, even in the absence of a manipulation or independent variable. Further, there is no particular reason to expect that the average response in the control condition, say, would be exactly the same as the average response in the experimental condition. If you were to randomly divide your friends into two groups and calculate the average attitudes toward gun control in the two groups, you would expect the two averages to differ a little bit. Similarly, in an experiment, just on the basis of the chance assignment of different people to different conditions you would expect the average response to the dependent measure in one condition to be a little more or a little less than the average in any other condition. Thus, to claim that your independent variable has had any effect on your dependent variable, you have to know whether the difference between conditions is greater than this variability due to chance. Basically, that is what statistical analysis will tell you—whether the difference between conditions is sufficiently large that you can rule out chance as a plausible explanation for that difference.

After chance, the things most likely to give you trouble in your efforts to establish the internal validity of an experiment have to do with the peculiar role that many people assume when they become a subject in an experiment. For most people, even most college students, it is a very unusual experience; and, as Silverman (1977) has noted, you should not be suprised to find that people behave in atypical ways when they are in atypical settings. Experimenters, of course, want to obtain responses to indendent variables that are natural or representative. In fact, many people justify the use of deception in research with precisely that reason, that is, that it is necessary to disguise the true purpose of the research so that people can respond to the independent variable in as unselfconscious or natural a manner as possible. Subjects, on the other hand, seem to approach the experimental situation with an attitude that is something like, "Tell me what you want me to do and I'll do it and we can get this over with as quickly as possible."

The sources of this compliance are, no doubt, complex. There is an element of respect for science and the attempt to learn about why people behave as they do. There is an element of simple politeness and courtesy to the, usually, older and higher status experimenter. But, whatever the sources, the results are usually distortions of behavior. It is as if most subjects assume that the experimenter is trying to prove something and they view their task as one of helping him or her do so. Thus, any cue that the setting or the experimenter gives off about what the hypothesis is, what the study is attempting to demonstrate, or how the subject is expected to behave is likely to be seized on by the subject, who is often all too ready to behave accordingly. The sum total of such cues are referred to as the demand characteristics of the experimental situation (Orne, 1962). They reveal to the subject what the situation demands. One of the major purposes of an experimental cover story, of course, is to keep demand characteristics to a minimum. If the true purpose of the experiment is hidden in the folds of the cover story, then it is less likely that subjects will be able to pick up cues that tell them how to respond. As you have seen however, cover stories can introduce confounding variables.

Even with a good clean cover story you may have problems. Rosenthal (1966, 1976) and his colleagues have found that in apparently well-controlled laboratory settings, experimenters who expect their subjects to respond in certain ways are more likely to obtain those responses than are experimenters with no such prior expectations. For example, in a number of studies, experimenters were asked to administer a person–perception task to subjects. The experimenters were to show a series of photos to each subject and ask the subject to rate each photo in terms of whether the person pictured had been experiencing success or failure. The ratings were to be made on a scale from -10 (extreme failure) to $+10$ (extreme success), and the photos had all been previously determined actually to be neutral on this scale. However, some experimenters were led to believe that the subjects' ratings would average about $+5$, whereas others were led to believe they would average about -5. In study after study, it was found that experimenters with the former expectation obtained significantly more positive ratings from their subjects than experimenters with the latter. Note that this happened even though the experimenters all read precisely the same instructions to their subjects, a feature of the procedure that Rosenthal took pains to confirm by recording the experimenter–subject interactions. Thus, however experimenters were conveying their expectations, it was apparently being done by some very subtle cues.

As you might expect, advocates of laboratory experimentation as *the* method for the social and behavioral sciences were not too pleased with the implications of Rosenthal's data, and critics were quick to point out flaws in the research (cf. Barber & Silver, 1968). However, the evidence that such experimenter expectancy effects are real and can indeed bias experimental results has become so overwhelming that even Rosenthal's erstwhile critics now concede that the effects can be a problem (Barber, 1976). The problem is, in fact, quite serious because research has demonstrated that there are not just one or two aspects of the experimenter's behavior that convey cues to subjects. Rather, it seems to be the case that almost everything the experimenter does may unintentionally convey what he or she expects—tone of voice, relative emphasis on certain words, leaning forward or backward at certain points in the procedure, looking at subjects, nodding, frowning, smiling (cf. Friedman, 1967; Jones & Cooper, 1971; Duncan & Rosenthal, 1968).

What all this means for you is that any experiment you design must include some way of avoiding such effects, and there are several ways you can do that. The first, which is not recommended, is to automate everything. Greet the subjects, put them in a booth with a computer terminal, and turn it on. Your manipulation(s) can be delivered via the screen, and subjects can type out their responses to your dependent measure on the keyboard. Ronis, Baumgardner, Leippe, Cacioppo, and Greenwald (1977) have, in fact, used this approach to study persuasion. They presented messages on the screen for subjects to read and then subjects answered opinion questions by punching in numbers. The virtue of this approach, of course, is standardization. Everything that each subject sees is exactly the same. The drawback, which I believe outweighs that virtue, is that it lacks what Aronson and Carlsmith (1968) have called EXPERIMENTAL REALISM. It is not very involving, it seems to have no impact on subjects. In fact, from the subjects' point of view, it is likely to be downright boring. A better way of avoiding experimenter expectancy effects is to retain a live experimenter for interacting with and directing subjects, but devise ways to keep the experimenter from knowing which condition any given subject has been assigned to. If the experimenter does not know how the subject is expected to respond, the likelihood of influencing that response is reduced. The term used to describe this situation is BLIND: the experimenter is kept blind as to the condition to which the subject has been assigned. Exactly how you do that depends on your procedure, but it can usually be done without too much trouble. You might, for example, have the manipulation and the dependent measure administered by different experimenters.

In addition to the overly compliant, helpful attitude that seems to characterize many subjects in laboratory experiments, there is another factor that plays a part in their eager search for cues about what is expected of them. Rosenberg (1965) has suggested that many subjects suffer from EVALUATION APPREHENSION. That is, many seem to be anxious about not only getting through the experiment as smoothly and as quickly as possible, but also about winning a positive evaluation from the experimenter. They want the experimenter to approve of them, to like them, to believe they have a good personality. Thus, they may be particularly attentive to cues about how the experimenter expects them to behave. Using the photo-rating task described earlier, Minor (1970) has demonstrated that when subjects are not apprehensive about being evaluated, experimenters fail to obtain results in line with their expectations. Fifteen male graduate students were used as experimenters, and some were led to believe that rating of the photos would average about +5, whereas others were led to believe the ratings would average about −5. The subjects were male and female student volunteers who either were led to believe they would be psychologically maladjusted on the task if they did not do well (high-evaluation apprehension) or were told that they were part of a control group whose data would simply be lumped together with everyone else's (low-evaluation apprehension). The results appear in Figure 3, where it can be seen that subjects who were concerned about their performances were much more sensitive to cues about what the experimenter expected.

When people first began to use experimentation as a tool to investigate social and behavioral processes, it was used rather naively. It was assumed that because the experiment had proved to be so successful in physics and chemistry—and even with animal behavior—it could be employed with humans as subjects. There was little attempt to control for or to assess the sorts of contaminating influences we have been discussing. However, when critics began to point out that experiments on human behavior and social processes might be a little more complicated than had been thought, that there were certain problems that needed looking into, you would have thought they had called for a return to the dark ages—researchers were

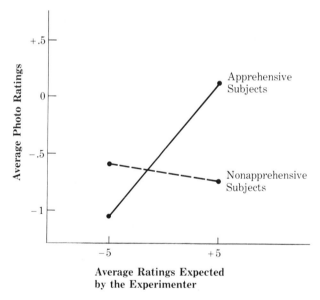

Figure 3 MEAN RATINGS OF NEUTRAL PHOTOGRAPHS. Subjects in the experiment who were more concerned about the importance of their own performance of the task were much more sensitive to cues that conveyed what the experimenter expected. (From Minor, 1970.)

vying to outdo each other in denouncing the critics as backsliders and turncoats.

Critics of experimentation usually emphasized one or the other of two major points, both of which seem reasonable. The first is that experiments need to be done more carefully than they have been in the past. The purpose of the last few pages, of course, was to alert you to some of the more pervasive difficulties that have been encountered and to suggest a few ways in which you can avoid them. Suls and Gastorf (1980) reported that in terms of controlling for experimenter effects, for example, there has indeed been an improvement in the quality of published research since 1960. So, things are looking up; but all too many experiments still yield ambiguous results because of the failure to include adequate controls. The second major point emphasized by critics of experimentation is that experiments need to be more selectively employed than they have been in the past. There is an old quote from Abraham Maslow that runs, "if the only tool you have is a hammer, it is tempting to treat everything as if it were a nail." As you have seen from the preceding chapters, experimentation is certainly not the only tool available. So the question is, When is experimentation appropriate?

What Experiments Can and Cannot Do for You

It has already been pointed out that, of all the research methods discussed, an experiment can provide you with the clearest evidence of a cause-and-effect relationship. It achieves that distinction, of course, by allowing you to manipulate one variable and observe what happens to another, under conditions that (you hope) enable you to rule out all other plausible reasons for changes in the latter. Experimentation is usually considered vastly superior to correlational research in this respect, and rightly so. Naturally occurring events are often a complicated mesh of several variables, and it is impossible to tell which are essential to producing the effect in question. Experimentation enables you to systematically untie such knots, manipulate the variables one at a time, and separate the essential from the nonessential.

For example, in the mid-1960s there was a murder on the streets of New York that caused a wave of national indignation. It was not the murder *per se* that was so unusual. What aroused the national conscience was that it later came to light that a number of people had heard the victim's cries, some had even witnessed the crime from their apartment windows, but none had done anything to help. None had even bothered to call the police. Newspapers and magazines picked up the story and proclaimed it to be yet another horrible example of urban apathy, of not wanting to be involved, and, generally, of the impending disintegration of civilized society. If you think about it for a moment, you can probably come up with several reasons why someone might not have helped the woman in distress. Maybe the newspapers were right. The witnesses just did not care. Maybe they were afraid for their own safety should they try to intervene. Maybe they were reluctant to get caught up in the identification, prosecution, and trial of the criminal. Maybe they thought someone else had already notified the police. Using this actual event as a stimulus to their thinking, Latané and Darley (1970) designed and carried out a series of laboratory experiments on the latter point, which they conceptualized as diffusion of responsibility. They were able to show that when a person believes a number of others are aware of an emergency situation, the person is much less likely to help than when he or she believes no one else knows that help is needed. In other words, what Latané and Darley did was to single out one component of a complex stimulus situation. They then designed an experiment in which they could manipulate that one component to see what effect it (alone) had on the dependent variable of interest (helping behavior in emergency situations). Such analysis of complex variables is one of the most appropriate uses of experimentation. For another example of this use of experimentation, see BEAUTY AND THE BEHAVIOR OF THE BEHOLDER on the next page.

In addition to the analytic use of experiments, Gergen (1978) has suggested another role that might be referred to as the SENSITIZING FUNCTION. As he put it, occasionally an experimental demonstration can unsettle the way we look at things. Here the task of the experiment is really to bring up into awareness certain aspects of behavior that need to be dealt with, to sensitize us to the consequences of some facets of social life. According to Gergen, Asch's research on conformity and Milgram's on obedience to authority really served this consciousness-raising function. They sensitized people to the tremendously powerful influences of groups and authority figures in producing conformity to norms and obedience, respectively. Since the publication of the results of those experiments, it has been more difficult for the smug to make glib assertions that what happened in Germany during World War II was due to a quirk of the German personality. It could indeed happen here. Thus, the experiments did more than merely reproduce in the lab behavior already known to exist; they created a new self-consciousness.

There is no guarantee, of course, that just because you can produce a finding in the lab it has anything at all to do with how people behave outside of the experimental situation. A great deal of criticism of experiments on social and behavioral processes has focused on this point. Experiments are often said to be artificial and to lack EXTERNAL VALIDITY. Experiments are said to have external validity when the obtained results hold

BEAUTY AND THE BEHAVIOR OF THE BEHOLDER

A typical interaction between two people is very complex. Physical characteristics, personal styles, verbal and nonverbal behaviors, and previously existing beliefs all contribute to the impressions each person develops of the other. Snyder, Tanke, and Berschied (1977) suggested that initial impressions may be particularly important here because you may unknowingly induce others to treat you in such a way that your initial impression of them is confirmed, a process they refer to as BEHAVIORAL CONFIRMATION. If you believe Sam is cold and hostile, you may be less friendly than if you believe he is warm and generous. Sam may be offended by your aloofness and reciprocate in kind. Thus, your initial impression of his lack of warmth is confirmed, although the confirmation is brought about by your own behavior.

To see whether this sort of self-fulfilling prophecy occurs with stereotypes about the physically attractive, Snyder et al. designed an experiment in which male college students were to try to get acquainted with a female college student over the telephone. The male–female pairs who took part were not allowed to see each other prior to their phone conversation. However, each male student was given some information about the woman he would be talking with and shown a photo that had supposedly just been taken with a Polaroid camera. The female phone partners were in another room. All of the information furnished the males was supplied by the actual person they were to get acquainted with over the phone. The photos, however, were selected from one of two sets of photos: attractive or relatively unattractive females.

Each male–female pair engaged in a 10-minute phone conversation, which was recorded. Later, raters were asked to listen to the tape tracks that contained the female voices and answer a number of questions about the females. Note that raters heard only the females, and they did not know whether a particular female was believed to be attractive or unattractive.

Before the phone conversations took place, the male students had indicated their initial impressions of their partners, based on the information and (phony) photos. Those who saw an attractive photo expected, for example, that their partner would be poised, humorous, and sociable. These expectations were indeed fulfilled. The raters listening to the phone conversations rated the females whose partners thought they were attractive as sounding more poised, more humorous, more sociable, and generally more socially adept than the females whose partners believed them to be unattractive. Those believed to be attractive actually came to behave in a more friendly, likable, and pleasant manner.

Note that the importance of the previously existing beliefs in producing this effect could never have been clearly established by observation of interactions alone. In the typical interaction, too many things vary simultaneously.

true in different settings, with different subjects, and/or under altered conditions. In addition, it is sometimes pointed out that your ability to demonstrate that A caused B under one set of conditions does not preclude the possibility that B causes A under a different set of conditions. Even though it may be true that any particular experiment may be artificial and leave specific questions (such as whether B can cause A) unanswered, blanket criticisms of experimentation such as these strike me as silly. Artificiality may be a desirable characteristic in many instances. Henshel (1980) pointed out, for example, that much of what is now known about biofeedback and our ability to control bodily functions previously thought to be beyond the realm of voluntary control were learned under extremely artificial experimental conditions. Similarly, Campbell and Stanley (1966) noted that artificiality is essential to the analytic separation of variables discussed earlier and that such analytic separation has been fundamental to advancing our understanding in many fields. Campbell and Stanley also noted that those who complain of the low external validity of experiments may be expecting too much from each experiment. They suggested that such critics adopt a somewhat longer time perspective and that experimenters explore the generality of findings by conceptual replications.

Summary

The advantages of experimentation can be illustrated by old research on competition. By taking the phenomenon that he had observed among bicycle racers into the lab, Triplett was able to manipulate the variable of interest, avoid self-selection of subjects to conditions, and control a number of extraneous variables. Thus, he could rule out a number of explanations for the observation that competition led to improved performance.

In several ways an experiment is simply an extension of the other methods discussed. Experimentation, too, is a technique that helps you be very percise and explicit about the conditions under which your observations take place and is based on the assumption that all knowledge involves comparison. Where experimentation first goes beyond the other methods is by introducing the notion of manipulation, of changing something to see what will happen. That aspect of the environment that is manipulated in an experiment is the independent variable and that which you examine to see whether your manipulation has had any effect is the dependent variable.

One of the key choices facing a would-be experimenter is how to manipulate the independent variable: by instructions to the subjects or by an event that happens to the subjects. The latter is more likely to get and hold the subjects' attention, but the former is less likely to introduce extraneous, confounding variables. Because the purpose of an experiment is to see whether changes in the independent variable produce changes in the dependent variable, other things that might plausibly be expected to have an effect on the dependent variable must be controlled. In a typical experiment, then, you must be able to rule out the possibility of preexisting differences among subjects assigned to the different conditions. Two techniques for doing this are matching and random assignment. Generally, random assignment is preferable, but it might not work too well when you only have a small number of subjects. Use of a table of random numbers, such as that found in the Appendix, can help you assign subjects to conditions randomly.

An experiment by Cohen illustrates the detailed planning that often goes into a well-done experiment and also introduces some additional concepts. Experimenters often design their research so that they can investigate the effects of more than one independent variable on the dependent variable. Such designs typically take the form of a factorial experiment, which has the advantage of letting the experimenter explore interactions among the variables. The posttest-only control group design, the pretest–posttest control group design, and the Solomon four-group design are standard designs. However, the most common practice is to add as many or as few conditions as are necessary to test the hypothesis.

Once you have decided how many conditions you need, the real work (and art) of experimentation begins. You have to lay out a detailed procedure, making sure that you do not introduce confounding variables in the process. At some point in the procedure, deception may be necessary, but it should be avoided if possible. Next, several general alternative explantions were discussed that are the bane of most experimenters: chance, demand charactistics, experimenter expectancy effects, and evaluation apprehension. Those do not exhaust the list, of course, but they will give you enough to worry about for awhile.

By far the most common use of experimentation is the dissection of complex variables, a use referred to as its analytic function. Although less frequently used, it is also possible to employ experimentation as a technique for sensitizing people to certain consequences of normal behavior. Asch's research on conformity served such a function. It alerted people to the power of groups to induce conformity.

Recommended Reading

Aronson, E., & Carlsmith, J. M. Experimentation in social psychology. In G. Lindzey and E. Aronson (Eds.), *Handbook of social psychology* (2nd ed.). Reading, MA: Addison-Wesley, 1968.

This chapter is probably the best source for a discussion of the art of experimentation on social behavior. The authors brought their considerable experience as innovative experimenters to bear on the nitty-gritty problems of staging an experiment in such a manner that it is so involving for a subject that he or she will respond naturally. With the help of numerous examples and illustrations, they discuss issues such as building a plausible cover story, delivering the independent variable by instructions versus an event that happens to the subject, the use of deception, and the advantages of a live experimenter. The authors are more than willing to stick their necks out and take (and defend) a number of unpopular positions. For example, they argue cogently that rigid adherence to a set script is less important for the experimenter than making sure that the independent variable has an impact on each subject, even if the experimenter has to improvise and repeat and elaborate parts of the script for some subjects. Critics, of course, claim that this opens the floodgates of bias, but Aronson and Carlsmith have discussed several ways of combating bias without losing the advantages of the live, sensitive experimenter. They also have pointed out that the best way to learn about how to do experiments is to try it—but read this chapter before you do.

Gergen, K. J. Experimentation in social psychology: a reappraisal. *European Journal of Social Psychology*, 1978, *8*, 507–527.

In the last few years, Ken Gergen, a psychologist at Swarthmore College, has emerged as an eloquent and pointed critic of the overreliance on the laboratory experiment in social psychology. Although Gergen would not have us abandon experimentation altogether, he has argued that there are certain important features of everyday social life that are impossible for the experimenter to duplicate in the laboratory. For example, he noted that what we do in a typical social setting is usually one of many different possible things. In his words, social events are competitive and how we respond to any given stimulus depends on what else is competing for our attention. An experiment, however, is usually designed to determine whether a given stimulus has any effect on our behavior. It leaves us in the dark (usually) about the relative power of one stimulus in comparison with others in the normal circumstances of daily life. Gergen also has noted that social events are sequentially embedded. Any given social act, even something as bland as saying "Good Morning" to your neighbor, is part of an ongoing sequence, and the meaning of that act is in part a function of the behaviors that preceded it and those that follow it. Experiments, of course, are usually very brief and cannot hope to capture extended interaction patterns, which Gergen says are the most important. Gergen has pointed up a number of other limitations of the experiment. His ideas are thought-provoking and timely.

Hendrick, C., & Jones, R. A. *The nature of theory and research in social psychology.* New York: Academic Press, 1972

Needless to say, I am biased about this book, but for a detailed analysis of experimentation on social behavior it is hard to beat. The first five chapters cover the basic ingredients of hypothesis testing and experimentation, including such topics as demand characteristics, internal validity, control, deception, pretesting, pilot studies, and all the other things you need to be aware of to do an experiment well. The novel part of the book, however, consists of Chapters Six through Ten. In each of these chapters, the literature in one specific area of research, such as Primary-Recency in Personality Impression Formation, is reviewed. Following the review an experiment in that tradition is reprinted, and following the experiment a detailed analysis of the shortcomings of the experiment is presented. A second experiment, which attempted to improve on the first, is then reprinted and it, too, is shown to have certain flaws. A third experiment, which attempted to improve on the first two, is given and, alas, how it, too, fell short of perfection is also made plain. The point, of course, is to convey how research is a process of gradual approximation to clarity and understanding and how any given piece of research may be flawed but still contribute to this process of refinement of knowledge.

Rosenthal, R. *Experimenter effects in behavioral research* (2nd ed.). New York: Halsted Press, 1976.

When the first edition of this book came out, it created quite a stir. Laboratory experimenters had always been annoyingly smug about how well-controlled their research was and how bias was something that confounded other kinds of research, but not the lab experiment. Here was Rosenthal claiming that the vaunted lab experiment was rife with bias. In a variety of ways experimenters seemed to be inducing subjects to behave as they (the experimenters) expected. Rosenthal was not just arguing that this was a possibility, he had evidence (and a lot of it). For example, in one task subjects were asked to rate (from -10 to $+10$) the amount of success or failure recently experienced by people depicted in a series of photos. The photos had previously been determined to be neutral on the dimension, but some experimenters administering this task were led to believe the subjects' ratings would average about $+5$ whereas others were led to believe the subjects' ratings would average about -5. In fact, the former experimenters did indeed obtain significantly higher ratings from their subjects than the latter. As you might guess, Rosenthal's work was vociferously attacked by defenders of the experiment. Many of their criticisms have turned out to be valid, but in spite of that Rosenthal's major point has stood the test of time. Unintentional bias induced by the experimenters' expectancies can invalidate the findings of laboratory research. Thus, the good experimenter must find a way to avoid letting his or her expectancies influence the results. Rosenthal also made a number of good suggestions about how this can be done.

Schachter, S. *The psychology of affiliation: Experimental studies of the sources of gregariousness*. Stanford, CA: Stanford Unversity Press, 1959.

One of the most appropriate and informative ways in which experiments on social behavior can be employed is to help sharpen our thinking about phenomena that we observe in daily life. In this classic volume, Schachter provided a model of how that can be done. Beginning with some observations and anecdotes about the consequences of social isolation, he designed a series of simple experiments that revealed that anxiety increases the tendency to affiliate with others and that that tendency is especially pronounced when one can affiliate with others who are in similar circumstances. "Misery doesn't just love any company, only miserable company." He then proposed a series of possible explanations as to why this should be so and designed some additional conditions to gather evidence on the validity of these. One of the major appeals of the volume is the clear manner in which the reasons behind each successive step in the program of research are laid out. The book also provided an exciting account of how one can capitalize on an unexpected finding. Almost by accident Schachter found that first-born and only children showed a much greater tendency to affiliate when anxious than later born children. The hypotheses that followed that discovery eventually led to a discussion of the performance of fighter pilots in Korea and psychotherapy dropouts. You will have to read the book to get the connections.

10

Simulation

Scientific Metaphors

Evaluating Simulations

Summary

Recommended Readings

One of the thoughts that may have occurred to you by now is that the research methods in this book could be arrayed along a continuum. We began with that most open, unstructured of procedures, participant observation, and have worked our way along to the controlled environment of the laboratory experiment. With each new method, techniques for refining and structuring your observations of behavior were introduced. The purpose of each new methodological nicety, of course, was to help keep you from kidding yourself, from falling into the trap of concluding more than you should from your own research. Each method has built on and extended those that preceded it. In doing so, each has opened up new opportunities for learning about people and behavior, but each has also brought new restrictions on which behaviors could be studied and a gradual shift away from the study of ongoing real-life activities. The price of increased methodological rigor seems to have been an increased remoteness from everyday life.

Another, somewhat more subtle, shift has occurred in moving from participant observation to experimentation. The examples cited, and they are reasonably representative, seem to have conveyed a waning interest in discovering what the social world is like and a growing focus on what was described in Chapter One as verification—the testing of specific hypotheses.

Of course, you might say that these two shifts in emphasis underscore the point that has been made repeatedly in the preceding pages. There is no one superior method, no single avenue to truth. The method of choice depends on the question of interest. However, advocates of the research techniques to be discussed in this final chapter claim that a compromise choice is possible. Their argument is that simulations take advantage of the rigor and precision of the experimental approach while at the same time allowing you to investigate some of the more complex, dynamic processes usually thought of as the province of some of the less-structured methods. Let us see.

Scientific Metaphors

The *American Heritage Dictionary* (1971) defines the verb *simulate* as "to have an appearance of; imitate; to make a pretense of." The noun *simulation* is defined as "an imitation; the assumption of a false appearance; a feigning or pretending." As Abelson (1968) noted, such definitions are a potential source of embarrassment to those who would like to use simulations in research. The cliché is that scientific research is a quest for truth. How can you arrive at the truth via a method the very name of which has such a strong connotation of phoniness? Needless to say, critics of the various simulation techniques find the dictionary definitions of simulate and simulation to be a source of wry amusement. Those definitions are precisely the point, so they say. SIMULATIONS are imitations.

Why not study the real thing? Why bother with an imitation when you know ahead of time that it is only an imitation—and probably an imperfect one at that? One answer, of course, is that sometimes it is just completely impractical to study the real thing directly. For example, suppose you were interested in the sorts of errors made by pilot trainees in their first attempts to fly a plane. Putting trainees into a multimillion-dollar aircraft for their first attempts would not be a sound economic policy, although it would probably ensure that the more uncoordinated trainees would quickly be eliminated from the program. Rather, it would be a better idea to use a flight simulator, which is a detailed physical model of the cockpit of an airplane. Such simulations are useful for both training and research. As for the training aspects, would-be pilots can practice reading the instruments and manipulating the controls until they have the entire arrangement of dials, meters, knobs, and switches so well in mind that they do not waste precious seconds trying to decide whether that little green dial with the red letters is their altitude or their airspeed. As for the research aspect, such simulators have proved invaluable in human factors engineering (the designing of those very dials, meters, knobs and switches so as to minimize misreading and mishandling and maximize comfort for the human operator).

Palys (1978) has noted that the notion of modeling, of constructing an analogy of some system, is the key to simulation. But, most of the simulations of interest in the social and behavioral sciences do not involve physical models. They involve models that are looser, more abstract, models that do not attempt to duplicate every single detail of the real thing, as the flight simulator does. Rather, the models of interest are like scientific metaphors, analogues that attempt to capture and represent in a different form the basic characteristics of the thing modeled. The hope, of course, is that the model will be easier to study than the real thing and that by learning how the model works you will, in fact, be learning about the real McCoy.[1] See A COMMON(S) DILEMMA, on page 328.

Following Abelson (1968), then, a simulation is an imitation of the processes and products of a system, an imitation that is intended to expose the basic operating characteristics of the system being simulated. Note that there are two central features here. First, there is a focus on processes. Something dynamic is modeled, something that changes over time. Second, there is a focus on discovery. The purpose of a simulation is to uncover the essence of the phenomenon being modeled, to see how it works.

---

[1]The real McCoy, by the way, was a rum runner during the prohibition era. He was noted for the high quality of his imported goods, which were in stark contrast to the tasteless imitations of his competition (Coffey, 1975).

A COMMON(S) DILEMMA

In recent years a social phenomenon known as the tragedy of the commons has been the topic of much discussion (Hardin, 1968) and research (Dawes, McTavish, & Shaklee, 1977). The name comes from jointly held lands (commons) in old New England on which all villagers could allow their cattle to graze, free of charge. The potentially tragic part was that if individual villagers got greedy and increased the size of their herds, they might profit more–so long as nobody else got the same idea. If many people increased the size of their herds, the land would quickly be overgrazed and everyone's cows would get thinner instead of fatter. The dilemma, then, is that short-term profit for the individual is pitted against long-term profit for the community. This basic dilemma occurs in many areas of life, from disposal of toxic wastes and control of exhaust emissions to overpopulation. It is easiest (i.e., most profitable) for a manufacturer to dump wastes in the nearest river, but we all suffer when that is allowed. Many people believe everyone should be free to have as many children as they like; but if that continues much longer, the world will run out of food.

Edney and Harper (1978) argued that the essential characteristics of the dilemma can be captured, and studied, in a simple game in which a small number of people are seated around a bowl containing marbles. The game is so constructed that the marbles have some real value–say, each can be exchanged for 10 cents at the end of the game. The aim of the game is simple, each person is to get as many marbles as possible. This is done by just reaching in and grabbing a handful whenever the spirit moves you. Every 10 seconds, the number of marbles in the bowl is doubled (by the game's equivalent of God); but if the bowl is ever completely emptied by the players, the game is over. One other detail, the players may not talk to each other during the game.

Think about that for a moment. If everyone would exercise a little restraint, then all the players could turn a handsome profit. But, at any instant, one or two greedy grabbers could ruin it. To the extent that the game represents the same basic dilemma as that involved in the tragedy of the commons, it is an apt scientific metaphor. It is a model that may prove useful in understanding the dynamics of reactions to the dilemma.

There is no point in going to all the time and effort required to conduct a simulation when you know ahead of time how the thing is going to turn out. As Abelson (1968) put it, a simulation is most worthwhile when it produces unanticipated results.

The stage was set for the modern use of simulation as a research tool only about 50 years ago. As Inbar and Stoll (1972) pointed out, it was via work in electrical engineering that the now familiar concepts of system and feedback were introduced. The resulting systems approach was crucial in pointing the way toward conceptualizing problems in holistic terms. To understand a system, you have to look at the overall configuration, at all the elements and all the processes by which a change in one results in changes in the others. Simulations, then, are usually attempts to model entire systems.

There is more involved. In fact, there are several varieties of simulations, each of which seems to have sprung from somewhat different sources. Three basic types will be discussed in this chapter, and an example of each will be given. I have omitted computer simulations, that is, simulations in which a computer is programmed to manipulate the data of interest in ways suggested by the model you have constructed. Although such simulations can lead to unanticipated outcomes, especially when the model is a complex one, they have been omitted for two reasons. First, a usable understanding of computer simulations requires a degree of sophistication about programming that is beyond the scope of an introduction to research methods. Second, and more important, computer simulations simply do not yet seem to have lived up to the expectation that they would become a generally useful tool for the social and behavioral sciences. They remain rare birds, and their uses, relatively esoteric.

Controlled Freedom

Probably the most common type of simulation is a variation of the experiment, a variation introduced into research by Kurt Lewin in the 1930s. Experimentation per se was, of course, already familiar by then. What was new was Lewin's insistence that entire social constellations could profitably be studied via the experimental approach. The key is what he referred to as transposition, the carrying over of the essential structural characteristics of some real-world phenomenon into the experimental setting. Thus, the basic overall pattern, not simply one or two of its elements, must be abstracted and recaptured by the experimenter on a smaller scale and in a relatively well-controlled environment. Lewin (1951) felt that experiments become artificial and unlifelike when only one or two aspects of a phenomenon were realized in the research and not the essential pattern.

There is a relatively subtle distinction between the experiment, as described in the last chapter and as usually practiced, and the sort of experimental simulation we are discussing here. As described in the last chapter, an experiment is usually focused on establishing cause–effect relationships between variables, on testing specific hypotheses; if A, then B. Experimental simulations usually allow subjects greater freedom of behavior. The focus is on observing what will happen when the social phenomenon is transposed (with all essential characteristics intact) to the controlled setting and set in motion. How will the processes work themselves out? If A, then what? To help make this distinction clearer, look at the Discussion on the next page.

One of the best early examples of the Lewinian ideal of transposition is some research on rumor transmission, research that had its origins in the months following the attack on Pearl Harbor at the beginning of World War II. As you can imagine, that was a time of great anxiety. People were unsure of exactly what to expect, and rumors were flying. Rumors about the losses in the Pacific, for example, were widespread, and the losses were usually greatly exaggerated. Such rumors, of course, were destructive to morale and hurt the mobilization effort. If the entire Pacific Fleet had been sunk at Pearl Harbor, there was little hope of successfully waging war against Japan.

Rumors became such a serious problem in the early months of the war that a number of campaigns were mounted to combat their pernicious effects. President Roosevelt personally tried to squelch them in his "Fireside Chat" of February 23, 1942. The Office of War Information attempted to stop them by flooding the country with accurate news and by trying to convince people that loose talk was dangerous. Catchy slogans were invented: "Zip your lip and save a ship." Posters, such as one of Uncle Sam holding a finger to his lips and another of Hitler with a hand cupped behind his ear, appeared everywhere. Newspapers ran columns called "The Rumor Clinic," which not only discussed the destructive effects of rumors, generally, but repudiated specific rumors with accurate information.

In spite of all this intense antirumor activity, very little was actually known about the nature of rumors or why they took the particular forms that they did. There was a great deal of more or less plausible speculation but little systematic knowledge. That state of affairs prompted two Harvard psychologists, Gordon Allport and Leo Postman, to look into the issue. They began with a careful analysis of what seemed to be involved. First, it was clear that rumors were a social phenomenon. Two or more people were always involved, and the rumor, or the proposition of interest, was passed along from person to person. Second, it was usually the case that whatever the proposition was, it was something about which there was no clear evidence easily available. Thus, the person to whom a rumor was told could not assess its accuracy against the facts. It also seemed to be the case that many of the wartime rumors were quite concise. In fact, many of them seemed to have a certain slogan-like quality. Another intriguing feature was that there was often a kernel of truth, some residual particle of fact that had been distorted almost beyond recognition. One other characteristic was that people seemed most likely to tell rumors to others within their own social circle, that is, to people who were generally similar

WHAT IS IT THAT MOCK JURY RESEARCH IS MOCKING?

In recent years one of the most active areas of social psychological research has been that on mock juries. The research was at least partly motivated by an understandable, even laudable, desire among psychologists and sociologists for their research to have some immediate, real-world impact. By simulating the legal system in the lab, it could be analyzed under controlled conditions and something could be learned about the psychological and sociological phenomena that occur in courtrooms. At least, that was the idea. A typical mock jury study, for example, might examine how the attractiveness of the defendant and the victim in a criminal case influence the jurors' verdict about the defendant's guilt. The study might be carried out, again typically, by asking college students (mock jurors) to read a brief presentation of a case. The variables of interest – here, the attractiveness of the victim and defendant – would be manipulated by varying the descriptions that different subjects read. After reading the material, each subject is asked to rate the extent to which he or she believes the defendant to be guilty.

Does that sound like a typical laboratory experiment? It should, because that is exactly what it is. As Dillehay and Nietzel (1980a, 1980b) have pointed out, it is certainly not a simulation of anything that goes on in a courtroom. Think about what really goes on in a courtroom. Evidence, for example, is not presented in a brief, written summary. Testimony comes from witnesses, who often contradict each other. Jurors do not render individual verdicts. They deliberate, they argue with each other. When, and if, they reach agreement, the judgment is dichotomous: guilty or not guilty. They are not allowed to decide that, "Oh, I'd give it about a 6.7 on a 10-point scale." Also, whatever a real jury decides, it is a decision that they know has consequences for the defendant. It is not a decision to be made lightly. The point, of course, is that mock jury research seems to be relevant by proclamation only. What has been missing from such research is the careful analysis of the trial context, an analysis that must precede any attempts at simulation.

Note that the objections to what has been called mock jury research are not blanket objections to analogies and simulations in research. The objections are to poor analogies, analogies that are not based on careful diagnosis of the social and psychological processes operating in the domain of interest.

to themselves in a variety of ways. All of these things seemed to define rumors, but there simply was not much known about the processes involved in rumor transmission.

It occurred to Allport and Postman (1947) that some earlier research on the psychology of testimony might be relevant. That earlier research had found that testimony about events one had witnessed was often quite inaccurate. Further, most of the inaccuracies appeared to be traceable to errors of perception and memory. People were not only unable to take in and remember all the details present in some event, but what was remembered was often a distorted version of the event. Bartlett (1932), for example, had found that attitudes and expectations play an important part in what we attend to and remember. Thus, Allport and Postman reasoned that the basic pattern of perception–retention–report that had been used in the research on eyewitness testimony might be the key to the processes implicated in rumor transmission. However, instead of one individual witnessing, remembering, and then telling about an event, with rumors there are a series of individuals. What each subsequent individual witnesses is simply the report of the previous individual.

Out of this perspective grew a very simple simulation of rumor transmission, a simulation that seemed to capture the essential structural pattern involved: some information is passed along from person to person, by word of mouth, in the absence of evidence against which the information can be checked. It was done like this. A group of six or seven people was selected from a class or an audience and asked to leave the room. Then a picture, such as that in Figure 1, was projected on a screen. One of those asked to leave the room was brought back in, placed so that he or she could not see the screen and asked to listen while a member of the audience described, in great detail, what was on the screen. A second person was brought back into the room and asked to listen while the first repeated, as accurately as possible, what had been heard. A third person was brought back in and asked to listen to the second person's description, and so on. Each description was recorded in full so that it could be compared with those that preceded and followed it.

That is it, except for the fact that this simulation was carried out many, many times with different groups and different pictures as the stimulus for the initial description. Before mentioning the results, however, there are several things to note. First, like most models, the Allport and Postman simulation was a stripped-down version of the real thing. A number of variables that could have been included, that might have made a difference even, were simply ignored. For example, with real rumors, people are not asked to repeat them in front of an audience. They usually select to whom, where, and when they will repeat the rumor. Also, the setting of the simulation and the instructions given each subject emphasized accuracy, an emphasis that is probably absent under more natural circumstances. The simulation also ignored time as a variable. With actual rumors, someone may wait weeks or even months before repeating them. Even so, Allport and Postman believed that their simulation was a reasonable facsimile of the basic phenomenon of rumor transmission and that, as such, it might reveal some of the processes involved.

Figure 1   PICTURE WITH MANY DETAILS was used to study rumor transmission. When subjects were asked to relay descriptions from person to person, three basic phenomena occurred. First, the vast majority of details in the scene were lost (a process known as leveling). Second, one or two features were exaggerated (sharpening). Finally, the details that did survive were often shaped to conform with previously existing attitudes and expectations (assimilation). (From Allport & Postman, 1947.)

It did. Comparisons of the subsequent descriptions revealed three basic processes that, acting conjointly, produced versions of the initial scene that were remarkably rumor-like. First, each description tended to be shorter, more concise, more easily remembered and told than the one that had preceded it. This resulted primarily from the progressive dropping out of details and qualifications, a process that Allport and Postman termed LEVELING. However, leveling never continued to the point of total obliteration, only to that point at which the originally verbose description had been reduced to a short concise statement that could easily be remembered. For example, by the time it reached the seventh or eighth person, the entire scene in Figure 1 might be reduced to, "There's a boy stealing fruit from a push cart. A policeman is after him." Second, as leveling progresses, the items that are retained become relatively more prominent, more central to the description, a process Allport and Postman referred to as SHARPEN-ING. Leveling and sharpening, of course, are two sides of the same coin.

One cannot occur without the other. Finally, the protocols revealed the powerful effects of existing attitudes, interests, and expectations of the listener–transmitter, a process known as ASSIMILATION. Females retelling descriptions of the scene in Figure 1 were much more likely to focus on the dresses in the store window than were males; nearly everyone who mentioned it at all converted the name on the movie marquee to Gene Autry, a popular singing cowboy at the time. Details were thus distorted, items chosen for emphasis, and whole scenes gradually shifted as a function of what piqued the next listener's interest (see Figure 2).

Before going on, let us summarize what Allport and Postman did. They created a stripped-down analogy of rumor transmision, a model that could be studied in a setting free of extraneous influences to see how it worked. On the basis of their impressions of the results, they identified three processes that could plausibly be used to account for the results and, by argument, seem to account for what happens with real-life rumors. The hard-nosed would balk at all this. Their *impressions*! *By argument*! But, simulations are not intended to prove anything. They are better thought of as theory-building devices, techniques that help you get a grasp on what may be involved. In the end, of course, you will have to deal with that "may." How can you establish that the processes identified in a simulation really correspond to the processes operating in the system simulated? The question is one of validity, which is discussed below. But first, let us examine two other varieties of simulations. As you will see, the same question arises with both.

Role-Playing

As you are no doubt aware, the importance of the concepts of role and norm in the study of social behavior can hardly be exaggerated. Norms, of course, are rules about what constitutes appropriate behavior in particular situations, and they are based on agreement or consensus. They change over time, just as do other aspects of society. In that connection, it is both instructive and amusing to read through an old book of etiquette in which the norms of some bygone era have been cast into sets of dos and don'ts for the socially anxious. There are norms about nearly every aspect of social behavior, from the type of clothes we wear to the side of the street we drive on–that last one is an official norm in that we have made it into a law. People who are similarly categorized by having the same subset of norms applied to them are said to occupy the same role. And once a person has been categorized as occupying a certain role– automobile driver, father, student, raconteur–certain definite behaviors are expected. The concept of role calls attention to the normative nature of our expectation about the behaviors of someone occupying a particular

Figure 2 MESSAGE TRANSFORMATION as it passes from person to person appears to be related to the process involved in rumor transmission. (Drawing by Ziegler © The New Yorker Magazine, Inc.)

role – whether that someone is oneself or another person (cf. Jones, 1982a).

Much of our social behavior, then, is governed by the norms, or rules, that define what is appropriate for someone acting out a particular role. We are, as Harré and Secord (1973) put it, rule-following agents. The intriguing thing about this is that in many situations we may behave appropriately without knowing precisely which rule we are following, why we are doing what we are doing. There are many ways in which this state of affairs could come about. We may, for example, have learned what to do in a particular situation by simply watching what everybody else does and imitating them. Or, there may be nonverbal cues from others in some situations to guide our actions, cues so subtle that we never consciously recognize their power. For much of our interpersonal behavior, it appears that we never take that step back that would give us the perspective necessary to analyze what we are doing. We muddle through, however, doing what appears to come naturally.

According to Ginsburg (1979), role-playing can give us that necessary perspective. ROLE-PLAYING involves having someone act out those behaviors thought to be associated with a particular role. And, since roles are defined in terms of norms having to do with behavior towards other people, there is usually a reciprocal or complementary role. The reciprocal role might be acted out by the experimenter or by another naive research participant. Further, when you ask someone to act out a role, you usually ask them to act the way they themselves would behave in that role. But there are other possibilities. As Hendrick (1977) pointed out, you might ask someone to act the role in the manner they believe an average person would or in the manner a specific other person would, for example, the way their husband or their mother would. It is also possible to ask a person to imagine how they or someone else would act in a given situation instead of having them actually engage in the overt acting. Needless to say, overt role-playing tends to be more involving (and revealing). Whichever option is chosen, the purpose is to use role-playing to uncover the situational features that guide behavior, including the implicit rules governing behavior, that is, what Harré and Secord referred to as the ROLE/RULE FRAMEWORK within which behavior takes place.

But, be forewarned! It is not that simple. You are not going to be able to just assign roles and then sit back and watch the performance unfold. You are going to have to dig for that role/rule framework. You are going to have to focus every analytic device you can think of on those performances. Videotape, audiotape, coding, content analyses, and, yes, questioning the role-players about details of their performances. Consider this example.

One of the more controversial uses of overt role-playing to appear in recent years is a study by Zimbardo and his colleagues (Haney, Banks, & Zimbardo, 1973; Zimbardo, Haney, Banks, & Jaffee, 1982). The study was conducted in a simulated prison cell block constructed in the basement of the Psychology Building at Stanford University. There were three small (6×9 ft) cells with steel-barred doors, an unlit (2×2×7 ft) solitary confinement closet, guards' quarters in an adjacent wing, an observation screen at the end of the main corridor, and video cameras and tape recorders. *Prisoners* wore loose-fitted smocks, numbers, and nylon stocking caps. *Guards* wore khaki uniforms and reflecting sunglasses and carried whistles and police nightsticks. Both prisoners and guards were paid $15 a day for their participation: for the guards, a day meant an 8-hour shift; prisoners were kept around the clock. Other than being told that they would receive a minimally adequate diet for the duration of the study and that they should expect to be under surveillance, prisoners were given no further instructions about appropriate behavior. Guards were given a little additional direction about administrative details, work shifts, and filling out daily reports. The study was to run for two weeks and began with prisoners actually being arrested by the Palo Alto, California police. They were handcuffed, searched, advised of their rights, and taken off to the police station. Once there, they were blindfolded and transported to the simulated prison for the duration.

The prisoners and guards were chosen from a pool of male college students[2] who had answered a newspaper ad for volunteers to participate

---

[2]The study was conducted during the summer vacation.

in a study of prison life. Seventy-five applied and the 21 selected were the survivors of a careful screening process designed to eliminate all but the most mature, stable individuals. That is an important point because one of the major things that Zimbardo and his associates were interested in finding was whether there is something about prison life that produces pathological behavior. Prisons are commonly considered to be sinkholes of depravity and interpersonal aggression. The usual explanation given for this is the character of the people who inhabit prisons. That is, both prisoners and guards are in prisons precisely because of their willingness to use aggressive, antisocial behavior in their dealings with other people. Hence, it is no surprise that prisons are violent, unpleasant, hostile places. By putting in those roles – of prisoners and guards – persons who were not in any way abnormal, Zimbardo made it impossible to explain any bizarre developments by citing the personality dispositions of the people involved. They were all normal, intelligent human beings, chosen because of their maturity of outlook and stability of mind.

But, bizarre things did begin to happen – and quickly. The study began on a Sunday and was scheduled to run for two weeks. Six days later the study was terminated because of the unusual reactions that had begun to emerge among both the prisoners and the guards. Five prisoners had to be released even prior to that because of extreme depression, crying, and acute anxiety. In contrast, the guards wanted to continue; and, in fact, several had already become so involved in their roles that they would stay around after their official shifts were over, apparently because they enjoyed the power and control associated with their roles.

During that brief six-day period, 12 hours of videotape and over 30 hours of audio recordings were made of interactions between prisoners and guards. These two types of recordings were scored by judges for the presence of a variety of behavioral and verbal indices, for example, the presence of questions, insults, resistance, commands, threats, and self-evaluative statements. In addition, mood adjective checklists were administered to all participants on several occasions. Personality data were obtained prior to the beginning of the simulation. Guards were required to make daily reports of their observations. The experimenters kept informal diaries (in their capacities as prison warden and superintendent). Finally, all subjects completed post-experimental questionnaires about a month after the study was over.

The point in collecting all those data, of course, was to provide some documentation of the role/rule framework implicit in the situation and to see how that framework affected interactions and participants' views of themselves. The very fact of early termination testifies to the extent that prisoners, at least, were affected by the situation. The pervasive sense of helplessness that characterized their position in the simulated prison quickly produced genuine depressive reactions. Their overall outlook, moods, and self-evaluations plummeted downward within days of the start of the study. Note that it was the prisoners' role, their situation, that produced these reactions. Guards had been randomly assigned to their role from the same group of volunteers, and they (the guards) responded quite differently. Their evaluations of themselves also became more negative, but for different reasons. Many were unpleasantly surprised at how much they actually seemed to enjoy their roles. They reveled in the control and power they had over the prisoners and began to go beyond the call of duty in harrassing the prisoners. Of particular interest, of course, were those interactions between the guards and prisoners. In spite of the fact that they were free to engage in any form of interaction, analyses of the video and audio recordings revealed that the characteristic interactions were negative, hostile, and confrontational.

Zimbardo and his colleagues argued that the key to understanding what happened in their simulated prison—and, by inference, what happens in real prisons—is the conferring of differential power to the roles of guard and of prisoner. That differential power had the apparent backing of the researchers and Stanford University in the simulation. In the real world, of course, it is backed by the will of society at large. The simulation ruled out the possibility of accounting for the results by attributing sadistic disposition to the guards, for example. The guards (and the prisoners) were selected for participation because of their very normality, their mature and stable dispositions. As Haney et al. (1973) put it, "the negative, antisocial reactions observed were not the product of an environment created by combining a collection of deviant personalities, but rather, the result of an intrinsically pathological situation which could distort and rechannel the behavior of essentially normal individuals."

Critics of the simulated prison research say there is a simple explanation for the results. Banuazizi and Movahedi (1975), for example, pointed out that the interpersonal brutality that occurs in prisons has received so much publicity, has been graphically depicted in so many movies, and is the stuff of so many novels that everybody knows how tough guards are and how prisoners are supposed to act. Thus, the subjects in the prison research probably had clear stereotypes of how prisoners and guards behave and, when asked to play those roles, they did. In other words, the subjects understood what was expected of them and they performed as expected. This, of course, is a version of what was described earlier as a demand characteristic interpretation (Orne, 1962, 1969). When subjects understand, or figure out, what research situations demand of them, they often do it just to help out. After all, it is presumably for a good cause and they are being paid for their time. Zimbardo and his colleagues attempt to counter this interpretation by noting that even when the subjects did not know that they were being monitored, they behaved in role. The critics, however, remain unconvinced.

The issue, then, is whether anything has really been learned about the power of the prison environment to shape the behavior of prisoners and guards. Whether or not this particular simulation was successful in revealing the essence of the real-world phenomenon, it is important to note what was attempted. The intention was to set up the research in such a way that the effects of two variables, confounded in the real world, could be teased apart in the simulation. That is, in reality prisons (1) are inhabited by many antisocial, violent people and (2) have a rigid two-class social system in which one class has all power and one class has none. In the simulation, the first of these was simply eliminated, stripped away as a possible explanation for anything that might happen in the simulation. The fact that models and simulations allow you to do that, to dispense with variables you think may be extraneous and to "see what happens if . . . ." is one of their greatest appeals and sources of usefulness. The problem is to avoid introducing new variables into the simulation, variables that have no counterpart in the reality being simulated. Such variables, of course, raise questions about the validity of the simulation. But, again, before taking up the question of validity, let us describe one more variety of simulation.

Games as Research Settings

War games, which have been used as training exercises for hundreds of years, seem to have been among the first full-blown simulations. These large-scale tactical operations, complete with umpires and scorekeepers, provide an opportunity for armed forces personnel to try out equipment and maneuvers under combat-like conditions. They are, of course, a form of role-playing. With increased television coverage, the analogy with the theater seems nearly complete in that many of these displays now enjoy an audience. In 1981, for example, thousands of soldiers were airlifted to Egypt for desert training, an exercise that was viewed by millions via the evening news. In the tradition of war games, but on a smaller scale, there are now a variety of simulation games available, games primarily intended as learning devices for the people involved. There is a Life Career Game and a Legislative Game (Boocook, 1968), a Simulated Society Game (Gamson, 1978a, 1978b), games for teaching American history (Baker, 1968), and, literally, scores of others. The intention of the inventors of such games is to provide the players with some holistic insights into the issues and forces involved in the topic of concern. Rather than simply being told about legitimate conflicts of interest in society, for example, the game player might be put in the position of having to deal with diametrically opposed demands from other players representing those interests.

The simulation games most useful for research, as opposed to teaching, are somewhat different. They are actual contests between two (or more) people, who are not asked to role-play anyone or anything. They are simply to play the game according to the rules. As Vinacke (1969) has noted, the outcome is usually not known in advance. It depends upon the actions of the participants. Thus, the usual focus of research using such games is on the social interactions that occur between players. The hope is that the game will provide a structured, well-defined task by means of which the dynamics of interaction may be studied (see Figure 3).

A great deal of the research employing games has used some variation of an interpersonal situation termed the prisoner's dilemma. The name stems from the following setting: Suppose that two people are arrested on suspicion of committing a crime—say, armed robbery. They are taken to the police station and put in separate rooms for questioning. Suppose further that they are guilty and that each is sincerely interested in putting in as little time as possible behind bars. The problem is that neither can be sure of what the other is going to do. If neither confesses, both are likely to be charged with a lesser offense, such as illegal possession of weapons. Thus, both will get off with minimum sentences because the evidence on the armed robbery charge was only circumstantial. If both confess, both are likely to get a long jail term. However, if one confesses and the other does not, the one who confesses will get a light sentence in return for providing evidence against his or her (former) colleague, whereas the latter will be penalized much more severely. Each prisoner's

Figure 3 HIDDEN ASSUMPTIONS are likely to be guiding individuals' social interactions. When developing games as research settings you are forced to make the rules of the game explicit, such as, "no calling for outside help." Making such implicit understandings explicit is a key to all model building and theory development. (© 1979 King Features Syndicate, Inc.)

(A)

Prisoner A Can:

		Refuse to Confess	Confess
Prisoner B Can:	Refuse to Confess (Cooperative)	A gets 6 months B gets 6 months	A gets 90 days B gets 10 years
	Confess (Competitive)	A gets 10 years B gets 90 days	A gets 5 years B gets 5 years

(B)

Response of Player A

Response of Player B		Cooperative	Competitive
	Cooperative	+5 / +5	+10 / −20
	Competitive	−20 / +10	−5 / −5

Figure 4 THE PRISONER'S DILEMMA in real life and as a game for studying social interaction. (A) The basic structure of the prisoner's dilemma. Each prisoner must decide whether to act competitively (confess) or cooperatively (refuse to confess), but the outcome is also affected by what the other prisoner decides to do. (B) Possible combinations of responses and rewards in a game modeled after the prisoner's dilemma. Player B's payoff is shown to the left of the slash, Player A's response is on the right.

dilemma, then, is whether to trust the partner not to confess and not confess oneself (that is, to cooperate with one's partner) or to confess and save oneself before the partner confesses (that is, to compete with one's partner). The situation is called a mixed motive situation because it pits the motivation to cooperate against the motivation to compete. The basic structure of the dilemma is depicted in Figure 4A.

The rewards involved in simulation games modeled after the prisoner's dilemma are not jail terms, of course, but prizes of various sorts – usually points or money. In these analogies, such games are usually played by two people for a series of trials. On a given trial, each player is confronted with a choice between a cooperative and a competitive response and is also faced with the puzzle of what the other player will choose on that trial. The reason that puzzle is so important is that the outcome of a given trial is determined by what both players choose. This can be seen in Figure 4B, which depicts a general pattern of the various possible combinations of responses and rewards. If mutual cooperation occurs on a given trial, both players win a moderate amount (+5); if mutual competition occurs, both players lose (−5). The opportunity also exists for one to exploit a cooperative opponent by making a competitive choice when one's opponent makes a cooperative choice. In the latter case, the person making the competitive choice comes out way ahead (+10) and the person making the cooperative choice loses badly (−20).

As an example of how such a simple game can be useful in learning about social interaction, consider some research by Kelley and Stahelski (1970). By asking people how they would behave in the game, Kelley and Stahelski identified groups who indicated (prior to the start) that they intended to be cooperative or competitive. They were then paired off in one of three ways for the actual game: two competitive players, two cooperative players, or one competitive and one cooperative player. After playing for a number of trials, the players were asked, individually, about what they believed their opponents' initial orientation had been. The most frequent error in the cooperative–competitive pairs was a judgment by the initially competitive member of such pairs that his or her (initially cooperative) opponent was also competitive. By examining the trial-by-trial choices, Kelly and Stahelski found that when paired with a competitor, the initially cooperative players had indeed become competitive. They termed this effect BEHAVIORAL ASSIMILATION, to reflect the fact that the behavior of the person who intended to be cooperative had been assimilated to the competitive style of his or her opponent. In fact, it appears that overassimilation occurs; that is, when paired with a competitively oriented partner, the initially cooperative person behaves even more competitively than the competitor. The cooperative player, exploited every time he or she tried to be nice, seems to have a limit. Then, "No more Mr. Nice Guy!" On the other hand, when two cooperative players were paired, they maintained cooperation throughout the game.

Of particular importance, however, is how Kelley and Stahelski used their findings in the course of further theory development. As Palys (1978) and others have noted, this is one of the areas in which simulations can be most helpful. The results with the prisoner's dilemma seemed to indicate that competitively oriented people influence their social worlds in such a way that the behaviors they are reacting to in others are determined by their own behavior. It follows that they are likely to develop a view of what other people are like that is different from that developed by cooperators. That is, cooperators will be aware that there is variability in interpersonal style, that some people are cooperative and some competitive. Competitors will not be aware of this variability because they force all those with whom they interact to be competitive.

Note that the latter was put forth as a tentative suggestion, a hypothesis stemming from the results of the simulation. Note, also, that it is based on the assumption that the goals and orientations people adopt for themselves in laboratory tasks such as the prisoner's dilemma reflect the goals and orientations they generally adopt in interactions with others. Kelley and Stahelski (1970) cited some data from studies employing the F-scale in support of this assumption. The F-scale is a personality assessment instrument designed to measure one's degree of authoritarianism, which we discussed in connection with archival research. Several studies (e.g., Scodel & Mussen, 1953) have shown that people scoring low on the F-scale (nonauthoritarians) tend to see others as being heterogeneous in their degree of authoritarianism. Those who score high on the F-scale (authoritarians) tend to believe that everyone is as authoritarian as they are themselves. Further, evidence indicates that people scoring low on the F-scale tend to be cooperative in the prisoner's dilemma game. When playing opposite a high F-scorer, however, they tend to be behaviorally assimilated to the high scorer, who tends to be competitive in play. The evidence is certainly not conclusive, but it is intriguing. As Kelley and Stahelski put it:

> One wonders whether, in general, the belief that other people are very much alike may not be a clue that the person holding that belief plays a very influential causal role in his interpersonal relationships . . . . The interaction process described here would . . . constitute a mechanism by which the authoritarian interpersonal orientation is a self-fulfilling prophecy, maintaining and justifying itself by causing the person to experience a world in which the orientation is shared and, therefore, necessary and justified.

It appears that the behavior of someone engaged in social interaction cannot be interpreted except as part of a system, a system composed of the individual's own behaviors as well as the behaviors of others.

The prisoner's dilemma is just one of a variety of games that can be useful in research. They are all models, analogies. Each is structured so as to capture what the investigator believes to be the essence of some real-life situation, such as in the Commons Dilemma described on page 328. Once the rules of the game are clearly specified, the manner in which interaction preceeds can be studied—usually much more easily than in the real-life setting. The influence of different types of participants, different payoffs, different rules can be examined. The latter is particularly important and is one of the genuine advantages of simulations. You can see what happens when you change the rules, something that is difficult to do in most natural settings. Of course, there are problems with the use of games such as the prisoner's dilemma. But, the problems are common to nearly all types of simulations in research (cf. Jones, Howard, & Haley, 1984).

Evaluating Simulations

The use of simulation in research has been the target of much criticism over the years. Part of the reason for this is that there are so many varieties of simulations, for example, different types of role-playing, and scores of different experimental games. Critics addressing themselves to one particular type of simulation or one particular use or both have sometimes not been sufficiently cautious in making clear the boundaries of their critiques. They often seem to imply that because one particular simulation was flawed or inappropriately used, all simulations must be useless. Freedman (1969), for example, pointed out that role-playing research in which people are simply asked to imagine themselves in a particular role and to report how they would behave is not likely to be very useful, especially if it is intended as a substitute for observing how they really behave in that role. Few would disagree with that. There is a vast literature demonstrating that what people say they will do and what they actually do are often quite different (e.g., Deutscher, 1966). But, as you have seen, there are other varieties of role-playing that evoke greater involvement and spontaneity and that can be informative. (For another example, consider the research discussed on the next page.) Similarly, Nemeth (1972) argued that the prisoner's dilemma game is not a good vehicle for studying bargaining, which many of its promoters believed it would be. Nemeth's point is that the game is too abstract and ambiguous. By eliminating the possibility of direct communication, aspects essential to bargaining as a process are also eliminated. You cannot make clear to your opponent in the game what your plans are, your goals, the reasons behind your choices. But, again, as we have seen, the game can be useful to help understand other phenomena. The key to assessing any particular simulation, then, is to ask yourself two questions: (1) Was simulation called for in this instance? (2) If so, was it done well enough for the results to have some bearing on the phenomenon of interest? A few comments on each of these issues might help you answer the questions.

When to Simulate

It is important to remember that simulations may be used for a variety of purposes. They can be quite useful as teaching tools, especially when those participating are induced to behave in self-surprising ways. Kelley and Stahelski's cooperative subjects, for example, may have learned something about themselves when they realized they had been provoked into out-competing the competitors. Similarly, simulations such as war games can yield valuable insights into the dynamics (and problems) of mov-

LONG-TERM EFFECTS OF ROLE-PLAYING

Critics of role-playing as a research tool have often focused on its "as if" quality, arguing that subjects view it as a few moments apart from life and do not take it too seriously. There is much anecdotal evidence to the contrary, however. Participants in simulation games sometimes get so involved in their roles that arguments and confrontations spill over into the postgame period. Palys (1978), in fact, claimed that involvement is frequently so great that ethical questions need to be raised about creating situations that are too powerful. Animosities engendered during some of the simulations may be left undissipated, a result suggesting the need for postgame debriefings.

If such impact can be achieved via role-playing, it may be possible to use it beneficially. An example of research that has done just that is found in the work of Janis and Mann (1965; Mann & Janis, 1968). The simulation was a relatively simple one in which each of a group of young females who were heavy smokers was asked to play the role of a patient who had just been informed she had cancer of the lung. The experimenter played the role of a physician, and several scenes were acted out in the doctor's office to ensure that each subject focused on the threat of painful illness, hospitalization, and an untimely death. The subjects were encouraged to improvise and really try to get into the role, to put themselves in the patient's shoes. Members of another group of subjects were exposed to the same information about cancer and smoking, via listening to tape recordings of the role-playing sessions. However, the latter subjects were given no opportunity themselves to play the role of cancer patients.

The initial study found that both in terms of changing attitudes toward smoking and in terms of changing actual smoking habits, the emotional role-playing was much more effective than passive exposure to the same information. The role-players, for example, reported a greater decrease in number of cigarettes smoked each day, from an average of about 25 to an average of 14. A follow-up study 18 months later found that this lower level of smoking was maintained. After 18 months, the role-players had decreased their consumption by about 13 cigarettes a day, whereas the passive controls were only down about 5 a day. As Mann and Janis (1968) noted, "Insofar as the subjects' verbal reports about their current cigarette consumption can be trusted, the evidence indicates that there was a sustained effect of the emotional role-playing procedure over a 1½ year period." That is quite an effect to get from 30 or 40 minutes of make-believe.

ing large bodies of troops—insights that can be obtained in no other way, short of war itself. When used for teaching, the important considerations in evaluating simulations are, of course, what and how much was learned by whom. Another use of simulations is as a vehicle for testing specific hypotheses. Many of the simulation games, such as the prisoner's dilemma, are used in this way. Does physiological arousal increase the frequency of competitive choices? Does the reward structure (i.e., how much players can win by exploiting their opponents) make a difference? Does cooperation fade as the stakes go up? When used in this way, the important considerations in evaluating a simulation are generally the same as those discussed in connection with experimentation (Chapter Nine).

But, the most important use of simulation methods, and the most difficult use to evaluate, is something that simulations share with participant observation. They are both great goads to theory development. They get your mind churning about what is really involved in rumor transmission or social interaction or whatever it is that interests you. Of course, with participant observation you are supposedly focused on taking in what is going on in the situation and with simulation development you are focused on explaining it (via building a model). Most people find these two activities difficult to separate. As soon as they see something interesting, they begin reaching for an explanation.

As noted earlier, a simulation is a scientific metaphor, an analogy. But, as Kaplan (1964) has said, the key question is whether there is something to be learned from the analogy if you choose to draw it. To suggest that getting married is like buying a car on time is pointless, unless that leads you to aspects of the marriage situation that you might not have thought of otherwise. That could, in fact, be a worthwhile analogy to pursue because marriage has one of the features that Abelson (1968) said is essential among candidates for simulation. That is, it involves a variety of forces interacting in complex ways that make the outcomes very difficult to predict. The hope in such situations is that an analogy, a model of the processes that might be involved, will both strip away much of the irrelevant and reveal something of the essential underlying character of the phenomenon. Note that the model will, almost by definition, be an oversimplification. But, do not let that scare you.

Try another example. Take some complex aspect of individual behavior or some complicated social situation and develop a model for it. Ask yourself if the analogy leads you to any new implications, any unanticipated aspects of the situation, any previously unconsidered dimensions. If it does not, it is useless. But, do not give up too quickly. Mull it over, twist it around, pursue it. If the model does suggest something new, you are well on your way to simulation. Thus, a partial answer to the question of when simulation is an appropriate strategy is when something new can be learned from the model you develop. Further, that is most likely to occur when the situation being modeled is a complex one, involving a variety of forces.

Another way of saying this is that simulations should be evaluated in terms of their HEURISTIC FERTILITY, that is, the extent to which they suggest new observations, research, and ideas. If nothing new is suggested by the model you develop, then you have wasted your time. That is why a model of some situation involving no more than one or two variables is not likely to be useful. It follows that much of the value of developing a simulation occurs before the simulation is ever actually carried out. It occurs during what Palys (1978) referred to as the confrontation and explication process. That occurs when you sit down, pen in hand, all ready to whip out a model, and you realize how much you do not know about the phenomenon that piqued your interest. You are confronted by your own ignorance. Painful though it is , that is really a crucial first step. It is there that the processes of model building and simulation begin. What, after all, is really involved in dating choices or white flight to the suburbs or the bandwagon effect in national elections? You will find you have to get your assumptions out on the table, define terms, fill in gaps, resolve inconsistencies. In other words, as Abelson (1968) put it, the most important part of simulation is the formulation of detailed ideas about the processes involved. So, when evaluation time rolls around, forget all the stage settings, and the fancy mathematics, and the magnificent machines. Ask yourself, what were the ideas behind this simulation? What social and behavioral processes have been clarified?

There are a couple of other things you might want to think about in assessing a simulation, or in developing your own. The first is related to the fact that models are simplifications of some more complex reality. Because of that, when you get to the explication phase of the confrontation–explication process, you probably will have to go a lot further than you would like in specifying assumptions. Everything must be made precise for the model, no ambiguities are allowed. There is good reason for that, of course. As Kaplan (1964) put it, the precision demanded in models keeps you from fooling yourself about what you know. You must be able to trace every process, every transition from start to finish. If you cannot, if you reach a point at which it is not clear how you got there, something is wrong, something has been left out. In Allport and Postman's study of rumors, for example, the protocols obtained from successive subjects were studied side-by-side, and the transitions from one to the next were all accounted for in terms of leveling, sharpening, and assimilation. The other point is that all of this takes time. All of the attention to detail, specifications of assumptions, coming to grips with what is really involved. It is usually time well spent, but it can be frustrating. You can end up after a day of staring at blank pieces of paper and crumpling up false starts with the feeling that nothing has been accomplished. But, do not give up. Keep thinking about it. Tomorrow you may have that Aha! experience.

Validity

Several years ago Abelson (1968) coined the term SIMULATION GAP. It refers to the frequently large differences between the nature of simulations and the nature of the systems they are supposedly imitating. Computers, for example, can be programmed to do some things that give them the appearance of having human intelligence, such as playing chess. But, the way in which the computer decides on its next move at any particular juncture in the game may bear no resemblance to the way a human player would decide. Although such a chess-playing computer could be lots of fun to have around, as a model of human chess playing, it would have little value.

The problem of bridging the simulation gap is, of course, a problem of validity, and it is the most serious difficulty with simulations. Once you have developed a model of some system, how can you be sure that what happens in the model is really the same as what happens in the system itself? Strictly speaking, you cannot. There will always be an element of uncertainty, a leap of faith required to get from the model back to the system modeled. But, what you can do is be aware of some of the ways in which models and simulations are likely to fool you. Then your judgment about the validity of a particular simulation will, at least, be well-informed.

It has already been noted that a model is, by definition, a simplification. Kaplan (1964) has suggested that, rather than thinking of a model as an oversimplification, it might be more useful in assessing validity to think of the model as an undercomplication. Such a twist not only calls attention to the fact that some variables have been left out, but—if you will pardon the pun—that, when included, those variables may complicate things. For example, the serial reproduction simulation set up by Allport and Postman seemed to yield transformations in rumors that paraleled those found in real rumors. But, Allport and Postmand left out several potentially important variables, variables that they themselves had identified as crucial in the transmission of wartime rumors. One was that the rumors always had a great deal of significance for the lives of those who transmitted them. People did not seem to pass on rumors about things that did not concern them. Thus, there is the possibility that subjects in the Allport and Postman study would have been much more accurate (i.e., much less leveling would have occurred) if they had been dealing with materials of some personal significance to them.

Dillehay and Nietzel (1980a) introduced a concept of importance in this connection, the notion of APPLIED EXPLANATORY POWER. The idea is that a simulation may be perfectly valid, in the sense that the processes involved correspond to processes operating in the system modeled. Yet, that knowledge may not be very useful because of other, more powerful factors that dominate the actual system. The distinction, of course, is between theoretical and practical significance. If your intention is merely to develop an understanding of the system, then you may not be too concerned with applied explanatory power. But if you want to use your theoretical system as a guide for social action, then the applied explanatory power of your concepts becomes a key to their validity. As Dillehay and Nietzel (1980a) put it, "What is statistically significant and theoretically valid for a given situation may yet be of little or no practical value because the relationship described accounts for so little of the variance in the focal outcome variable . . . what is of importance to a practitioner is the amount of variation in the behavior he/she confronts that is accounted for by the relationship specified in the proposition."

One final thing to remember in evaluating simulations is that any particular model is only one way of representing something. There may be many other ways of doing precisely the same thing. Thus, even though you may have a completely appropriate model of some large system, it is not necessarily the case that all of the model's properties correspond to aspects of that larger system. The fallacy that may tempt you here is what Kaplan (1964) referred to as "map reading." Just because Texas appears in green on your map of the United States, do not expect it to be covered with grass. The map, as a representation of reality, has properties that do not correspond to reality.

Summary

Simulations and models are imitations of convenience, scaled-down versions of social and behavioral systems. They can be useful for teaching, research, and theoretical elaboration. The purpose of a simulation, of course, is to help you understand how the system being modeled operates; how it works. Simulations are most useful when they lead to unanticipated consequences. They are most likely to do that when the system being simulated is a complex one, involving a variety of competing forces.

There are several varities of simulations. The simulation may be an extension of the laboratory experiment. The key to the extension is that, in contrast to the typical hypothesis-testing experiment, laboratory simulation involves greater freedom for the participants. The focus is on observing what will happen when some social phenomenon is transposed to the relatively well-controlled environment and set in motion. How will the processes work themselves out? Allport and Postman's study of rumor transmission illustrates this type of simulation.

A second type of simulation is role-playing, of which there are several different varieties. In general, role-playing is quite useful in helping you uncover the implicit understandings that guide social interaction in specific situations—what is referred to as the role/rule framework. Zimbardo's simulated prison illustrates one use of role-playing. By staffing and stocking his basement prison with normal, intelligent college students, Zimbardo was able to argue that not all of the pathology in prisons can be attributed to the personalities of guards and prisoners. The ability to thus manipulate some aspects of the system being modeled is one of the prime advantages of simulations. You can see "what would happen if. . . ." A third type of simulation involves the use of games, that is, structured tasks over which participants interact according to sets of rules. The key to each game is that the rules are constructed to capture the essence of some real-life situation, and the game provides a vehicle for studying the dynamics of social interaction via a simulation of that situation. The best known of the games is the prisoner's dilemma, a game designed to put each player in a bind between cooperation and competition. Other games have different structures, of course; but the attempt in each is to define the rules in order to capture the essential dynamics of the interaction of interest.

Some problems are associated with the evaluation of simulations. It is important to keep in mind that simulations are partial; they are not intended to duplicate everything about the system being modeled. Some aspects of the system will, of necessity, have been left out. Thus, it will always be necessary to ask how the results of the simulation would be influenced by those other processes and pieces that help make up the larger system. Investigators also need to be clear about what they hope to achieve via simulation. Do they just want to understand what is going on? Or do they want to use that understanding to change the world?

Recommended Readings

Not all of the items in this list are about simulations. A couple are more general. They are here because they cover some things that any good researcher ought to know, that is, they agree with my biases, and this is my last chance to recommend them to you. One of the articles in the collection edited by McGrath contains the following paradox (which you should be able to resolve by now—if not, check out pages 209 and 210 of that collection):

> There is no such thing as too much research!
> There is no such thing as flawless research!
> But: Poor research is much worse than none at all.

Want a hint? Poor research is different from flawed research.

Elstein, A. S., Shulman, L. S., & Sprafka, S. A. *Medical problem solving: An analysis of clinical reasoning.* Cambridge, MA: Harvard University Press, 1978.

Using what they referred to as high-fidelity simulations, the authors of this book studied the diagnostic problem-solving behavior of experienced physicians. They were particularly interested in finding out whether physicians reputed to be good diagnosticians went about diagnosing a case differently from physicians without such reputations. To make the necessary comparisons, it was deemed necessary to have members of the two groups of physicians diagnose the same cases. This was done by training actors to play the roles of patients. Scripts for the actors were developed from actual cases, and the actors memorized medical histories of the patients involved. The research consisted of having physicians interview the actors and make a diagnosis. It was completely up to the physicians to decide which questions to ask, how many to ask, and in what order. If lab tests were requested by the physicians, results of those tests were provided without comment. The interviews were recorded on videotape so that they could be analyzed at leisure and repeatedly – one of the great advantages of recordings is that you can go back to them with a new coding system and some new ideas later on. The results of the simulations suggested that successful diagnosticians generate hypotheses about possible problems and/or diseases quite early in an encounter with a patient. They then progressively home in on the most likely diagnosis by selectively seeking certain types of information. The use of trained actors with memorized case material was an excellent way of simulating physician–patient interviews. It allowed the investigators to learn something about the diagnostic process under controlled conditions that seemed to capture the essential pattern of the real-life situation.

Huff, D. *How to lie with statistics.* New York: Norton, 1954.

Several years ago a book salesman from Norton told me that this slim paperback has outsold all of their other books and continues to sell quite well. That is hard to believe about a book with the word *statistics* in the title. But, read it and you will see why. It is not really about statistics as much as it is about clear thinking, logic, and appropriate comparisons. It is also written in a delightful, semi-cynical style – poking fun at some of the ridiculous facts and figures we are confronted with every day. For example, during the Spanish-American War, the death rate in the U.S. Navy was 9 per thousand. Among the civilian population of New York City, the death rate at the time was 16 per thousand. The Navy actually used these figures to show that the Navy was safer than the streets of New York. The comparison, of course, was absurd. The Navy is predominantly made up of young men in top physical condition. A civilian population includes infants, the elderly, and the ill. Consider another example. Huff points out that many magazines and newspapers use illustrations that are unintentionally deceptive. Suppose you draw two cows, one three times the height of the other, to illustrate the increase in the number of cows in the United States from 1860 (8 million) to 1935 (25 million). The taller cow will have an apparent bulk or mass many times greater than the shorter figure and, thus, will give an exaggerated impression of the difference. Try it. Also try reading the book.

McGrath, J. E. (Ed.) Judgment calls: An unorthodox view of the research process. *American Behavioral Scientist*, 1981, *25*, 123–232.

Methodology text books and journal articles always seem to make research appear to be such a rational process, so clean-cut, and, well, SCIENTIFIC. Appearances are often deceiving, as the authors of this special issue of *ABS* pointed out. They argue that research does not get carried out in the way it is later described as having been carried out. It is heavily determined by all sorts of supposedly extraneous factors and involves a series of compromises between the ideal and the possible. Available resources, for example, are supposed to facilitate research, but they do much more. They constrain both the choice of problems to be investigated and how the research will be carried out. How likely is it that someone who has spent several years equipping a nice experimental lab is going to select a method other than experimentation for research? Not very. McGrath and his colleagues forcefully present the case for triangulation of methods that has been advocated since Chapter One. Their view is that not only are all methods flawed, they are each so seriously flawed as to be almost worthless *when used alone*. Salvation lies in multi-methods. The continued use of a particular instrument or method simply because other researchers in the area have used it is one of the most heinous of sins. Build a new instrument, try a new method. DO SOMETHING DIFFERENT!

Schelling, T. C. *Micromotives and macrobehavior.* New York: Norton, 1978.

Consider some aggregate of people, such as the audience in a movie theater that is only about half full. Try to figure out what combination of individual motives would account for the way in which they distribute themselves around the theater. Where would the first arrivals be most likely to sit? Which areas of the auditorium would people be likely to avoid? How far apart would people sit if there is plenty of room? Schelling's book consists of a series of such analyses, all exploring the relation between the behavior of the individuals who constitute some social aggregate and the characteristics of the aggregate. He speculated about individual motives, desires, and goals to piece together models that would account for the nature of aggregates in a variety of situations. One of the most valuable aspects of the book is that it conveys an enthusiasm for speculation. You begin to see that there is an underlying order in much that previously appeared to be random and chaotic. In spite of what the author claims, however, there is more than just one part of the book that is a little slow-going. But read it twice if you have to. Your social world will appear much more interesting afterward.

Stogdill, R. M. (Ed.) *The process of model building in the behavioral sciences.* Columbus, OH: Ohio State University Press, 1970.

This small volume contains the proceedings of a symposium on models and simulations held at Ohio State several years ago. In the words of the editor, the purpose of the symposium was not to provide a cookbook for the aspiring model-builder, but rather to examine the intellectual operations and requisite skills involved. The focus was on the creative process, and several of the authors took an explicitly autobiographical approach, relating their own experiences with model development and simulations. The authors, by the way, were all leading lights in the field, and the organizer of the symposium was quite correct in thinking we might learn something from their experiences. My favorite chapter is entitled "Making artists out of pedants." It is by James G. March and is about the development of a course on model-building at the University of California, Irvine. March begins by sketching his own model of why the social and behavioral sciences seem to recruit more than their share of students who are not analytically oriented. The course he and some colleagues developed at Irvine was designed specifically to enhance those analytic skills so essential to model-building. It was a course in which the ratio of thinking–creating to reading–regurgitation was significantly higher than normal, and it sounds as if it would have been great fun. This book also has a long appendix of exercises by March on which you can hone your model-building skills.

Table of Random Numbers

On the following two pages are 5632 numbers between zero and nine. They are grouped into sets of four merely to help you keep your place and to make the table somewhat easier to read. As an example of how you might use the table, consider the following. Suppose that you had 30 people, each of whom you wanted to assign randomly to one of two groups, say, an experimental group and a control group. First, you would assign each person a number, 01–30. Second, you pick an arbitrary starting point in the table, such as the thirteenth number in the twenty-first row of the first page (it should be the first 9 of 9966, unless I miscounted). Third, beginning at that number you look at two digit numbers 99, 66, 83, 50, 03, 38, . . . and assign the first 15 persons whose numbers you come across in this manner to the experimental group. Those people should be numbers 03, 08, 28, 19, 09, 16, (starting on the next row) 30, 22, 05, 15, 11, 10, 29 (starting on the next row) 27, and 24. The other 15 people would be assigned to the control group.

As another example, suppose you had 100 people you wanted to interview and five interviewers. To randomly assign interviewees to interviewers, you would first assign a number (00–99) to each person to be interviewed. Then, starting at some arbitrary point in the table and reading two-digit numbers, you would assign the first 20 people whose numbers you came across to Interviewer 1, the second 20 whose numbers you found to Interviewer 2, and so on.

8915 7829 5908 2605 8614 9658 9162 8096 3221 5131 3062 0649 2029 2018 4122 4473
2105 1170 1800 8165 7671 9233 0009 4817 8072 2905 1277 5801 6116 8276 8821 8712
5054 6239 5249 2123 5688 2978 1469 4973 6891 5688 7193 6112 4611 6150 1519 7640
8303 9793 0554 1603 3281 1499 9082 9902 5809 0760 0849 0149 4944 3460 0297 9294

2216 0982 3201 8329 7989 7583 0992 7920 2019 9110 9843 8989 0209 1462 8268 1352
9404 1244 4847 6660 2249 3364 4758 9388 3568 3813 3235 0327 7367 1627 0481 0162
6577 8819 0569 8569 3649 1162 2539 6588 0364 3994 6351 1846 0241 3944 2449 4708
2248 9282 9113 6833 6073 3597 7829 8104 7041 6935 2263 3250 6133 4935 4133 8516

1663 5576 3803 8878 4893 5002 2926 2098 5244 7962 8242 2814 2182 5476 8656 8174
8312 3201 9580 4528 2422 9507 1511 5044 7531 9737 2860 4524 5248 5301 3665 2503
3630 1852 3385 8452 3412 2024 5393 4576 1347 4232 7502 8109 6645 6952 4318 0708
3946 6852 0371 0355 1916 1110 9342 7518 3729 9754 0377 2284 1780 5341 4061 5866

2588 0245 3261 4267 9646 6666 8676 8051 4196 4019 1668 6790 8290 4686 2799 8744
7837 1831 8353 4959 3673 3931 0037 7944 0947 0392 8885 8950 1596 3594 7194 4619
2345 7493 4809 2431 0514 5612 7024 3951 9128 2420 7503 2529 7363 8545 3230 9517
0192 9321 7591 3371 9320 6693 0948 3203 5361 8664 5179 6731 4577 6528 6301 0632

7774 5110 9871 8258 1483 1028 8543 7393 9190 3272 2290 5010 0824 4520 3758 8019
4384 7106 7389 2738 7773 3669 9659 4923 1720 1621 8955 8103 1708 1334 7387 8729
4783 5058 8854 4001 4553 8517 1277 7818 7254 4471 1379 5086 6328 0688 6233 7338
7201 2579 7839 8585 3214 8403 3381 6207 6799 0706 9727 0812 2941 6374 3484 4422

8374 5137 1591 9966 8350 0338 4570 0887 9648 8092 2819 7431 0957 3169 8132 8216
5092 7630 5296 2216 3370 0373 0528 0515 1111 0098 4310 9019 2954 5150 0859 6946
3671 1116 5333 1940 2762 7827 2265 4924 3812 9943 7253 0439 3082 9895 7284 3932
0988 2936 2350 7979 4755 2602 3990 6520 8043 7572 6177 5401 9781 6547 6288 5193

2007 8566 5202 6359 9404 9731 4344 3318 4414 0795 6538 3683 2561 5868 2378 8108
1961 6059 9390 3460 0467 0454 3676 8873 8224 7238 7938 2550 1087 4360 4076 3289
6897 0150 1509 6409 9831 3897 5532 2435 3558 4954 9217 6719 1570 2365 7766 7695
0655 2019 0574 5284 7999 3931 5545 7836 5969 6505 7511 3907 9951 3862 5910 6863

2388 2668 9163 4880 4846 9195 8282 9927 3258 8617 7617 2313 5676 6293 2210 7405
2869 5749 7337 7533 2397 3640 8844 2309 1674 0038 1928 0500 2991 0483 0795 5241
9282 3180 8625 3479 3852 5832 4289 0053 2545 0673 6889 7987 7595 9172 2084 6877
6119 2933 6812 5025 4490 9370 5289 4295 3115 6160 9606 3596 9601 3093 7923 5763

7024 0463 8889 2412 7401 9781 6411 1215 5850 1080 4170 1847 3143 3805 8653 1105
2875 3775 1988 7073 3982 9691 0143 0979 2011 3443 6045 4025 7198 4782 6611 5525
5419 1638 2581 1028 4488 5806 2462 6024 9058 0531 1099 0798 9663 7890 4922 5519
7612 9196 5836 8061 8597 4566 6481 8035 6379 0301 6501 6386 5774 8684 5904 4348

6545 0532 5524 3247 9367 2851 6202 2819 3484 9375 6297 3260 8973 7320 7625 9809
6650 1763 5204 7818 1537 5719 0382 0818 8339 3619 3844 4794 4593 3577 1936 1561
7891 2170 0255 4366 1647 9503 5036 4076 7289 0535 2208 7486 4967 2740 4763 1236
0821 0518 8280 3439 8234 4412 1122 3378 8184 5755 8820 4148 7743 5960 5853 4510

6384 1575 4974 4807 9354 7243 2049 5103 8661 1010 6344 7753 1966 0018 5969 6509
4477 4908 8421 3109 6790 8855 1421 6543 5533 2240 8751 5071 7307 6391 1253 8574
6005 7290 4890 1234 8334 6070 0255 1126 9758 8607 5832 1587 8739 6605 7310 0847
1033 2827 1671 9637 6867 5856 5992 2027 7132 4539 8266 0047 4297 7982 4529 4480

```
7537 9411 3187 2807 1514 6346 0935 1642 8074 6420 8922 4764 4242 2673 2769 0640
7932 4739 0271 2888 1003 4397 6375 8768 3940 5729 4240 9273 4371 9712 9572 8743
7009 8784 8199 8199 1586 5979 3749 0443 3734 4893 9186 8304 2683 8961 2230 7046
3468 5007 4391 3033 0013 7463 5803 0636 5514 0724 4870 5742 5764 0200 7839 4405

5311 1902 8291 7051 6746 5657 9475 2359 6205 0886 5936 1020 0064 3303 0766 3927
8681 5263 9716 5500 3867 7368 1118 0845 2523 5585 7536 4971 7583 1181 1795 8010
2300 0300 4984 5229 2049 5418 7955 9112 8773 1215 3964 8424 0075 6166 7572 9589
5109 6534 0210 7810 5195 9331 3636 7438 6988 0647 1269 3817 3414 6309 0690 7985

4983 9859 8102 2787 5725 0818 7359 1140 8908 7571 3149 9692 9196 7783 5066 7590
3953 1599 4789 9602 4360 2560 1071 4242 4164 6797 3563 6203 0212 9132 7144 2274
1731 3387 4968 7213 8336 8037 7634 5781 7350 5762 9168 1134 4449 9130 1503 6454
3311 3719 6241 0975 9308 7640 4673 6446 0296 7053 1905 1498 0074 5000 6898 5476

9514 0767 8975 9216 6882 2223 4315 2222 5103 9683 9643 9266 0543 3703 5049 8667
8797 2706 9011 2967 3346 0057 6600 9343 0325 4857 0673 8558 1763 0811 4701 2548
1768 5723 1776 2576 2266 4498 6697 9406 5364 4250 9267 9235 9307 7480 1054 4828
4228 6263 2045 2360 0509 2364 6340 7014 1609 7712 9265 0388 6970 8603 5553 1290

6551 1515 7999 7531 4452 8806 4104 1252 4113 1306 2320 5324 4945 9385 5195 2008
4732 6399 6623 8811 6707 6661 7462 3981 0161 1902 2951 8780 7613 9103 8828 7199
1258 0570 2893 5368 2469 0924 5455 0489 1985 1612 2824 4897 6759 9575 4032 2115
7940 8497 3205 5971 3896 5343 3099 3338 3578 5419 4848 9747 3007 0587 8666 5939

4868 3491 2967 5297 4576 9792 5316 1741 4019 3263 3653 8739 4191 4081 6235 7517
2338 8562 9203 8438 5026 4353 4430 7901 6035 4539 8382 6661 5100 9679 5037 5877
4294 1847 2865 5411 0779 0357 3898 6022 8239 2459 0843 5296 4992 7456 9116 6573
6062 1705 1853 5549 5104 2500 5184 7037 6756 5851 7662 6316 2622 6648 3664 3767

2885 9734 3182 7811 0088 0764 1981 5379 4295 5674 6052 4364 8289 6148 6003 8828
9198 6904 9248 4319 1037 1841 1945 6361 4735 2911 8431 4390 4196 0692 9302 8841
8116 7035 7690 8337 9091 5111 6098 3509 4384 4009 2432 1264 3167 6507 5921 1375
9380 3072 7111 1506 2177 7512 6636 7300 6376 8923 5434 3167 1878 2342 2352 5714

1433 1489 6308 8673 9910 3268 7462 3457 7462 5297 8417 0379 7031 1474 2028 7735
6925 3927 7124 9584 9320 0543 8254 3062 2915 0600 2932 9609 9500 4493 3838 4577
1825 6093 4496 2558 4446 6250 3732 3283 8729 1399 7216 6359 4003 7725 6620 2681
7244 7044 2720 4556 3766 6382 4346 2467 9839 0660 7590 1533 1485 7991 2336 9549

9355 0103 0123 8586 8300 5742 5497 6006 4208 3424 2810 6796 8899 7990 8359 6106
2748 7511 9242 2655 0401 7082 9791 6949 2985 3503 1084 8787 3910 7619 1294 6750
2773 9051 9524 8478 6115 4466 7362 4363 5526 0447 8788 8339 2615 6226 4237 9916
4126 8830 6934 2605 7480 3283 3271 0871 3419 5194 2980 8332 9342 8944 1216 3440

6780 2061 1138 9155 0608 4680 7945 9709 3231 6813 6055 4552 4284 0440 9041 5225
4785 2441 4977 5112 5971 0883 1766 1977 1539 0321 5456 2921 2294 6733 9699 3843
8725 8566 7481 9260 3812 7053 2088 8202 7078 6132 0506 8278 6937 2943 2759 8953
5449 4252 8083 9451 3481 3403 1593 4396 1346 3579 4402 9619 1996 9210 8597 3290

9528 1517 0047 5774 4616 1248 0391 2244 1550 3812 6602 1681 6254 9514 5668 8176
7008 4741 5559 6020 1958 0240 6311 4136 1283 3948 4546 3322 0938 2028 8099 6574
1560 9850 2023 4256 4013 8331 8845 2018 5392 6078 4757 9545 7830 0641 5604 7860
1966 8976 8770 5215 1158 6216 3128 9413 7935 2154 6437 0252 3473 0217 6958 9189
```

Glossary

Accosting. A technique for securing the participation of subjects in field experiments. Individual subjects are simply confronted with a request that they answer a few questions, say, or are confronted with a situation to which they, personally, must respond. *See* Street theater strategy.

Alternative explanation. To make a case that a change in one variable (say, perceived similarity) produces change in another (say, attraction), you must be able to rule out the possibility that other, extraneous variables (such as sexual stimulation) produced the change (in attraction). Those other, extraneous variables are possible alternative explanations for the similarity-action effect. *See* Plausible alternative explanation.

Analogy. A similarity between things that are usually thought of as being quite different. Explicitly noting an analogy may help you discover further similarities between the objects or events in question.

Analytic files. Used for sorting and storing portions of notes taken by participant observers. As ideas occur about processes being observed, the files are created to store examples from the field notes of those processes in operation.

Aphorism. A concise statement usually thought of as expressing an important principle. "Nothing ventured, nothing gained."

Applied explanatory power. A concept having to do with the practical significance of research findings. A theoretically important relationship may be valid in a particular setting, but not explain much of the variation in behavior that occurs in that setting. Its applied explanatory power would be low.

Applied research. Research intended to obtain information that will help you make an intelligent decision in a specific situation. Usually contrasted with basic, or theoretical, research

Archives. Public and private documents recording any aspect of an organization's, institution's, or individual's activities.

Archival research. An investigation that makes use of public or private documents pertaining to the past.

Assimilation. The process, often subconscious, of transforming your perceptions of a person or event to make them fit a previously existing expectation of what they are, or should be, like.

Attention. The focusing of your consciousness on some object, event, or person. In participant observation, there is a danger of paying too much attention to the most salient aspects of a setting.

Attention–feedback–regulation cycle. One possible mechanism that may help explain the fact that observing someone's behavior often causes that behavior to change. That is, by observing someone's behavior, you call their attention to what they are doing. That, in turn, may cause them to change, that is, they may regulate their behavior.

Attrition. In longitudinal research in which subjects are to be contacted repeatedly, attrition refers to the fact that some may just disappear between contacts with the researcher. Some may die, some may move away or leave no forwarding address, and some may just change their mind about continuing to participate in the research. The problem is that attrition may introduce a bias into your data. Those who tolerate three or four interviews, for example, may be quite different from those who will not.

Balanced replication. When you believe the results of an experiment were produced by some flaw in the procedure you need to redo the experiment precisely, flaw and all, to demonstrate that fact. You also need to add a condition that has everything the first experiment had except the flaw. Such a design is a balanced replication. With the flawed condition you should obtain the same results as in the original experiment. With the new, unflawed condition, you should not – you hope.

Basic research. Research that is intended to test or refine some theoretical proposition. Usually contrasted with applied research.

Behavioral assimilation. In interacting with others, we sometimes induce them to act toward us as we are acting toward them. When that occurs, behavioral assimilation is said to have taken place.

Behavioral confirmation. This involves behaving toward another person in such a way that you induce them to confirm your expectations about them. If you expect them to be cold and aloof, you may be sufficiently unpleasant in your interaction with them that you induce them to be, sure enough, cold and aloof.

Behavior code. The descriptions and definitions of the behaviors you intend to observe. Also included in the code are the rules that tell you how to apply the definitions and examples of behaviors that represent each type or category to be noted.

Behavior *in situ*. Behavior in its natural setting, that is, in the place where it usually occurs.

Bias. Any of a number of forms of systematic distortions that may occur in your perceptions. It is usually thought of as a set of preferences that keep you from making an impartial judgment.

Blind scoring. In content analysis, for example, you may want some verbal material coded to see whether certain categories or types of information are present. However, you do not want the persons doing the coding to know the source of the material because it might bias their interpretations of what they are reading. The process of scoring (or coding) the material while remaining unaware of its sources is referred to as blind scoring.

Blocking. When the members of a sample of subjects differ in identifiable ways, it may be advisable to divide them into subsamples, such as high school males, high school females, college males, college females. Then, by allotting equal numbers from each subsample to each experimental condition, say, you reduce the possibility of having different types of subjects in different conditions, a set up that, of course, would invalidate your experiment before you begin.

Bogus pipeline. A technique or procedure by which you convince others that you will be able to tell, for example, what their *true* attitude or feeling is on an issue, when you really cannot do that. The hope is that if they believe you, they will then simply tell you the truth.

Case study. An intensive, in-depth analysis of the characteristics and history of one individual patient or subject. Case studies can be fruitful sources of hypotheses, but you should beware of using material from case studies as evidence for general hypotheses. The particular case you examined may be unique.

Category construction. The process of deciding which particular behaviors you are going to observe and defining precisely what you mean by each. No ambiguities are allowed. Each type of behavior will form a category.

Category system. In content analysis, the material of interest is read and scored for the presence or absence of certain interrelated concepts. That set of concepts is variously referred to as the coding or category system.

Closed-ended questions. Questions that require the respondent to select one of a small number of previously set answers, such as Yes or No or Strongly agree, Agree, Disagree, Strongly disagree.

Coding. In content analysis, coding refers to the process of reading the material of interest, noting the presence or absence of certain concepts specified by the coding scheme or category system, and assigning a score to the material.

Cohort study. A type of survey that allows you to examine longitudinal changes. In a cohort study, different samples are selected from the same (it is hoped) population. The samples are selected so that some have and some have not experienced certain events. Tenth and twelfth graders from the same school system may be selected to examine the effects of high school education on prejudice. The danger is that the 10th graders of 2 years ago (i.e., todays twelfth graders) may not really be from the same population as today's tenth graders.

Common sense. The body of knowledge and level of intelligence that a normal person should have and be able to use in making decisions in day-to-day life.

Concealed identity. A type of participant observation in which you do not tell the people in the setting that you are actually doing research. Rather, you simply move into the setting and pass yourself off as a regular member.

Conceptual replication. The process whereby an experiment on a particular topic is redone but the way in which the independent and/or dependent variables are operationalized is changed.

Conceptualization. The process of thinking, of formulating ideas and hypotheses. Probably the single most important part of research.

Confounding variable. A variable that actually includes a mixture of two or more potentially separate things is said to be a confounded variable. For example, if you put the tall people in your class in one group and the short people in a second group, you would probably have confounded sex and height in the two groups. Males are usually, but not always, taller than females.

Content analysis. A research method in which verbal (usually written) material is examined for the presence or absence of certain specified types of information or concepts.

Context. That which surrounds a given item. In an interview, the context may be thought of as the questions that precede and follow a particular question. Context may also refer to the qualifications and explanations within which the answer to a question is embedded. To ignore those explanations in citing what someone said may leave you open to the charge of "quoting out of context," which is a form of misrepresentation.

Contingency questions. Those questions in survey research that are to be answered only by those subjects who answer a previous question in a certain way. Thus, whether or not the respondent is asked the second question depends on, or is contingent upon, how he or she answered the first.

Contingency table. A way of displaying the relationships among two or more variables. The contingency table allows you to inspect the extent to which positive or negative attitudes, for example, depend upon the sex of the respondent.

Control. To control something usually means to be able to regulate it, to have power over it. In an experiment, to control a certain variable means to keep it from influencing the results and this can be done in several ways. Random assignment of subjects to conditions, for example, is intended to control for individual differences among subjects in the various conditions.

Convenience sample. In survey research, a convenience sample consists of those respondents who are easiest for you to contact, that is, the most convenient ones. When you limit your sample to these people, it is likely to be biased.

Cost–benefit analysis. A procedure for measuring the effectiveness or efficiency of a program. The final value is obtained by calculating the cost required to produce a given benefit. In cost–benefit analysis the effects of the program must be converted to a dollar value. That often requires the experimenter to make some very arbitrary assumptions.

Cost–effectiveness analysis. A technique for assessing the efficiency of a program. It is carried out by calculating the cost of the program per unit of change produced. For example, you might determine how much it costs to raise the average reading scores of first graders by 10 points.

Cover story. Some experiments involve deception and the most common type of deception is the use of a cover story, which is a plausible, but false, explanation to the subject of the purpose of the experiment. The point is to keep the subject unaware of the true purpose of the experiment. In some cases, awareness of the true purpose would influence the subject's response to the independent variable.

Creativity. The capacity for thinking up new ideas and ways of doing things. Creativity often involves breaking with traditional ways of perceiving objects and events.

Criticism. The art of making discriminating judgments, of finding the faults and merits of an idea or a research report.

Cross-sectional survey. A survey in which members of the sample are interviewed, or administered a questionnaire, one time only. Conversely, in a panel study, members of the sample are interviewed repeatedly in order to trace changes over time.

Curiosity. The desire to find out how things work, why they are as they are. Curiosity is one of the prime motive forces behind research.

Debriefing. At the end of an experiment, particularly if any deception was involved, it is essential to explain everything to the subjects – including the reasons for deception. Such explanations and the answering of any questions the subjects have about the research is referred to as debriefing.

Deduction. The act of inferring how a given general principle would apply in a particular situation.

Demand characteristics. Those cues that tell a subject how he or she is expected to respond in an experimental or interview situation, that is, cues that demand a particular type of response. Care should be taken to eliminate all such cues from the situation. Otherwise, you will not know whether your result is evidence of the variable of interest or simply evidence that the subject did what he or she thought you wanted.

Demographics. The characteristics of human populations, such as age, sex, and educational level.

Dependent variable. The point of an experiment is to determine whether changes in one or more variables (independent variables) produce changes in another (dependent variable). That is, the experimenter wants to see whether changes in the dependent variable depend on changes in the independent variables.

Description. The act of attending to and recording the details of situations, events, and people. One of the most difficult things about learning how to describe well is learning to pay attention not only to what is present in a situation you are trying to describe but also to what is absent.

Differentiation. The ability to see different aspects of a problem and to take those various factors into account in making a decision. *See* Integration.

Disciplined abstractions. Analytic concepts grounded in your observations of a particular setting. When developing disciplined abstractions, you ask yourself what general concept a particular behavior is an example of. Banging one's fist on the table at a meeting may be related to "commitment to an ideal." It may also be an example of rudeness.

Ego-threatening questions. In an interview, ego-threatening questions are those that arouse anxiety in the respondent. They should be avoided, if possible, because they are likely to result in evasiveness or antagonism to the interviewer. If such questions are necessary, they should be broached cautiously and only after a relationship of trust and respect has been established.

Elements. The individual units that make up a population. In sampling, you select elements from the population in such a way that the sample is representative of the population.

Elite interview. An interview with someone who is acknowledged to be a leader in his or her field. In such an interview, the interviewee may take the lead in defining areas of importance for discussion.

Emergent context. The events that follow a given social act and help you to interpret what the act really meant.

Empirical approach. The gathering of information about the way the world is, that is, relying on experience and observation. The empirical approach is usually contrasted with the rational approach in which you seek specific information that bears on a particular theory or idea.

Empirical relationship. Observed associations among things. If you were to note that every Monday the stock market goes up and every Wednesday it goes down, you would have observed a relationship between day of the week and stock prices. Discovering an empirical relationship may serve as a nudge to your curiosity and get you started trying to explain it.

Epidemiology. The study of the causes and transmission mechanisms of diseases in human populations.

Equifinality. A word used to describe the fact that a given behavior may be produced by many causes. Hence, you cannot rely only on the behavior itself if you want to understand what it means. Quite often you must examine what occurred prior to and after the behavior in question.

Ethics. The study of the values that guide our actions and influence our choices. In research on human subjects there is often an ethical dilemma produced by a conflict between the fact that we value obtaining new knowledge and also value the individual's right to privacy.

Ethnography. A detailed descriptive account of life in a particular cultural setting. Usually an ethnography is written by someone who has employed participant observation and has lived in the particular setting for some period of time.

Ethology. A field of study concerned with the behavior of animals in their natural settings.

Evaluation apprehension. A concern of many subjects participating in an experiment or an interview. Wanting to make a good impression, they may be worried about how you—as the experimenter or interviewer—are going to evaluate them. As a result, their behavior may not be natural.

Evaluation research. Any of a variety of techniques, methods, and procedures used to assess the effects of social, educational, and medical innovations. Usually, evaluation research is focused on a particular program and is designed to see whether the program is producing the effects anticipated.

Exact replication. Repeating an experiment precisely, with all the details the same as the first time.

Expectations. Our anticipations of relationships among things. They are likely to get us into trouble in observation because they may induce us to read into what we are observing, things that are not there.

Experiment. A form of research in which you manipulate one variable to see whether changes in it have any effect on another variable. The variable you manipulate is the independent variable, the one you observe (or measure) for changes is the dependent variable.

Experimental realism. The extent to which the activity a subject is asked to do in an experiment is involving and captures his or her attention.

Experimenter effects. An experiment usually involves interactions between two people: the experimenter and the subject. As a person with certain characteristics (age, sex, style, beliefs) the experimenter may unintentionally influence how the subject responds. The sum total of such influence is referred to as experienter effects. Ideally, of course, only the independent variable should influence how the subject responds.

Explanation. To explain something means to make it understandable. Explanation in research is the process of clarifying the relationships among variables, thereby showing how one influences another.

Exploratory studies. Also referred to as pilot studies. Relatively informal preliminary research in which you can try out questions for an interview, for example, to see how people perceive the questions. With an experiment, you might try several ways of operationalizing the independent variable during the exploratory phase.

External validity. The question of external validity is the question of generalizability: to what other settings or populations can the results of research be generalized. Research findings that completely lack external validity would not hold up in any other situation or among any other group of subjects. Variables that interfere with your ability to generalize to another setting or subject population are referred to as threats to external validity.

Extinction. A term that comes from learning theory. It refers to the finding that behavior that is not followed by some form of reinforcement will sooner or later cease to be performed–probably sooner.

Extralinguistic behavior. Behavior accompanying speech–other than the content or substantive aspects of speech inself. Some examples of extralinguistic behavior that may tell you things about the speaker are pauses, tone of voice, and accent.

Extraneous variables. Variables other than the ones of interest that you must find a way to control or, at least keep from influencing your results. If they cannot be controlled or neutralized you will have to come up with a plausible argument about why they were not important in your research.

Factorial design. An experimental design in which more than one independent variable is manipulated. Conditions are so constructed that a given level of each independent variable occurs in conjunction once (and only once) with each level of the other independent variables. Also called a crossed design.

Field experiments. Research conducted in field or naturalistic settings in which you manipulate one or more variables to see what effect that will have. The variable manipulated is the independent variable.

Field notes. The copious, descriptive notes taken by participant observers of the things they observe. The taking of good, complete field notes is an essential component of participant observation.

Field research. Another name for participant observation. The research method in which one immerses oneself in the ongoing social life of a setting and systematically records (see field notes) all that is seen and heard. The point is to reach an understanding of the how of social life in the setting and to develop a set of disciplined abstractions (analytic concepts that can account for what has been observed).

Fieldwork. Yet another name for participant observation. See Field research.

Focused interview. An interview in which you, as the investigator, define what it is you want to know but allow the respondent some latitude to express pertinent ideas and volunteer information. The focus is on the interviewee's attitudes and experiences relevant to the topic(s) of interest to you.

Formative evaluation. To assess the impact of social, educational, or medical programs, it is first necessary to establish that the program in question has actually been put into place and is operating as planned. This initial assessment is referred to as formative evaluation.

Funnel sequence. In interviewing, a funnel sequence is an order of the set of questions; in this sequence you begin with the broadest, most general, question and gradually narrow down to the most minute details.

Hawthorne effect. When subjects believe that you have taken an interest in them and their well being, they may exert more effort than normal to try to do whatever it is they think you want them to do. This is referred to as the Hawthorne effect because it was first documented in the 1920s at the Hawthorne plant of Western Electric Company.

Heuristic fertility. Something is said to have heuristic fertility if it suggests new ways of doing things, or new ideas for research, or new theoretical developments.

Hypothesis. A proposed explanation for a relationship between events or things. You might hypothesize, for example, that Professor Jones's courses are always filled with students because he is such an excellent lecturer. On the other hand, they may simply be required courses.

Hypothesis testing. The purpose of a great deal of research, especially experimentation. Hypothesis testing refers to the designing and carrying out of research in such a way that it will yield some evidence, yea or nay, on the validity of a proposed explanation for a relationship between two variables. Hypothesis testing is contrasted with descriptive research.

Idiographic. Research designed to explore an individual instance or case in great detail. Idiographic research is usually contrasted with nomothetic research.

Illusion of control. The belief that you can exercise control over events when, in reality, you cannot. Some research by Langer has demonstrated that we often act as if we are able to influence events that are really determined by chance.

Independent variable. In an experiment, the independent variable is the one you manipulate or change to see what will happen.

Index. In archival research you must decide what items of information you are going to use as an index, or marker, of the thing you are interested in. Making that decision is all that is meant by index construction. For example, allotments to police budgets may be used as an index of authoritarian attitudes in a community. Remember, however, that such indices may be flawed. In survey research, *index* has a different meaning. There an index is the combination of answers to two or more questions assessing the same thing. Such combinations are useful because they help create response variability and because it is sometimes difficult to measure concepts with a single question.

Induction. The act of inferring a general principle from isolated observations of examples of the principle in action.

Informants. Informants are the people in a community who are used by participant observers to gather information about the setting and the people in it. Having good informants can be very important to the progress and quality of fieldwork.

Informed consent. A procedure in which potential research participants are told what the research will involve and any harm it might do to them, and are then given a free choice about whether or not they want to take part.

Inoculation. The process by which a person is exposed to a weakened form of a disease-producing agent and the body's defenses stimulated so that later exposure to a more virulent form of the agent will not produce the disease. The principle of this process has been used, by analogy, in McGuire's research on resistance to persuasive communications.

Integration. As used in the text, integration refers to the perception of links or connections among the differentiated aspects of a problem. *See* Differentiation.

Interaction. A statistical term used to refer to the joint effect of two or more independent variables in an experiment. The presence of an interaction means that independent variable 1 has a different effect on the dependent variable at different levels of independent variable 2.

Interaction process analysis. A set of categories and procedures developed by Robert Bales for coding the ongoing interactions of small groups. The original IPA system had 12 categories, including "Disagrees," "Asks for orientation," and "Gives opinion."

Internal replication. An experiment within an experiment. Having two experimenters run half the subjects in each condition would be an example. The experiment carried out by Experimenter 1 would have been replicated by Experimenter 2–assuming both results were the same.

Internal validity. The question of internal validity is the question of whether or not the independent variable in an experiment is what really made a difference in the dependent variable. Did you manipulate what you thought you did? Did you measure what you thought you were measuring? Artifacts and other variables that interfere with your ability to show that the independent variable really was what produced the change in the dependent variable are referred to as threats to internal validity.

Interobserver agreement. When an observer watches and codes a set of events into categories, it is important to know how much of what he or she says occurred really occurred. One way to do this is to have two or more observers watch and code the same events. If their codings are similar, you can be more certain that the codings reflect reality and not some figment of the observers' imaginations. The degree of similarity of their codings is a measure of interobserver agreement.

Interrupted time series. A group of designs in which observations are made at several intervals before and after an intervention or manipulation. The manipulation constitutes the interruption in the series of observations.

Interrupted time series with switching replications. A time series design in which repeated observations are made on two groups and the manipulation is introduced to each of the two groups at different points in time.

Interview guide. A list of topics to be covered in an unscheduled interview.

Intimate familiarity. What participant observers must develop with respect to the setting they are observing, that is, a thorough knowledge of the setting and the people in it.

Invasion of privacy. Invasion of someone's privacy occurs when they are denied control over how much about themselves, their feelings, their history, their beliefs, or their behavior will be revealed to others. It is to be avoided in research–or in any other activity, for that matter.

Inverted funnel sequence. The order of questions within an interview schedule that starts with very narrow, circumscribed topics and gradually broadens out to more general topics.

Investigative reporting. A type of reporting, exemplified in Woodward and Bernstein's *All the President's Men*, in which evidence is sought that will justify the publication of a story. As noted in the text, it has a number of parallels with qualitative scientific research.

Leading question. A question asked in a manner calculated to encourage the respondent to give a particular answer.

Leveling. A phenomenon said to occur when the details of a story are lost as the story is passed from one person to another.

Levels. A statistical term referring to the number of degrees or stages of the independent variable present in an experiment. When the independent variable is simply present or absent, you have two levels. When there are low, medium, and high amounts of the independent variable in different conditions, you have three levels, and so on.

Likert scale. A question format often used in survey research in which the respondent is read a statement and then asked to indicate the degree of his or her agreement or disagreement with the statement. When several such items address the same topic, an individual's answers to all of them may be summed to provide an index of his or her attitude toward the topic.

Longitudinal study. Research in which data are collected over a period of time in order to examine changes that occur in the intervening periods.

Main effect. A statistical term referring to a certain type of effect that an independent variable has on the dependent variable in an experiment. A main effect means that independent variable 1, say, has the same effect on the dependent variable regardless of which level of independent variable 2 is present.

Manipulation. In an experiment, manipulation means changing the independent variable to see what effect the change has on the dependent variable.

Marginal status. In a community, having marginal status means that you are not a fully accepted, well-integrated member of the community. Their marginal status is often a problem for participant observers.

Matching. A type of assignment of subjects to conditions in an experiment in which information about the subjects' standing on some variable is used to equate subjects in the various conditions on that variable. For example, suppose you knew the IQ scores of all potential subjects. Then for every subject with an IQ of 130 assigned to one condition, you would have to assign a subject with an IQ of 130 to each of the other conditions.

Mean. The value arrived at by summing all the scores on one variable and dividing by the total number of scores. Also called an average.

Memory distortion. A bias that is particularly problematic for participant observers who must try to reconstruct what they have seen and heard during the course of a day when they sit down to write out their field notes. The distortion arises because we tend to remember things as being more in line with our preexisting beliefs about what-is-related-to-what than they really were.

MENSA. An elitist organization for people with very high IQs. They will not take your word for it, you must take an IQ test to get in.

Method of multiple working hypotheses. An approach to research in which you generate several possible explanations for the phenomenon of interest and gather evidence bearing on them all. The idea is that if you have several hypotheses you are entertaining, you will not become so fond of any particular one that you ignore contrary evidence.

Mnemonic. Any device, slogan, or technique that will help you remember something. How many days in November? Well, "30 days hath September, April, June, and November" is a useful mnemonic. So is counting the knuckles and spaces on your fist.

Multidisciplinary. Literally this means many disciplines, many ways of studying a problem. The word is usually used in a phrase such as *multidisciplinary research* and means that the research involves collaboration of representatives from several disciplines such as psychology, sociology, physiology, and education.

Multiple operationism. Devising several ways to measure the thing of interest. As a measure of interpersonal attraction, for example, you might use self-reports, heart rate increases, and eye contact.

Multistage cluster sample. With some populations it is difficult to construct a sample frame or to list all of the elements of the populatioin. It may be possible to divide the population into groups, or clusters, of elements. Then you can select a sample of clusters. Next, you select a sample of elements within each of the clusters selected in the first stage. You would then have a two-stage cluster sample.

Mundane files. A set of files used by fieldworkers for keeping track of all the information they have about specific people, organizations, and events in the setting they are observing. There might be a file for a specific person, for example, and each time that person appeared in a day's field notes, a copy of that day's notes would be put in the file.

No treatment control subjects. In experimental and quasi-experimental designs, some subjects are exposed to a manipulation in order to see if the manipulation makes a difference. Other subjects are not exposed to the manipution. The latter are referred to as No Treatment Control Subjects. The function they serve is to give you something to compare against the results from those exposed to the manipulation.

Nomothetic. A general type of research in which the goal is to arrive at general principles of behavior by extracting the commonalities from large numbers of cases. Nomothetic research is usually contrasted with idiographic research, the detailed study of individual cases.

Nonequivalent groups. In designing certain quasi-experiments, it is often necessary to use different, intact groups for the treatment and control conditions. Because these groups are different at the outset, they are referred to as nonequivalent. The problem is that when the treatment and control groups differ *after* your intervention, you may not know if it was the intervention that produced the difference or whether it was that initial nonequivalence that caused the difference.

Nonreactive. Research that neither creates in subjects an awareness that they are taking part in research nor does anything that would alter their natural responses is said to be nonreactive. It does not create a reaction in subjects.

Nonresponse bias. In survey research, this is a distortion created when some members of a sample choose not to respond to your questions. The problem is that the people who choose not to respond may differ in some systematic way from the people who respond. Thus, absence of data from the nonresponders makes the information you have unrepresentative of the population.

Nonverbal behavior. Any behavior other than vocalization, that is, all of the gestures, manners of dress, posture, tics, facial expressions, ways of walking that tell you something (maybe) about the person in question.

Objectives. Once policy has been established in evaluation research it is necessary to set specific objectives. These are particular goals to be accomplished in the implementation of the policy.

Observation. The act of attending to the people or situation of interest. Observation is so commonplace that we tend to forget how important it is. We also develop rather sloppy habits of observation because quite often we do not need to attend to every detail of a situation. For good research, detailed observation is a must.

Observational research. Research in which you do not manipulate anything, but simply look at or listen to (or both) what is going on. It comes in two basic varieties: participant and nonparticipant. In the former, you enter into the setting of interest and try to learn all there is to learn about it. In the latter, your interest is usually somewhat more focused on a few behaviors in the hope that observing those will answer one or two specific questions.

Observational systems. Very similar to behavior code, which was defined earlier. An observational system is a set of definitions of behaviors you intend to observe and some rules about the conditions under which your observations are to be made.

Observer drift. When two or more observers are watching and coding the same sequences of behaviors, it has often been found that they come increasingly to agree with each other, but gradually to move away from the strict definitions and rules specified in the behavior code; that is, they drift. One way to solve the problem is to have frequent reviews and drills on the behavior code. Observer drift can, of course, occur when there is only one observer.

Observer training. What all good observers need–lots and lots. Training involves memorization of the behavior code or observer's manual and practice using the code. But practice is not enough. The *sine qua non* is practice with corrective feedback, that is, going over mistakes and trying to do a better job next time.

Obtrusive. In research, this is something that you do not want to be. (If you have any taste, you do not want to be obtrusive in your personal life, either.) Webster defines obtrusive as calling attention to oneself. For an investigator, this is undesirable because it may change the behavior of the people being observed. Making them too aware of the fact that they are being observed (or tested, or listened to, or experimented upon) is likely to decrease the spontaneity of their behavior.

One group pretest–posttest design. A quasi-experimental design in which observations are made on one group of subjects before and after some intervention or manipulation. This design is not as good as the pretest–posttest design with control group for inferring whether or not the intervention really made a difference.

One-shot case study. A form of research in which you make some observations or measurements or both on the members of a group after an event has occurred to the group. The problem is that you have nothing with which to compare your observations. The group might have been precisely the same before the event occurred, but you have no way of knowing.

Open-ended questions. Questions that cannot be answered with a simple yes or no statement of fact. The point of open-ended questions is to encourage subjects to elaborate, to give fuller information. An example is, "How do you feel about the President's economic program?"

Operant. This is a term from learning theory. It refers to a behavior that is emitted or performed spontaneosly, that is, with no apparent provocation. Such behaviors are of interest because it has been found that once they are emitted, the probability of their future occurence can be increased if they are followed by some form of reinforcement.

Operationalization. Picking a measure or index that you are willing to accept as an indicator of the concept you are interested in. For example, you might select grade point average as your way of measuring intelligence. If you did, a lot of people would argue with you about it because GPA reflects many things in addition to intelligence. For example, it is also a function of effort.

Optical illusion. An effect by which what you think you see is different from what is really out there. Good magicians are masters at creating optical illusions. You think you see them pull a dollar from behind someone's ear, but they really pull it from between their own fingers.

Outcropping. A geological term referring to projections of underlying rock strata that break through the topsoil at various points. In connection with archival research, the term refers to the fact that many social phenomena are manifest in a variety of ways. Hence, quite different indices might plausibly be used to measure the same underlying phenomenon. Increased authoritarianism of an age, for example, might be reflected in police budgets (going up) or library withdrawals of books on psychology (going down). Both of those would be outcroppings of the same thing.

Panel study. A type of survey in which members of a sample are interviewed repeatedly. The purpose is to trace changes over time in the variables of interest.

Participant observation. A general research method, most often used by anthropologists, in which the researcher immerses himself or herself in the day-to-day activities of the people he or she wishes to study. Margaret Mead, for example, lived among the natives of Samoa while doing the research that served as the basis of her book *Coming of Age in Samoa*.

Patched-up design. The basic all-purpose design for the versatile experimenter. A patched-up design is constructed by adding the conditions and measures that are required in the particular circumstances confronting you. You add whatever is needed to make the comparisons that need to be made and rule out any and all plausible alternative explanations.

Perception. The process of taking-in information by a human. Perception includes a variety of subprocesses such as attention, short-term memory, and rehearsal of short-term memory.

Plausible alternative explanation. In an experiment, one or more plausible alternative explanations are reasons other than the manipulation that can reasonably be argued to have produced the change observed in the dependent variable.

Policy. In the context of evaluation research, policy is the general statement of goals deemed desirable. Usually, one or more programs may be implemented to accomplish those goals.

Population of interest. The complete collection of elements constituting a group: all the people in the United States; all the left handed biology majors at Slippery Rock State College.

Posttest only design with nonequivalent groups. A quasi-experimental design in which members of an intact group are exposed to an intervention or manipulation. Subsequent observations of that group are then compared to observations of another group that was not exposed to the intervention. The basic problem with this design is that you often have no way of knowing if the two groups were really equivalent before the intervention occurred.

Preexisting conceptual scheme. Beliefs that we all carry around in our heads about what-is-likely-to-be-related-to-what. Such beliefs can fog our perceptions by making it easier for us to think that we have observed something when, in fact, we have not. Expectations and stereotypes are closely related and exert similar biasing influences.

Premises. Underlying assumptions that one usually does not feel the need to test or gather evidence on. I assume, for example, that you are a reasonable person. Of course, I have been wrong before.

Pretesting. The relatively informal trying out of a set of questions (say, for an interview schedule) to see whether they are eliciting the type of information you are after or to make sure they are understandable. In an experiment, you might pretest your manipulation on a few people to see whether or not it is perceived as intended. The word pretest is also used to refer to the initial measurement of attitudes or beliefs or behavior in some research in which the design is pretest-manipulation-posttest. The point, of course, is to see whether the manipulation makes a difference in whatever it is you are measuring on the pretest and the posttest.

Pretest–posttest control group design. A design in which observations are made on two groups, before and after an intervention or manipulation occurs to one of the groups. If subjects can be randomly assigned to the two groups, it will be a true experiment.

Primacy effect. The tendency of the first information we obtain about another person or event to be given undue weight; the reason so many people think it is important to make a good first impression on others.

Principle of specification. When asking questions in an interview, it is important to be precise about the context of the question. Otherwise, the respondent may not understand exactly what information you are seeking.

Principle of tacit assumption. In asking questions, it is important to recognize that there are certain common understandings, assumptions that are shared by most members of a culture. Thus, if your question touches on one of these, it is likely to be ignored because the respondent will not bother to mention something that everybody knows and takes for granted. The question must be worded to make clear precisely what you are after.

Proactive records. Records biased by their keepers for any of a variety of reasons. Record keepers are people and they may bias the records they are keeping. Whether the motive is simply to make themselves look good or to protect their job, you need to be aware that records do serve the purposes of their keepers and, hence, may be biased.

Probes. Follow-up questions or comments used to try to get people to elaborate on answers given in an interview, for example, "Could you tell me a little more about that?" "And what did you do then?"

Programs. The means for realizing policy in evaluation research. Programs are the particular procedures and plans for achieving a certain social, educational, or medical effect.

Proxemics. A word popularized by the anthropologist Edward Hall. It refers to the study of the way in which people (and animals) use and structure the space around them. It comes from the word proximity, which Webster defines as the state or quality of being near or close. As a little exercise in proxemics, you might try standing about six inches away from your course instructor when you tell him or her what you thought of this course.

Quantification. The process of transforming concepts and ideas into measurable entities.

Quasi-experimental designs. Research designs that only approximate being truly experimental. For example, in some situations you may not be able to randomly assign subjects to conditions. Or, you may not be able to manipulate the independent variable, but rather you may be forced to rely on some naturally occurring change.

Quota matrix. An array used to classify subjects on several different variables, such as age and sex. A quota matrix is useful in assigning subjects to the conditions of an experiment. If you have four conditions, for example, but only three females between the ages of 16 and 21, you will not be able to use those subjects in your experiment because you do not have enough to assign one to each condition.

Radio telemetry. The use of radio transmitters to monitor the movements, vocalizations, and other behaviors of subjects.

Randomized trials. A phrase used in medical and epidemiological research to refer to experiments in which subjects are randomly assigned to conditions. Usually such research is intended as a trial of a new drug or treatment or life-style change. Randomized trials are vastly superior to clinical impressions in establishing that the new drug or procedure is effective.

Randomization. The process of assigning subjects to conditions in such a way that each subject has an equal chance to be assigned to each condition. Also referred to as random assignment.

Random numbers. The numbers in an array (usually a table) in which each digit has an equal chance of being followed by each of the digits 0 through 9. Such tables are useful in the process of randomization (*see* above). For instructions on how to use a table of random numbers, see the Appendix.

Random sampling. Selecting your sample in such a way that every element in the population of interest has an equal chance of being included in the sample.

Rational approach. Research in which you decide ahead of time exactly which behaviors you are going to observe in order to obtain some evidence on the question of interest to you. Rational approach is usually contrasted with empirical approach.

Reactive research. Research that produces a change in the way a subject would "naturally" respond is said to be reactive. In general, experimentation is much more reactive than archival research, for example.

Reader's Guide to Periodical Literature. A useful publication that you may find in your library. It lists current and past magazine and journal articles from about 180 general and nontechnical periodicals published in the United States.

Reinforcement. Anything that follows a given behavior and increases the probability that that behavior will occur again is said to have reinforced the performance of the behavior. If you receive an A on tests after you study hard, you will study hard for the next test, thus, receiving A's reinforces studying (assuming, of course, that you value good grades).

Reliability. A measure is said to be reliable if it gives the same result when used again under the same conditions.

Reliability of coders. In content analysis, a coder is the person who reads the material and scores it for the presence or absence of certain concepts. A coder is reliable if on rereading and rescoring the same material, he or she produces the same results, that is, scores the same concepts as having been present. With two coders reading the same material, reliability refers to how similar their results are. Do they score the same concepts as having been present in the material scored?

Replication. This is a term meaning repeatability. One of the requirements of a good science is that the observations and experiments that form its foundation be repeatable or replicable. If Newton were the only person who had ever seen apples fall to earth, physics would be in trouble.

Representative sample. A sample is representative of a population if the nature and distribution of attributes within the sample correspond to the nature and distribution of those same attributes in the population.

Research design. The process of deciding what procedures, measures, subjects, and paraphenalia you will need to test your hypotheses. Often the most creative, exciting part of the entire research process.

Research interview. A social interaction between two people in which the interviewer initiates and varyingly controls the exchange with the respondent for the purpose of obtaining quantifiable and comparable information relevent to an emerging or stated hypothesis.

Respondent. A person who is interviewed or administered a questionnaire in survey research. He or she who responds to the questions.

Response variability. When different people respond to a stimulus, such as a question in an interview, they may respond differently . Some will be positive and some negative, some will agree and some will disagree. The distribution of those responses is what is referred to as response variability.

Retrospective context. To understand what a given behavior means, the researcher must consider the events that preceded it. Those prior events from which the behavior emerged are referred to as the retrospective context.

Return rate. In survey research in which questionnaires are mailed to respondents who are asked to fill them out and mail them back, the return rate is the percentage of the entire sample who actually return the questionnaires. If 100 were sent out and 69 came back, the return rate would be 69 percent.

Reversed items. In measuring some concepts in survey research, it is often useful to have two or more items attempting to assess the same thing. Changing the structure of the items so that a person who would agree with one would be expected to disagree with another is what is meant by reversing items. It is useful as a check that respondents are really answering to the best of their ability and not just saying yes (or no) to everything.

Role playing. Research in which subjects are asked to imagine themselves in a certain situation and tell you how they would respond. If you decide to use this approach, which I do not recommend, just be very careful about what you conclude. Remember, you will have *no* evidence about how subjects *actually* respond in those situations. What people say and what they do are often quite different.

Rube Goldberg. A cartoonist of the early twentieth century who was famous for his inventions of elaborate, intricate, awkward devices that were designed to accomplish very simple things, such as watering a flower or putting out a candle. Some theories of social behavior appear to have been devised by Rube's intellectual descendants.

Role/rule framework. The norms and implicit rules that govern behavior in specific situations.

Rule of thumb. A bit of advice based on practical experience. An example of a rule of thumb is that past performance is the best predictor of future performance.

Salience. Having a quality of standing out, being distinctive. For the participant observer, the salience of certain people or features in a setting is a source of bias. There is some evidence that we tend to devote too much attention to salient features of a setting. Hence, some less salient but, perhaps, more important things may escape our attention.

Sample. A subset of the elements of a population, chosen for study with the hope that what is found to be true of the sample will be true for the population.

Sampling. The process of selecting the units of interest. In content analysis, for example, it is often necessary to select texts to be analyzed. In survey research, one must select respondents to be interviewed. There are a variety of different techniques for sampling and a variety of different types of samples.

Sampling frame. A list of all the elements in a population. Used as a basis for selecting a sample.

Sampling interval. If all the elements in a population are arranged in a list and you decide to take every *nth* element as your sample, then *n* is your sampling interval.

Schedule. The set of questions to be asked in an interview.

Scheduled interview. An interview in which you have a fixed set of questions and ask them in the same order of all respondents.

Selective deposit. A problem for archival researchers is that some of the things of interest may never have gotten put down on paper; only certain parts of the past make their way into records. This is what is referred to as selective deposit.

Selective survival. Many records of the past simply do not survive very long. They rot or are damaged by fire or are thrown out. Thus, the available records in archives are not necessarily all that were once available. Only some survive.

Self report. Much of the data in the social and behavioral sciences is obtained by simply asking people questions or having them fill out questionnaires. Such data are self reports; people tell you about themselves, their attitudes, opinions, behaviors. There are a number of biases that may make such data suspect, including the understandable desire of people to present themselves in the best possible light. Thus, whenever possible, it is a good idea to obtain other kinds of data to validate self reports.

Self-selected sample. When the members of a sample that you have selected decide for themselves who will and who will not respond, the result is a self-selected sample. The problem is that you have no way of knowing how the respondents differ from the nonrespondents.

Self symbolizing behaviors. Behaviors that people perform in order to let others know who and what they are. People who want others to know that they are joggers, for example, might wear jogging shoes all the time, that is, even when they are not actively huffing and puffing down the road.

Sensitizing function of research and theory. One of the functions that research or theory can serve is to heighten people's awareness about what is possible. Milgram's research, in which relatively minimal pressure was sufficient to induce normal people to inflict great pain on another, served such a function.

Sharpening. When people retell a story or passage from memory, it has been found that they often accentuate one or two details and make them the focus of the story. This is referred to as sharpening.

Simple random sample. A sample selected from a population without the use of a sampling interval, but in which every member of the population has an equal chance of appearing in the sample. One way to select such a sample would be to number all the members of the population, put the numbers on slips of paper in a hat, and draw out as many slips as you want in your sample. The members of the population whose numbers you draw out would be your simple random sample.

Simulation. A model that attempts to capture and represent in a different, usually smaller and simpler, form the essential characteristics of the thing modeled.

Simulation gap. The differences between the nature of simulations and the nature of the systems they are supposedly imitating.

Single factor design. An experiment in which there is only one independent variable.

Social facilitation. In has been found that the presence of other people affects behavior. Generally, the presence of others will enhance the performance of well-known responses and this enhancement is referred to a social facilitation.

Social desirability bias. The tendency of people to want the approval of others can distort research findings. In Survey research, for example, respondents may be reluctant to tell you anything negative about themselves because they fear you might disapprove. Thus, they may give you a socially desirable answer that differs from the truth.

Socially desirable behaviors. Socially desirable behaviors are those behaviors that are approved and accepted by the society around you: making good grades, being polite, dressing neatly.

Solomon four group design. An experimental design in which two groups are pretested and two are not. Then one pretested and one non-pretested group are exposed to the intervention or manipulation. Subsequently, all four groups are tested.

Spatial behavior. Behavior that has to do with the way in which people structure and use the space around them. Such behaviors can often be used as the focus of your observation or the dependent variable in experimental research.

Specifications. The guidelines for dealing with problems in fitting interview respondents' answers into categories.

Standardization. Refers to the processes involved in making and keeping the components of research the same for all subjects.

Static group comparison. A quasi-experimental design in which one group has been exposed to an intervention or manipulation and you have some observations on that group after the fact. In addition you have observations on another group not exposed to the intervention.

Stereotyping. Attributing characteristics to objects, people, and events on the basis of your beliefs about what they are usually like. A bad thing to do, of course, because it can blind you to what they are really like.

Stratification variable. In survey research, a stratification variable is used to divide a sample into subgroups, such as males and females (sex would be the stratification variable in that case). Stratification variables enable the researcher to see whether the results are the same in different subgroups. They are also of use in explanatory analysis.

Stratified sampling. If the population of interest to you contains two or more distinct subgroups, such as males and females, you may select your sample in a manner designed to insure that the members of the subgroups are represented in the sample in proportion to their presence in the population. If you do, you will have a stratified sample.

Street theater strategy. A method of securing the participation of subjects in field experiments. A minidrama is enacted in public in a manner designed to attract the attention of everyone in the immediate vicinity. The reactions of those who witness such events are usually the variables of interest.

Subgroup analysis. In survey research, subgroup analysis involves dividing your sample into two or more subsamples on the basis of a stratification variable. For example, when sex is the stratification variable, you divide your sample into males and females to see whether what you found for the sample as a whole holds true for both males and females.

Summative evaluation. The determination of the effectiveness of a social, educational, or medical program. Also referred to as impact assessment.

Survey research. The most well known of the methodologies of social science. It involves interviewing, or admininstering a questionnaire, to a sample of respondents chosen to represent a population of interest.

Syllogism. A format for the expression of logical deductions. There are three parts: a major premise, a minor premise, and a conclusion. The major premise usually states a general principle (All men are mortal). The minor premise usually states a fact (Dogood P. Osborne is a man). The conclusion states what one can conclude from the preceding (Even ole' Dogood is going to cash in his chips one day – er, ahem. Dogood is mortal).

Systematic random sampling. In survey research, the basis for selecting a sample is often a list of all the elements in the population. The list is referred to as a sampling frame. You take a systematic sample by selecting every *nth* element on the list as your sample. You get to choose *n*, also.

Theoretical elaboration. One of the major purposes of research, to increase our understanding by the process of proposing and testing explanations and formulating those that are verified into ever more comprehensive theories. Theories help us make sense of facts and guide us in our search for more.

Theory. A proposed explanation for some empirical (observed) phenomena. A theory is usually thought of as being a little more elaborate than an hypothesis. One way to think of it might be that one proposed explanation constitutes an hypothesis. Two or more related hypotheses constitute a theory.

Threats to external validity. Sources of bias that would prevent you from generalizing the results of your research to other places, other times, or other subjects. Specific threats to external validity are enumerated in Chapters Nine and Ten.

Threats to internal validity. Sources of bias that would prevent you from claiming that your independent variable really made a difference in your dependent variable. Specific threats to internal validity are enumerated in Chapter Seven.

Treatments. A statistical term referring to different degrees or stages of the independent variable present in an experiment. If the independent variable is simply present or absent, there are two treatments. If you have low, medium, and high amounts of the independent variable in different conditions, you have three treatments, and so on. Same as levels.

Triangulation of measurement. Very similar to multiple operationism. The basic idea is that you should measure the things of interest in more than one way – just in case one of your measuring sticks is warped. If you are interested in loyalty within groups, for example, you should think of several different ways of assessing how loyal group members are: How long do they stay in the group? Do they say bad things about the group to others? How hard do they work on group projects?

Unit of analysis. In survey research, the unit of analysis usually corresponds to an element of the population of interest. The entities about which you want to find out something: people, families, cities, countries.

Unobtrusive. Similar to nonreactive. Measures or procedures of research that do not interfere with or change the natural responses of a subject.

Unrepresentative sample. Some instances of the things or events or people of interest that are generally different from most of them. The people who are consistently late to a class are probably an unrepresentative sample of the entire class. Perpetual tardiness probably indicates lack of interest or an inability to plan one's time well—qualities that other members of the class might not share.

Unscheduled interview. An interview in which you do not follow a script with instructions for your presentation, wording, and sequence of questions. You have some freedom in fitting the questions to the respondent and the situation.

Unscheduled standardized interview. An interview that seeks to achieve comparability of responses by asking each respondent questions in an appropriate vocabulary, order, and manner so that the interview will mean the identical thing to all respondents.

Unscheduled unstandardized interview. An interview in which you ask different respondents different questions as you find out what and how much they can contribute to your knowledge of the topic of interest.

Validity. A measure is valid to the extent that it really measures what it is supposed to—nothing more and nothing less. A valid indicator of self-esteem, for example, would be one on which only those people with high self-esteem scored high and only those people who thought poorly of themselves scored low.

Verification. The process of testing proposed explanations and theories to see whether they are, in fact, accurate. Verification is a crucial step in the research process.

Bibliography

Abelson, R. P. (1968). Simulation of social behavior. In G. Lindzey & E. Aronson (Eds.), *Handbook of social psychology* (2nd ed.). Reading, MA: Addison-Wesley.

Abelson, R. P., & Miller, J. C. (1967). Negative persuasion via personal insult. *Journal of Experimental Social Psychology, 3,* 321–333.

Abt, C. C. (1979). Government constraints on evaluation quality. In L. E. Datta & R. Perloff (Eds.), *Improving evaluations* (pp. 43 – 52). Beverly Hills, CA: Sage.

Adams, J. L. (1980). *Conceptual blockbusting: A guide to better ideas* (2nd ed.). New York: Norton.

Adorno, T. W., Frenkel-Brunswik, E., Levinson, D., & Sanford, R. N. (1950). *The authoritarian personality.* New York: Harper.

Allport, G. W. (1937). *Pattern and growth in personality.* New York: Holt, Rinehart & Winston.

Allport, G. W. (1942). *The use of personal documents in psychological science.* New York: Social Science Research Council.

Allport, G. W., & Postman, L. (1947). *The psychology of rumor.* New York: Holt, Rinehart & Winston.

Altman, I. (1975). *The environment and social behavior: Privacy, personal space, territory, crowding.* Monterey, CA: Brooks/Cole.

American Psychological Association. (1973). *Ethical principles in the conduct of research with human subjects.* Washington, DC: American Psychological Association.

Archer, D., Gartner, R., Akert, R., & Lockwood, T. (1978). Cities and homicide: A new look at an old paradox. *Comparative Studies in Sociology, 1,* 73–95.

Aronson, E., & Carlsmith, J. M. (1968). Experimentation in social psychology. In G. Lindzey & E. Aronson (Eds.), *Handbook of Social Psychology* (2nd ed.). Reading, MA: Addison-Wesley.

Asch, S. (1952). *Social psychology.* New York: Prentice-Hall.

Associated Press. (1983, March 10). Electronic bracelet will let offenders do time at home. *Lexington Herald-Leader,* p. A–15

Auden, W. H., & Kronenberger, L. (1966). *The Viking book of aphorisms.* New York: Viking Press.

Automobile Manufacturers' Association, Inc. (1966). *The state of the art of traffic safety: A critical review and analysis of the technical information on factors affecting traffic safety.* Cambridge, England: Arthur D. Little.

Babbie, E. R. (1973). *Survey research methods.* Belmont, CA: Wadsworth.

Baker, E. H. (1968). A pre-civil war simulation for teaching American history. In S. S. Boocock & E. O. Schild (Eds.), *Simulation games in learning*. Beverly Hills, CA: Sage.

Bales, R. F. (1950). *Interaction process analysis*. Cambridge, MA: Addison-Wesley.

Bales, R. F. (1970). *Personality and interpersonal behavior*. New York: Holt, Rinehart & Winston.

Banuazizi, A., & Movahedi, S. (1975). Interpersonal dynamics in a simulated prison: A methodological analysis. *American Psychologist, 30,* 152–160.

Barber, T. X. (1976). *Pitfalls in human research: Ten pivotal points*. New York: Pergamon.

Barber, T. X., & Silver, M. J. (1968). Fact, fiction and the experimenter bias effect. *Psychological Bulletin Monograph Supplement, 70,* 1–29.

Bartlett, F. C. (1932). *Remembering*. Cambridge: Cambridge University Press.

Barton, E. M., Baltes, M. M., & Orzech, M. J. (1980). Etiology of dependence in older nursing home residents during morning care: The role of staff behavior. *Journal of Personality and Social Psychology, 38,* 423–431.

Baum, A., Fleming, R., & Singer, J. E. (1982). Stress at three mile island: Applying psychological impact analysis. In L. Bickman (Ed.), *Applied Social Psychology Annual (Vol. 3)* (pp. 217–248). Beverly Hills, CA: Sage.

Baumrind, D. (1964). Some thoughts on ethics of research: After reading Milgram's behavioral study of obedience. *American Psychologist, 19,* 421–423.

Becker, H. S., & Geer, B. (1970). Participant observation and interviewing: A comparison. In W. J. Filstead (Ed.), *Qualitative methodology: Firsthand involvement with the social world*. Chicago: Markham.

Benney, M., Riesman, D., & Star, S. A. (1956). Age and sex in the interview. *American Journal of Sociology, 62,* 143–152.

Bergmann, B. R. (1982, December 12). The failures of a chair-bound science. *The New York Times*, Section 3, page 3.

Berkun, M. M., Bialek, H. M., Kern, R. P., & Yagi, K. (1962). Experimental studies of psychological stress in man. *Psychological Monographs, 76,* 1–39.

Beveridge, W. I. B. (1957). *The art of scientific investigation* (3rd ed.). New York: Vintage Books.

Bochner, S. (1979). Designing unobtrusive field experiments in social psychology. In L. Sechrest (Ed.), *Unobtrusive measurement today. New Directions for Methodology of Behavioral Science* (No. 1). San Francisco: Jossey-Bass.

Boice, R. (1983). Observational skills. *Psychological Bulletin, 93,* 3–29.

Boocock, S. S. (1968). An experimental study of the learning effects of two games with simulated environments. In S. S. Boocock & E. O. Schild (Eds.), *Simulation games in learning*. Beverly Hills, CA: Sage.

Bowers, K. S. (1973). Situationism in psychology: An analysis and a critique. *Psychological Review, 80,* 307–336.

Box, G. E. P., Hunter, W. G., & Hunter, J. S. (1978). *Statistics for experimenters: An introduction to design, data analysis, and model building*. New York: Wiley.

Bradburn, N. M. (1982). Question wording effects in surveys. In R. M. Hogarth (Ed.), Question framing and response consistency. *New Directions for Methodology of Social and Behavioral Science* (No. 11). San Francisco: Jossey-Bass.

Bruner, J. S. (1951). Personality dynamics and the process of perceiving. In R. R. Blake & G. V. Ramsey (Eds.), *Perception—An Approach to Personality*. New York: Ronald Press.

Brush, S. G. (1974). Should the history of science be rated X? *Science, 183*, 1164–1172.

Burchard, W. (1958). Lawyers, political scientists, sociologists—and concealed microphones. *American Sociological Review, 23*, 686–691.

Burger, J. M., Oakman, J. A., & Bullard, N. G. (1983). Desire for control and the perception of crowding. *Personality and Social Psychology Bulletin, 9*, 475–479.

Byrne, D. (1971). *The attraction paradigm.* New York: Academic Press.

Campbell, B. M. (1982, December 12). Black executives and corporate stress. *The New York Times Magazine*, 36–39, 100, 102, 104–107.

Campbell, D. T. (1957). Factors relevant to the validity of experiments in social settings. *Psychological Bulletin, 54*, 297–312.

Campbell, D. T. (1969a). Prospective: Artifact and control. In R. Rosenthal & R. L. Rosnow (Eds.), *Artifact in behavioral research.* New York: Academic Press.

Campbell, D. T. (1969b). Reforms as experiments. *American Psychologist, 24*, 409–429.

Campbell, D. T., & Stanley, J. (1966). *Experimental and quasi-experimental designs for research.* Chicago: Rand McNally.

Cannell, C. F., & Kahn, R. L. (1968). Interviewing. In G. Lindzey & E. Aronson (Eds.), *Handbook of social psychology* (2nd ed.). Reading, MA: Addison-Wesley.

Carpenter, E. (1965). Comment on "Research among the Eskimo." *Current Anthropology, 6* (1), 55–60.

Cartwright, D. (1953). Analysis of qualitative material. In L. Festinger & D. Katz (Eds.), *Research methods in the behavioral sciences.* New York: Holt, Rinehart & Winston.

Center for Disease Control. (1979). *Reported morbidity and mortality in the United States, 1978.* Atlanta, GA: U. S. Department of Health, Education & Welfare Publication No. (CDC) 79-8241.

Chamberlain, T. C. (1965). The method of multiple working hypotheses. *Science, 148*, 754–759. (Original work published 1890.)

Cochran, N. (1978). Grandma Moses and the 'corruption' of data. *Evaluation Quarterly, 2*, 363–373.

Cochran, N. (1980). Society as emergent and more than rational: An essay on the inappropriateness of program evaluation. *Policy Sciences, 12*, 113–129.

Cochran, N., Gordon, A. C., & Krause, M. S. (1980). Proactive records: Reflections on the village watchman. *Knowledge, 2* (1), 5–18.

Cohen, C. E. (1977). Cognitive basis of stereotyping. Paper presented at the 85th Annual Convention of the American Psychological Association, San Francisco, CA.

Cohen, C. E. (1981). Person categories and social perception: Testing some boundaries of the processing effects of prior knowledge. *Journal of Personality and Social Psychology, 40*, 441–452.

Cohen, J. L., & Davis, J. H. (1973). Effects of audience status, evaluation, and time of action on performance with hidden-word problems. *Journal of Personality and Social Psychology, 27*, 74–85.

Coffey, T. M. (1975). *The long thirst: Prohibition in America: 1920–1933.* New York: Dell.

Cole, S. (1969). *The unionization of teachers: A case study of the UFT.* New York: Praeger.

Cole, S. (1972). *The sociological method.* Chicago: Markham.

Collins, B. E., Whalen, C. K., & Henker, B. (1980). Ecological and pharmacological influences on behaviors in the classrooom: The hyperkinetic syndrome. In S. Salziner, J. Antrobus, & J. Glick (Eds.), *The ecosystem of the "sick child."* New York: Academic Press.

Cone, J. D., & Foster, S. L. (1982). Direct observation in clinical psychology. In P. C. Kendall and J. N. Butcher (Eds.), *Handbook of research methods in clinical psychology.* New York: Wiley.

Cook, T. D., & Campbell, D. T. (1979). *Quasi-experimentation: Design and analysis issues for field settings.* Chicago: Rand McNally.

Coombs, R. H. & Goldman, L. J. (1973). Maintenance and discontinuity of coping mechanisms in an intensive care unit. *Social Problems, 20,* 342–355.

Cooper, J., & Jones, R. A. (1970). Self-esteem and consistency as determinants of anticipatory opinion change. *Journal of Personality and Social Psychology, 14,* 312–320.

Cottrell, N. B. (1968). Performance in the presence of other human beings: Mere presence, audience, and affiliation effects. In E. C. Simmel, R. A. Hoppe, & G. A. Milton (Eds.), *Social facilitation and imitative behavior.* Boston: Allyn & Bacon.

Cronbach, L. J. (1957). The two disciplines of scientific psychology. *American Psychologist, 12,* 671–684.

Cronbach, L. J. (1975). Beyond the two disciplines of scientific psychology. *American Psychologist, 30,* 116–127.

Cronbach, L. J. (1977). Remarks to the new society. *Evaluation Research Society Newsletter, 1*(1), 1–3.

Cronbach, L. J., Ambron, S. R., Dornbusch, S. M., Hess, R. D., Hornik, R. C., Phillips, D. C., Walker, D. F., & Weiner, S. S. (1981). *Toward reform of program evaluation.* San Francisco: Jossey-Bass.

Crowne, D. & Marlowe, D. (1964). *The approval motive.* New York: Wiley.

Dailey, C. A. (1952). The effects of premature conclusions upon the acquisition of understanding of a person. *Journal of Psychology, 33,* 133–152.

Darwin, C. (1972). *The voyage of the Beagle.* New York: Bantam Books, (Original work published 1835).

Dawes, R. M. (1972). *Fundamentals of attitude measurement.* New York: Wiley.

Dawes, R. M., McTavish, J., & Shaklee, H. (1977). Behavior, communication, and assumptions about other people's behavior in a commons dilemma situation. *Journal of Personality and Social Psychology, 35,* 1–11.

Deci, E. L., Betley, G., Kahle, J., Abrams, L., & Porac, J. (1981). When trying to win: Competition and intrinsic motivation. *Personality and Social Psychology Bulletin, 7,* 79–83.

Deutscher, I. (1966). Words and deeds: Social science and social policy. *Social Problems, 13,* 233–254.

Dexter, L. A. (1970). *Elite and specialized interviewing.* Evanston, IL: Northwestern University Press.

Dickson, P. (1978). *The official rules.* New York: Delacorte Press.

Diener, E., & Crandall, R. (1978). *Ethics in social and behavioral research.* Chicago: University of Chicago Press.

Dillehay, R. C. (1973). On the irrelevance of the classical negative evidence concerning the effect of attitudes on behavior. *American Psychologist, 28,* 887–891.

Dillehay, R. C., & Nietzel, M. T. (1980a). Constructing a science of jury behavior. In L. Wheeler (Ed.), *Review of Personality and Social Psychology* (Vol. 1). Beverly Hills, CA: Sage.

Dillehay, R. C., & Nietzel, M. T. (1980b). Conceptualizing mock jury/juror research: Critique and illustration. In K. S. Larsen (Ed.), *Social psychology: Crisis or failure.* Monmouth, OR: Institute for Theoretical History.

Dillehay, R. C., & Nietzel, M. T. (1982). The influence of juror experience on jury decision making. A research proposal submitted to the National Science Foundation.

Doob, A. N., Carlsmith, J. M., Freedman, J. L., Landauer, T. K., & Soleng, T. (1969). Effects of initial selling price on subsequent sales. *Journal of Personality and Social Psychology, 11,* 345–350.

Doob, A. N., & MacDonald, G. E. (1979). Television viewing and fear of victimization: Is the relationship causal? *Journal of Personality and Social Psychology, 37,* 170–179.

Dowd, M. (1983, December 4). Work and motherhood tie in survey of women's values. *Lexington Herald-Leader,* p. A–29.

Duncan, S. & Rosenthal, R. (1968). Vocal emphasis in experimenters' instruction reading as unintended determinant of subjects' responses. *Language and Speech, 11,* 20–26.

Dykman, B. M., & Reis, H. T. (1979). Personality and correlation of classroom seating position. *Journal of Educational Psychology, 71,* 346–354.

Edney, J. J., & Harper, C. S. (1978). The commons dilemma: A review of contributions from psychology. *Environmental Management, 2,* 491–507.

Eichna, L. W. (1980). Medical-school education, 1975–1979: A student's perspective. *New England Journal of Medicine, 303,* 727–734.

Eisenberg, L. (1972). The *human* nature of human nature. *Science, 176,* 123–128.

Ellsworth, P. C. (1977). From abstract ideas to concrete instances: Some guidelines for choosing natural settings. *American Psychologist, 32,* 604–615.

Erdelyi, M. H. (1974). A new look at the new look: Perceptual defense and vigilance. *Psychological Review, 81,* 1–25.

Erlich, J., & Riesman, D. (1961). Age and authority in the interview. *Public Opinion Quarterly, 25,* 39–56.

Evans, R. I. (1976). *The making of psychology.* New York: Alfred A. Knopf.

Evans, R. I., Hanson, W. B., & Mittelmark, M. B. (1977). Increasing the validity of self-reports of smoking behavior in children. *Journal of Applied Psychology, 62,* 521–523.

Eysenck, H. J. (1965). *Smoking, health, and personality.* New York: Basic Books.

Eysenck, H. J. (1980). *The causes and effects of smoking.* London: Maurice Temple Smith.

Farrell, B. (1975). George in the afternoon: An adventure in group journalism. *Harper's, 251,* 81–82.

Festinger, L., Riecken, H. W., & Schachter, S. (1956). *When prophecy fails: A social and psychological study of a modern group that predicted the destruction of the world.* New York: Harper & Row.

Fiedler, F. E. (1955). The influence of leader-keyman relations on combat crew effectiveness. *Journal of Abnormal and Social Psychology, 51,* 227–235.

Fiedler, F. E. (1973). Predicting the effects of leadership training and experience from the contingency model: A clarification. *Journal of Applied Psychology, 57,* 110–113.

Fischhoff, B. (1980). For those condemned to study the past: Reflections on historical judgment. In R. A. Shweder (Ed.), Fallible judgment in behavior research. *New Directions for Methodology of Social and Behavioral Science* (No. 4). San Francisco: Jossey-Bass.

Fiske, D. W. (1980). When are verbal reports veridical? In R. A. Shweder (Ed.), Fallible judgment in behavioral research. *New Directions for Methodology of Social and Behavioral Science* (No. 4). San Francisco: Jossey-Bass.

Ford, T. R. (1977). The production of social knowledge for public use. *Social Forces, 56,* 504–518.

Fox, D. (1967). *Expansion of the more effective schools program.* New York: Center for Urban Education.

Freedman, J. L. (1969). Role playing: Psychology by consensus. *Journal of Personality and Social Psychology, 13,* 107–114.

Freud, S. (1938). *The basic writings of Sigmund Freud* (Edited by A. A. Brill). New York: Random House.

Friedman, H. S. (1982). Nonverbal communication in medical interaction. In H. S. Friedman & M. R. DiMatteo (Eds.), *Interpersonal issues in health care.* New York: Academic Press.

Friedman, N. (1967). *The social nature of psychological research: The psychological experiment as a social interaction.* New York: Basic Books.

Frost, R. (1949). *The complete poems of Robert Frost.* New York: Henry Holt & Company, p. 131.

Gamson, W. A. (1978). *SIMSOC; Coordinator's Manual* (3rd ed.). New York: The Free Press.

Gamson, W. A. (1978). *SIMSOC; Participant's Manual* (3rd ed.). New York: The Free Press.

Gerbner, G., & Gross, L. (1976). The scary world of TV's heavy viewer. *Psychology Today* (April), 41–45, 89.

Gergen, K. J. (1973). Social psychology as history. *Journal of Personality and Social Psychology, 26,* 309–320.

Gergen, K. J. (1978). Experimentation in social psychology: A reappraisal. *European Journal of Social Psychology, 8,* 507–527.

Gergen, K. J. (1980). Toward intellectual audacity in social psychology. In R. Gilmour & S. Duck (Eds.), *The development of social psychology.* London: Academic Press.

Ginsberg, G. P. (1979). The effective use of role-playing in social psychological research. In G. P. Ginsberg (Ed.), *Emerging strategies in social psychological research*. New York: Wiley.

Glaser, B. G., & Straus, A. L. (1967). *The discovery of grounded theory: Strategies for qualitative research*. New York: Aldine.

Glass, D. (1977). *Behavior patterns, stress, and coronary disease*. Hillsdale, NJ: Erlbaum.

Glass, D., & Singer, J. (1972). *Urban stress: Experiments on noise and social stressors*. New York: Academic Press.

Glenn, N. D. (1977). *Cohort analysis*. Beverly Hills, CA: Sage.

Goffman, E. (1959). *The presentation of self in everyday life*. Garden City, NY: Doubleday Anchor.

Goffman, E. (1961). *Asylums*. Garden City, NY: Doubleday Anchor.

Gorden, R. L. (1956). Dimensions of the depth interview. *American Journal of Sociology, 62*, 158–164.

Gorden, R. L. (1969). *Interviewing: Strategy, techniques, and tactics*. Homewood, IL: Dorsey Press.

Gordis, L., & Gold, E. (1980). Privacy, confidentiality, and the use of medical records in research. *Science, 207*, 153–156.

Hall, E. T. (1966). *The hidden dimension*. Garden City, NY: Doubleday.

Haney, C., Banks, C., & Zimbardo, P. (1973). Interpersonal dynamics in a simulated prison. *International Journal of Criminology and Penology, 1*, 69–97.

Hans, V. P. & Slater, D. (1983). John Hinckley, Jr. and the insanity defense: The public's verdict. *Public Opinion Quarterly, 47*, 202–212.

Hardin, G. (1968). The tragedy of the commons. *Science, 166*, 1103–1107.

Harré, R., & Secord, P. (1973). *The explanation of social behavior*. Totowa, NJ: Littlefield, Adams.

Harris, M. (1974). *Cows, pigs, wars, and witches: The riddles of culture*. New York: Crowell.

Hartman, D. P. (1982). Assessing the dependability of observational data. In D. P. Hartman (Ed.), Using observers to study behavior. *New Directions for Methodology of Social and Behavioral Science*, (No. 14). San Francisco: Jossey-Bass.

Hawkins, R. P. (1982). Developing a behavior code. In D. P. Hartman (Ed.), Using observers to study behavior. *New Directions for Methodology of Social and Behavioral Science*, (No. 14). San Francisco: Jossey-Bass.

Hendrick, C. (1977). Role-taking, role-playing, and the laboratory experiment. *Personality and Social Psychology Bulletin, 3*, 467–478.

Hendrick, C., & Jones, R. A. (1972). *The nature of theory and research in social psychology*. New York: Academic Press.

Henle, M., & Hubble, M. B. (1938). "Egocentricity" in adult conversation. *Journal of Social Psychology, 9*, 227–234.

Henshel, R. L. (1980). The purposes of laboratory experimentation and the virtues of deliberate artificiality. *Journal of Experimental Social Psychology, 16*, 466–478.

Heyns, R. W., & Lippitt, R. (1954). Systematic observational techniques. In G. Lindzey (Ed.), *Handbook of social psychology*. Reading, MA: Addison-Wesley.

Higbee, K. L., Lott, W. J., & Graves, J. P. (1976). Experimentation and college students in social psychology research. *Personality and Social Psychology Bulletin, 2*, 239–241.

Hildum, D., & Brown, R. W. (1956). Verbal reinforcement and interviewer bias. *Journal of Abnormal and Social Psychology, 53*, 108–111.

Hite, S. (1976). *The Hite report: A nationwide study of female sexuality.* New York: Macmillan.

Hite, S. (1981). *The Hite report on male sexuality.* New York: Knopf.

Holsti, O. R. (1969). *Content analysis for the social sciences and humanities.* Reading, MA. Addison-Wesley.

Hovland, C. I. (1959). Reconciling conflicting results derived from experimental and survey studies of attitude change. *American Psychologist, 14*, 8–17.

Humphrey, L. (1970). *Tearoom trade: Impersonal sex in public places.* Chicago: Aldine.

Hyman, H. (1954). *Interviewing in social research.* Chicago: University of Chicago Press.

Inbar, M., & Stoll, C. S. (1972). *Simulation and gaming in social science.* New York: The Free Press.

Janis, I.L., & Frick, F. (1943). The relationship between attitudes toward conclusions and errors in judging the logical validity of syllogisms. *Journal of Experimental Psychology, 33*, 73–77.

Janis, I. L., & Mann, L. (1965). Effectiveness of emotional role playing in modifying smoking habits and attitudes. *Journal of Experimental Research in Personality, 1*, 84–90.

Jones, E. E. (1966, August 1–7). Conceptual generality and experimental strategy in social psychology. Paper presented at the International Congress of Psychology, Moscow, USSR.

Jones, E. E., & Gerard, H. B. (1967). *Foundations of social psychology.* New York: Wiley.

Jones, F. (1984, August 23). Summer and drink don't mix. *Toronto Star,* p. A–19.

Jones, R. A. (1977). *Self-fulfilling prophecies: Social, psychological, and physiological effects of expectancies.* Hillsdale, NJ: Erlbaum.

Jones, R. A. (1982a). Expectations and illness. In M. R. DiMatteo & H. S. Friedman (Eds.), *Interpersonal relations in health care.* New York: Academic Press.

Jones, R. A. (1982b). Stereotyping as a process of social cognition. In A. R. Miller (Ed.), *In the eye of the beholder: Contemporary issues in stereotyping.* New York: Praeger.

Jones, R. A., & Cooper, J. (1971). Mediation of experimenter effects. *Journal of Personality and Social Psychology, 20*, 70–74.

Jones, R. A., Hendrick, C., & Epstein, Y. (1979). *Introduction to social psychology.* Sunderland, MA: Sinauer.

Jones, R. A., Howard, P. H., & Haley, J. V. (1984). Outcome desirability and probability distortions: An experimental verification of medical folklore. *Journal of Applied Social Psychology, 14*, 319–333.

Jones, R. A., Wekstein, D. R., & Morris, B. R. (1985). Concerns of the elderly. Unpublished manuscript, University of Kentucky.

Kahn, R. L., & Cannell, C. F. (1957). *The dynamics of interviewing.* New York: Wiley.

Kanter, R. M. (1977a). *Men and women of the corporation.* New York: Basic Books.

Kanter, R. M. (1977b). Some effects of proportions on group life: Skewed sex ratios and responses to token women. *American Journal of Sociology, 82,* 965–990.

Kaplan, A. (1964). *The conduct of inquiry: Methodology for behavioral science.* San Francisco: Chandler.

Katz, D. (1942). Do interviewers bias poll results? *Public Opinion Quarterly, 6,* 248–268.

Kazdin, A. E. (1982). Observer effects: Reactivity of direct observation. In D. P. Hartman (Ed.), Using observers to study behavior, *New Directions for Methodology of Social and Behavioral Science* (No. 14). San Francisco: Jossey-Bass.

Kelman, H. C. (1977). Privacy and research with human beings. *Journal of Social Issues, 33,* 169–195.

Kelley, H. H., & Stahelski, A. J. (1970). Social interaction basis of cooperators' and competitors' beliefs about others. *Journal of Personality and Social Psychology, 16,* 66–91.

Kershaw, D., & Fair, J. (1976). *The New Jersey income–maintenance experiment,* Vol. 1. New York: Academic Press.

Kinsey, A. C., Pomeroy, W. B., & Martin, C. E. (1948). *Sexual behavior in the human male.* Philadelphia: Saunders.

Kinsey, A. C., Pomeroy, W. B., Martin, C. E., & Gebhard, P. H. (1953). *Sexual behavior in the human female.* Philadelphia: Saunders.

Knox, R. A. (1980). Heart transplants: To pay or not to pay. *Science, 209,* 570–572, 575.

Koestler, A. (1976). *The act of creation.* London: Hutchinson Danube Edition.

Kolata, G. B. (1981). Clinical trial of psychotherapies is under way. *Science, 212,* 432–433.

Krippendorff, K. (1980). *Content analysis: An introduction to its methodology.* Beverly Hills, CA: Sage.

Kruskal, W., & Mosteller, F. (1981). Ideas of representative sampling. In D. W. Fiske (Ed.), Problems with language imprecision. *New Directions for Methodology of Social and Behavioral Science* (No. 9.). San Francisco: Jossey-Bass.

Kuhn, T. S. (1970). *The structure of scientific revolutions (2nd. ed.).* Chicago: University of Chicago Press.

Kutner, N. G. (1982). Cost–benefit issues in U.S. national health legislation:The case of end stage renal disease program. *Social Problems, 30,* 51–64.

Labov, W. (1970). The study of language in its social context. *Studium Generale, 23,* 30–87.

Lana, R. E. (1969). Pretest sensitization. In R. Rosenthal & R. L. Rosnow (Eds.), *Artifact in behavioral research.* New York: Academic Press.

Langer, E. J. (1975). The illusion of control. *Journal of Personality and Social Psychology, 32,* 311–328.

Latané, B., & Darley, J. M. (1970). *The unresponsive bystander.* New York: Appleton-Century-Crofts.

Latané, B., & Elman, D. (1970). The bystander and the thief. In B. Latané & J. M. Darley, (Eds.), *The unresponsive bystander: Why doesn't he help?* New York: Appleton-Century-Crofts.

Lazarsfeld, P. F. (1944). The controversy over detailed interviews—an offer for negotiation. *Public Opinion Quarterly, 8,* 38–60.

Lenski, G. E., & Leggett, J. C. (1960). Caste, class, and deference in the research interview. *American Journal of Sociology, 65,* 463–467.

Levine, M. (1980). Investigative reporting as a research method. An analysis of Bernstein and Woodward's "All the President's Men." *American Psychologist, 35,* 626–638.

Lewin, K. (1951). Problems of research in social psychology. In D. Cartwright (Ed.), *Field theory in social science.* New York: Harper & Row.

Lieberman, M. A. (1961). Relationship of mortality rates to entrance to a home for the aged. *Geriatrics, 16,* 515–519.

Liebow, E. (1967). *Tally's corner: A study of Negro streetcorner men.* Boston: Little, Brown & Company.

Lippmann, W. (1922). *Public opinion.* New York: Harcourt Brace.

Lofland, J. (1971). *Analyzing social settings: A guide to qualitative observation and analysis.* Belmont, CA: Wadsworth.

Lofland, J. (1976). *Doing social life: The qualitative study of human interaction in natural settings.* New York: Wiley.

Loftus, E. F. (1975). Leading questions and the eyewitness report. *Cognitive Psychology, 7,* 560–572.

Mann, L., & Janis, I. L. (1968). A follow-up study on the long-term effects of emotional role playing. *Journal of Personality and Social Psychology, 8,* 339–342.

Markus, G. B. (1979). *Analyzing panel data.* Beverly Hills, CA: Sage.

Marshall, E. (1980). Psychotherapy works, but for whom? *Science, 207,* 506–508.

Mazur-Hart, S. F., & Berman, J. J. (1977). Changing from fault to no-fault divorce: An interrupted time series analysis. *Journal of Applied Social Psychology, 7,* 300–312.

McArthur, L. Z., & Eisen, S. V. (1976). Achievements of male and female storybook characters as determinants of achievement behavior by boys and girls. *Journal of Personality and Social Psychology, 33,* 467–473.

McCarthy, C. R. (1981). The development of federal regulations for social science research. In A. J. Kimmel (Ed.), Ethics of human subject research, *New Directions for Methodology of Social and Behavioral Science,* (No. 10). San Francisco: Jossey-Bass.

McDavid, J. W. (1965). Approval-seeking motivation and the volunteer subject. *Journal of Personality and Social Psychology, 2,* 115–117.

McGuire, W. J. (1964). Inducing resistance to persuasion: Some contemporary approaches. In L. Berkowitz (Ed.), *Advances in Experimental Social Psychology* (Vol. 11). New York: Academic Press.

McGuire, W. J. (1969). Theory-oriented research in natural settings: The best of both worlds for social psychology. In M. Sherif & C.W. Sherif (Eds.), *Interdisciplinary relationships in the social sciences.* Chicago: Aldine.

McGuire, W. J. (1973). The yin and yang of progress in social psychology: Seven koan. *Journal of Personality and Social Psychology, 26,* 446–456.

McKearney, J. W. (1977–1978). Asking questions about behavior. *Perspectives in Biology and Medicine, 21,* 109–119.

McKinlay, J. B. (1981). From "promising report" to "standard procedure": Seven stages in the career of a medical innovation. *Milbank Memorial Fund Quarterly/Health and Society, 59*(3), 374–411.

Mead, M. (1949). *Coming of age in Samoa: A study of adolescence and sex in primitive society.* New York: Mentor. (Original work published 1928)

Mead, M. (1949). Preface to the 1949 Edition. In *Coming of age in Samoa.* New York: Mentor.

Merton, R. K., Fiske, M., & Kendall, P. L. (1956). *The focused interview.* Glencoe, IL: The Free Press.

Miklich, D. R. (1975). Radio telemetry in clinical psychology and related areas. *American Psychologist, 30,* 418–425.

Miklich, D. R., Chai, H., Purcell, K., Weiss, J. H., & Brady, J. (1974). Naturalistic observation of emotions preceding low pulmonary flow rates. *Journal of Allergy and Clinical Immunology, 54,* 102 (Abstract).

Milgram, S. (1963). Behavioral study of obedience. *Journal of Abnormal and Social Psychology, 67,* 371–378.

Milgram, S. (1964). Group pressure and action against a person. *Journal of Abnormal and Social Psychology, 69,* 137–143.

Milgram, S. (1969). The lost letter technique. *Psychology Today,* June, pp. 30–33, 66, 68.

Milgram, S. (1974). *Obedience to authority.* New York: Harper & Row.

Miller, D. B. (1977). Roles of naturalistic observation in comparative psychology. *American Psychologist, 32,* 211–219.

Miller, R. (1927, March 23). Precipitation and presidents. *The Nation, 124,* (No. 3220), 315–316.

Minor, M. W. (1970). Experimenter expectancy effect as a factor of evaluation apprehension. *Journal of Personality and Social Psychology, 15,* 326–332.

Moore, R. W. (1981). Hospital stress and patient recovery in two ward settings. Unpublished doctoral dissertation, University of Kentucky.

Mosteller, F. (1981). Innovation and evaluation. *Science, 211,* 881–886.

Murray, J. P., & Kippax, S. (1979). From the early window to the late night show: International trends in the study of television's impact on children and adults. In L. Berkowitz (Ed.), *Advances in Experimental Social Psychology* (Vol. 12), New York: Academic Press.

Myers, D. G., & Bishop, G. D. (1970). Discussion effects on racial attitudes. *Science, 169,* 778–789.

Neisser, U. (1981). John Dean's memory: A case study. *Cognition, 9,* 1–22.

Nemeth, C. (1972). A critical analysis of research utilizing the prisoner's dilemma paradigm for the study of bargaining. In L. Berkowitz (Ed.), *Advances in Experimental Social Psychology* (Vol. 6). New York: Academic Press.

Newberry, B. H. (1973). Truth telling in subjects with information about experiments: Who is being deceived? *Journal of Personality and Social Psychology, 25*, 364–374.

Newcomb, T. M. (1929). The consistency of certain extrovert–introvert behavior patterns in 51 problem boys. *Teachers College contributions to education* (No. 382). New York: Teachers College.

Newtson, D. (1973). Attribution and the unit of perception of ongoing behavior. *Journal of Personality and Social Psychology, 28*, 28–38.

Newtson, D. (1976). Foundations of attribution: The perception of ongoing behavior. In J. H. Harvey, W. J. Ickes, & R. F. Kidd (Eds.), *New directions in attribution research* (Vol. 1). Hillsdale, NJ: Erlbaum.

Newtson, D., Engquist, G., & Bois, J. (1977). The objective basis of behavior units. *Journal of Personality and Social Psychology, 35*, 847–862.

New York Times News Service (1984, May 3). Swimming, walking are favorite activities. *Lexington Herald-Leader*, p. C–10.

Nisbett, R. E., Borgida, E., Crandall, R., & Reed, H. (1976). Popular induction: Information is not always informative. In J. S. Carroll & J. W. Payne (Eds.), *Cognition and social behavior*. Hillsdale, NJ: Erlbaum.

Nisbett, R. E., & Ross, L. (1980). *Human inference: Strategies and shortcomings of social judgment*. Englewood Cliffs, NJ: Prentice-Hall.

Orne, M. T. (1962). On the social psychology of the psychological experiment: With particular reference to demand characteristics. *American Psychologist, 17*, 776–786.

Orne, M. T. (1969). Demand characteristics and the concept of quasi-controls. In R. Rosenthal & R. L. Rosnow (Eds.), *Artifact in behavioral research*. New York: Academic Press.

Orwell, G. (1961). *1984*. New York: New American Library. (Original work published 1949)

Padgett, V. R., & Jorgenson, D. O. (1982). Superstition and economic threat: Germany 1918–1940. *Personality and Social Psychology Bulletin, 8*, 736–741.

Palys, T. S. (1978). Simulation methods and social psychology. *Journal for the Theory of Social Behavior, 8*, 341–368.

Pearsall, M. (1970). Participant observation as role and method in behavioral research. In W. J. Filstead (Ed.), *Qualitative methodology: Firsthand involvement with the social world*. Chicago: Markham.

Pennebaker, J. W., & Newtson, D. (1983). Observation of a unique event: The psychological impact of the Mount Saint Helens volcano. In H. T. Reis (Ed.), *New Directions for Methodology of Social and Behavioral Science* (No. 15). San Francisco: Jossey-Bass.

Pepper, S. (1981). Problems in the quantification of frequency expressions. In D. W. Fiske (Ed.), Problems with language imprecision. *New Directions for Methodology of Social and Behavioral Science* (No. 9). San Francisco: Jossey-Bass.

Petersen, J. (1983). The Playboy readers' sex survey. Part One. *Playboy, 30*, 108, 241, 242, 244, 246, 248, 250.

Phillips, D. P., & Feldman, K. A. (1973). A dip in deaths before ceremonial occasions: Some new relationships between social integration and mortality. *American Sociological Review, 38*, 678–696.

Piliavin, I. M., Rodin, J., & Piliavin, J. A. (1969). Good Samaritanism: An underground phenomenon? *Journal of Personality and Social Psychology, 13,* 289–299.

Pirsig, R. M. (1974). *Zen and the art of motorcycle maintenance: An inquiry into values.* New York: Morrow.

Polsky, N. (1969). *Hustlers, beats, and others.* Garden City, NY: Doubleday.

Purcell, K., & Brady, K. (1966). Adaptation to the invasion of privacy: Monitoring behavior with a miniature radio transmitter. *Merrill-Palmer Quarterly, 12,* 242–254.

Rathje, W. L. (1979). Trace measures. In L. Sechrest (Ed.), Unobtrusive measures today. *New Directions for Methodology of Social and Behavioral Science* (No. 1). San Francisco: Jossey-Bass.

Reid, J. B. (1982). Observer training in naturalistic research. In D. P. Hartman (Ed.), Using observers to study behavior. *New Directions for Methodology of Social and Behavioral Science* (No. 14). San Francisco: Jossey-Bass.

Rice, S. A. (1929). Contagious bias in the interview: A methodological note. *American Journal of Sociology, 35,* 420–423.

Richardson, S. A., Dohrenwend, B. S., & Klein, D. (1965). *Interviewing.* New York: Basic Books.

Ring, K. (1967). Experimental social psychology: Some sober questions about some frivolous values. *Journal of Experimental Social Psychology, 3,* 113–123.

Roberts, R. R., & Renzaglia, G. A. (1965). The influence of tape recording on counseling. *Journal of Counseling Psychology, 12,* 10–16.

Robinson, D., & Rohde, S. (1946). Two experiments with an anti-semitism poll. *Journal of Abnormal and Social Psychology, 41,* 136–144.

Rodin, J., & Langer, E. (1977). Long-term effects of a control-relevant intervention with the institutionalized aged. *Journal of Personality and Social Psychology, 35,* 897–902.

Roethlisberger, F.F., & Dickson, W. J. (1939). *Management and the worker.* New York: Wiley.

Ronis, D. L., Baumgardner, M. H., Leippe, M. R., Cacioppo, J. T., & Greenwald, A. G. (1977). In search of reliable persuasion effects: I. A computer controlled procedure for studying persuasion. *Journal of Personality and Social Psychology, 35,* 548–569.

Rose, R. M., Jenkins, C. D., & Hurst, N. W. (1978). Health change in air traffic controllers: A prospective study. *Psychosomatic Medicine, 40,* 142–165.

Rosenberg, M. J. (1965). When dissonance fails: On eliminating evaluation apprehension from attitude measurement. *Journal of Personality and Social Psychology, 1,* 28–42.

Rosenberg, S., & Cohen, B. D. (1967). Toward a psychological analysis of verbal communication skills. In R. L. Schiefelbusch, R. H. Copeland, & J. O. Smith (Eds.), *Language and Mental Retardation.* New York: Holt, Rinehart & Winston.

Rosenberg, S., & Jones, R. A. (1972). A method for investigating and representing as person's implicit theory of personality: Theodore Dreiser's view of people. *Journal of Personality and Social Psychology, 22,* 372–386.

Rosenhan, D. L. (1973). On being sane in insane places. *Science, 179,* 250–258.

Rosenthal, R. (1966). *Experimenter effects in behavioral research.* New York: Appleton-Century-Crofts.

Rosenthal, R. (1976). *Experimenter effects in behavioral research* (rev. ed.). Hillsdale, NJ: Erlbaum.

Rosenthal, R., Hall, J. A., DiMatteo, M. R., Rogers, P. L., & Archer, D. (1979). *Sensitivity to nonverbal communication: The PONS test.* Baltimore: Johns Hopkins University Press.

Ross, H. L., Campbell, D. T., & Glass, G. V. (1970). Determining the social effects of a legal reform: The British "breathalyser" crackdown of 1967. *American Behavioral Scientist, 13,* 493–509.

Ross, L. (1981). *Reporting.* New York: Dodd, Mead, & Co.

Ross, L. D., Amabile, T. M., & Steinmetz, J. L. (1977). Social roles, social control, and biases in social perception processes. *Journal of Personality and Social Psychology, 35,* 485–494.

Rossi, P. H., Freeman, H. E., & Wright, S. R. (1979). *Evaluation: A systematic approach.* Beverly Hills, CA: Sage.

Rubin, J., Provenzano, F., & Luria, Z. (1974). The eye of the beholder: Parents' views on sex of newborns. *American Journal of Orthopsychiatry, 44,* 512–519.

Rubin, L. B. (1976). *Worlds of pain: Life in the working class family.* New York: Basic Books.

Rubin, Z. (1973). *Liking and loving: An invitation to social psychology.* New York: Holt, Rinehart & Winston.

Rubin, Z., & Mitchell, C. (1976). Couples research as couples counseling: Some unintended effects of studying close relationships. *American Psychologist, 31,* 17–25.

Ruebhausen, O. M., & Brim, O. G., Jr. (1965). Privacy and behavioral research. *Columbia Law Review, 65,* 1184–1211.

Sales, S. M. (1973). Threat as a factor in authoritarianism: An analysis of archival data. *Journal of Personality and Social Psychology, 28,* 44–57.

Samelson, F. (1980). J. B. Watson's Little Albert, Cyril Burt's twins, and the need for a critical science. *American Psychologist, 35,* 619–625.

Schaps, E. (1972). Cost, dependency, and helping. *Journal of Personality and Social Psychology, 21,* 74–78.

Schachter, S., Redington, K., Grunberg, N., Apple, W., & Schindler, S. (1980). Springtime, suicide, and wills. Unpublished manuscript, Columbia University.

Schegloff, E. A. (1972). Notes on a conversational practice: Formulating place. In D. Sudnow (Ed.), *Studies in social interaction.* New York: The Free Press.

Schlenker, B. R. (1980) *Impression management: The self-concept, social identity, and interpersonal relations.* Monterey, CA: Brooks/Cole.

Schmidt, C. F. (1972). Multidimensional scaling analysis of the printed media's explanations of the riots of the summer of 1967. *Journal of Personality and Social Psychology, 24,* 59–67.

Scodel, A., & Mussen, P. (1953). Social perceptions of authoritarians and non-authoritarians. *Journal of Abnormal and Social Psychology, 48,* 181–184.

Schroder, H. M., Driver, M. J., & Streufert, S. (1967). *Human information processing.* New York: Holt, Rinehart & Winston.

Schulz, R., & Bazerman, M. (1980). Ceremonial occasions and mortality: A second look. *American Psychologist, 1980, 35,* 253–261.

Scott, G. C. (1980). Playboy interview. *Playboy, 27*(12), 81–138.

Sechrest, L., & Phillips, M. (1979). Unobtrusive measures: An overview. In L. Sechrest (Ed.), Unobtrusive measurement today. *New Directions for Methodology of Behavioral Science, 1,* 1–18.

Seeman, J. (1969). Deception in psychological research. *American Psychologist, 24,* 1025–1028.

Serbin, L. A., Citron, C., & Connor, J. M. (1978). Covert assessment of observer agreement: An application and extension. *Journal of Genetic Psychology, 133,* 155–161.

Sexton, M. M. (1979). Behavioral epidemiology. In O. F. Pomerleau & J. P. Brady (Eds.), *Behavioral medicine: Theory and practice.* Baltimore: Williams & Wilkins.

Shortell, S. M., & Richardson, W. C. (1978). *Health program evaluation.* St. Louis: Mosby.

Shweder, R. A. (1975). How relevant is an individual difference theory of personality? *Journal of Personality, 43,* 455–484.

Shweder, R. A., & D'Andrade, R. G. (1980). The systematic distortion hypothesis. In R. A. Shweder (Ed.), *New Directions for Methodology of Social and Behavioral Science, 4,* 37–58.

Sigall, H., & Page, R. (1971). Current stereotypes: A little fading, a little faking. *Journal of Personality and Social Psychology, 18,* 247–255.

Silverman, I. (1977). *The human subject in the psychological laboratory.* New York: Pergamon.

Skinner, B. F. (1938). *The behavior of organisms.* New York: Appleton-Century-Crofts.

Snyder, M., & Swann, W. B., Jr. (1978). Behavioral confirmation in social interaction: From social perception to social reality. *Journal of Experimental Social Psychology, 14,* 148–162.

Snyder, M., Tanke, E. D., & Berschied, E. (1977). Social perception and interpersonal behavior: On the self-fulfilling nature of social stereotypes. *Journal of Personality and Social Psychology, 35,* 656–666.

Solomon, R. L. (1949). An extension of control group design. *Psychological Bulletin, 46,* 137–150.

Sommer, R. (1969). *Personal space.* Englewood Cliffs, NJ: Prentice-Hall.

Stone, P. J., Dunphy, D. C., Smith, M. S., & Ogilvie, D. M. (1966). *The general inquirer: A computer approach to content analysis.* Cambridge, MA: MIT Press.

Straus, R. (1973). Departments and disciplines: Stasis and change. *Science, 182,* 895–898.

Strodtbeck, F. L., James, R. M., & Hawkins, C. (1957). Social status in jury deliberation. *American Sociological Review, 24,* 713–719.

Sudman, S., & Bradburn, N. M. (1982). *Asking questions: A practical guide to questionnaire construction.* San Francisco: Jossey-Bass.

Suedfeld, P., & Rank, A. D. (1976). Revolutionary leaders: Long-term success as a function of changes in conceptual complexity. *Journal of Personality and Social Psychology, 34,* 169–178.

Suls, J., & Gastorf, J. (1980). Has the social psychology of the experiment influenced how research is conducted? *European Journal of Social Psychology, 10,* 291–294.

Swanberg, W. A. (1965). *Dreiser.* New York: Scribners.

Taylor, S. E., & Fiske, S. T. (1975). Point of view and perceptions of causality. *Journal of Personality and Social Psychology, 32,* 439–445.

Taylor, S. E., & Fiske, S. T. (1978). Salience, attention, and attribution: Top of the head phenomena. In L. Berkowitz (Ed.), *Advances in Experimental Social Psychology* (Vol. 11). New York: Academic Press.

Terkel, S. (1975). *Working.* New York: Avon Books.

Tetlock, P. E. (1981). Pre- to postelection shifts in presidential rhetoric: Impression management or cognitive adjustment. *Journal of Personality and Social Psychology, 41,* 207–212.

Toffler, A. (1971). *Future shock.* New York: Bantam.

Touhey, J. C. (1974). Effects of additional women professionals on ratings of occupational prestige and desirability. *Journal of Personality and Social Psychology, 29,* 86–89.

Triplett, N. (1897–1898). The dynamogenic factors in pacemaking and competition. *American Journal of Psychology, 9,* 507–533.

Trow, M. (1970). Comment on "Participant observation and interviewing: A comparison." In W. J. Filstead (Ed.), *Qualitative methodology: Firsthand involvement with the social world.* Chicago: Markham.

Van Lawick-Goodall, J. (1971). *In the shadow of man.* Boston: Houghton Mifflin.

Vinacke, W. E. (1969). Variables in experimental games: Toward a field theory. *Psychological Bulletin, 71,* 293–318.

Volicer, B. J. (1978). Hospital stress and patient reports of pain and physical status. *Journal of Human Stress, 4,* 28–37.

von Hoffman, N. (1970). Sociological snoopers. *Transaction, 7,* 4–6.

Wallace, A., Wallechinsky, D., & Wallace, I. (1983). *The book of lists #3.* New York: William Morrow & Co.

Wallace, I., Wallechinsky, D., & Wallace, A. (1982, February 7). Exclusive: The worst household tasks. *Parade,* p. 21.

Wallace, I., Wallechinsky, D., Wallace, A., & Wallace, S. (1979). *The book of lists #2.* New York: William Morrow & Co.

Wallechinsky, D., Wallace, I., & Wallace, A. (1977). *The book of lists.* New York: William Morrow & Co.

Watson, J. B. (1924). *Behaviorism.* Chicago: University of Chicago Press.

Watzlawick, P., Beavin, J. H., & Jackson, D. D. (1967). *Pragmatics of human communication: A study of interactional patterns, pathologies, and paradoxes.* New York: Norton.

Wax, R. H. (1971). *Doing fieldwork: Warnings and advice.* Chicago: University of Chicago Press.

Webb, E. J., Campbell, D. T., Schwartz, R. D., & Sechrest, L. (1966). *Unobtrusive measures: Nonreactive research in the social sciences.* Chicago: Rand McNally.

Webb, E. J., Campbell, D. T., Schwartz, R. D., Sechrest, L., & Grove, J. B. (1981). *Nonreactive measures in the social sciences (2nd ed.).* Boston: Houghton Mifflin.

Weick, K. E. (1968). Systematic observational methods. In G. Lindzey and E. Aronson (Eds.), *Handbook of social psychology* (2nd ed.). Reading, MA: Addison-Wesley.

Weiss, C. H. (1972). *Evaluation research: Methods of assessing program effectiveness.* Englewood Cliffs, NJ: Prentice-Hall.

Wenar, C. (1961). The reliability of mothers' histories. *Child Development, 32,* 491-500.

Wharton, Y. L. (1977). *List of hypotheses advanced to explain the SAT score decline.* New York: College Entrance Examination Board.

Wholey, J. S., Nay, J. N., Scanlon, J. W., & Schmidt, R. E. (1975). Evaluation: When is it really needed? *Evaluation, 2*(2), 89-93.

Whyte, W. T. (1951). Observational field work methods. In M. Jahoda, M. Deutsch, & S. W. Cook (Eds.), *Research methods in the social sciences.* New York: Dryden Press.

Wicklund, R. A., & Brehm, J. W. (1976). *Perspectives on cognitive dissonance.* Hillsdale, NJ: Erlbaum.

Wicklund, R. A., & Gollwitzer, P. M. (1982). *Symbolic self-completion.* Hillsdale, NJ: Erlbaum.

Williams, J. A., Jr. (1964). Interviewer-respondent interaction: A study of bias in the information interview. *Sociometry, 27,* 338-352.

Williams, W. (1975). Implementation analysis and assessment. *Policy Analysis, 1,* 531-566.

Willer, B. S. (1977). Individual patient programming: An experiment in the use of evaluation and feedback for hospital psychology. *Evaluation Quarterly, 1,* 587-608.

Wilson, D. M., & Donnerstein, E. (1976). Legal and ethical aspects of nonreactive social psychological research: An excursion into the public mind. *American Psychologist, 31,* 765-773.

Wolfe, T. (1974). Why they aren't writing the great American novel anymore: A treatise on the varieties of realistic experience. *Esquire,* 152-158, 272.

Wolfe, T. (1976). *Mauve gloves & madmen, clutter & vine.* New York: Farrar, Straus & Giroux.

Wortman, P. M. (1983). Evaluation research: A methodological perspective. *Annual Review of Psychology, 34,* 223-260.

Wrightsman, L. (1981). Personal documents as data in conceptualizing adult personality development. *Personality and Social Psychology Bulletin, 7,* 367-385.

Zajonc, R. B. (1965). Social facilitation. *Science, 149,* 269-274.

Zimbardo, P. G., Haney, C., Banks, W. C., & Jaffe, D. (1982). The psychology of imprisonment: Privation, power, and pathology. In J. C. Brigham & L. S. Wrightsman (Eds.), *Contemporary issues in social psychology* (4th ed.). Monterey, CA: Brooks/Cole.

Quotation Credits

CHAPTER 1

p. 8: From L. Eisenberg, "The human nature of human nature," *Science 176* (pp. 123–124). Copyright 1972 by the American Association for the Advancement of Science.

p. 12: From W.I.B. Beveridge, *The Art of Scientific Investigation*, Third Edition (p. 100). Heinemann Educational Books Ltd., 1957. Used also with the permission of W.W. Norton & Co.

p. 20: From R.E. Nisbett et al., "Population induction: Information is not always informative," in J.S. Carroll and J.W. Payne (eds.), *Cognition and Social Behavior* (p. 129). Copyright 1980 by Lawrence Erlbaum Associates.

p. 30: From L. Ross, *Reporting* (p. 11). Dodd, Mead & Co., 1981. Used with the permission of Lillian Ross.

p. 31: From T. Wolfe, *Mauve Gloves and Madmen, Clutter and Vine* (p. 139). Farrar, Straus & Giroux, Inc., 1976.

p. 33: From E. Liebow, *Tally's Corner: A Study of Negro Streetcorner Men* (pp. 37–38). Little, Brown & Co., 1967.

CHAPTER 2

p. 46: From R.M. Kanter, *Men and Women of the Corporation* (p. 121). Copyright 1977 by Rosabeth Moss Kanter. Reprinted by permission of Basic Books Inc.

p. 59: From B. Farrell, "George in the afternoon" (pp. 81–82). Copyright 1975 by *Harper's* Magazine. All rights reserved. Reprinted from the August 1975 issue by special permission.

CHAPTER 3

p. 92: From R.F. Bales, *Personality and Interpersonal Behavior* (pp. 123–124). Copyright 1970 by Holt, Rinehart and Winston, Inc. Reprinted by permission of CBS College Publishing.

CHAPTER 4

p. 126: From P.J. Stone, D.C. Dunphy, M.S. Smith, and D.M. Ogilvie, *The General Inquirer: A Computer Approach to Content Analysis* (pp. 7–8). M.I.T. Press, 1966.

CHAPTER 5

p. 152: From R.I. Evans, *The Making of Psychology* (pp. 86, 109, 136, 214). Alfred A. Knopf Inc., 1976.

p. 165: From E.A. Schegloff, "Notes on a conversational practice: Formulating place," in D. Sudnow (ed.), *Studies in Social Interaction* (pp. 83–84). Copyright 1972 by The Free Press, a division of Macmillan, Inc.

p. 168: From P. Farb, *Word Play: What Happens When People Talk* (p. 97). Alfred A. Knopf Inc., 1973.

CHAPTER 6

p. 176: From S. Sudman and N.M. Bradburn, *Asking Questions: A Practical Guide to Questionnaire Construction* (pp. 13–14). Jossey-Bass, 1983.

p. 199: From G. Gerbner and L. Gross, "The scary world of TV's heavy viewer," *Psychology Today*, April 1976 (p. 44).

CHAPTER 7

p. 226: From P.C. Ellsworth, "From abstract ideas to concrete instances: Some guidelines for choosing natural settings," *American Psychologist 32* (p. 611). Copyright 1977 by the American Psychological Association.

p. 240: From D.M. Wilson and E. Donnerstein, "Legal and ethical aspects of nonreactive social psychological research: An excursion into the public mind," *American Psychologist 31* (p. 767). Copyright 1976 by the American Psychological Association.

CHAPTER 8

p. 255: From S.M. Shortell and W.C. Richardson, *Health Program Evaluation* (pp. 11–12). The C.V. Mosby Company, 1978. Used by permission.

CHAPTER 9

p. 285: From *The Poetry of Robert Frost*, edited by Edward Connery Latham. Copyright 1916, 1969 by Holt, Rinehart and Winston. Copyright 1944 by Robert Frost. Reprinted by permission of Holt, Rinehart and Winston, Publishers.

CHAPTER 10

p. 343: From H.H. Kelley and A.J. Stahelski, "Social interaction basis of cooperators' and competitors' beliefs about others," *Journal of Personality and Social Psychology 16* (pp. 88–89). Copyright 1970 by the American Psychological Association.

Name Index

Subject Index

Affricative, 76–77
Age
  interviewer/interviewee, 162
  survey question, 153
Air traffic controllers, 263–264
Alternatives, closed-ended questions and, 153
Ambiguity, about direction of causality, 222, 225
Analogy
  hypothesis formation and, 18
  simulation as, 327, 346
Analytic files, 54–56
APA, Committee on Ethical Practices in Research, 82, 84
Aphorisms, hypothesis formation and, 19
Applied explanatory power, 348–349
Archival research
  defined, 104
  nonreactive nature of, 104, 117
Archives
  defined, 105
  proactivity of, 116
  selective deposit and survival, 115–116
Artillery, experiment on Army recruits, 34–35
Assessment
  observer reliability and, 96–98
  program evaluation and, 257, 258–261
Assimilation
  behavioral, 342
  tokenism and, 47
  rumor transmission and, 333, 334
Astrology books, as authoritarian index, 108–109
Attention, observation and, 56–58
Attention-feedback-regulation, 80
Attitude change, 215
Attribution, internal validity and, 218–220
Attrition
  panel studies and, 188

threat to internal validity, 221, 225, 302
Authoritarianism
  F-scale and, 343
  threatening times and, 106–110

Balanced replication, 301
Behavior
  coding categories, 89–94
  context of, 4–5
  dependent/dependence-supportive, 85–88
  of experiment subjects, 313–316
  extralinguistic, 75–77
  nonverbal, 74–75
  operant paradigm and, 86
  patterns of, 51, 52
  socially desirable, 80
  spatial, 77
Behavior coding, 85
  categories for, 89–94
Behavioral assimilation, 342
Behavioral confirmation, 319
Betrayal funnel, 26
Bias
  interview questions and, 160–161
  nonresponse, 185–186
  participant observation and, 56–65
  self-selection, 186
  social desirability, 193
  see also Distortion
Bicycle racing, 282–283
"Blind," 315
Blocking, 291
Blue Cross, 259–261
Bogus pipeline, 202–203
Brainwashing, 2
Breathalyser, 236–239
Broad Street Pump, 219

"Candid Camera," 84
Caste (social), 162–164

405